AUSTRALIA BREAKS APART

JOHN STAPLETON

Australia Breaks Apart
Copyright © 2023 John Stapleton
All rights reserved.

Print ISBN: 978-06-45-0394-8-4
Ebook ISBN: 978-06-45-0394-7-4

Published by A Sense of Place Publishing 2023

Reviewers and editors may use up to 1000 words of this book with attribution. Any larger extracts or other usage should be negotiated with the publisher.

Otherwise no parts of this publication may be reproduced, stored in a retrieval system, or transmitted in any form or by any means, electronic, mechanical, photocopying, recording, or otherwise, without the prior written permission of the copyright owner or the publisher.

This book is sold subject to the condition that it shall not, by way of trade or otherwise, be lent, resold, hired out, or otherwise circulated without the publisher's prior consent in any form of binding or cover other than that in which it is published and without a similar condition including this condition being imposed on the subsequent purchaser. Under no circumstances may any part of this book be photocopied for resale.

This is the fifth book in the series of snapshots of contemporary Australian history which began with *Terror in Australia: Workers' Paradise Lost* in 2015, and was followed by *Hideout in the Apocalypse*, *Dark Dark Policing* and *Unfolding Catastrophe: Australia*.

While canvassing a wide range of experts and commentators and factually accurate, partly for legal reasons the books tell the story through the eyes of a retired reporter, Old Alex, and thereby use novelistic techniques to cover this pivotal point in the nation's history.

Cover design by Jessica Bell
Cover images from Asanka Ratnayake of Getty Images

 A catalogue record for this book is available from the National Library of Australia

TABLE OF CONTENTS

Preface 7
One Prison Island. 9
Two How It All Ends 18
Three The Derangement of Battle. 33
Four The Lone Sentinel. 54
Five A Narrow Valley Threads Down to the Sea. 69
Six Violence Grips Australia 90
Seven The River Rushes By 111
Eight The Shrine of Remembrance 132
Nine We Weep for You and You Are Not Yet Born 153
Ten The Imperial Battleship Has Landed 174
Eleven Partial to that Partial Light 194
Twelve Shattered Ground. 218
Thirteen SOS Australia: The New World Order 233
Fourteen Convoy to Canberra 261
Fifteen A Time for All Time 293
Sixteen Blessed Art Thou 321
Seventeen Perpetrators in Power 354
Eighteen Factcheck This: Bombshell Revelations 378
Nineteen After the Tribulation Trust No Man 407
Acknowledgements 445
About the Author. 447

PREFACE

No book can do anything but scratch this remarkably complex, two-faced period of Australian history, a time when hypocrisy reigned and the nation became infamous around the world for its draconian response to Covid.

This book is set in the period from mid-2021 to early 2023.

It is the direct sequel to the 2021 book *Unfolding Catastrophe: Australia* and is the fifth in a series of snapshots of Australian history which began in 2015 with *Terror in Australia: Workers' Paradise Lost*, and was followed by *Hideout in the Apocalypse* and *Dark Dark Policing*.

Unlike its predecessors, this book is not footnoted. While *Australia Breaks Apart*, as with the others in the series, occasionally uses subjective narrative techniques to help tell the story, every single word in this book is true and accurate as far as the author is aware.

A number of Australia's leading public intellectuals have contributed to this text, usually through the initial mechanism of having their work published in A Sense of Place Magazine, which the author edits.

In the age of the internet, the quotations from various sources, including academics, commentators and journalists are clearly defined, on the public record and easy to find. Any researcher having difficulty locating a source is welcome to contact the author.

While the majority of the book is direct reportage, the narrative is constructed through the eyes of the central character Old Alex, a retired journalist.

The author is one of Australia's most experienced news reporters, having worked on mainstream mastheads, particularly *The Sydney Morning Herald* and *The Australian*, for more than a quarter of a century, making him uniquely placed to tell this story. He continues to write and publish in retirement.

In this third person style of telling the nation's story, the author employs a narrative device which allows for a vivid evocation of the tectonic shifts in our cultural landscape, the spiritual reformation driven by the excessive authoritarianism and population wide abuses of the period and which feeds into the human story as a whole.

According to the most recent research, more than half the population think in pictures and equally more than half the population experience lucid or waking dreams akin to hallucinations, at least to some degree.

Old Alex is thus afflicted. This condition inspires the more subjective or lyrical interludes and allows for a symbolism and reflection on a wide scale medical and societal fraud which until recent times almost everyone has struggled to comprehend and digest.

While they may sometimes seem fantastical, these episodes are an accurate record of the author's experiences, made more intense by Australia's prolonged lockdowns.

Outside a small pond of populist literature, almost all book publishing in Australia is government funded. Despite an abundance of documentary material from this period, including podcasts and a blizzard of personal testimony on social media, there are unlikely to be many histories of this era in Australia because none of the major players, including politicians, health bureaucrats, regulators, media personnel, police, the military and the intelligence agencies emerge as innocent parties.

Hopefully this book will help to shed some light on one of the darkest periods of Australia's history.

ONE
PRISON ISLAND

This massive edifice of evil was too complex, and, really, too elegant, to assign to just human awfulness and human inventiveness. It suggested a spiritual dimension of evil. This evil was like a giant cultural spaceship which landed on Earth, with a technology to unfold and almost at once to set foot upon the egalitarian, post-enlightenment West a global dystopia run on cruelty and cognitive dissonance.

How could otherwise nice people have come to do such evil?

Naomi Wolf. *The Bodies of Others.*

As someone long prepared for this to happen
Go firmly to the window. Drink it in
Exquisite music. Alexandra laughing
Your first commitments tangible again

Leonard Cohen. *Alexandra Leaving.*

OLD ALEX SAT on that sunlit step in an unfanciful suburb called Oak Flats; flooded with light, exhausted, perhaps, to be fanciful about it all, as if he'd just written *1984* and was basking in creative satisfaction, and the glory. Except, of course, there was no glory, and George Orwell aka Eric Blair never lived to see the stunning success of his anti-totalitarian novel. He was suffering the effects of tuberculosis even as he wrote it. There is no glory in the grave.

That most curious of books, a book which would have never have found a mainstream publisher in the 21st Century, became the most referenced work in the English Canon in 2020; and even more so in 2021, the year he sat on that doorstep in Oak Flats.

The country was at the height of its totalitarian derangement, where every single aspect of life was controlled by the government.

Half the country, 12 million people, were now officially in lockdown. His neighbours were encouraged to report him if he spent more than two hours away from home. The mainstream media delivered a blizzard of Covid fear mongering, hour in, hour out, day in, day out. The population was confused, terrified and remarkably compliant. They turned on each other, on anyone who did not comply.

Politicians and Chief Health Officers placed themselves front and centre of the nightly news bulletins; and panic, everywhere there was panic.

Hundreds of military personnel now patrolled the streets of Sydney, searching for anyone who might not have a legitimate excuse for being outside their home. The overweight New South Wales Police Commissioner announced with apparent delight that they had issued more than 600 fines for non-compliance the previous day, an abuse of the citizenry of which, as far as Old Alex was concerned, the dictatorial Commissioner and his political masters should have been absolutely ashamed.

But of course, shame wasn't in the lexicon. Nor was honesty, proportionality, decency, compassion.

The authoritarian derangement overtaking Australia was without precedent, and every sign of collapse came jumping out through the voices all around, the electronic blather that filled the air, a terrible threat whispered on a bed of deceit.

On his private newsfeed there was a steady stream of outrage and scepticism. Everywhere else there was a shuttered, terrible silence, an acquiescence he struggled to understand.

Eighteen months on from the country's first Covid death Australia was almost unrecognisable. The nation had seen the most violent demonstrations in its history and a brutality of policing only ever seen in the first days of colonisation when the natives were shot and the convicts whipped till blood filled their boots. Australians had been turned against Australians, divided by race, wealth, education, cognitive ability, and most recently vaccine status. Police blanketing the suburbs across Australia were now enforcing the equivalent of martial law.

All in the name of keeping Australians "safe".

Australia had become a laughing stock around the world, a warning of the consequences of Covid overreach. The massaged image of Australia as an egalitarian and welcoming tourist destination populated with colourful animals and equally colourful people vanished as police bashed, arrested and pepper sprayed protestors. The courts would be clogged for years to come; for none of this was done with consent.

Where was the evidence that putting millions of people under house arrest, unable to visit friends and family, unable in many cases to work, to see elderly relatives in their dying days, destroying tens of thousands of businesses, throwing vast swathes of the population on to welfare, quadrupling the national debt, destroying the education of millions of Australian children, where was the evidence that these actions were an appropriate response to the coronavirus?

Where was the evidence that instituting curfews on millions of Australians was effective or appropriate? Or proportionate?

Even to question these multiple insanities was considered unpatriotic.

The mainstream media in which he had worked all his life trumpeted the government's propaganda, while real journalism died on the Covid altar.

Australia! This really was happening in the land of kangaroos, crocodiles and poisonous snakes, homesteads and sprawling sheep stations.

***

Evidence?

Australia's public servants like to talk about "evidence-based" policy. It usually meant the exact opposite.

In the case of Covid, and the insane level of micromanagement recklessly imposed on long-suffering suburbanites, the so-called evidence was all kept secret from the public. Following the science or following the medical advice, as the politicians repeatedly claimed they were doing, actually meant nothing of the kind. Old Alex believed not a word they said.

Across the country's most populous states, in Victoria, New South Wales and Queensland, indeed across the entire country, there had been the same charade: the implementation of draconian law enforcement and massive restrictions on personal liberty, but state and federal governments were all refusing to release the medical evidence on which these decisions were based.

For the simple reason: It didn't exist. Not one single Australian politician could produce the evidence that their government's actions were appropriate.

Setting the conspiracy theorists alight, the ridiculously dictatorial New South Wales Health Minister Brad Hazzard spoke of the New World Order, where everyone would be forced to be vaccinated, where everyone must comply, but was refusing to release the "medical advice" he was relying on to institute a statewide lockdown.

Because, of course, Health Hazzard was off and running on his own lousy railway.

You can lock them up, destroy their livelihoods, businesses, and mental health; but you are too arrogant, too incompetent, or perhaps just too conflicted, to reveal to those whose lives you are destroying exactly why you are doing it.

Reach not far to find a vaccine manufacturer.

Let this madness wither in the light, or emerge from behind your bodyguard of tame journalists and grossly manipulated mainstream media outlets; and face your critics.

Around Oak Flats Alex heard the eerie comment from people faced with the Hobbesian choice of getting injected with a controversial vaccine they did not want, or losing their jobs. "They're culling us."

Trust was zero.

With their jobs went their homes, their mortgages, their sense of self-worth and the ability to care for their children.

**

While horror stories of vaccine injuries and lost employment mounted around him, the disfiguring of the society cast multiple absurdities into his own life. Unable to go to the pub or a restaurant, forbidden to even leave his own Local Government Areas.

The authorities and the politicians Australians so unwisely trusted had betrayed their own people, leaving a polity racked with pain, raked daily with a kind of frothing insanity.

"The central government will collapse in 2047," Old Alex said a number of times for no particular reason, except that he believed it to be true.

To him, as a newspaper reporter a longtime observer of base human conduct, none of the politician's behaviour, their fevered, demented attempts to get the entire population vaccinated, made any sense whatsoever; unless those who claimed the political class were in receipt of millions of dollars in bribes from vaccine manufacturers happened to be accurate.

Almost every other conspiracy theory had come true in this benighted era.

You couldn't convince Old Alex these people actually cared about the welfare of their constituents, their safety and well being; the same poor bastards being imprisoned in their own homes, whose careers and businesses were being destroyed, whose voices were ignored. Punitive fines were dished out to anyone who dared to protest.

Diktat after diktat rained down on an imprisoned population.

***

With "Health Hazzard", as NSW Health Minister Brad Hazzard was rapidly dubbed, riding wingman at their morning press conferences, the lunatic, at least to Old Alex's inflamed imagination, Chief Medical Officer Dr Kerry Chant, with a mad germaphobic glaze in her eyes, issued what were to his mind an endless stream of utterly pointless but nonetheless life-altering decisions: Citizens could not cross state or international borders, could not visit their dying parents or children in hospital, go to church or go dancing, had to wear masks, practise social distancing, and for the sake of the welfare of the community, get vaccinated, once, twice, thrice.

As the black joke of the day went: "What do the vaccinated and unvaccinated have in common?"

"Neither will ever be fully vaccinated."

Lie after lie after lie; that's what, in the end, it all amounted to, because nothing the government did worked.

Tracking the rationale for decision-making back to Big Pharma wasn't difficult; nor was uncovering the fact that everything happening "in this space", as the public service expression went, was highly contested by some of the world's most eminently qualified practitioners, academics and researchers.

But power drunk apparatchiks across Australia saw no need to explain themselves to "the great unwashed", that is, the voters, their constituents.

One might have thought that as a class there was not much point in politicians and health bureaucrats placing themselves front and centre of everybody's life if the principal result was to leave a frustrated, angry and disillusioned population; which was exactly what Australia's state and federal governments were doing.

"You can't catch the virus if you just stay home," Dr Kerry Chant declared.

A siren went off in the distance and he thought: "Another person just died of boredom."

***

It felt as if the country was breaking apart; caught in an evil rustle of insanity, the population led down the garden path by some of the most malignant personalities to ever grace the political stage.

The world's only Pentecostal leader, Australian Prime Minister Scott Morrison, was at the height, or the depths, of his destructive power; and while sooner or later he would have to face the electorate, right now his personality traits, his autocratic tendencies, his slithering out of all personal responsibility, his lowbrow intellectuality, his ability to play to the cheap seats, his dishonesty, as some saw the endless corporate and government rorting that went on under his watch, the funnelling of tens of billions of dollars to corporate mates, all these factors were now in play.

Old Alex, and many others, were left with that deadening sensation: You know you're being ripped off, there's just nothing you can do about it.

Once regarded as a Federation, as one country, it had been news to him, just as it had been news to most Australians, that the states could shut their borders at will; but that's exactly what had happened.

He couldn't leave Australia, now little better than a Prison Island, he couldn't leave his home state of New South Wales, the borders to the neighbouring states of Queensland, Victoria and South Australia all being shut; and he couldn't even legally travel more than 10 kilometres.

We were all confined to quarters.

The atmosphere was intensely hermetic, we were all trapped in our own domestic situation, cosy, deteriorating or alone.

His was just a small thing, desperately ridiculous, that was all, nothing compared to the much of the rest of the country, but still he felt it most intensely as he sat on that step; behind him the broken flyscreen, and inside broken doors and broken furniture, after the tradie who had been living there rent-free for six months decided to smash up his house as a thank you note.

Messy lives, messy people. Invite chaos into your life and that is exactly what you get.

He had been lonely. The house was full of ghosts; and he repeatedly thought of that line: "Be careful who you pray to."

Humans may be able to summon the spirits, but who knew that these dark forces could be so easily stirred?

That's how it felt, in that freezing, miserable house; and so he had indeed invited chaos into his life; and was well served. The tradie, Connor, had been a good drinking buddy if nothing else, a bong and beer for breakfast kind of guy, a dispeller of ghosts, a Ghost Buster extraordinaire, and so Alex came to smile on the reasons for the domestic ruin, and his own role in it.

The book was over, the first copies of *Unfolding Catastrophe: Australia* had arrived, he was proud of the effort, and in the wake of it all he had declared he was giving up drinking; and had gifted a bottle of bourbon to Connor; to add to the bottle he was already drinking.

Fast forward a few hours and Connor was out on the back verandah screaming at all the neighbours that they could all "go and get fucked"; in between smashing up cupboards, doors and walls.

Through the violent tirades Alex made a dash to his car; and spent the night down at the beach.

Needless to say, that was the end of Connor as a house guest.

Meshneks. Black, insect-like creatures phasing in and out of that moment in time and place. The ones that come at the time of an impending death. He had been able to see them in the corridors. Summoned from the dark. Summoned from the God-fearing nature of his elderly parent; literally a house full of ghosts.

They were gone now.

And he had one mad bastard to thank for that: Connor.

***

That same day the NSW government announced that an easing of restrictions would begin in 18 days; as if we should all kiss the hand that destroyed us.

"New freedoms for vaccinated first step on state roadmap out of COVID" read the headline on the government missive: "People across NSW who have received both doses of a COVID-19 vaccine will be allowed more freedoms next month after NSW hit the target of six million jabs. This is the first step in the roadmap and further freedoms will follow for those who have had the jab when the state hits new vaccination targets of 70 and 80 per cent."

None of it applied to him. The unvaccinated. The new pariah class refusing to get a "jab" which didn't stop you getting this most feared of diseases, didn't stop you spreading it, and was developed by some of the most scandal-plagued companies on Earth. As lonely as he was, he'd take his chances.

"Following consultation with Dr Kerry Chant and her team, as well as the NSW Chief Psychiatrist Dr Murray Wright, the following individual freedoms will be allowed for adults who have received both doses of the COVID-19 vaccine.

From 12.01 am, Monday, 13 September:

For those who live outside the LGAs of concern, outdoor gatherings of up to five people (including children, all adults must be vaccinated) will be allowed in a person's LGA or within 5km of home.

For those who live in the LGAs of concern households with all adults vaccinated will be able to gather outdoors for recreation (including picnics) within the existing rules (for one hour only, outside curfew hours and within 5km of home). This is in addition to the one hour allowed for exercise.

***

The then Premier of NSW Gladys Berejiklian, who held a press conference each morning at 11 am, making herself a feminist icon or a blight on the state, however you saw it, thanked the millions of people across NSW.

"We are so grateful for every person who comes forward to get vaccinated because the more jabs we get into arms, the sooner we can lift restrictions,"

Ms Berejiklian said. "We appreciate the community's patience in the lead up to 13 September, this additional time will allow the recent surge of vaccines to take effect."

While it all turned out to be based on lies that the vaccine stopped infection and transmission, at the time the public had no idea.

As part of the so-called "roadmap" when the following targets were hit, the promised freedoms would be:

70 percent full vaccination: a range of family, industry, community and economic restrictions to be lifted for those who are vaccinated.

80 percent full vaccination: further easing of restrictions on industry, community and the economy.

Simple as that, Australia introduced medical apartheid. It was a dangerous path, fully embraced. The terrible health fascism of the era was now in play.

The release continued: "The government is also investigating trials of certain industries in coming months, as a proof-of-concept measure to prepare the businesses to open up and operate in a COVID-safe way."

Deputy Premier John Barilaro said the "roadmap" was the path to freedom and the biggest incentive yet to get vaccinated.

"The roadmap announced today outlines a clear pathway forward in which a range of family, industry, community and economic restrictions will be lifted for those that are fully vaccinated when NSW hits 70 per cent," Mr Barilaro said. "Having a meal with loved ones, or having a drink with friends is just around the corner, but to get there, we need to keep up momentum in the vaccination rollout."

Snake Oil salesmen, that is all they had become.

Was it true that Pfizer was somehow secretly funnelling millions of dollars of influence to politicians, as was rumoured at the time?

Who knew?

Soon enough both the Premier and Deputy Premier would be gone, with accusations of corruption, albeit not to do with the vaccines, buzzing around both of them.

TWO
HOW IT ALL ENDS

Often think of the rapidity with which things pass by and disappear, both the things which are and the things which are produced. For substance is like a river in a continual flow, and the activities of things are in constant change, and the causes work in infinite varieties; and there is hardly anything which stands still. And consider that which is near to thee, this boundless abyss of the past and the future in which all things disappear. How then is he not a fool who is puffed up with such things or plagued about them and makes himself miserable? For they vex him only for a time, and a short time.

Marcus Aurelius. *Meditations*.

A FREEZING WINTER, diabolically bad weather, lockdowns, and the unparalleled brutality of Australia's malfunctioning political system.

All of it combined; in those days before it went feral.

"Its surprising people aren't more angry," was a common enough comment; having endured a period of time when it seemed as if every little fascist in the country had been unleashed, officials strutting their temporary power and their temporary illusion of moral ground. In this little edifice, or place, Oak Flats, this little ledge on a diminishing authority. In this place which, unlike much of the country, would, if his waking dreams were correct, see great prosperity in the years, the decades, the centuries to come. While much about this period of Australian history was incredibly confused, those visions of a prosperous future, of a highly developed culture, of soaring buildings giving all the appearance of floating against the sky, those visions never contradicted themselves.

In the Australia of Old Alex's time, that time in between, evil got rewarded. Cognitive dissonance reigned. And the feeling that frequently besieged him, of having been taken hostage by a seer from the future, cast back into a primitive time and place, of being utterly intrigued by what he saw, as if an anthropologist fascinated by a stone age tribe, or a biologist fascinated by another lifeform, never left him.

For years the biggest story in the country had been the slow-motion collapse of the Australia of old into a country of uber surveillance caught in an all embracing bureaucratic stranglehold..

Now, with the country imprisoned by the world's most extreme lockdowns and insane levels of social restrictions, introduced without debate or parliamentary approval in what was tantamount to martial law, it had all come to pass, seemingly in an instant.

The previous four books he had written on this pivotal point in Australian history, *Terror in Australia: Workers' Paradise Lost*, *Hideout in the Apocalypse*, *Dark Dark Policing* and *Unfolding Catastrophe: Australia*, all warned of a darkening time.

He had felt compelled to write them, he was never quite sure why.

Now, when he looked back, it was as if someone else had actually written them; that all he did was act as a transmission point.

Let me be an instrument of your peace; except this had nothing to do with peace. This was all about conflict. The Imperial Battleship had landed. For some it was the Second Coming. View it as you like.

These were darkening times, and these books, switching from street scenes to fantastical flights of the imagination to reportage, all had a certain prophetic tone to them.

Shocking even to him, who had written them, mostly in the early hours of the morning, was how quickly it had all come to pass.

The books were all written in the third person. Alex, a dishevelled retired newspaper reporter who bore a passing resemblance to the author, was the vehicle through which the nation's story was told.

All four books ended with a warning of a totalitarian future.

By way of background, here are the closing episodes in sequence.

This is the ending of *Terror in Australia: Workers' Paradise Lost*.

***

"It's terrible what's happened to this city," Old Alex said to the Vietnamese woman making his coffee at the late night cafe in Kings Cross, once a vibrant entertainment district in the heart of Sydney. "You not only one say terrible," she said. "Many people say the same. The government, so many rules."

Alex was sad, he explained because he had been born here; had some identity with the country. The city he once treated as his own backyard was lost.

"Maybe it get better in the future," the Vietnamese woman said, handing him his coffee and his change.

"I don't think so," he replied. "I doubt it very much."

Walking back to the office where he commonly worked from midnight to dawn, a time when the buzz of humans all around him was less intense, he passed, again and again, derelict scenes in the street; and wanted to be long gone.

A group of Middle Eastern men drove past in a spanking new Bentley. They barely noticed the societal collapse they were driving through; more than comfortable inside their own world. You didn't drive around this town in a brand new Bentley because you worked nine to five. This was a city where crime had always paid.

Walking once again past the promotional "Building the Future" signs erected by the Sydney City Council, he knew for certain: this was Paradise Lost, and it was never coming back.

Whatever form the society would take in the future, and there would be considerable chaos and bloodshed before the final outcome, it was not the world he had grown up in, and it was not the world the social engineers had hoodwinked the people into believing it was.

Screwed by the left and screwed by the right. Jihad within and jihad without. Terror within and terror without. The freedoms of thought, expression, conduct, enterprise, character which had once been so much a part of Australia had vanished.

In those weeks and months that held breath, it felt as if the battle between those trying to trigger an enlightenment and those trying to trigger an apocalypse could go either way.

Signs and portents were everywhere.

For some reason an expression by a rough sleeper he had become friendly with in the Nepalese lakeside city of Pokhara kept popping into his head:

"You think you the only tiger in the jungle. Not possible."

The fanatical, the fantastical and the theological, all had far too much to do with the present circumstance. Alex scanned the news and despaired. He read easily accessible advice to jihadists on the best smartphones and encryption programs, while the Australian government pounded on about terror.

Increasingly appalled, he read account after account of massacres, tortures, murders, looked at pictures, as millions of people in the West had done, of those about to die.

Imagine a world where it was impossible to lie.

In those days before, Alex sincerely hoped, an ultimate grace would settle upon mankind, a grace that would not be at the behest of any faith, that would not be held within the frame of any belief. There were too many deaths, too much butchery. In that microcosm of Australia where he had been born, a depressed population, muttering in its own frustrations, abandoned all hope that the wider world would ever make sense; and watched football instead.

"There are more things in heaven and on earth, Horatio, than are dreamt of in your philosophy," went the Shakespeare line, while the words "Apocryphal" and "Apocalypse" shimmered in the middle distance.

The world he had known was gone.

"Be happy that you knew it," an old friend advised when he expressed his anger at the empty streets, the impoverished state of the country, the hapless state of the media, the gathering strength of the Sharia, the contempt for native spiritualities, the barbarians inside the gate, the horror that had enveloped the world. "Be grateful that you knew it when it was good."

Alex, he would sometimes mutter to himself, was dyslexic across time and space. Tell him to do one thing and he would do another, turn left and he would turn right. He didn't like being told what to think, on spiritual matters or anything else. Nor had most of the people he had ever known.

"Be happy," he thought, "that many of your friends died before they could be stoned to death. Be happy that they weren't faced with the choice, convert or die. Be happy that as apostates they weren't crucified or beheaded. Because they would never have converted. It wasn't in their nature."

Over his lifespan he had seen the wheel turn several times: everything he and that initial little band he had partied with so hard back in the sixties and seventies had believed in, all of it had been dumped from the buckets of the Ferris wheel into a vacant allotment. The rise of the wowsers. The rise of middle-class probity. The rise of the politically correct. The rise of the Christians. The rise of Islamic State.

This time around it wasn't just melancholy at the loss of a few souls, or the loss of a scene or demimonde. This time around he grieved for the loss of everything, his home, Australia, a place, the spirits of old, the landscapes that had breathed a timeless spirituality and the inner-city demimondaines which had breathed a licentious thrill, a place where all delinquent, time-sliding souls met before departure; in the once crowded streets which had been so much a part of his youth.

A place where they had laughed, genuinely and freely, in delight at each other's physical forms. A place where they could love; and be loved. A place where they had been, for however a brief a time in the firmament, free.

***

Five years on, "The world's gone mad," the old newspaper reporter said as he passed people on his morning walk.

"Didn't make any sense anyway," came the response.

Australia was shutting down. Empowered by tough new laws and public pressure, police forces were testing how far they could go in punishing behaviour that was ordinarily routine, keeping their political masters happy while increasing their own power.

In Australia, the authorities had threatened people sitting alone drinking coffee with six months in jail, or for sitting in their cars, for not having a good reason to have left their house, for eating a kebab alone on a park bench.

Under these conditions, where basic humanity is lost, the perpetrators act like predators and the targets act like prey.

As Paul Gregoire pointed out in the Sydney Criminal Lawyers Blog, the government was making criminals out of ordinary people.

"When NSW police commissioner Mick Fuller explained during a budget estimates hearing on 1 September, 2021, that, in relation to COVID-19, his force is treating the virus itself like a criminal, it seemed a little odd.

"The top cop added that as he's treating this tiny biological entity that's spread across the entire globe like a human who's broken the law, 'therefore, wherever the virus is, you will see an increased police presence'.

"But the truth of the matter is COVID isn't a criminal and it doesn't abide by human-imposed laws.

"So, it would seem that more to the point, the Commissioner is actually saying his officers are treating people who are infected by COVID-19 or have the potential to be infected by the virus as if they have done something illegal.

"Indeed, one only has to think back over the past 18 months, with the heavy police presence on the streets, checking IDs and handing out penalty infringement notices, to come to the conclusion that in the COVID-19 pandemic era, we are all guilty until proven uninfected."

***

Hideout in the Apocalypse was about surveillance and the crushing of Australia's larrikin spirit. The government knew when it introduced the panopticon, universal surveillance, that it would have a devastating impact on the culture.

If people know they are being watched they behave differently. Dissent is stifled, conformity becomes the norm, the population easier to manage.

At the same time the Australian government had prosecuted the greatest assault on freedom of speech in the nation's history. The media was highly manipulated, and journalists closely monitored. They were now classified as Persons of Interest for the nation's security agencies, an outlandish assault on the Fourth Estate.

A democracy in name only, in Australia the war on terror became a war on the people's right to know, justifying an unprecedented expansion of state power. Now we had Covid-19.

Below is the closing sequence for *Hideout*.

***

At the Tables of Knowledge scattered across the country there was nothing but contempt for their political leaders from a stubborn, resentful, disillusioned and increasingly embittered population.

The once staunch left-leaning Labor voters who populated the beer garden at the Lakeview Hotel, builders, labourers, concreters, plasterers, truckies, electricians, carpenters, mixed with subsiding alcoholics in poor health, switched their vote.

A year or two before, few of them would have ever admitted publicly their politically incorrect support for ultra-nationalist anti-mass immigration advocate Senator Pauline Hanson, leader of One Nation.

Now, she garnered the protest vote, and they supported her to a man, or woman.

Fueled by resentment, some of the often vacuous chatter was now vicious: "I can't wait to watch Pauline string up the first rope."

But the vast majority of it was simply the voices of people who had had enough; sick of a country where nothing worked, where everything was expensive, where government mangled into every part of their lives, where fat cats and politicians stole their taxes, where their own opinions and hard work were regarded as of no account.

The identity politics of the day, refugees, lesbian mothers, Aboriginals in custody, ignored the muddling middle.

Not one politician stood up and declared to ordinary workers: "I am going to make your life better."

The social engineers, their tertiary acquired groupthink theories failing to take in the real world, reaped what they had sowed: contempt.

One of Australia's most esteemed writers, Richard Flanagan, delivered a heartfelt condemnation of the country in which he dwelled: "Every day we hear grim and grimmer news that suggests we are passing through the winter of the world. Everywhere man is tormented, the globe reels from multitudes of suffering and horror, and, worst, we no longer know with confidence what our answer might be. And yet we understand that the time approaches when an answer must be made or a terrible reckoning will be ours."

Resentment curdled everywhere.

A petition went up online for returned soldiers, sent to war by the very government which now ignored them: "When you slip into your warm bed tonight, over 100 veterans of Iraq and Afghanistan wars will sleep rough in parks around Australia. Cold, hungry and suffering Post Traumatic Stress Disorder as a result of service to their country, these brave veterans deserve better. They need a place to shower, to eat, to sleep and to talk to other veterans who understand what they are going through. But where do they go? How can the government justify spending millions and millions on refugees yet forget those who were prepared to lay down their lives for the country they love???

The horsemen wheeled out onto the plains of Dabiq.

> And when he had opened the fourth seal, I heard the voice of the fourth beast say, Come and see. And I looked, and behold a pale horse: and his name that sat on him was Death, and Hell followed with him. And power was given unto them over the fourth part of the earth, to kill with sword, and with hunger, and with death, and with the beasts of the earth.

The drones flew overhead. Western bombs rained down on crying children.

The massacres grew worse. Talk of a World War was everywhere in the wind.

> So the angel swung his sickle over the earth and gathered the grapes of the earth, and he threw them into the great winepress of God's wrath. And the winepress was trodden outside the city, and the blood that flowed from it rose as high as the bridles of the horses…

In those waking dreams which continued to haunt the old news reporter, the attempts by those who had sent him and hundreds of others like him to rescue a race from an apocalypse, to avoid the gifting of billions of souls to the Dark Lords, stood on the precipice of failure.

The world had ignored the warnings of the town criers. The Enlightenment had failed. Time was running out.

The books he had loved as a youth began to recycle rapidly through his brain. Ask not For Whom the Bell Tolls, it tolls for thee.

The policies and procedures were in place, the rules and regulations drafted. The place had been prepared. The plane was on the tarmac. There was a gap in the air, that intake of breath prior to calamity.

We will meet in the place where there is no darkness, in the middle of the torture chamber.

But it would all avail the torturers nought; their feeble souls the flashes of light at the edge of a firestorm, barely existing before they were gone, destroyed in the maelstrom they themselves had helped create.

Above, as it had done all year, the sky burned.

***

All of the books warned of a darkening time; and unimaginable as it once was, the implausible was now becoming the reality. Below is the closing sequence for *Dark Dark Policing*.

***

"Swampie", as he was so appropriately called, a former bikie and a member of Oak Flats royalty, was back for a brief stint from his FIFO, Fly In Fly Out work in the Northern Territory.

"Plunder the poor, give to the rich." The retired news reporter repeated the old line when the conversation drifted to the government of the day.

"Why haven't they risen up?" Swampie asked, gesturing towards the lines of suburban houses surrounding them. "Why hasn't there been a revolution already?"

Alex shrugged: "There will be. Millions more unemployed in a chronically mismanaged economy, that will do it. You can only treat people like dirt for so long."

All around where he was staying the once bucolic hills and pastures of a dairy farm were being scraped for a $700 million freeway. Wind whipped the topsoil into mini dust storms while thousands of houses sprung up out of the surrounding farmlands, seemingly overnight.

"Where are these people going to find work?" Alex asked, only to be met with a shrug.

The democratic contract was broken; Prime Minister Scott Morrison and his predecessors had perpetrated the crime.

The media hunts in packs. And every journalist in the country now had Morrison in their sights. Shameless as he was, politics would prove just as big a public humiliation for the current Prime Minister as it had for his predecessor and mate, Malcolm Turnbull. And his predecessor in turn, Tony Abbott. The worst Australia's political class had to offer. The worst of the worst.

The public and the media were "woke", as the expression of the moment went, and no amount of "nothing to see here" shuffle could save this hapless brand of conservatism.

Now the talk was not of Recession but a Depression, a belated acceptance of a reality already gripping many parts of Australia.

The headlines told it all: "Chinese company approved to run water-mining operation in drought-stricken Queensland", "Australia's vast household debt a giant economic millstone", "The economic outlook for Australia has tanked", "International Monetary Fund has sharply downgraded forecasts for the Australian economy", "Australian economy to limp along as consumers struggle".

"Our plunging economy", "How the Government protects its donors and tax dodgers", "Government caves to a few 'big interests."

"Morrison government paid empathy consultant $190,000."

"Mining giant given millions in grant by Coalition from fund for Indigenous disadvantage."

As for Alex's own story, trapped as he sometimes felt in one mortal frame after another, it was about to take a giant, joyful leap.

But for those both brief and interminable months, caught in the suburbs where he had never wanted to be, unable to tell friend from foe, depressed by the state of the country and damaged by the harassment of the so-called "national security" agencies, he was forced to summon help from that far-off place, from those who had conquered quantum entanglement long ago.

Old Alex kept asking for that idol of his youth Bertrand Russell, for high intellect and compassionate insight, and instead got the curmudgeonly Eric Blair, aka George Orwell, a man who wrote beautifully about the downtrodden and the working poor but who in truth was not of them.

A prophet who did not live to see his most famous book, *Nineteen Eighty-Four*, have the profound impact that it did. And who in this era, almost seventy years after his death from tuberculosis, was quoted more than any living writer.

Old Alex kept asking for an ability to see the flows of history, and instead got drunken poets, Dylan Thomas, Malcolm Lowry, Henry Lawson, so many thousands of others who had died their own remote, unkind deaths; alcoholics, street junkies, the most isolated and denigrated of mankind. And especially here, in this cold, windy place, the spirits whose names he could not decipher, the ancestors of this place, the wise and courageous, noble and poor, those who had loved and been loved, warriors who had seen their own tribes conquered and who grieved to this very day.

Old Alex left that jinn-soaked place, with its harsh winters and the sad whispering of its ancients, the trees fringing the lake, the working man's cottages, all the stories of the sometimes funny-as, inevitably drunken exploits of its denizens. He left the uber surveillance perpetrated by the most patently corrupt and appallingly mismanaged government in the nation's history. And flew free.

"Take it as a badge of honour they even noticed you," he was advised. "Do what I told you to do a long time ago: laugh at them. You are one. They are thousands. And you know what you've got on your side that they do not? Truth."

Prophecies are warnings; frightening moments of clairvoyance. The vision-soaked dreams of the strange and the restless, the food riots of the future, desert gulags, soldiers in black riot gear manning every street corner, sad, derelict cities, the gleaming edifices which rose and fell far out to sea, they were already twisting into the present.

His prophecies were unlikely to be heeded; for greed is blind. Even as those borne-aloft intelligences he was gifted to see circled in otherworldly anger, attempting to change the course of nations and the course of history, they knew that humans were fatally flawed. Most particularly in this place, so far from the centre of things; where the worst of the worst prayed for a righteous nation in flights of delusion as they rigged a government replete with malevolent spirits and staffed with those of unparalleled greed and self-aggrandisement, characterised from top to bottom by malfeasance and incompetence, by a grand ignorance of the people they purported to represent and who, instead, they robbed.

Historians would look back and wonder how it was that a country's ruling elites could so savagely betray, so audaciously rob, their fellow countrymen. How integrity and decency were so easily abandoned. How they could with such blundering idiocy and staggering incompetence destroy the very place which had made them rich.

Why the population did not rise up even quicker than they did.

How a once optimistic country lost its way.

The evil that men do lives after them.

You did not need the gift of prophecy to know that future historians would view the Abbott–Turnbull–Morrison era as the worst period of governance in Australia's history, a time when a terrible brutality was born.

***

And then Covid hit, the brutality, indeed the insanity of Australia's response making headlines around the world. Here are the closing sequences for *Unfolding Catastrophe: Australia*.

***

The national derangement was complete.

A Melbourne hospital prevented a mother from seeing her son, who was suffering from a severe brain injury after a motor crash.

"We haven't been able to see our son since he woke up from a coma. We just want to hug our son."

Police were filmed arresting and pepper-spraying a bunch of ratbag kids, average age perhaps twelve, after one of them refused to wear a mask into a shop and the rest gave them "a bit of lip".

The largely deserted working-class shopping mall saw yet another conflagration between police and the citizenry; every last one of the tweens involved under age.

They might have been too young to legally have sex, but they weren't too young to be pepper-sprayed and arrested in what the authorities had been assuring us was the new COVID normal.

This was the unravelling. This was one of the cascading moments in time, in that kaleidoscope of incidents when the authorities lost control of their own behaviour, the public lost all faith in the authorities, and the official narrative lost all credibility.

A man was fined $5000 for drinking a cup of takeaway coffee in the street, in the remote central Australian town of Alice Springs. Surrounded by some of the world's most beautiful desert country, there was not and had never been, a single solitary case of Covid in the town. Footage showed the man being wrestled to the ground and his coffee spilling onto the street.

This was the hell you created.

There is an old Jesuit saying, "Set the world alight!"

Well, so you did. But how can anyone bow down to these false, lunatic gods?

The prime minister was spending a lot of time "on his prayer knees", as he told a slavish media. The result: the rest of the country was enduring an End Time delusion.

Twelve million in lockdown for the panicked fear of a disease few had any chance of catching, and those who did, an even remoter chance of dying from. How is that not the Angel of Death? How is that not a national derangement? How is this not *The Origins of Totalitarianism*?

Where the darkest of Lords reap the souls of men.

The actions of the Australian authorities impugned through our every sense of self; of the familiarity and comfort of routines which humans establish by their very nature.

As many other writers had commented; there was a strange spirituality to the season, a dangerous dementia of the occult; or so it often felt.

And in all of this, this utterly lunatic time, there was the absolute immediate consequence; of lives and futures destroyed.

***

Close to home, Old Alex's local cafe, The Village Fix, was shut after the owner was arrested for not wearing a mask; the dozen or so police coordinating with the local daily newspaper, *The Illawarra Mercury*, to make sure the dramatic scenes were splashed all over their front page.

The paper breathlessly reported that some people were frightened to come into town because someone wasn't wearing a mask. There might have been little or no scientific evidence that masks were effective in stopping the spread of Covid, but they were very good at instilling fear and a heightened sense of danger into a population; in manufacturing a psychic derangement.

Officers fined owner Anthony Reale, 41, $1000 for not wearing a face mask or ensuring that three of his employees wore masks.

His wife, Natalie, mother of their three young children, was also arrested. "We have been put through the wringer," she told him. "Now we have to deal with all the expense of courts and lawyers. We have done nothing wrong. It was a setup. Putting us on the front page has meant we have had threats; as have other organic stores who have adopted the same stance."

A world upside down.

"What sort of police involve themselves in activities against ordinary citizens which can lead to them being threatened, to endangering my family like this? None of the stories mention the struggles of small business, or that have some mask exemptions, which are very bad for some people's health.

"We have quite a bit of support across the world. Cafes from across Australia and America have messaged us, and we have also had threats, but the support outweighs the threats. We have been dragged through hell; I was treated like a dog."

NSW Deputy Police Commissioner Gary Worboys said the cafe was flagrantly disregarding Covid-19 protocols.

"There was an absolute clear resistance from the cafe owner and those people at front-of-house to actually wear a mask," Mr Worboys said. "It is clearly irresponsible."

What was clearly irresponsible policing in this derangement spreading through the entire society was the destruction of perfectly decent people's lives and livelihoods; their public shaming, exposing a family with young children to public threat.

Wherever Old Alex happened to be, he frequented the earliest opening cafe, which is how he got to know the family which ran Village Fix. You couldn't find more decent, harder-working people. And just like him, they didn't believe the government narrative either.

What was truly irresponsible was the amount of stress government functionaries were placing on ordinary citizens; a derangement of the era causing scenes of conflict between citizens and police right across the country.

***

The veneer of civilisation proved virus-thin. The consequences of lockdowns and the remaking of Australian society would spill down the generations. The derangement that took over the political class and the absolute mismanagement of the Covid crisis, beginning in early 2020, would seriously damage the welfare of hundreds of thousands of families; and mark the nation's descent into a totalitarian hell. For out of the humus of that destructive time, new kinds of leaders and forms of government would arise. A new kind of apartheid; a new kind of mass psychosis would reshape a subjugated population, the towns, the communities, families, the isolated and the much loved, transforming the way Australians interacted and cared for each other. The era would birth a new kind of cruelty.

And those who inherited this future would wonder, above all else, how anyone of conscience could have let this happen?

THREE
THE DERANGEMENT OF BATTLE

If you come to
Heaven's Torrents
Heaven's Wells,
Heaven's Prisons,
Heaven's Traps
Heaven's Cracks:
Quit such places
With all speed.

Sun Tzu. *The Art of War*.

The sky seemed somehow airless – as though all the air had been pumped out and there was nothing but dry dust overhead. And the pump was continuing its work: together with the air, faith and hope had now disappeared; nothing was left but a small mound of grey, frozen earth. A soul can live in torment for years and years, even decades, as it slowly, stone by stone, builds a mound over a grave; as it moves towards the apprehension of eternal loss and bows down before reality.

Vasily Grossman, *Life and Fate*.

WE WERE BARELY conscious, struggling into a lifeform, compelled, inadequate, unable to comprehend this most peculiar time in history. How did any of it make sense?

3 July, 2021 was the initial Saturday of the "soft" Sydney lockdown. Premier Gladys Berejiklian jovially empathised with locals at her 11 am media briefing about the weather being "great" and asked those exercising outdoors to keep to groups of 10 and not let it become 20; one of only hundreds of endlessly changing nonsensical diktats issued in the interminable course of the government's exploitation of Covid. Nothing to do with contagion.

Old Alex kept asking himself: What happens when they realise it was all for nothing?

Informed commentators had been asking that same question for more than a year. We still hadn't got there. Instead, the derangement was complete.

There had been week after week, month after month of government generated diktats and the so-called health emergency led every news bulletin, creating a kind of breathless hysteria. Even if they could, nobody wanted to talk.

Unable to legally leave his house for more than two hours a day, and his neighbours encouraged to report him to the authorities if he did, Old Alex spent a lot of time sitting on the doorstep; imprisoned by both foul weather and a foul government. All around a terrifying silence, or acquiescence. Herd behaviour, thugs afoot.

That doorstep. Those lonely patches of winter sunlight. The world shrank.

Those who believed it was all a lie from the beginning were shunned; or isolated, although it was a crime hiding in plain sight.

The entire weekend saw sunny mid-winter weather and residents of Sydney's affluent Eastern Suburbs, residents of the inner city and the inner west flocked to parks and beaches. People exercised, played sport and had picnics; a wonderful return to normality after all those bizarre visitations, those terrible lockdowns of previous months.

Despite the parks being more crowded than usual, despite months of government and media promoted hysteria, there were no police patrols, no fines, and indeed, "no worries". Needless to say, this whiff of freedom did not last.

***

Each morning at around 11 am, ensuring maximum coverage on news bulletins throughout the remainder of the day, came the ritual morning press conference; Covid theatre in full throttle, ensuring Premier Gladys Berejiklian and her henchwoman, Chief Medical Officer Dr Kerry Chant, remained front and centre of the news cycle, warning of yet more restrictions.

Heavily masked, and backed up by a showy police presence, carrying important looking files, these women announced case numbers and death tolls and an ever-shifting regime of rule changes.

As they spoke millions of people endured some of the harshest, and as it turned out most pointless lockdowns in the world. Lives, businesses, careers destroyed as those two grandstanded in front of the cameras.

Old Alex wasn't the only one truly disgusted by the daily charade.

"Gladys at 11" read the billboard on the front of one shuttered cinema.

During these days of the initial laxed lockdown, the Covid-19 Delta variant managed to spread from the sun-bathing region of the Bondi cluster and found its way out to the communities of Sydney's southwestern region by Thursday, 8 July.

As Paul Gregoire at the Sydney Criminal Lawyers Blog reported: "State authorities freaked. And NSW police announced it would be deploying 100 extra officers into the region, with the idea repeatedly flagged that the virus roaming around the less affluent and more ethnic communities of southwest Sydney posed a greater risk."

And the soft lockdown was made hard.

Migrant communities were scapegoated, and the millions of residents of Sydney's sprawling western suburbs felt deeply insulted by the super toffs of the Eastern suburbs; a city, a country, a place deeply riven; a society more divided than ever before.

At 5 pm on 8 July, NSW police released a statement outlining it would "launch a major high-visibility operation across Sydney's south-west" to ensure restrictions were being followed.

"The understanding here being that migrant communities who were locked down for three months last year, somehow didn't get it this time around," Gregoire wrote. "So, mounted police, the dog unit, traffic and highway patrol cops, PolAir, traffic police and general duties officers were all being sent to Fairfield, Canterbury-Bankstown and Liverpool local government areas."

NSW Police Minister David Elliott said the "Delta strain is a game changer". He made no mention of the thousands of Sydneysiders from eastern parts of Sydney, who evidently did not watch mainstream media either and were flocking to the parks and beaches, in that part of Sydney where finding a house for under a million dollars was literally an impossibility.

The sprawling reaches of western Sydney contain large migrant communities, with some areas having 70% of their populations born overseas, hardly a recipe for social cohesion; all the easier to crush you.

Berejiklian, at the height of her power, urged the communities to stay at home. She said police would be asking people who were outside their homes what their reasonable excuse was, and would be cracking down on activities like unnecessary shopping.

"You don't need that pair of shoes today," said police local commander Assistant Commissioner Tony Cooke.

Now there's a manifest evil, excessive shopping.

In the wealthy eastern suburbs, citizens were going about their lives more or less as usual.

In the large tracts of the not so wealthy west, they were compelled inwards into a nightmare of common suffering; an anger that would last a very long time.

As Thucydides had put it more than 2400 years before: "The strong do what they can and the weak suffer what they must." A saying which was being picked up in various translations by contemporary commentators, for it had become frighteningly apposite.

***

Racial justice organisation Democracy in Colour decried the decision, describing the operation as "thinly veiled racism".

"This isn't a public health response, it's explicitly targeting people of colour and working-class communities in the western suburbs," said National Director Neha Madhok. "Inner-city suburbs and the Northern Beaches have had significant cases, but they have not been harshly policed like this."

Assistant Commissioner Cooke claimed he had been in constant contact with community leaders and there was no excuse for not complying with restrictions at this point in the pandemic.

"Our multicultural liaison officers have been deployed for weeks now across the community, sending the message, we have paraphernalia in 56 languages distributed to communities," he said. "This is about us working together to comply with these orders ... When we do not get the compliance we will enforce."

Premier Gladys Berejiklian warned of consequences if case numbers continued to grow due to 'disobedience".

Berejiklian attributed the spike in cases to "non-compliance" in the community and illegal household interactions.

***

The nature of it, the size of the scam, was confounding; and as Old Alex wandered through the remnants of an ancient forest nearby, the shocking truth ran through his head like alarm bells, springing to attention, shrieking to be heard; and yet it remained, in a sense, almost incomprehensible, that humans could care so little for the welfare of their brethren.

Naomi Wolf, in her stunning book *The Bodies of Others*, expressed it all far more coherently than his own jumbled thoughts, when she wrote of this "harrowing civilisational crossroads – engaged in a war against vast impersonal forces with limitless power over our lives ... how those forces seized upon two years of COVID-19 panic in sinister new ways and how, yet, against overwhelming odds, we still might win.

"Others have looked at this war from a biomedical perspective, or from a strictly political one. My focus is on how this ongoing war against us is far more basic, aimed at nothing less than dissolving the meaning of humanity itself and undoing the rich cultural legacy we in the West have long treasured and passed on to succeeding generations.

"In those two years, the COVID-19 pandemic, which began unfolding with the unprecedented global lockdown in March 2020, has fundamentally remade human relations, capitalism, and culture in the West.

"In 2020-22, we entered a time in which the post-World War II organising principle of human affairs, the democratic nation-state, was being intentionally diluted in power and undermined in the interest of constructing a replacement meta-structure of unaccountable loosely aligned global nonprofits, Big Tech corporations, the WEF, and the Chinese Communist Party (CCP).

"Their aim was to construct engines of history designed to dissolve human culture, closeness and community. United in an alliance of convenience, these forces see human beings and the troublesome individualistic West, with its stubborn insistence on human rights, on joy, on spontaneity, on quirkiness, acceptance and tolerance, as obstacles to be managed, drained of power and resources, and sidelined. Their goal is to subvert Western cultural norms and ultimately to alienate Western children from their families' influence and from Western history and freedoms generally.

"The war against 'the virus' has really been a war waged via technologies and their masters to dissolve human culture and disempower human beings. It is a war on free thought and free speech – a war against our most fundamental beliefs."

***

On that Thursday afternoon 8 July 2021, on the same day the government was announcing their high profile enforcement, police raided the Chester Hill headquarters of popular western Sydney restaurant chain Rashay's.

It was based on a tip-off that people weren't wearing masks in the office. Australia was now a nation of dobbers, encouraged by the risible performance of politicians and enforced by the police who did not, or could not, stand up against the lunacy they were being asked to inflict on the population.

Many were known to be unhappy with the duties they were being asked to perform. Great choice: act like a dickhead or lose your job and your ability to look after your kids. The attending officers found two call centre operators allegedly unmasked while eating lunch.

Owner of the chain of 30 restaurants Rami Ykmour wasn't taking any of it lying down.

"I'm here to follow the law,' Mr Ykmour tells a heavily kitted out and armed officer in his foyer. "You've just got to understand that these people here are here supporting people who are unemployed. That's what we're doing, during a pandemic."

The argument escalated after Ykmour asked a police officer to wait outside.

The officer refused and insisted on waiting in the lobby as "an offence has been committed".

Moments later he was joined by several more police officers who crowded into the front office.

You don't get to be the owner of a chain of restaurants in a rough house like Western Sydney by being shy, and Ykmour live streamed the entire incident to Facebook, where the footage remains available, another piece of evidence of authorities harassing small business owners, driving many of them to bankruptcy; instilling a savage divide between the police and the community.

"He's calling for backup," Ykmour says to the camera. "Look how many police officers he's got. He's got 10 officers. "One, two, three, four. There's 20 people here for a young girl."

As the Australian edition of the ever bolshie UK Daily Mail, which did a damn sight better job of covering these incidents than any of the local outlets, recorded: "A staff member sitting behind the reception desk begins to break down as the commotion escalates. The woman then collapses onto the floor and Mr Ykmour pulls out his phone to call an ambulance while telling off the officers.

"Another officer raises his voice at Mr Ykmour to stop arguing with police and focus on the call."

Shortly afterwards Ykmour was arrested and taken away in a paddy wagon for not having produced the ID of one of the allegedly unmasked employees.

A NSW Police spokesperson later said two staff members had been issued $200 fines for not wearing face masks.

This was the New Covid Normal. This was Australia.

***

As every day the country descended further into a totalitarian hell, if Old Alex had one hope for *Unfolding Catastrophe* it was that it marked a white line amidst the chaos that had enveloped the populace, that it forced politicians to rethink their actions and for the public to reassess their politicians.

No such luck, of course. He was too easy to ignore. The ship of state sailed on, indifferent to the swirling eddies through which it ploughed. And with their cruelty and divorce from reality, indifferent to the populace itself.

Numerous writers had observed that the single most frightening thing about COVID had not been the virus itself, but the public's willingness to comply with a blizzard of irrational diktats. That the single most selfish thing any citizen could do was to follow their leaders blindly; and let them get away with their absurd destruction.

In Australia the ugly face of Covid totalitarianism was the soon to be disgraced Prime Minister Scott Morrison, who seized on the panic as a chance to rehabilitate his damaged political career while at the same time accreting ever more power to himself, quadrupling the national debt and forking out tens of billions of dollars to the corporate sector.

It was the rest of the population that was paying, that is the 12 million people under what was tantamount to house arrest; many no longer able to take care of themselves and their families, having lost either the dignity of labour or the pride of running their own businesses.

Yet, the rich in Australia, as in other countries, were many billions of dollars richer than they were 18 months before; with a massive transfer of wealth from the middle class upwards to the oligarchs.

Unfolding Catastrophe asked: What will happen when the population realises they have been lied to? The answer? They will riot in the street.

Which is exactly what happened; with unparalleled scenes of violent protests around the country.

The history of government hysteria and the implementation of lockdowns began with Imperial College London, and was mirrored in Australia with similar modelling by the Bill Gates funded Peter Doherty Institute, which originally and inaccurately predicted 50,000 to 150,000 deaths.

Australian authorities must have known within weeks that the hysteria being visited upon the country was being done under either false or highly disputed premises; that the forecasts of both the Imperial College London and the Peter Doherty Institute in Australia were wildly inaccurate.

It was obvious from very early on that the projected death toll, the excuse for Scott Morrison placing himself front and centre of the fear campaign, the rationale behind the massive destruction of Australian life, was false.

Why did no one call him out? Not his political comrades in arms. Not his wealthy political donors. Not the Premiers now shutting down their entire states and masquerading as heroes of the moment. Not the senior bureaucrats peddling a message of alarmism; and only very, very few in the nation's media.

It was the world's most famous whistleblower, Edward Snowden, who had warned more than a year previously: "We are seeing new powers being claimed. We are seeing new powers being abused.

"You know, they always say these are temporary, it is for this reason and that reason. But there is nothing more permanent than a temporary measure."

No government should ever again have the power to shut down lives, businesses, culture, and liberties with such a wanton disregard for the welfare of their citizenry.

That was the warning he wished to convey. In the slipstream, shouting in the wind, as all cautionary voices were ignored.

***

Another friend was dying. Most of those he had partied with as a young man were long gone, AIDS and overdoses, and now, of course, the afflictions of old age. This one cancer. So to visit him, he revisited Sydney's once bohemian entertainment centre, Kings Cross, where once, as a hyperactive teenager, he had known every back alley.

His dreams turned vivid in a waking flash.

He was plunged 47 floors to the planet surface. Into profane circumstances. Into their realm.

Just like that. He was sore from the jolt for days to come.

He did the same thing he always did. He visited the old haunts. The siren call. Appear near when you are far. Appear far when you are near.

Once, he would have thought of it as being deserted from above. Now those red lights blinked slowly as supremely intelligent machines gathered on the horizon.

Now we walk through the valley, and will permit no evil.

Cruised by the intelligence agencies, sometimes he was walking through that pond of black eels. Sometimes he was swimming through it. Sometimes he just looked from afar, and waited for them to leave.

His head was so full of voices he had no idea who to trust.

The currents were dangerous. Ditto their Psyop programs.

And their manipulation and control of the public narrative, despite all their tech wizardry and high IQs, was also very very dangerous; for they knew not what they did.

He went down to the little park at the back of Elizabeth Bay, where the carp he remembered as a youth, or at least their descendants, still swam through the water feature.

Much preferable to be a delinquent child seeking shelter; someone with youth and life ahead of them.

Australia, those areas he had seen in recent days at least, remained in a false twilight. The rich drank their fancy beers, well-creamed faces, well-laundered clothes; nice restaurants, cars, houses, certainty of belief.

Old Alex, like those old carp, rose to the surface for oxygen; swam indifferent to the surrounding swarm. In the end we all became humus on the forest floor, the culture's floor.

We are chameleons. We adopt the local patina. We come at nighttime and in the dawn. We are reluctant to appear at such crisis ridden crossroads, with deception everywhere.

He rose to walk, and could see no more.

Let us sing then, let us sing, the idiot songs of an idiot savant, the languishing, anguished if you will, attempts to save a population, a country, a dream of subsistence and self-reliance; a dream of comradeship and community.

While a silence, a frightening silence, gripped all their lives.

***

Instead of being in the middle of the action, as he might once have been as a city reporter, all Old Alex could do was watch from his aerie in the remote suburbs, the urban fringe beneath a sandstone escarpment, as military helicopters flew from the base at Nowra further south up to Sydney and back; and feel, if his mind was in flying mode, the high technical literacy of the pilot and the military intent of those on board, and feel in some ways the wonder of the ancients as they watched, through his eyes, those flying warships streaming through the sky.

A frightening pall; and truly, nothing made sense. Something else was afoot. He knew perfectly well the government apparatchiks did not care for the welfare of the populace, despite all the protestations of the show pony politicians parading in front of the cameras; if they did care they would have mingled with the common people, and never have rorted those billions of dollars off the backs of a slave population, just to squander it. He had been frightened long before they were born, long before humans.

***

Whether you could leave home, go to work, go to a restaurant, avoid being masked or jabbed, it was all at government behest.

Melbourne was well on the way to becoming the most locked-down city on Earth, with the Victorian Premier, North Korean leader Kim Jong-un lookalike Daniel Andrews, placing himself front and centre of the catastrophe on a daily basis, setting, surely, a world record for the longest continuous stretch of press conferences in the world, more than 100 days in a row.

Melbourne became a byword worldwide for absurd Covid overreach, for state violence and brutality.

Literally half the country was now shut down.

At midnight on Thursday 15th of July, 2021, Melbourne entered its fifth lockdown; originally for a five day period.

There were no Covid cases in hospitals in Victoria on the day of the announcement, yet these power drunk fools were shutting down the entire state.

Premier Daniel Andrews, who still had his supporters, all scared witless of "the virus" and turning to a "strong man" to save them, said: "We now have new cases, new exposure sites and a strain of this virus that is wildly infectious.

"We've seen this strain before – and you probably already know what we need to do next. Victoria will not wait to act. We know that not much good comes from waiting.

"Waiting could see more people infected and the number of exposure sites explode.

"If we act now – while we're right on the heels of this outbreak – we can give ourselves every chance of getting ahead of it. If we wait – we lose that option.

"Which is why, on the advice of the Acting Chief Health Officer, Victoria will go into lockdown tonight, meaning there are only five reasons to leave home from 11:59 pm on Thursday 15 of July 2021.

"That means you can only leave home to get the food and the supplies you need, for exercise for up to two hours and no more than five kilometres from your home, for care or caregiving, work or education if you can't do it from home or to get vaccinated at the nearest possible location.

"These restrictions will be in place for five days."

Only a week earlier the Victorian government had been announcing an easing of restrictions and a relaxing of their "traffic light" system which classified other sections of the country depending on their perceived danger. All of Western Australia and the Northern Territory had become green zones.

Then the departmental advice had read: "Existing red zone arrivals from areas that are now orange zones who have had a test since arriving in Victoria and have received a negative result no longer have to quarantine unless they have been in contact with a confirmed case or a known exposure site. If they haven't had a test since arriving back into Victoria, they must continue to isolate, get tested, and stay isolated until they receive a negative result."

A week later and the Victoria's Health Department was declaring: 'Engagement teams, supported by Defence personnel, made 350 household visits to permit holders yesterday. Of those, 337 were red zone permit holders, 328 from NSW and 9 from the ACT. A small number were found not to be isolating and will be referred to authorities for appropriate action.

"You must have a valid permit, exception or exemption to enter Victoria, even if entering from a green zone."

It was no wonder the public was confused. Unsettled. Frightened. Couldn't keep track of the endlessly changing diktats, had no idea who or what to believe, and were willing to roll up their sleeves for an experimental "vaccine" which, as it turned out, stopped neither infection nor transmission and for which the long term consequences were entirely unknown.

***

On the streets of Melbourne, just hours before the city entered its fifth lockdown, protesters marched through the Central Business District. Demonstrators called for an end to draconian measures. Hours before Victorian Premier Daniel Andrews announced the state would enter a five-day snap lockdown from midnight.

Protesters on social media described lockdowns as "human rights abuses", with many claiming they were just regular everyday people who have had enough.

Hundreds numbering into the thousands chanted "Sack Dan Andrews" on the steps of historic Flinders Street Station, reputed to be the world's busiest train station back in the 1920s. They then marched from the station to Parliament House, chanting "Freedom" and shadowed by a large police presence.

Signs read: "You Can Say No", "I Have a Choice", "Lockdown Kills", "This All Ends When We Say No", "No Common Sense!", "Government Lies! This Is A War! Injections the Weapon!" and "Indict the Real Criminals: Soros, Gates, Fauci."

TOTT News, which unlike most of Australia's bought and sold media were on top of the story from the beginning, editorialised: "The frustration is understandable. So many people have lost their businesses, their homes and have had their families ripped apart. Many more are in a really bad way.

"How many more waves can be survived by this perpetual operation?

"Lockdown 5.0 for Melbourne. 16 months into this pandemic saga. What an absolute farce.

"The Victorian government wants to replace temporary state of emergency laws – which need to be passed through parliament to be extended or changed – with new permanent powers. As predicted, the Orwellian 'war' against the 'invisible enemy' was never meant to ever end. Rather, the narrative was always designed to morph into a state of indefinite propaganda.

"It is all by design, and only will change when people say enough is enough."

One speaker was heard yelling: "Here we go again. Once again, Daniel Andrews has jumped at his own shadow and thrown millions of people's lives into chaos."

Another conservatively dressed middle-aged man shouted through a loudspeaker: "We need a pathway out of this, a way for it to end. I propose to set a date. When the Emergency Powers end. When the restrictions end. When all the coercion and human rights abuses end."

One young man addressing the crowd declared: "What has been going on in this country has no place in a free society." Yet another: "Ladies and gentlemen. Our backs are up against the wall. If we do not get involved our country will be lost forever.

Addressing the crowd Topher Field, later to produce the powerful documentary Battleground Melbourne, said: "Make no mistake, lockdowns are not helping us get through this pandemic. They are keeping us locked in the pandemic."

***

With the impending release of *Unfolding Catastrophe*, Old Alex was asked to give a speech, on Zoom, no such thing as in the flesh these days, and so he struck as hard as he could; in part, incensed, because of his own situation, miserable, locked down. The tradie with his non-stop talking and drinking at least filled the cold reaches of the house where his elderly parent had been obsessively praying to a stern, unforgiving, Abrahamic God for decades.

Believe what you will, the house really had been full of ghosts, the spirit ectoplasmic, that is, forming on invocation, and if nothing else, a lonely woman, she had been earnestly summoning her particular god for decades, and claimed a direct connection. "Ask and it will be given to you; seek and you will find; knock and the door will be opened to you."

Now there was a different kind of spookiness, not just the terror being visited upon them every day by the authorities, but an uncanny feeling, of stalking evil, incomprehensible evil, powerful, all enveloping; and they were in the last place to be safe, for there was no escape.

Unfolding Catastrophe had stuck closely to the issue of lockdowns, which he regarded as demonstrably incorrect public policy, while the vaccine rollout led the country's few independent minded journalists to hesitate, because any threat to the rollout was seen as a threat to public health, and thereby deeply irresponsible. Who were we, mere citizens, to doubt the word of epidemiologists, doctors, health experts? To doubt the word of The World Health Organisation? The vaccine hesitant, such as himself, were regarded as no better than sociopaths. In any case, if you dared doubt, the algorithms would delete you.

Soon enough the idea that men could control the algorithms would come to seem as plausible as men controlling the gods.

And besides, he had already had his brush with Big Tech censorship, having been thrown off the publishing platform Medium for a story over Bill Gates and eugenics, another story which would become pretty much common wisdom in the months and years ahead. He didn't want his magazine thrown off Facebook and Twitter.

Wisdom, or cowardice, or both.

Time moves rapidly, the river upends the boat, the passengers drown, few make it to shore. Restrictions multiplied dizzyingly, left people flailing, tossed about by unknowable currents, affliction streaming from Pandora's box.

***

Being of a certain age, he was forty when computers came into common use, the speech he was asked to give was his first encounter with Zoom, the messaging app which allowed online meetings and which every bright young thing was already taking for granted.

He managed to cut himself shaving just before the Forum started, and the cut refused to heal. He spent half the meeting dabbing himself with a towel as the blood kept pouring. He was such a novice he didn't even realise his every gesture could be seen by the other participants, including three Islamic doctors all promoting the virtues of vaccines.

The Forum was called "Coronavirus: A Conversation Beyond The Hype and Fear: Addressing Concerns about CoronaVirus, Vaccines & Lockdowns."

Other speakers included the Grand Mufti of Australia, the Assistant Minister for Community Safety and Multicultural Affairs Jason Wood and senior Opposition figure Jim Chalmers, soon enough to become the nation's Treasurer. Three Muslim doctors extolled the importance of getting vaccinated.

All sang true to the Covid songbook; all except him.

He had been invited by Keysar Trad, the then President of the Australian Federation of Islamic Councils and over the decades one of the most famous or infamous of the nation's Muslim spokesmen. He had read *Unfolding* and knew exactly what Old Alex was like. That's why he was invited. To sing out of tune to the mass hypnosis; a psyop program on an unprecedented scale.

Western Sydney, parts of which were almost entirely Islamic, had suffered enormously through the lockdowns, unable to attend the mosque or see their families, the two cornerstones of their lives.

Here's an edited version of the speech.

***

We have seen across the last 18 months, and particularly in recent weeks, the most violent demonstrations in Australian history.

Australians have been turned against Australians.

With hundreds of military personnel on the street, with police blanketing suburbs across Australia now enforcing the equivalent of martial law, not one single Australian politician can produce the evidence that this action is appropriate.

At the same time as Australia has become a laughing stock around the world, with the most excoriating coverage this country has ever attracted. In America, the idea that under Australia's covid restrictions dogs in animal refuges are being shot rather than given to loving homes touched a sympathetic chord.

An ill informed, frightened and confused Australian population, many of them without the literacy or media skills to know when they are being lied to, have been bludgeoned into accepting the loss of all their freedoms, while unbelievably arrogant and utterly out of touch politicians, many of them earning some 40 or 50 times the income of a welfare recipient, have escaped scot free.

They never meet, except at controlled events during election campaigns, the ordinary working Australians most devastated by their insane and self-aggrandising responses to Covid.

When this is all over, let's not forget this crisis was man made. That it wasn't the virus that did all this damage, but governments' response to it.

It's the rest of the population that is paying. And paying big time. Millions of people can no longer take care of their families, have lost the pride of running their own businesses and the ability to care for their own families. Are facing massive debts and the destruction of all they have ever worked for.

The Australian government ignored all the cautionary tales emanating from some of the world's leading tertiary institutions, including Princeton, Harvard, Oxford and Stanford, all warning that lockdowns were a dangerous social experiment which went against decades of epidemiological wisdom and would do more harm than good. The result has been an authoritarian derangement, with military on the streets, unprecedented levels of highly aggressive policing, a dramatic loss of liberties, thousands marching in repeated demonstrations and uber surveillance at a level previously unimaginable.

Under Covid, the rich in Australia are now many billions of dollars richer than they were 18 months ago.

***

There was a queue of international and Australian experts decrying the lockdowns Australia was so forcefully implementing. Because he could, because it was a scandal from the very beginning of this whole dismal sleet-laced saga, Old Alex looked for and published in his online journal as many doubters of the official narrative as he could.

As, in a prior time, any normal journalist would have done.

It was during those first bewildering months when the official narrative came to seem so improbable that Old Alex that he came across Professor Ramesh Thakur, who had written extensively on Covid for publications both in his adopted country and around the world.

When it comes down to Australia's vast ocean of commentary and government backed propaganda during the Covid period, Ramesh stood out for his bold, erudite and highly intelligent analysis, his level of statistical and numerical literacy without peer.

To quote Thakur: "The harsh lockdown measures were instituted in response to the fear-mongering projections of mathematical modelling that bear hardly any resemblance to the reality that has unfolded across the world.

"The result has been disastrous for millions of people around the world. Rather than focusing protective measures on the people at heightened risk of illness, governments around the world imposed and continue to impose severe restrictions on their entire population.

"With routine medical care disrupted, businesses shuttered, curfews imposed, travel restricted, socialisation criminalised, we are causing a devastating amount of harm."

Many people, both in Australia and around the world, were warning, a year or more before, that the unilateral actions being taken by the authorities would lead to an authoritarian derangement. That's exactly what is happening in Australia.

It was the world's most famous whistleblower, Edward Snowden, who warned in May of last year: "Everybody who looks around right now, they can see, they can feel what's in the air. Everything is changing rapidly. We are seeing new powers being claimed. We are seeing new powers being abused.

"And we are seeing governments tearing open new avenues into our private lives under the justification of emergency measures.

"You know, they always say these are temporary, it is for this reason and that reason... But there is nothing more permanent than a temporary measure. The system is now failing."

It is not just the political and bureaucratic classes which have behaved so badly, but the media profession itself. As one group of doctors quoted in *Unfolding Catastrophe* recorded: "The relentless bombardment of numbers, unleashed on the population day after day, hour after hour, without indicating those numbers, without comparing them with flu deaths in other years, without comparing them with deaths from other causes, has induced true anxiety psychosis in the population."

There have already been, and will continue to be, many, many scandals associated with the political, administrative and medical responses to Covid.

The old dictum, "do no harm" has been abandoned, as many in the medical profession have overseen or acted as political shields for the massive damage now being done to millions and millions of Australians.

The history of government hysteria and the implementation of lockdowns began with Imperial College London and was mirrored in Australia with similar modelling by the Doherty Institute, which was predicting 50,000 to 150,000 deaths in this country.

The director of the research Niel Ferguson is the same man who predicted in 2005 that 150 million people would be killed from bird flu. In the end, 282 people died worldwide.

Australian authorities must have known within weeks that the hysteria being visited upon the country was being done under either false or highly disputed premises; that both the Imperial College London and the Doherty Institute in Australia were wildly inaccurate.

This is the same institute the government is now relying on to set its vaccine thresholds.

It was obvious from very early on that the projected death tolls, the excuse for Scott Morrison placing himself front and centre of the fear campaign, the rationale behind the massive destruction of Australian life, was false.

Why did no one call him out? Not his political comrades in arms. Not his wealthy political donors. Not the premiers now shutting down their entire states and masquerading as heroes of the moment. Not the senior bureaucrats peddling a message of alarmism; and only very, very few in the nation's media.

Politicians ignored all the warnings, seized the advice that suited them and have absolutely destroyed the country. Goodbye democracy. Goodbye decency.

***

Yes, it was true, we stood for you on a distant shore.

Stranded in a valley, his human life in brief turmoil, the latitude, the longitude, the geo-spatial distortion, the fact that even the greatest sceptics knew that something was coming, that these styles of consciousness, as much studied as they were, remained rare.

Old Alex, in his inflamed imagination, conflicting images accreting in the silence of that valley, had ignored all entreaties.

He had ignored the super smart and the gracious, the military gronks and the esoterics; and they ran across thousands of variations until they found a match. For if there had been prophets throughout human history, which there had been, then these were unique humans who one way or another linked to elements which stood outside of time, a universal spirit of one kind or another; featured in multiple manifestations through multiple generations.

Those who sought the mystery, the hi-tech wizards who wished to exploit these connection points to a universal spirit, who knew humans were on the verge of great change, queried him time and again. And he ignored them. They, the spirits, would do exactly as they liked, when they liked, when the tides were right; when they chose to grant the greatest of all gifts, beyond mere life.

That was the way the story appeared to Old Alex, in those recesses where the ancients walked, in a realm beyond the realm. That the travails of this so-called pandemic, of the relentless deceit that had enveloped all their lives, the pointless lockdowns, the utterly corrupt mass vaccination of the population and the brutality of the state in the abrogation of virtually all liberties, that this was a forge in which a new world was born.

Imprisoned in his own home day after day, allowed out for only two hours a day, where else could imagination fly?

The daily derangement of government press conferences provoked fear and confusion into the population and placed their own utterly dysfunctional incompetence front and centre of everybody's lives.

Derangement. It was a derangement. Overstepping the mark. Plundering. Perhaps it was always thus, the conquerors took the spoils, but here the parasites were imprisoning their own populations, with millions upon millions of Australians now in what amounted to a permanent lockdown, imprisoned in their own homes, monitored, surveilled, abused, imprisoned, fined. That it had come to this seemed too improbable to be real, but thus it was.

He reached backwards and forwards, saw in that valley an unimaginable hi-tech future, a teleport, vessels coming and going, staggering technologies, he smelt, or at least saw, the incense of thousands of years gone and the future they now fought so desperately to preserve.

For here they were at the limits of what was possible; even for them, fluid in time. Ex tempore. Not so much out of time, as outside time.

We come at the End of Empire. And for a human marooned, so it seemed to be; amidst these dispirited, beaten people. Amidst their humble dreams, their impoverishment, their backward, primitive technologies.

These were a people who had lost all faith in their leaders and their government; the instabilities in the system building by the day.

Millions and millions in lockdown; their own futures destroyed, their children's futures destroyed, while the fat cats grew fatter, oilier, more unctuous.

While the man at the centre of this debacle, that worshipper of false Gods, the Pentecostal Prime Minister Scott Morrison, flew between his taxpayer funded mansions in taxpayer funded planes, with taxpayer funded security increasingly deployed to hold back the anger of the mob.

Which was about to upend the fabric of a country once known as Australia.

FOUR
THE LONE SENTINEL

I think they've, well they've gathered here for me
I am within you, you are within me
I am beside you, you are beside me
I think they're singing to be free, I think they're singing to be free

Nick Cave. Ghosteen.

Lockdowns distort time. The few people Old Alex encountered were depressed, dispirited and disillusioned. Some believed the government messaging. The New South Wales Government issued an endless stream of diktats, updates and what appeared in hindsight to be a deliberate attempt to confuse and frighten the population during the entirety of that truly dismal winter.

Apart from the early period of colonisation, this was the most violent, coercive and despairing period in the nation's history.

We were all in isolation.

A locked down, frightened population became a different beast to the Australia of old, easy to manipulate, coerce or bludgeon into submission.

You could fill entire encyclopaedias with the daily announcements erupting out of the Australia's Health Departments; the pantomime of daily press conferences adding to the absurd sense of derangement.

Here is a small sampling of some of the statements out of New South Wales. Perhaps, as future historians look back across this blizzard of ever changing diktats from the state and territory governments, these documents, thousands of pages of them, will become the foundation texts for how to create a nationwide psychosis, one element in the study of the rise of totalitarianism in Australia:

NSW Health. Statistics. 7 July, 2021: NSW recorded 27 new locally acquired cases of COVID-19 in the 24 hours to 8 pm last night.

Of these locally acquired cases, 18 are linked to a known case or cluster – seven are household contacts and 11 are close contacts – and the source of infection for nine cases remain under investigation.

One new overseas-acquired case was recorded in the same period. The total number of cases in NSW since the beginning of the pandemic is 5,836.

There have been 357 locally acquired cases reported since 16 June 2021, when the first case of the Bondi cluster was reported.

There are now 264 cases directly linked to known cases in the Bondi cluster.

There are 25 cases that are unlinked to a known case or cluster, with a further 68 who are linked to these 25 unlinked cases.

There are currently 37 COVID-19 cases admitted to hospital, with seven people in intensive care, two of whom require ventilation.

There were 45,000 tests reported to 8 pm last night, compared with the previous day's total of 32,136.

NSW Health administered 20,564 COVID-19 vaccines in the 24 hours to 8 pm last night, including 7,135 at the vaccination centre at Sydney Olympic Park.

The total number of vaccines administered in NSW is now 2,474,124, with 962,785 doses administered by NSW Health to 8 pm last night and 1,511,339 administered by the GP network and other providers to 11.59 pm on Monday 5 July.

NSW Health's ongoing sewage surveillance program has detected traces of the virus that causes COVID-19 at a number of locations around Sydney. The detections at Minto and Marrickville sewage treatment plants are of particular concern, as there are no known cases in these catchments. A detection in the Cronulla catchment is also of concern as it has had no new cases in the past week. People who have recently recovered from COVID-19 can continue to shed fragments of the virus for several weeks.

Hundreds of more words for that day's announcements alone.

NSW Health Minister Brad Hazzard: Given the ongoing number of infectious cases in the community, the current lockdown will be extended for at least another two weeks until 11:59 pm on Friday, 30 July.

We are constantly reviewing the health advice and will continue to update the community if any changes are required.

This means the restrictions currently in place across Greater Sydney including the Central Coast, Blue Mountains, Wollongong and Shellharbour will remain in place until this time.

In these areas, online learning for students will also continue for an additional two weeks.

We understand this is a difficult time for the community and appreciate their ongoing patience.

It is vital people continue to come forward for testing to help us find any COVID-19 cases in the community.

***

Public Health Alert 23 July 2020: 23 July 2021: NSW Health has been notified of a number of new and updated venues of concern and public transport routes associated with confirmed cases of COVID-19, and of a new sewage detection.

NSW Health's ongoing sewage surveillance program has detected fragments of the virus that causes COVID-19 at the sewage treatment plant at Moss Vale in the Southern Highlands.

There are no known cases in this area, which is of great concern.

Everyone in the Moss Vale area is asked to be especially vigilant for any symptoms that could signal COVID-19, and if they appear, to immediately be tested and isolate until a negative result is received. If symptoms appear again, please be tested and isolate again.

Old Alex's unvaxxed relatives in the Southern Highlands, on the other side of the sandstone escarpment, could not go to bars or restaurants and were also enduring a profound period of extended isolation.

No known cases.

How absurd it all was in hindsight; and those bureaucrats on their massive public service salaries had, if not the benefit of hindsight the benefit of easily accessible data on the overseas experience and easy access to some of the world's leading analysts, who mounted forceful, cogent and damaging arguments demonstrating that all this hysteria was truly pointless, creating a derangement in the community which served no purpose other than accreting power to the state.

***

On the same day the NSW Health Department announced that anyone who attended various venues at the times listed was classified as a casual contact and must immediately get tested and isolate until a negative result is received.

"If your date of exposure at this venue occurred in the past four days, you must get another test on day five from the date of exposure. Wear a mask around others and limit your movements until you get another negative result. You should continue to monitor for symptoms and if any symptoms occur, get tested again."

Here's a small sampling of some of the venues and times listed for 23 July 2021, all breathlessly reported in the government-funded and manipulated mainstream media:

> Rust Bucket, Belmore, Saturday 17 July, 11:05 am to 11:25 am.
>
> Mr Liquor, Earlwood, 17 July, 5.30 to 5.40 pm.
>
> 85C Daily Cafe, Campsie, 17 July, 7.35 to 7.55 am.
>
> Afghan Sufra, Lakemba, Sunday 18 July, 12:00 to 1:00 pm.
>
> Paradise Grocery, Lakemba, 12 to 1.00 pm.
>
> Leaf Cafe, Burwood, 1.00 to 1.05 pm.
>
> Afford Disability, Belmore, 19-22 July, All Day.
>
> Pharmacy 4 Less, Burwood Westfield, 12.50 to 1.00 pm.
>
> Family Medical Practice, Campsie, 10 to 11 am.

On and on and on it went. Day in and day out. Week in week out. Month in month out.

Driven mad by the isolation, drinking at dangerous levels, in Old Alex's waking dreams a lone standard bearer, mounted on a stallion and dressed in full ceremonial regalia, would appear high up in the valley opposite, look across to where he was camped, watch a while, then turn his steed and disappear.

At first he assumed it was a scout for a greater army.

But in the end the sadness of the soldier's expression bore fruit, and he realised that far from a scout, the vision was the equivalent of an envoy, for the spirits spoke in images that humans could understand, animals, birds, armies, royal houses, and that this one had come to check on his well being, to see if he was awake, to see if he could hear and see and respond to the spirits, and when it was clear that in his debilitated, dispirited, often enough drunken state he was unresponsive and unreceptive, would turn and disappear, there to await another time.

**

Massive protests became a feature of Australian life. Emotions were running high. All round the country, millions of Australians were imprisoned in their own homes and repeatedly told that the only way out of lockdowns was vaccination; a terrible societal wide fraud inflicted on the gullible and the unwilling. That was for a vaccine which did not stop infection, transmission or death.

The protests were duly ignored by the mainstream media hostage to government and vaccine funding, but widely covered and celebrated in the nation's burgeoning independent media.

These protests were some of the largest, most energetic, and most heavily policed in Australia's history; and unlike climate and anti-racism protests generated by government funded narratives, were essentially organic in nature.

At first they were lonely, isolated and decried, by their governments, their friends, their family and the nation's media, feeling the full weight of the loneliness of protest, of standing up for something you believe in, the human spirit refusing to be crushed. The protestors were alone no more.

On 24 July 2021, tens of thousands of people turned out across the country, producing dramatic scenes which should have at least given pause to the nation's politicians. Instead, at least in the halls of power, it produced obfuscation, denial and ever greater waste of public funds as millions of dollars were expended in the crackdowns.

A war against their own people.

"Country in Distress" read one banner, waved one banner, held high above a seething crowd.

"Drop Your Mask, Free Your Voice" read another.

At the time people in Greater Sydney and its surrounds had been living in lockdown for exactly four weeks. No amount of protest was going to bring those pointless lockdowns to an end.

TOTT News reported: "A crowd stretching as far as the eye can see moved through the CBD towards Town Hall amid a massive police presence — estimates suggest as many as 15,000 people taking part in the march.

"Footage on social media shows the demonstrators walking down Broadway, one of the main arteries through Sydney's inner-west, as part of the worldwide rallies.

"Entire families can be seen among the crowd and few people are wearing face masks, making their voices heard against lockdown madness, vaccine coercion, loss of livelihoods and more."

In Melbourne, thousands of protesters turned out in the central business district chanting "freedom".

Protesters broke through the barricades due to sheer numbers in the area and began marching down the street towards Parliament House.

Makeshift banners included one that read: "This is not about a virus it's about total government control of the people."

The then Health minister in Victoria Martin Foley blasted the mass gathering, saying those taking part "are on the side of the virus. Please. be on the side of humanity, not the side of the virus."

TOTT News observed: "More Orwellian language being used in a state already attempting to entrench permanent restrictions. As predicted, the Orwellian war against the invisible enemy was never meant to ever end. Rather, the narrative was always designed to morph into a state of indefinite propaganda."

Police estimated 7,500 people gathered in the Botanic Gardens and marched through the city, many of whom were not wearing masks, in another successful Brisbane rally.

Placards included "The Truth Variant Is Here", "Don't Believe the Covid-19 Hoax Pandemic", "Coercion is Not Consent", "Freedom Over Fear" and "For Our Children".

Others, indicating the surprising spiritual undertow of the events, included "Jesus Is Near" and "God Wins".

***

A tearful nurse addressed a gathering in the regional centre of Coffs Harbour, saying: "I'm on my own. I started nursing because I wanted to get a house. Now we are all being told we can't continue unless we get the vaccine. We are fighting it."

Harsh weather conditions didn't deter protesters from heading to the lawns of Parliament House in the nation's capital Canberra, where a large crowd gathered for speeches and an awareness campaign.

Signs and banners included: "Millions March Against Mandatory Vaccination", "Since When Was Two Weeks to Flatten the Curve Consent for the World's Biggest Medical Experiment?" and "Forty Cycles of PCR is Fraud",, referring to the testing regime known to produce a large number of false positives.

Already, perhaps for his own sanity, perhaps for the benefit of the at this point diminished number of Watchers on the Watch, equally caught up by the blizzard of insane diktats, Old Alex took to repeatedly muttering under his breath, "the biggest medical fraud in history".

"Is it true?", a younger member of the surveillance team asked.

His more senior colleague nodded, "Yes."

The intelligence agencies already knew this was fraud. Their role, and why they were so involved, might be a question for another day. But there was no doubt they knew.

Neither they, nor the bureaucrats, nor their political masters, put a stop to any of it.

**

From the 21st of August people who lived alone were forced to register their "singles bubble" in New South Wales if they wanted to spend time with a friend or lover.

Increased fines for Public Health Order breaches came into force from 12.01 am, Monday, 16 August:
- $5,000 on the spot fine for breaching self-isolation rules;
- $5,000 on the spot fine for lying on a permit;
- $5,000 on the spot fine for lying to a contact tracer;
- $3,000 on the spot fine for breaching the two person outdoor exercise/recreation rule; and
- $3,000 on the spot fine for breaching rules around entry into regional NSW for authorised work, inspecting real estate and travelling to your second home.

All outdoor recreation was banned and only exercise and supervision of children allowed.

**

New South Wales Premier Gladys Berejiklian said non-compliance was a major issue extending the state's lockdown and said police and the Australian Defence Force had more personnel on the ground than ever before. "We don't apologise for having that strong presence," she said.

"The future of our freedom relies on it.

"In one day alone, more than 400 people police know of across the state left their house for the wrong reason."

Some 18,000 police officers were backed up with the support of 800 Australian Defence Force members in the three-week crackdown on non-compliance of public health orders.

Police Minister David Elliot warned that officers would be out in full force and any anti-lockdown protesters faced arrest.

"We're temporarily living with restrictions that we all want to see lifted, but the mass gathering of a group of idiots could mean that day moves further into the future," he said.

"We've had to tighten the current public health orders because of the minority who exploited them. In the Local Government Areas of concern it will no longer be acceptable to leave your home for outdoor recreation, meaning gathering at parks or outside takeaway shops or cafes is not on. Enough is enough. If you do it, you will get fined," Mr Elliott said.

"Residents across Greater Sydney and lockdown areas can also expect to see enhanced random police checkpoints on roads, to ensure people are complying with the stay at home rules aimed to protect the community."

NSW Police Commissioner Mick Fuller said the joint NSW Police Force and Australian Defence Force operation – STAY AT HOME – would commence on Monday, 16 August.

"These are some of the strongest powers we've ever had in the history of the NSW Police Force, as part of the government's strategy to get in front of the virus in the coming weeks – it's all about getting ahead of Delta, not chasing it," Commissioner Fuller said.

"From this week we'll be issuing $5,000 fines to people and closing premises which continue to break the health orders. Don't complain if this happens to you – police are over the rule breakers."

***

Steve Waterson at *The Australian* wrote that he had recently watched two mounted police ride their large horses south along the middle of

Bondi Beach, stopping at the towels of two young mothers and their four toddlers, tiny beside the horses' hoofs, to order them to pack up buckets and spades and leave the beach.

"Thanks for keeping us safe. The madness toggles between sinister and comical. Especially hilarious are the comedy stylings of the bullying dolt (Premier Daniel Andrews) who is turning Victoria into a post-apocalyptic wasteland: it's acceptable to remove your useless mask to drink coffee on the street, he declares, but an offence to do so to drink alcohol. It must be excruciating for black-clad Melburnians, paralysed indecision warming their espresso martinis.

"We're urged to get vaccinated as the only way out of this nightmare, as though the restrictions were imposed by some external enemy, while what's really happening is that our leaders create this misery, steal our freedoms, then command us to obey their orders in order to regain them.

"There will surely come a point when people robbed of their livelihoods will have literally nothing left to lose.

"So here we are, worse off than when all the hysteria began, a risible counterweight to the return to normality spreading all over the world, slumped into a manufactured psychosis. Australians are being deliberately and methodically terrified, while enforced isolation weakens our resilience.

"It renders us more susceptible to the howls of panic, unchallenged by normal debate and conversation, forbidden to meet, discuss or express our disagreement.

"We are turning on each other like mediaeval city-states, while our basic human decency dissolves into brawls over toilet paper."

***

"Australia is going full Fascist" the Off-Guardian declared in one of the many negative headlines the country was now attracting worldwide.

Journalist Kit Knightly wrote that Covid19 had been used as an excuse to increase government control of pretty much everything, pretty much everywhere.

"It is, without question, the greatest campaign to seize power, and greatest assault on personal freedom, of my lifetime. With countries seemingly in a contest to outdo each other's clampdowns, lockdowns, quarantines and surveillance programs.

"From the beginning of the 'pandemic' three countries, in particular, have set the pace on this – Canada, Australia and New Zealand. Since last spring these three have been one-upping each other in a race to the fascist finish line. And right now, Australia is putting a sprint in to pull away from the pack.

"Cities are going into full lockdown for just one positive test. Some Australian cities and states aren't just under total lockdowns, but also ever-extending curfews. The details of which read like a dystopian novel.

"People are not permitted to leave the state, let alone the country. They're not even permitted more than 5km from their home. They're not allowed out at all after 9 pm or before 5 am. Masks are mandatory everywhere for everyone. Outdoors and in. No religious services. No weddings. Shoot stray dogs, just in case.

"Police barge into 'unapproved' shops and fine business owners, or go house-to-house making sure no one has gone out. People who test positive are taken from homes for indefinite stays at quarantine hotels. The army has been deployed to check papers and vaccine status at road checkpoints."

"Increasingly their rules and limitations are becoming not just tyrannical but literally insane. It seems, just about every day, one or another Australian politician or health 'expert' is on the news saying something crazy.

"Don't take your masks off to drink. Don't be friendly. Don't watch the sunset. Tape your balcony shut."

***

In his piece for *The Daily Sceptic* that August, the final month of what had been a truly dismal winter in the Land Down Under, Guy de la Bédoyère wrote: "As an historian, what really strikes me now is how brief the Covid crisis has been so far. Yes, I know it seems like 500 years since we were last able to travel freely and not hear about the pandemic on the nightly news. But in historical terms this is nothing.

"What will define the era is the social, political, and economic fallout and, trust me, that's barely started. Governments are going to fall, millions of people are going to be ruined while others make fortunes, and some countries are going to disintegrate. But when, where or how is yet to be seen. This will take years – decades – but I think you can see the signs of fragmentation and epic change already – almost all self-inflicted as a result of the hysteria that has consumed us since early 2020.

"I have watched with apprehension and astonishment at the direction Australia and New Zealand have travelled in the last 18 months. One thing I know very well is that those in the present never learn from the past.

"My fear though is that Australia, of all the developed modern democratic states, has set out down a path that could in extremis result in the country breaking apart.

"The national infrastructure is ramshackle. It was already the case that individual states are more interested in their own futures than the country's.

"The destruction of individual freedoms in Australia and the epic speed with which that has happened has no parallel in the modern world in a modern democratic state."

***

The lioness purred through Old Alex's waking dreams. That magnificent animal, in her physical prime, at the height of her powers, muscled, lean, handsome, her belly full from a recent kill, dozed in the savanna sun. Her young cubs, their bellies full of milk, lolled or played beside her. Sometimes a protective paw would reach out to encompass them, or bat them away if they became too frisky. Mostly it was about love. We were all in love, in these ravishing times.

The surveillance team he dubbed the Watchers on the Watch, bored witless as they often were, never left him.

They leaked across half the hemisphere, and so obvious were they Old Alex hadn't even realised their call signs, aubergine, poppadom, oregano, were meant to be secret. He was tired of them anyway; their endless boasting and ribbing about sexual conquests, their endless dirty talk, their arrogance, for they thought they were so damn clever, with their above average IQs and whiz bang technologies, these humans who thought they were the future of the race.

He would repeat for the dullards amongst them: We are not for capture, copy or acquisition.

This will go down, is already going down, on our terms, exactly as we say it will.

As for the country, it was mired in scandal; up to their necks in it.

In the meantime, their sense of time different to ours, they would watch the rise and fall of these snarling, backstabbing hypocrites calling themselves politicians, their greed manifest, their incompetence writ in banners across the sky, it was so blatant, we would ride the banners of history and let others do the work, for every journalist out there was now on the hunt; for different reasons, but on the hunt.

The centre could not hold. The status quo could not be maintained. We are everywhere and nowhere. We stalk your every waking thought.

The lioness stirred. As beautiful as she was, as peaceful as the scene appeared, she could turn dangerous in an instant. And no more quickly than if her cubs were threatened.

They were birthing a new world. A world where it was impossible to lie. Then watch the collapse; as this sorry sorry government wrote its own demise; the obituaries already being written and it wasn't even dead yet.

***

Prime Minister Scott Morrison, who had placed himself front and centre of the Covid melodrama, would, if he could, skulk off into the nation's boardrooms, where his complete lack of administrative talent, his abject failure to understand the voting public, his unalloyed greed and corporate cronyism would all be welcomed.

A den of thieves. Throw the moneylenders from the temple. Our temple.

In Australian terms, in any terms, this truly was a winter of the soul.

The same repeating line breathing through the text: We weep for you and you are not yet born.

"We come at the End of Empire," the spirits whispered, a mixture of cruel Assyrian gods and native spirits, of a swirling construction, the ultimate evolution.

August in Australia is the final month of winter, and often a kind of pre-Spring which some call a fifth season, but not this time, when one cold, wet, windy day froze into another; when, in the middle of lockdown, our dreams felt frighteningly real. As Nick Cave once put it: "This much I know to be true."

It was a complex story of deceit in dishonest times.

August 2021 was a month like no other, a groundbreaking, historic month where the entire country stepped straight to the edge of the abyss of totalitarianism. And all too many played along.

We were all, in a sense, a long way from home.

Australia's freedom movement was on the move. A rolling stream of protests reached one of its many crests on the 21 August, 2021, with protestors being showered in pepper spray and met with thousands of police across the country. No one was left with any illusion that the right to protest, once regarded as a sacred right, an inherent part of being Australian, had been abolished.

From a generation which grew up on Vietnam War protests of the 1970s, another social movement which ultimately and undeniably proved to be on the right side of history, for Old Alex it was nothing short of sacrilege.

Slowly coming back into focus after the strange rushing all encompassing torrent that was book writing, as if at the mercy of the gods, he ran a piece in his magazine from the Sydney Criminal Lawyers Blog, one of the new forms of funding for journalism which was progressively replacing the sclerotic and heavily manipulated mainstream press.

The headline: "We can't arrest our way out of this." The piece was by Sonia Hickey and Ugur Nedim, two of the many talents coming to the fore in these times. Cursed art thou. As if the whole country had been cursed.

"It seems that hardly a week goes without the New South Wales government issuing a new public health order, or amending or adding to existing orders.

"As a consequence, it can be difficult to keep up with and digest the ever-changing, increasingly complex and frustratingly vague and ambiguous rules.

"So it's no surprise that in just one 24 hour period earlier this week, 22 people were issued with court attendance notices and will face court for allegedly failing to comply with a public health order and 240 were issued with on-the-spot fines.

"And it seems there will be no letup, as various branches of the New South Wales Police Force have made it clear they will be out in numbers to enforce the rules – be they general duties, water, traffic, transport or mounted groups of officers.

"But the latest changes have led to many comparing the approach taken by those in power to authoritarian governments of both today and yesteryear."

The mainstream media papered over the lie; time and time and time again. We had all entered an extremely dishonest world.

***

Old Alex found the place where in his inflamed imagination where the spirits would come, not a grazing of two worlds but a visitation, there at the edge of an ancient forest, a clearing where the amplifying power of the forest and the vortex of the surrounding cliffs all served a purpose.

Where, as the spirits gathered in power, for, as he had said so often, it was a geospatial phenomenon, it required time, it required a place, it required patience, humility and respect before a power torched beyond human imagining, and he had begun to go there each morning; with the future smell of incense and the chant of priests beginning to form in the primitive clime.

This was the future they were beginning to create, a blessing which would provide prosperity and wealth for generations to come, and ultimately lead to one of the greatest flowerings of civilisation in the short history of man; beginning two centuries hence, and ending in crisis 407, now 406 years into the future; where the messaging originated.

That's what his waking dreams told him.

He had found, one morning, a pair of cheap plastic Ray-Ban replica sunglasses on the path to the future sanctuary; already this ground taking on the feel of a sacred place, next to a sacred forest.

He thought no more of it, until one morning, in the midst of his rituals, with the powers gathering and the air already deep in flux, a dog, an old Border Collie cross, appeared at his feet and surprised, he leant down to pat the animal, which curled around his feet in affection, as animals did when these states took hold.

Shortly thereafter a woman appeared, with two other dogs.

There was no reason to be in that place. It was not a path to anywhere. He had never seen anyone there before.

He made some comment, as he always did to dog owners, about how nice their creatures were, and she asked: "Have you seen a pair of sunglasses?"

"Yes," he said. "They're in my car. I found them the other day."

She pretended surprise or delight; pretended to have lost and been searching for them, although they had been placed carefully and centrally on the path.

So he interrupted his ritual, like Buddha he had become comfortable with the mesh between heaven and Earth, with the grand sweep of sacred visions and the profanities of the material realm, and cheerfully said he would go and fetch them from the car.

She and her dogs joined him, truly, there was no reason why anyone would visit this place, certainly not a woman walking her dogs alone, and they walked together back down the 100 metres or so of the path to where his vehicle lay prominently parked at the closed gate.

He found the sunglasses in the side door of his vehicle, and handed them to her.

She expressed great delight, and donned the cheap five dollar glasses as if they really were originals, really were worth hundreds of dollars.

During their conversation he had expressed his utter frustration at the lockdowns destroying the country, the blizzard of absurd diktats destroying all normal life.

Health regulations now ran to more than 50 pages, and had been changed more than 50 times.

"I don't even know if I'm illegal," he said.

"Where do you live?" she asked, as if she didn't know.

"Oak Flats," he replied.

"You are, actually," she replied, explaining that the 10 kilometre limit had been reduced to five.

"Don't dob me in," he said light heartedly, for the absurdities of the evil enveloping Australia knew no limit to its minutiae.

"I won't," she said, in a pretence of warmth, a dog lover after all, but warned him that there were police in the area.

They said their pretend farewells.

He had no doubt if she saw his vehicle again she would report him to the authorities.

And he would face a hefty $5000 fine.

Trust No One.

It would be his only human interaction for the day.

FIVE
A NARROW VALLEY THREADS DOWN TO THE SEA

"The call for a new, hyper-strict government … emerged *from within the population itself.* Terrorists, climate change, heterosexual men, and, later, viruses were considered too dangerous to be tackled with old-fashioned means. The technological 'tracking and tracing' of populations became increasingly acceptable and was even deemed necessary. We associate totalitarianism mainly with labour, concentration and extermination camps, but those are merely the final, bewildering stage of a long process."

Mattias Desmet. *The Psychology of Totalitarianism.*

"I've tried to beat the system which destroys every writer, and from you have come only wounds and kicks in the face."

John Steinbeck. *Letters.*

ALREADY WORLD FAMOUS for the brutality of its lockdowns, the violent and abusive behaviour of its police officers and the supreme arrogance of its leader Daniel Andrews, the state of Victoria and its capital Melbourne went into its sixth, and by now record breaking lockdown on 5 August 2021.

A fear-stricken and breathtakingly compliant population had had enough.

Yet still they suffered.

And still the mainstream media recorded no objections as the by now greatly empowered politicians and bureaucrats paraded their madness at daily press conferences.

Highly credentialed experts from around the world were warning that lockdowns would not work, had never worked and went against decades of epidemiological wisdom, but Australian governments were in no mood to listen. Drunk on their own power, they were not for changing course.

The lockdown would last 78 days, until the 21st of October 2021. When it began seven people were in hospital, two in Intensive Care. Derisory numbers. History has an uncanny way of exposing fraud.

While chronological order is usually the best way to tell a story, let's for one moment jump a year ahead.

In 2022 Alex Berenson, former *New York Times* reporter and author of *Pandemia: How Coronavirus Hysteria Took Over Our Government, Rights, and Lives*, recorded the outcome of the authoritarian lunacy which overtook Victoria beginning in 2020 with a story headlined "Deaths are soaring in one of the world's most highly mRNA vaccinated areas".

For a time, banned from Twitter and reviled in the mainstream media, Berenson was very much a lone ranger among traditional, old style let-the-facts-fall-where-they-may journalists. Regulatory capture and the co-option of mainstream media by government and corporate interests, in particular Big Pharma, meant the mainstream media had entirely abandoned its traditional role.

With no doubt a little bit of chutzpah Berenson claimed that the best thing about his situation was that he had the biggest story on Earth almost entirely to himself.

While his focus was America, he was also well aware of what was happening in the Land Down Under.

"Deaths in the Australian state of Victoria, where 95 per cent of adults have received Covid vaccines and most are boosted with mRNA shots, soared to their highest level in at least 13 years in August – far above the five-year average. Victoria offers almost unique data: near-real-time reporting on death trends in millions of people who are heavily vaccinated but had little exposure to Covid before being jabbed.

"The picture is increasingly grim.

"Victoria registered 4,896 deaths from all causes in August, 27 per cent above the monthly average of the previous five Augusts. Mortality in Australia typically peaks June through August, the Southern Hemisphere's winter, but the figure is only the latest in a disturbing trend.

"So far in 2022, Victoria has registered 32,533 deaths, 20 percent above its average for the same eight-month period from 2017 through 2021. Victoria has had more than 4000 deaths in five months since February; it crossed that threshold only in seven months in the previous 12 years.

"In general, deaths in Victoria have typically fallen in a very narrow band. In each year from 2017 to 2021, the state reported between 26,350 and 27,800 deaths for the eight months from January to August.

"Not anymore."

***

So much for keeping Victorians safe!!!!!!!!!! As Kim Jong-un look-alike Daniel Andrews repeatedly told Victorians was the motive behind the lockdowns.

In 2022 the sight of Daniel Andrews smirking next to newly elected Australian Prime Minister Anthony Albanese during the so-called National Cabinet sent a chill through every freedom-loving Australian. And so it should have. The two, from the same side of politics, were said to be particularly close. By this time Andrews was deeply despised by significant sections of the Victorian community, and Albanese's absurd claim that Andrews was managing Melbourne well did nothing but destroy his own credibility.

The manipulation and concealment of figures on death rates suggested knowledge and culpability. That is, the bureaucrats and politicians knew perfectly well that their actions during the height of Covid hysteria had led to the deaths of thousands of Australians and did massive damage to society.

They never confessed. They never apologised. And the mainstream media, now reliant on tens of millions of dollars of tax breaks originally given for peddling Covid information, or more accurately disinformation, never held them to account.

It was left to the outliers to tell the truth.

***

You might say hindsight is a wonderful thing; also in 2022 the world's leading academic centre for examining government driven Covid narratives, the Brownstone Institute, published a piece titled A Big Picture Look at the Disastrous Public Health Response to COVID-19.

It read in part: "An underlying principle of public health is, or was, to provide the public with accurate information so that they can make good health choices for themselves and their community.

"The past three years have seen this paradigm turned on its head, with the public's money being used to deceive and coerce them, forcing them to follow public health dictates. The public has funded their own incarceration and impoverishment through their taxes, with public funds driving the unprecedented non-pharmaceutical, and then pharmaceutical, response to a virus that kills mainly old sick people near the end of their lives.

"Children have had their education downgraded, and economies have been mangled, ensuring future generations will also pay.

"Citizens have paid the bill via taxes for novel nonpharmaceutical interventions (lockdowns, mask mandates and frequent testing) and repeated vaccinations of immune people with rapidly waning vaccines, whilst seeing their own incomes reduced. The increase in the money supply to cover relief for forced unemployment has driven inflation, contributing to increased food, water, energy, health and insurance costs. These responses have disproportionately harmed low income families.

"Lockdowns may prove to be one of the gravest governmental failures of modern times. Mass business closures and restricted movement have affected billions of people globally through poverty, food insecurity, loneliness, unemployment, educational interruption, and interrupted healthcare. What did not make media headlines is the more than three million children who have died from malnutrition in the first year of the pandemic. Together with increasing malnutrition, the world is facing rising burdens of child marriage and child labor, developmental and mental problems, poverty, suicide and chronic disease.

"Reviews of the effects of lockdowns on COVID-19 mortality concluded there is no broad-based evidence of noticeable COVID-19 benefit. Pandemic models that guided poverty not only overestimated COVID-19 impact but failed to take into account the collateral damage of lockdowns. The sense of fear, anxiety and helplessness brought to families and 2.2 billion children around the globe with the removal of future earning capacity and limited access to healthcare will impact lives in an unprecedented manner for generations."

Yes, hindsight is a wonderful thing. But already in August 2021, there were a number of leading Australian academics warning against the lockdown mania which had overtaken Australian governments, leaving more than 12 million people prisoners in their own homes.

Including, much to his chagrin, Old Alex.

***

Driven to absolute distraction by lockdowns he absolutely did not agree with, his only human contact mediated by a computer, or brief exchanges in the few places it was possible to get away without wearing a mask, his house trashed by the departing tradie, Old Alex was just as demoralised as the broader population, depressed, distressed and deeply confused. Government-funded fear, extreme and ever changing diktats combined with free floating anxiety meant the otherwise innocuous world around him had curdled.

His waking dreams went into overdrive.

What was so astonishing was how much of it was out in the open. They crawled through trees and other lifeforms. Humans were just one thing on this planet. Genetically predisposed to hear them, well there was that, but so were many other things, if you could only read the wind blown leaves, if only we could surrender our own faulty dispositions, if only we could transcend for one tiny moment the mortality of these frames, the fleeting nature of it all.

He had been away, the geographical, geospatial or spiritual connection, call it what you will, broken. We became familiars. Or familiar. There were two sides to this, and he a bridge.

Bridges break. Bridges are trodden upon. Bridges are only appreciated as points of departure or connection, as places where one tethering is linked to another. In the trees, in the trees. "We know what you are," one of the Watchers on the Watch had told him days before. "You're not the only one."

It was for all to see, how ravishing this place, how the planet teamed with life, we were born here and would die here, and yet we were all, too, born very far away.

As for the country; a fool's paradise. The rampant dysfunction and connivance unbelievable. We weren't here to change that, because nothing could change it now.

The spirit that moved upon the water, well, that same water was lapping under the pier, was tangling through fishing lines, was home to yet more life.

And we came to whisper in your dreams, of a power way beyond yourself.

He watched. They watched. Game on.

And what would be preserved out of this time in history? What could save an unfulfilled nation? What could save a population deliberately de-educated?

Here in the reaches. There on the shore.

**

Way back in August of 2021 the Victorian Premier Daniel Andrews was up to the equally loathed smirker Prime Minister Scott Morrison, both men who clearly thought they were vastly superior "leaders" to the unwashed masses they led.

As one of those artists, writers and activists stirred into action through lockdowns and coerced vaccinations, Geoff Shaw, wrote in *Unmasked*, an unwavering book-length attack on Andrews, the state's sixth lockdown was all because there were six new cases the day before "suspected to be the highly infectious Delta variant".

"With only 80 active cases in the whole of Victoria, with only two in intensive care and on ventilators, Victoria was locked down from 8 pm that night. Supposedly for only seven days."

No one believed the short sharp shock rave anymore.

As Shaw expressed it, the ever-caring spiel by the despot was the same: "From 8:00 pm tonight, there are only five reasons to leave home: getting the food and the supplies you need, exercising for up to two hours, care or caregiving, authorised work or education if you can't do it from home, or to get vaccinated at the nearest possible location."

"Shopping and exercise must be done within five kilometres of your home or the nearest location.

"Face masks will remain mandatory indoors (not at home) and outdoors unless an exception applies – this includes all workplaces and secondary schools."

"Private gatherings are not permitted except for an intimate partner or nominated person visits. Public gatherings are not permitted. Exercise is limited to two people."

As Shaw so articulately put it: "Blah, blah, blah."

"Expectantly, seven days was never going to satisfy Dan. The world record for the most lockdowns was his. He now needed to focus on the world record for the number of days in lockdown.

"So, Dan extends the lockdown because 'the strategy is working'. Yet still, some people believed Dan."

In August Daniel Andrews brought back the night-time curfew and publically slammed people who broke his rules to go to the beach and watch a sunset. It's the middle of winter. Hardly anyone goes to the beach, and that beach is 100 kilometres away from Melbourne.

The entire country, the entire population, was being propelled into a nationwide psychosis.

***

There was a terrible air of resignation. They lined up to be vaccinated, they dismally stayed locked down in their homes, whipped into a state of terror and irrationality by the endless declamations and proclamations of media pundits, the portentous announcements of chief medical officers, the ridiculous grandstanding of the politicians.

During those brief encounters some of the conquered spoke virtuously of their own submission; with the weather cold, windy and wet.

Caught in a moral contagion, a mass panic driven entirely by the nation's politicians and bureaucrats, if it hadn't been for that modern marvel the internet Old Alex, and many others, would have felt entirely alone. It was no wonder so many succumbed.

They may have seemed weak minded, even moronic, in hindsight, but at that time many in the populace felt like they were doing the right thing, and still others simply went along to get along.

In an article titled The Covid Media Wars Down Under Paul Collits wrote that there were a number of supreme ironies in play in the Covid

Commonwealth of Australia, "where we have most of the population housebound, lockdown mania ever creeping from the cities into the back blocks as (typically) a single, wayward spreader visits a region, a dogged determination to just keep digging the zero Covid hole ever deeper, and ritual condemnations of wrong-thought now reaching the national Parliament."

There were breaks in the traffic, for anyone who cared to see. But no one cut through. In these strange times none of these sceptical, highly qualified voices springing up all round the world ever got through to the Australian masses. Amid the few strangers or acquaintances he engaged with, Old Alex encountered fear, or perplexity, at the very notion that someone might not get vaccinated.

Each morning as he drove down for his "takeaway only" coffee, no lingering for a morning catchup these days, all strangers were a danger, he would pass a queue of cars lining up at the local vaccination centre, stretching for hundreds of metres, sometimes kilometres, people willingly lining up to receive a vaccination for which they had no idea of the long term consequences and for which sceptics around the world were already sounding alarm bells.

When the unvaccinated were finally allowed back into the Lakeview Hotel Old Alex watched with a certain sad bemusement as a lean blonde "funny as fuck" tradie called Danny declared loudly in the beer garden at Lakeview: "I've had two shots. The second one made me sick as a dog. I did it for my mum. She wanted me to have it. I'm not having the booster."

Millions of Australians were convinced by their taxpayer funded representatives that lining up to take the vaccine was the socially responsible thing to do.

They had no idea of the risks they were taking. It would be some time before reality caught up with them, and then it would be all too late.

"Oh my God, what have I done?"

Resentment, alarm, regret, they all curdled on this rough road to Damascus.

***

The point of this discursive exercise being, the Australian authorities, highly paid, on salaries ten times the average worker, should have known, must have known, that none of their policies would bear up under scrutiny, not the masks, not the lockdowns, and certainly not the vaccines they did so much to coerce the population into taking.

And which they must have known at the time, with research tumbling out from multiple sources around the globe, were neither safe nor effective.

And for which the long term consequences were entirely unknown.

That made them culpable, and liable for damages.

And if they did know, which was their job, that made them either incompetent, dishonest, or corrupt; taken hostage by their own compromises, by bribes from Big Pharma and by the nationwide hysteria they themselves helped create.

***

August 21, 2021 was the day Victoria Police started using rubber bullets on protesters.

Matt Lawson, by all reports a very peaceable man, was one of those seriously injured on the streets of Melbourne. He made his way into history by dint of becoming the first person injured by the bullets. He was shot six times, and the resulting bruising and injuries made for graphic online images, and must have been extremely painful.

The nation was being seized with a violence perpetrated and propelled by the government itself, by those elected to serve.

"I was in an absolute state of shock that the police force I trusted to protect me had shot me repeatedly at point blank range," he later said in an address broadcast on YouTube for all to see. "I was broken. The internal bruising was agony. It would be months before I could lift my arms above my shoulders.

"Rubber bullets, also called less lethal weapons, have killed people before and at that close range they could very well have killed me that day.

"My government was willing to risk an act of murder for the sake of ensuring obedience. I was truly broken.

"It was months before I left my house again. For all the physical damage it was the mental damage that really took its toll."

Reignite Democracy Australia pursued a legal case against the officers involved, with no outcome more than a year on. The case, which sought exemplary damages, was funded through public donations. Managing

Director of RDA Monica Smit said: "It is about creating a situation where the police are accountable."

Whether pursuing elaborately complex legal cases through Australia's dysfunctional court system was the best use of donor funds, including the acquisition of high priced barrister Julian Burnside, remained to be seen.

Lawyer in the case Mani Shishineh said: "Police were shooting within three or four metres at unarmed civilians, mothers, children, elderly grandmothers. We never want that to happen again. If we were to see scenes like that in China, Brazil, even Germany, we would think wow, society has collapsed into chaos and savagery."

***

Pepper ball rounds were confirmed to have been used by Victoria Police during anti-lock down protests at various locations in Melbourne's central business district on the afternoon of Saturday, 21 August, 2021.

Melbourne Activist Legal Support, which had tracked the rise in coercive crowd control tactics by Victoria Police over several years, condemned the normalisation of harmful "non-lethal" weapons use by Victoria Police and the growing arsenal they had at their disposal.

The semi-automatic rifles used fire capsicum rounds, blunt force pellets the size of marbles, or dye markers that brand people for arrest later.

Video evidence also showed the use of baton round launchers being fired in the area around Queen Victoria Market during a protest event.

These weapons could fire different types of kinetic impact projectiles including rubber or plastic bullets.

"These pellets, and other types of kinetic projectiles, are incredibly dangerous and can blind, maim and leave permanent injuries depending on where they hit the body. Victorian police officers do not have unrestrained power to use weapons or any other force on members of the public.

"The emergency pandemic powers do not provide the police any greater powers to disperse crowds with 'non-lethal options'. Police are given powers to fine, to declare an area an 'emergency area', and to require people to move on, but emergency powers do not provide for greater use of force."

***

The lockdowns were crushing, spiritually, emotionally, physically; confined to the prison of their homes all Australians suffered, although by no means equally.

The public servants, able now to "work" from home, no longer obliged to front the office or do the daily commute, simply had to heat up their coffee machines on their marble benchtops before pretending to work for another day. Many of those jobs were unproductive, pointless, utterly useless Bullshit Jobs, as the book title went; but Australia's Public Service helped to maintain the illusion that those who thought something had gone terribly wrong were just delusional. Unenlightened. From some kind of lower social order.

Those in nice houses and comfortable domestic situations liked working from home. Their salaries did not suffer, indeed went up, as did their numbers.

The real world of work, of labouring and serving, had become a nightmare.

There would be a great deal of ducking and weaving, a stampede out the doors by the perpetrators, those responsible for this disaster being visited upon the country, but for now, all was a prison; the government front and centre of this crushing malfeasance, this derangement of the soul.

***

Front and centre of it all, whipping up hysteria on a daily basis, was the nation's media; now dependent on government largesse for their survival, and thereby doing the bidding of government, faithful lapdogs. The profession of which Old Alex had once been so proud to be a member were now little more than government propagandists, and the nation was already paying for their willing servitude, their betrayal of the truth.

They lied and they lied. And then they lied some more.

The result was a terrified populace; quivering, psychotic, depressed, dispirited, and with nowhere to go. There was no escape. There was no just getting on a plane and heading off to better fields, that, too, was verboten.

They were lonely keyboards, those who dared to disagree.

A Senate Committee in the nation's capital Canberra looking into media diversity hauled into one of its hearings executives of Sky News Australia, who were interrogated for having the temerity to broadcast diverse views on Australia's political and policy responses to the Covid virus.

They weren't perfect by any means, but their scepticism stood out in the sea of whitewash and official falsehoods that was mainstream media coverage.

Their views were routinely regarded as "misinformation" by those who should, and often probably did, know better.

Australia's ultimate caricature of ugly, high and mighty political correctness, Greens Senator Sarah Hanson-Young, declared: "Australians are rightly worried about the promotion and dissemination of Covid lies and conspiracy theories that put lives at risk and undermine public health."

As Collits wrote, Australians weren't "rightly worried". They were beguiled and confused by an utterly dysfunctional if not rampantly criminal government, acting not in the best interests of their people, but the best interests of pharmaceutical giants, most notably Pfizer and Moderna.

Two companies whose reputations and share prices, even back then, were plunging from the giddy heights of early Covid hysteria to the humus on the forest floor, more garbage for history to turn into compost.

"The Senator might also have mentioned the Australians 'rightly worried' about Covid totalitarianism, police brutality, public health mission creep, lost freedoms, trashed economies and the like, but to each her own.

"Sky has now been reported as having removed from its own website the 'offending' videos that may have been the cause of its banning for a week by YouTube."

In those shocking, benighted, cursed times there wasn't much good news around in the Land Down Under, "when Big Tech is coming for you, when the entire political class is a wholly owned subsidiary of Big Pharma, when Covid political correctness has taken root across the vast breadth of the land, when even the Murdoch empire cowers before its many critics."

***

There were many who saw a spiritual element to the changing zeitgeist. One of those was UK comedian come social and political commentator Russel Brand, who daily tore apart the Covid narrative and attracted millions of followers as a direct result.

"A human being is more than just information, a human being is more than just material, there is something sacred, something spiritual, you cannot be reduced to data points, there is something mystical, there is a ghost in the machine, there is a holy spirit, there is hope. We cannot allow centralised tech authority to turn us into just a list of binary code. We cannot allow powerful tech giants who are essentially modern day sovereigns, empires, tyrants, and kings astride the globe. Unable to be regulated, free to do whatever they want, free to travel the world, beyond nations. To have so much power that the needs and requirements of ordinary people are neglected."

A comedian who spoke about aggregated souls and the power of many.

There were people across the globe having similar visions.

Visited.

The gods were roiled.

And those who acted as gods, would soon enough be gone for good.

And so it was, and so it would be. This becoming. As if, in fact, a Second Coming.

***

Dodging around the outrageous censorship imposed by YouTube, owned by Google, blessed art thou, blessed are your government contracts, in one episode Russell Brand asks: "How much control does Bill Gates have over the media?

"We contest that Bill Gates has more power than any nation, certainly any government.

"We ask: What is the role of the Bill and Melinda Gates Foundation and the donations in particular they make to media organisations and organisations that train journalists? Whose misinformation is the most deadly misinformation?

"Is it the mainstream media misinformation which in my view could lead to all sorts of complications? For instance for those who believed the misinformation that the vaccines are 100% or 90% effective and stop transmission?"

At that point The Bill and Melinda Gates Foundation had made more than $300 million in donations to fund media projects.

Recipients of this cash included many of America's most important news outlets, including CNN, NBC, NPR, PBS and *The Atlantic*. Gates also sponsored a myriad of influential foreign organisations, including the *BBC*, *The Guardian*, *The Financial Times* and *The Daily Telegraph* in the United Kingdom; prominent European newspapers such as *Le Monde* (France), *Der Spiegel* (Germany) and *El País* (Spain); as well as big global broadcasters like *Al-Jazeera*. There were many others.

"What is the intention of this expenditure," Brand asked. "These are not charities. It's not like an endangered panda, is it? These are businesses. Why would you give money to a business? These are large media organisations. Are these donations transparent?"

In this case, Russell Brand was relying for his source on the work of Grayzone author Alan MacLeod, who listed not just a substantial number of news outlets but journalist organisations as well. These included the International Center for Journalists, Premium Times Centre for Investigative Journalism, The Pulitzer Center for Crisis Reporting, The Bureau of Investigative Journalism, the Institute for Advanced Journalism Studies, the Communications Consortium Media Center and the Institute for Advanced Journalism Studies. Among others.

In addition to this, the Gates Foundation also plied press and journalism associations with cash, including the National Newspaper Publishers Association, a group representing more than 200 outlets, as well as the Education Writers Association, the National Press Foundation, the American Society of News Editors Foundation and the Reporters Committee for Freedom of the Press.

Macleod reported: "The foundation also puts up the money to directly train journalists all over the world, in the form of scholarships, courses and workshops. Today, it is possible for an individual to train as a reporter thanks to a Gates Foundation grant, find work at a Gates-funded outlet, and belong to a press association funded by Gates. This is especially true of journalists working in the fields of health, education and global development, the ones Gates himself is most active in and where scrutiny of the billionaire's actions and motives are most necessary.

"It does introduce a glaring conflict of interest whereby the very institutions we rely on to hold accountable one of the richest and most powerful men in the planet's history are quietly being funded by him. This conflict of interest is one that corporate media have largely tried to ignore, while the supposedly altruistic philanthropist Gates just keeps getting richer, laughing all the way to the bank."

Gates Foundation grants pertaining to the instruction of journalists included Johns Hopkins University, the University of California Berkeley, the Institute for Advanced Journalism Studies, the Entertainment Industry Foundation, Harvard University, Development Media International, Boston University and Development Media International; Amongst a myriad of other organisations forming a vast global web of influence; a rigged game.

Macleod wrote that "while the Gates Foundation fosters an air of openness about itself, there is actually precious little public information about what happens to the money from each grant, save for a short, one or two sentence description written by the foundation itself on its website.

"Only donations to press organisations themselves or projects that could be identified from the information on the Gates Foundation's website as media campaigns were counted, meaning that thousands of grants having some media element do not appear in this list.

"That the Gates Foundation is underwriting a significant chunk of our media ecosystem leads to serious problems with objectivity."

***

Money might not buy you love, but it certainly buys you a lot of good coverage; obsequious, servile, adulatory, fawning coverage. Finding a critical word about Bill Gates in the mainstream media was impossible.

The Age, *The Sydney Morning Herald*, *The New Daily*, *Guardian Australia*, not a whisper of criticism. All the bad news stories about the vaccines, all the critiques, the alarm bells by some of the world's most well credentialed experts, all of it was ignored. The News Limited rags including *The Daily Telegraph*, the *Brisbane Courier* Mail and Melbourne's *Herald Sun*, offered some critical coverage, but Gates somehow got off scott free.

Lockdown, mask and vaccine sceptics were as scarce as a men's rights activist or a climate change sceptic on the $1.2 billion taxpayer-funded Australian Broadcasting Corporation, whose slavish devotion to the Covid narrative lost them relevance and viewers. Not for nothing were they known as the government's propaganda wing, no better than the communist or authoritarian countries they loved to criticise. Fearless journalism was nowhere to be found.

At the same time, Gates funded the Peter Doherty Institute, the government's go-to institute of choice for all things Covid, despite their wildly inaccurate predictions on the spread and lethality of the virus.

Gates also funded the academic journal *The Conversation* whose winning formula of running articles from publicly funded academics had been replicated in the US and the UK. With the help of Gates.

Throughout the Covid era academic after academic sang true to their funding sources, that is vaccine manufacturers. Story after story eulogised the vaccines as latter day miracles. Not a single question mark could be found. "What to tell your five-year-old about the vaccine."

How to prepare your child to be injected with a substance you as a human parent, without the gift of prophecy, could not possibly know the long-term consequences of.

It was truly sickening stuff.

And those who called it evil, well, what else was it?

The endless portentous pronouncements by the nation's servile bought and sold academics, regurgitated by an equally loyal and unquestioning media and acted upon by the nation's low grade politicians and dysfunctional bureaucracies, was a circumlocutious betrayal. In the public square it created a deadly concoction of hysteria and gullibility from one end of the country to the other; for millions of their less fortunate fellow Australians.

Here's a small sampling of headlines from the Gates funded *The Conversation*.

> Are you due for a booster?
>
> COVID vaccines: many people have had two doses but not their boosters. Lagging booster vaccine uptake in England means millions of people may not be optimally protected ahead of winter.
>
> The best way to stay healthy is vaccination.
>
> With a COVID 'variant soup' looming, New Zealand urgently needs another round of vaccine boosters.
>
> COVID vaccines don't just benefit physical health – they improve mental health too.

Misinformation will be rampant when it comes to COVID-19 shots for young children – here's what you can do to counter it.

At last, COVID-19 shots for little kids. The FDA's authorisation of COVID-19 shots for children ages 6 months to 4 years will bring relief for millions of parents.

I'm an infectious disease doctor. Yes, I'm vaccinating our 5-year-old against COVID-19. Here is why you should too.

Vaccinating teenagers is beneficial, even if their vulnerability to COVID-19 is low. Reducing transmission of the virus among younger people can help Britain reopen more quickly and reduce the risk of the virus infecting those most at risk.

The COVID-19 vaccines are a smash success.

When making the decision whether to vaccinate children aged five to 11 against COVID-19, regulators in Canada must rely on sound ethics as well as sound science.

Sound ethics and sound science. Well, that turned out to be a sad joke. The COVID-19 vaccines are a smash success. That's called lying for a living.

It was a tried and true formula. Governments find what they fund for and fund what they want to find.

The malign, all pervasive and extremely damaging influence of the Bill and Melinda Gates Foundation could be seen throughout Australia's politics, academia, health bureaucracies, research foundations and the corporate media.

We had been captured. We had allowed ourselves to be captured. Our foreign policy was mortgaged to the Americans. Our critical infrastructure, from the electricity grid to the nation's ports, had been sold to China. And our entire reaction to Covid and thereby the subsequent societal wide impacts to it had been handed over to Big Pharma and the vaccine profiteers.

By no small coincidence, Gates also happened to fund the so-called fact checkers, the World Health Organisation.

As wags put it, most billionaires buy themselves mansions and super yachts, Gates bought himself a UN Agency.

***

In widely reported comments, the US billionaire applauded Australia's pandemic strategy.

Speaking at the inaugural Munich Security Council, Bill Gates praised Australia's Covid response, claiming the quick implementation of restrictions allowed the island nation to suppress Covid cases early on.

"If every country does what Australia did, then you wouldn't be calling [the next outbreak] a pandemic," he said.

Yes, if only every country on Earth had blown tens of billions of dollars of public money purchasing ten vaccine doses for every man, woman and child, in Australia. That was 255 million doses for a population of 25 million for a product for which the manufacturers had no liability and which did not perform as advertised.

If only every country on Earth had held mass vaccination campaigns, and spent vast amounts of money mandating and dragooning their populations into receiving a vaccination they did not want. Then the world's vaccine-profiteer-in-chief Bill Gates would be even richer. Down at Old Alex's local cafe Joey, who worked at the local steel mill and always stopped there on his way to work, said: "I didn't want to get it, but I had to for work. My boss was crying. He really didn't want to get it."

As retired business analyst Richard Kelly would subsequently ask in a piece for the Brownstone Institute: :

> What about the injuries and deaths?
>
> What about the gagging of doctors?
>
> What about the suppression of treatments?
>
> What about the missed weddings and funerals?
>
> What about the denial of medical care?
>
> What will you say to the twin who grows up without her sister because her mother had to drive hundreds of kilometres to

Sydney rather than cross the border to Queensland and lost the baby?

What about stigmatising?

What about the money?

What about censorship?

What about the propaganda?

What about the coercion?

What about the businesses destroyed while idle nurses made dance videos for TikTok?

What about the increased mortality ?

What about the lost education?

What about the closed churches?

What about the global lockstep?

All the damage that was done to the social fabric of the country, and it was clear Bill Gates couldn't have cared less. Indeed, why would you when you were walking away with billions of dollars in profit pillaged from a gullible and bludgeoned population.

***

In that area, on the south coast of New South Wales where Old Alex had so surprisingly become ensconced, there were only remnants of the ancient vegetation, some of the most southern temperate rain forests in the world, slow growing, intensely beautiful.

The ancient stands were largely destroyed with the influx of white settlers during the 1800s, with timber cutters hacking down the forests, first the cedars highly prized for their timber; to make way for dairy farms, for which the area was uniquely suited

Those fields, once cleared, really did resemble parts of Wales.

The destruction of those forests left a void in the aching consciousness of the area; filled as it was with whispers from the past, and whispers from the future; as entities gathered like shrouds from the infinite to warn the denizens of today of their cataclysmic frailty, of their utter stupidity, their gullibility, and the depth of their betrayal.

As he walked sometimes through those ancient realms, it was the scale of the scam which he struggled most to comprehend.

Convinced that we were in the middle of a war against the human Naomi Wolf wrote in *The Bodies of Others*: "One of the reasons our current crisis feels so strange and disorienting to us humans, especially to Western humans, is that it was in some ways modelled by machines and by programmers and may well have been continually modified via machine learning. We are not living through organic human history as it has unfolded in the past.

"If you ask a computer program to define a human being or what supports human culture, it would likely spit out a list of all the relationships, attributes and spaces that were targeted by the policies of 2020-22. The machine program might respond: smiling, touching, hugging, praying, and speaking; the ability to read and to communicate via speech and facial expressions and touch; the ability to cooperate and to form bonds.

"If you asked a machine program, 'What are the building blocks of human culture?' It might spit out: 'Dancing, listening to music, watching concerts and theatrical productions, holy days and rituals, teaching children in a school, singing and worship.'

"So it is not for nothing that the bad actors have intentionally targeted the 'analog/humane world' of: physical books; physical bookstores; human-populated lecture halls; physical libraries; physical currency; physical maps; paper and metal money; human employees and human workplaces; concert halls and theatres; pubs, bars, and restaurants; in-person classrooms, churches, synagogues, mosques; dinner parties; non-electric cars; holy days and rituals."

From the beginning, mystified that this could even be allowed to happen, Old Alex had believed, as messages seeped through the fabric, that this was a crime perpetrated by lunar rightwing elements of America's secretive military and intelligence agencies.

They wanted to play God. They wanted to vaccinate the world. That way lay perfect control.

They wouldn't be the first gods to come crashing down to Earth; mired as they were in the biggest failure of government policy in their nation's history.

The biggest question, as with so many wings of government involved, became, who knew what, and why didn't they put a stop to it.

Or was it all intentional, this fiasco visited upon their own people?

SIX
VIOLENCE GRIPS AUSTRALIA

The disciples said to Jesus: "Tell us how our end will be." Jesus said: "Have you already discovered the beginning that you are now asking about the end? For where the beginning is, there the end will be too. Blessed is he who will stand at the beginning. And he will know the end, and he will not taste death. That resurrection which you are awaiting has already come, but you do not recognise it."

Gospel of Thomas.

"The outcome of my days is always the same; an infinite desire for what one never gets; a void one cannot fill; an utter yearning to produce in all ways, to battle against time that drags us along, and the distractions that throw a veil over our soul. One works not only to produce art but to give value to time."

Eugene Delacroix.

AUSTRALIA DESCENDED INTO its darkest days, a full totalitarian tilt into the abyss of government maladministration, a frightened, disoriented, confused population imprisoned in their own homes, and distrust everywhere. While a deluded and misinformed Australian public endured what on the face of it was a mass Psyop operation, a deliberately terrified population herded in one direction, towards mass vaccination and a singular loss of personal liberties, Australia's international reputation as a freedom loving easy going holiday destination was being trashed.

In August, that final month of winter, as the deranged Premier of Victoria Daniel Andrews plunged the state into its sixth, world record beating lockdown, the world's most successful podcaster, American Joe Rogan, lamented of Australia: "There's some crazy shit going on right now where the army is trying to keep people inside in Australia. They have full on government lockdowns where the government is flying helicopters over streets saying 'go back indoors, you're not allowed outside'."

Subsequently on Instagram he wrote: "Australia had the worst reaction to the pandemic with dystopian, police-state measures that are truly inconceivable to the rest of the civilised world."

For Old Alex all the violence that was enveloping the country was happening at some remove. For him it was a silent violence. He barely spoke to anyone; either in the flesh or on the phone. He didn't go to the demonstrations, he saw it all through some terrible filtered lens, tidbits on encrypted platforms, flashes of news, pieces that other people wrote, or he cherry picked for his online magazine.

Legally, he was not allowed more than five kilometres from his house. Psychologically, he could not bear the masks, which gave him instant panic attacks, and so the thought of two hours up to Sydney on a train, where many of the major demonstrations were held, was forbidding; foreboding. Perhaps it was just cowardice. Perhaps it was a frailty of spirit. Or wisdom. Or something else entirely.

He prayed for courage, strength, determination, good health, high intelligence, and occasionally, although it was forbidden, good fortune, resources, power in the land of the living, the mortals.

They didn't always arrive, these traits, gifts, whatever they were.

He watched from his aerie on the south coast, located between a military base further south and Sydney to the north, as the helicopters flew up and back, up and back, along that narrow reach between the sandstone cliffs and the coast, all for surveillance, for tracking, for the imprisonment of the population. A terrible brutality of the state.

Sydney and the area two hours south where Old Alex was marooned had been in lockdown for two months, despite almost zero cases, while the capital Canberra was also plunged into lockdown.

He wished, more than once, that he was still a reporter on one of Sydney's major newspapers, that he was out there, with a pen and a reporter's pad as his barrier against the world, his own weapons, in the thick of it all, but safe in the role. He didn't have to take sides. All he had to do was record. And he was good at it; had been good at it. Retirement didn't suit him much.

The lockdowns so beloved by Australia's politicians were already being decried by academics around the world, and would come to be seen as one of the greatest policy failures in the history of public health.

Hostage to vaccine manufacturers and their government collaborators, most of the mainstream media disparaged or ignored the gathering freedom movement around the country.

Across Australia protestors faced walls of police.

***

At the same time, the land of kangaroos and koalas, dangerous reptiles, cockatoos, budgerigars and surfers, that Australia of fond myth and legend, was being annihilated.

The international coverage was excoriating. The Qatar based Aljazeera news, for example, under a prominent picture of protestors carrying a banner "Country in Distress", recorded that there had been nationwide protests on 21 August, 2021, with more than 250 people protesting against coronavirus lockdowns in Australia having been arrested and many others facing fines for defying health orders.

"At least seven police officers were treated for injuries after skirmishes broke out at some of the demonstrations on Saturday, which took place in multiple cities nationwide. The largest and most violent protest was in Melbourne. Many were organised by people in encrypted online chat groups."

In Melbourne police arrested 218 people and issued more than 200 fines, each for an extremely punitive 5,400 Australian dollars, an extremely punitive level.

Six Victoria state police officers were hospitalised and three people remained in custody for allegedly assaulting police. Officers used pepper spray on several people, saying in a statement they were left with no choice.

In New South Wales state, police said they arrested 47 people and fined more than 260 in relation to demonstrations across the state. They also issued 137 tickets after stopping about 38,000 vehicles that approached the city.

New South Wales Deputy Commissioner Mal Lanyon said police expected to identify more people through security cameras and social media footage.

More than 2,000 people also gathered in Brisbane City Botanic Gardens to rally against the lockdown and vaccine measures, although Queensland state police said they did not make any arrests.

"Wake up sheeple," read one sign at a Brisbane protest. Another read: "Lockdowns Kill". And another in large letters simply: "Freedom".

A crime was committed here today; and no one was held to account.

***

In a piece badged "Insanity Down Under" one of America's most popular broadcasters, Tucker Carlson at Fox News, gave his take on Australia's Covid Regulations.

"One thing about Americans, they love Australia," he told his million plus followers. Most Americans have never been there, it's an awful long way away, but when Americans think of Australians, they imagine a freer, tougher version of themselves. Steve Irwin, Crocodile Dundee -- that kind of thing.

"So there is a huge reserve of affection in the United States for Australia, its culture and its people. It's also possible that most Americans, us included, have not updated our assumptions about Australia in a while and the modern reality is a little different from what we imagine.

"Australia looks a lot like China did at the beginning of the pandemic, that's the sad truth. People being welded inside their apartments to starve, the guys in hazmat suits forcing people into quarantine boxes and then driving away to some unknown destination.

"At the time, our public health officials told us that nothing like that could ever happen in our country or in the West, but that was wrong, because those things are now happening in Australia.

"Not everyone in the country is on board with this, but since Australians were completely disarmed by their government several years ago, there is precisely nothing they can do about it, so it has accelerated. Look at what's happening now? They're being crushed."

Would the population have been so compliant, and the authorities so utterly out of control, if the citizenry had been armed, as Americans so notoriously were?

It was a conversation Old Alex overheard repeatedly; and wondered about himself.

Few Australians possessed guns of their own; ever since a mentally ill man Martin Bryant killed 35 tourists in a shooting spree at the old penal colony of Port Arthur in Tasmania in 1996, one of the most brutal penal settlements in the entire fledgling nation.

Dark calls across a dark history.

The Prime Minister of the day, John Howard, used the opportunity to mount a massive gun buyback; to effectively disarm the population. A left leaning media joined the hurrah.

It was generally seen as a public good. The few sceptics were painted as gun toting rednecks. Nobody wanted to be like America, full of cowboys and massacres.

The English prison guards were remarkably cruel; and as the saying went in the Covid era, the problem about contemporary Australia was not that we were descended from convicts, but that we were descended from prison officers.

Old Alex had been working that Sunday as a general news reporter on the country's national newspaper *The Australian*, with his Chief of Staff Madonna King complaining that it was a slow day and fretting over what could possibly fill the next day's paper.

A perennial concern, particularly on Sundays.

Then all hell broke loose.

But there are always two sides to that story. Disarming a population makes them feel powerless, and leaves the only people with guns either thugs in uniform or gangsters with easy means of procuring illegal weaponry.

Either way, it was one more step in creating a compliant population reliant on the state for protection, and no coincidence that government propaganda in the latter days constantly repeated the message that they were "keeping Australians safe", a role which once belonged to communities and to families.

Carlson then went on to play several clips of scenes in Melbourne.

The first is of a wild street melee of running protesters and police. The next clip shows fully kitted out policemen with shields and helmets aggressively punching commuters as they try to enter a train station.

"We're trying to get home, we're trying to get home," one protestor repeatedly shouts.

"There is a lot of footage like this from Australia. In just two years, the Australian Police went from raiding newsrooms to beating people in the streets, so maybe the lesson is, things can change very quickly. One moment, the English-speaking world is mocking China for being dystopian and autocratic; the next moment, they are aping China and hunting people down."

***

This was a story told by outliers and outsiders. For Old Alex, weaned on the written word long before the Internet Age, all this was happening in some distant realm.

The violent scenes that engulfed Australia defied any rational sense; and were extremely difficult to describe in words.

If the God of the Bible had been speaking in the early 2020s, rather than "In the beginning was the Word", that is, a form of communication between the realms, "he" might well have said, "In the beginning was the Podcast".

For it was the images and voices of the era which carried the most power, and the most immediate documentors and most vital commentators were all working through video.

Words no longer carried the power they once did; and visual and verbal literacy became far more important than the arcane artform of books, or indeed newspapers, whose slavish devotion to the government narrative had left them entirely discredited and barely read.

Helpfully one of the outliers in the Australian media landscape TOTT News, one of the only outlets to have foreseen the truly dystopian nature of the Covid scare from the beginning, compiled a list of messages of concern on the social media platforms of the day from prominent personalities in support of Australia's protestors.

One of those was Tim Pocle, a journalist, singer and podcaster with 1.4 million followers who tweeted aerial footage of protests in Melbourne. The thread ignited protest from Australians still naïve enough to believe their government's narrative, and plenty of support: "Best thing to come out of this whole covid fiasco is that now many more people don't trust governments, media, police, big tech and big pharma."

Poole would later release a song Genocide, which he promoted with the words: "If the fascists had their way, people would have visited their loved ones as they were dying in hospital, making the pandemic much, much worse."

As the song went: "We follow, we follow, until it's our turn to die."

American television presenter Gillian McKeith also put out confronting footage from the heart of the demonstrations, with police in full riot gear facing down unarmed protestors with rubber bullets and pepper spray: "Governments that fire rubber bullets at their citizens must be dismantled now. The police are supposed to protect the people, not assault and abuse as they have done in Melbourne."

Another television presenter, Julia Hartley-Brewer, with more than 400,000 followers, tweeted: "Warriors for freedom. We salute you."

Multi-media personality and conservative pundit with more than 80,000 followers Carmine Sabia declared: "It is sad to see what has happened to the Communist Republic of Australia."

Author and comedian Tim Young told his almost three quarters of a million followers: "I'm praying for my friends in Australia who now protest for their freedom."

Director of Digital Platforms, author Darrell B. Harrison messaged: "Countries like New Zealand and Australia are going to extreme, illogical, and oppressive lengths to prevent even a single case of COVID-19 – as if that were even possible."

Swedish journalist Peter Imanuelsen told his more than 420,000 followers: "Australia is literally turning into a fascist police state before our very eyes."

And Canadian journalist Keean Bexte, with more than 230,000 followers, said: "Remember kids, our free society is only ever a generation away from becoming a police state like Australia."

***

In stark contrast to the messages of concern and empathy flooding in from around the world the New South Wales government went hell for leather to terrify the population. Then Police Minister David Elliot, a plump self-satisfied man characteristic of the breed, declared: "There is no doubt that these are the darkest days the people of NSW have had to face in nearly a century. But the high rate of vaccination means there is a pathway, a pathway of hope.

"Unfortunately there will be some obstacles on that pathway and one of those obstacles is the need to restrict public gatherings."

"So anybody who attends a protest tomorrow is going to be facing the full force of the New South Wales Police Force. You will also be endangering the lives of your loved ones. And prolonging this lockdown."

The violent, brutal suppression of dissent, not the virus, represented the state's darkest days.

Conveniently for the authorities, the right to protest had been abolished. A fundamental democratic right gone with the stroke of a pen. And a massive taxpayer funded fear campaign.

Elliott said he was "sick to death of people flouting the rules".

He told media outlets that it was no coincidence that there had been a "spike" in cases three weeks after thousands of people attended protests in Sydney's Central Business District on the 24th of July.

"There is no doubt in my mind at least some of these cases that we are seeing at the moment had their genesis at the protest," he said. "Which is why, if they try to do it again, the Police, with the assistance of any other agency we need, will make sure that the response is the same."

That is, violent, abusive, authoritarian, and provoking scenes that were now making headlines around the world, so utterly deranged were they.

***

At 12.01 on the 16th of August, the entire state, not just Sydney, was plunged into lockdown.

Tiny hamlets such as Come By Chance, population 167, in the middle of absolutely nowhere, were equally afflicted as crowded western Sydney suburbs.

Bush poet Banjo Patterson immortalised the town with the words:

"But my languid mood forsook me, when I found a name that took me,

Quite by chance I came across it – `Come-by-Chance' was what I read…"

Over the years of his wandering, Old Alex had passed through the hamlet repeatedly, stopping occasionally at the store or the local pub.

The joke about Come By Chance was that one half of the town didn't speak to the other. That's because there was a cemetery on one side of the road.

Locked down. There wasn't much else to do there but go to the pub, and you couldn't do that anymore.

Under the new measures random checkpoints were set up along key streets and roads in Sydney and more riot squad and highway patrol officers descended on the suburbs.

Singles who might want to scratch an increasingly lonely itch had to formally register their "bubble partner" with the government. If they were in a Local Government Area "of concern" they must also live within five kilometres of each other.

And there would be absolutely no travel to the regions without a government permit. People who fled Sydney for their holiday homes or to visit friends and relatives in the country were turned back to the city.

The state, the citizenry, everyone was haemorrhaging money.

The insanity was everywhere; and just down the road from where Old Alex was ensconced on the south coast police were knocking on doors to ensure that no one was escaping their places of residence in the city to seek shelter in their beach houses; sending them back to their miserable flats if they were sheltering in place, a place such as their second home.

The rationale? The logic? There was none.

Sprawling suburbs across Western Sydney, ultimately covering millions of people, were all declared to be "of concern", including Fairfield, Blacktown, Burwood, Liverpool and Parramatta.

There were $5000 on-the-spot fine for a "quarantine breach", up from $1000. A $5000 penalty also applied for lying on a permit, or for lying to a contact tracer.

The blizzard of announcements included $3000 fines for anyone exercising with more than one other person.

Shopping, exercise and outdoor recreation could only be done in a person's local government area or within five kilometres of home.

Random checkpoints on key roads were also increased.

Helicopters hovered ahead, ensuring that people were complying with the curfew orders.

It looked like, it was, martial law.

***

Police handed out more Covid fines in August, 2021 than they did in the previous 17 months – 25,687 fines worth $23.9 million.

New South Wales Deputy Police Commissioner Malcolm Lanyon declared: "Stay at home unless absolutely necessary. Tomorrow we will have over 1400 police involved in an operation to prevent those people who want to conduct an unlawful protest from doing so."

The statement from the Minister and the Commissioner was sent out in a social media message badged NSW Police Force: Poena Premit Comes Culpam. Punishment swiftly follows the crime.

The mass vaccination of the population was never justified and nothing to be proud of. But the perpetrators of this farce, those who used their public office to spread falsehoods, limit liberties and create panic in the population, never faced any penalty.

As history would prove soon enough, the vaccines were neither safe nor effective, nor did they prevent transmission, and nor were they a public good. They were, however, a massive source of profit for the pharmaceutical companies; and whether they engineered the situation or simply exploited it, the terrifying of an entire population suited them very well indeed. To profiteer was in their DNA.

Who knew?

And when did they know?

They would be the most significant questions as the repercussions sank in, and the recriminations began.

Along with many of his fellow perpetrators, from the Premier to the Health Minister and down the rank ranks, soon enough Police Minister David Elliott would be giving his valedictory address.

Indeed, mea culpa, David Elliot, who looked like he had never missed a meal in his life, should have been expressing shame, guilt, regret, remorse. And a heartfelt apology.

No such luck.

***

"We come at the End of Empire," the spirits whispered when Old Alex demanded to know why they were there, in that long, cold valley, in that unassuming suburb, in his unassuming house.

In this case the end of American empire.

As Australia's state and federal politicians imposed some of the harshest and most absurd lockdowns in the world, as they banned protests, monitored dissenters, bashed and fined all those who dared to defy their orders, the Taliban were seizing Kabul; fleeing citizens tumbled from a military plane taking off from the airport, and riotous scenes surrounding the airport were all too eerily reminiscent of the fall of Saigon, a place where sometimes the cries of the tortured were as vivid as if they were happening in the dark warrens in front of your eyes, not 50 years before.

How often could you make the same mistake?

Along with their never ending, disastrously managed wars, Old Alex was certain the collapse of America's credibility on the world stage was indelibly intertwined with the rampant corruption in their public health system, as the disastrous collusion between American government agencies and vaccine manufacturers and the consequent absurd overreach of Covid restrictions scarred the life of billions of people around the globe.

The gods were roiled, in this stricken time.

It was American money that funded the gain of function research on the virus and the resultant laboratory leak; thereby creating the "pandemic" which terrorised the world, and enabled these people to act like the gods they were not. It was American military and intelligence agencies which conducted pandemic simulations such as Operation Dark Winter which within months came to look uncannily like the real thing. It was American social media companies, including Twitter and Facebook, which censored anyone who dared to speak out against the prevailing hysteria, many of them highly distinguished, extremely well qualified experts in their fields.

It was American money which expedited the development of a Covid-19 vaccine whose harms became increasingly manifest, and it was American influence which led billions of people around the world to become injected with an experimental medical treatment, the long term consequences of which were at that point unknown.

All the warnings were ignored.

All of them.

It felt to Old Alex as if this infliction of harm on the populace had stirred ancient spirits into action. Who were these people to appoint themselves as Gods? Who were they to attempt population control, to tell us how many pin points it took to transmit a message of infinite wisdom, of grandeur, of love, of a kindness these pissants simply didn't understand.

Oh life. Glorious life.

At the time of writing, 68.4% of the world population had received at least one dose of a Covid-19 vaccine and 12.98 billion doses had been administered globally. In late 2022 1.7 million were being administered daily, despite the massive scandal around their research and development, serious doubts about their safety and efficacy, and public admissions that the "vaccines" did not stop infection or transmission.

The source of this information? The World in Data, a website funded, of course, by the Bill and Melinda Gates Foundation.

Their fingers were everywhere, and there would be a price, for our gullibility, for their tantamount evil.

***

Many people spoke of the evil inherent in the times and the spiritual element deep within the ferment. Pundits one might normally assume were agnostics spoke powerfully and repeatedly of the power of prayer, of Jesus Christ, of their God, or the gods, of a spiritual realm, and a spiritual context to what was happening worldwide.

One of those most unlikely was English comedian Russell Brand, whose daily impassioned rants against the Covid narrative, Bill Gates, Big Pharma, Klaus Schwab, the World Economic Forum, globalisation, digital IDs and the host of other Orwellian tendencies of the times had seen his popularity increase.

"Welcome you six million awakening wonders," he would begin his YouTube show, referring to the number of his followers on just one of his platforms.

He invited one of the spiritual gurus of the era, Eckhardt Tolle, author of *The Power of Now: A Guide to Spiritual Enlightenment*, on to the show.

The book had provided succour to people in crisis ever since it was first published in the late 1990s, and was particularly popular with former drug addicts, which Brand freely admitted to being.

Unlike his usual brash comedic style Brand himself appeared as if he was gobsmacked to be talking to one of the great spiritual gurus of the time. Perhaps he had read *The Power of Now* in rehab, many former heroin addicts had.

"You have become more political in recent times, which is fine," Eckhardt Tolle tells him. "Things have become so insane they need to be questioned.

"We are going through a period of increasing insanity collectively, it is like an illness, a collective mental illness has overtaken a significant section of society.

"Sometimes this happens, people, not just individuals but collectives, go through periods of insanity and this is what we are moving into now, an area of great turbulence.

"There is a deeper stupid and that is a complete lack of wisdom, and wisdom is what we need and wisdom arises out of awareness.

"How we dealt with the pandemic is an example of that. Just attacking this one thing, with complete disregard of secondary consequences which may be far worse than the original problem. Economic consequences, psychological consequences, complete lack of wisdom. That is unfortunately where we are.

"The crisis point is also great opportunity. We will experience a great reset, but not in the way it has been planned by certain groups or organisations. They will be very surprised. It will be a very different reset to the one they may be planning."

***

What was happening on the ground in Australia simply defied belief. The terrible silence. The brutality. The obsequiousness of the population. Compliance. Almost everyone Old Alex met believed their government. The dissidents, the few there were, emerged slowly, cautiously.

One of the only journalists in Australia to stand up against the tyranny of Covid mania in the Land Down Under was Rebecca Weisser of *Spectator Australia*. Old Alex used to work with her at the News Limited Headquarters in Sydney. The former opinion page editor at *The Australian* was a formidable intellect in her own right, and represented a threatened species in the Australian media landscape, a journalist not singing the demented tunes of vaccine manufacturers and their collaborators in the government sector.

At the beginning of that August, 2021, the final month of what had been a long dark winter for everybody, Weisser wrote: "New South Wales Premier Gladys Berejiklian made headlines around the world this week when she put soldiers on the streets of Sydney.

"The use of the military aptly illustrates that the government is not implementing a rational health policy, it is waging an all-out war in which no expense will be spared.

"Helicopters filled the skies. Loudspeakers warned citizens to leave the beaches. An elderly woman was arrested because, in wearing a 'Not Happy Gladys' tee-shirt, she was not just exercising, but exercising her right to protest. In Brisbane, also in lockdown, an elderly man was arrested by police who refused to believe that he couldn't wear a mask because of a heart condition until he collapsed of a heart attack.

"It is all justified by the decision of the national cabinet that Covid must be suppressed until 70 to 80 per cent of Australians over 16 get vaccinated. Only then will the return of vaccinated Australians from overseas be uncapped but there will still be lockdowns."

By the end of the month the situation had gotten a damn sight worse. A sense of dread filled every interaction, nothing made any sense, a darkness, if only it had been a simple darkness, an easy dread, an understandable evil; but this collapsing reality system, this desperate despair, this happenstance terror visited upon everybody, it was another level.

Weisser wrote: "Armed forces on the streets. Helicopters overhead. Sullen people unable to leave. Is it Saigon or Sydney? Kabul or Melbourne?

"Australians have been incarcerated in their continental prison for eighteen months. Sydneysiders are in their ninth week of home detention. Melburnians have clocked up 200 days in lockdown. Yet almost everywhere Delta is rising. Queensland, Canberra, even New Zealand, the home of the Covid elimination strategy, is battling an outbreak.

"As hopes of returning to zero Covid cases fade, Australia's increasingly unhinged premiers try to outdo each other in a bizarre state-of-origin competition to impose the most nonsensical restrictions on their constituents."

**

Even in the second year of this incomprehensible nightmare, many of the finest minds on the planet struggled to comprehend what was happening.

Beyond the size of the scam and its many moving parts, perhaps most incomprehensible, at least to Old Alex, was the behaviour, although he only knew it from online, of his old journalistic colleagues. They were meant to be smart, progressive types. They prided themselves on their independent thinking. And there they were, just like a low brow mob, pouring their privileged scorn on anyone who dared to disagree or even raise doubt about lockdowns, masks and social distancing; anyone who dared to disagree with the government sponsored orthodoxy.

He, personally, never deviated in his disbelief, perhaps because he had absolutely no reason to feel loyalty to a government spewing propaganda on inclusivity and diversity while meaning none of it. Just try disagreeing with them and you soon found out how diverse and inclusive they really were. He had never felt like one of them, the humans, surprised when he saw one staring back at him in the mirror, and the way he thought about it, which he never expressed, was that no human should feel this way; that the the way he felt or sensed things, the images and voices which filtered through him, that they weren't human at all.

We are only here for a brief span. And the gods will have their way.

Ishtar, that cruellest of gods, of love and war, as formless as any void, formed briefly and ran one brief tentacle like extension down the side of his face and across his neck, beauty and danger, intense and intent; but mostly the spirits spoke through the old ways, animal images, a lioness stalking through the tall grasses of the savannah, caution, extreme conflict, extreme peril, the guardian dogs barking at the temple gates, the sacred secrets, a high flying bird, mystical armies forming in the valley below.

***

In his groundbreaking book, *The Psychology of Totalitarianism*, Belgian professor of clinical psychology Mattias Desmet popularised the term "mass formation", postulating that most of the world population coalesced into a crowd in the early part of 2020.

As academics and sociologists puzzled over what they were witnessing, Desmet argued that the narrative of that crowd came to dominate the public sphere, the political sphere, and the private sphere, making it classically totalitarian.

He wrote: "The coronavirus crisis did not come out of the blue. It fits into a series of increasingly desperate and self-destructive societal responses to objects of fear: terrorists, global warming, coronavirus.

"Whenever a new object of fear arises in society, there is only one response and one defence in our current way of thinking: increased control. The fact that the human being can tolerate only a certain amount of control is completely overlooked.

"Coercive control leads to fear and fear leads to more coercive control. Just like that, society falls victim to a vicious circle that inevitably leads to totalitarianism, which means to extreme government control, eventually resulting in the radical destruction of both the psychological and physical integrity of human beings.

"This is the narrative of mechanistic science, in which man is reduced to a biological organism. A narrative that ignores the psychological, symbolic, and ethical dimensions of human beings and thereby has a devastating effect at the level of human relationships.

"Something in this narrative causes man to become isolated from his fellow man, and from nature; something in it causes man to stop resonating with the world around him; something in it turns the human being into an atomised subject. It is precisely this atomised subject that, according to Arendt, is the elementary building block of the totalitarian state.

"Totalitarianism is not a historical coincidence.

"In the final analysis, it is the logical consequence of mechanistic thinking and the delusional belief in the omnipotence of human rationality."

***

As that final month of winter in the Land Down Under wound to a close, through crushing lockdowns and political insanity, the thousands of protestors turning out in the streets, facing arrest and punitive fines, had become even more determined; just as the Covid narrative unravelled, and the corporate interests involved became clearer.

Thousands gathered in the Brisbane City Botanic Gardens to rally against what was now being referred to as a "reign of terror".

"Say No to the Pricks" read one sign, with a syringe encased in a Stop sign.

Another read: "All Risk, Zero Benefit: Mask, Lockdowns, Restrictions, Forced Jabs".

A banner was flown by a plane above Brisbane with the words "LOCKDOWN INSANITY = CHILD ABUSE".

Protesters passed by Queensland Parliament, shouting 'Freedom' in the direction of the building, before occupying the city. The streets, TOTT reported, were full as far as the eye could see.

In Darwin, police had their hands full confronting indigenous protesters, who formed a significant part of the Freedom Movement from the beginning.

One indigenous man Romper, who described himself as a member of the original sovereign tribal federation, addressed the camera and declared: "On the 21st of August, 2021, there were Freedom Day rallies held all over the planet and all across Australia.

"A lot of these rallies turned into violent episodes with the police perpetrating violence against the protesters and arresting and injuring a lot of people."

A police officer told him that there was an opportunity for the protest not to get out of hand, that they could do it another time, with a legal permit.

"We have the only lawful permit that is required, and that is tribal law," the indigenous man responded. "Your laws are fictitious. I should be making a citizen's arrest on you, that is the reality."

In Adelaide, the capital of South Australia, a crowd of more than 5000 turned out, a significant number for such a small city. The mood was generally jovial, with random cries of "Freedom" and many protestors pushing prams. "Wake up, people!" cried one. Placards included "Spread Facts Not Fear" and "Question Everything".

In Perth, the capital of Western Australia, protesters, flanked by police officers, carried signs denouncing lockdown measures and slamming Premier Mark McGowan for his hardline approach to lockdowns and State borders.

Campaigners were heard chanting "do not comply" and "the media is the virus", while children scampered around protesters carrying anti-vax placards.

Angry demonstrators chanted "tell the truth" after a speaker pointed out a Channel 7 journalist reporting on the rally.

Demonstrations were also held in Cairns, Townsville and other regional centres.

From here on in, the protests grew in size and intensity. The public were outraged, with very good cause.

***

The demonisation of the unvaxxed went into overdrive. New South Wales Premier Gladys Berejiklian told the state's citizens they were going to have to be vaccinated if they wanted to enjoy "the things we have missed".

"I wouldn't want to be in the room with lots of people who aren't vaccinated," Ms Berejiklian said. "And I certainly hope that all of our colleagues are vaccinated.

"That's the message we've been sending the community. And obviously as workplaces open up, every workplace will have their policies according to what the government is indicating.

"But I just want to make this point very clear: if people want to enjoy the things we have missed such as a meal or any other issue, or any other venue, they're going to have to be vaccinated."

That's flogging product.

A vaccine that didn't work as advertised; which was shoddily trialled, and which should never have made it to market. There they were, Australia's elected representatives, flogging it as hard as they could to a frightened, bewildered public, the very public they had terrified into submission, raped them of their taxes, and then used billions of their dollars to compel them to be injected with an experimental medical product they could not possibly have known the long term consequences of.

That's evil.

***

No one was more on the case than the Catholic writer Paul Collits, one of the single most intelligent commentators throughout this truly rotten period of Australian history, a religious man who knew evil when he saw it. In an absolute fury, he turned out a string of compelling articles condemning the government's actions.

In a piece called "Othering the Great Unvaccinated – a New Phase in the Blame Game", published in early August of 2021, he wrote: "Since the

Chinese Communist Virus arrived in the West, the puppet governments of the elites have been able, consistently, to get away with murder.

"One of the great Covid lies has been that it is the virus that has caused the economic pain, not the Government lockdowns and other non-medical interventions.

"This is passing the buck on a grand scale, deflecting the blame for their own stupidity, their evil totalitarianism and, perhaps worst of all, their blatant willingness to shut down their economies and smash the human rights of their citizens – all, seemingly, to avoid taking any responsibility for the shemozzle and so stay in power.

"And what about the social media killing fields of abuse, which can then be used as a resource for media types to reuse. This level of online abuse has been akin to The Lord of the Flies meeting The Madness of Crowds."

South Australian Member of Parliament Frank Pangallo opined of the unvaxxed: "They will need to be controlled or restricted."

The unvaccinated in Australia remained a political problem for governments that saw vaccines as the silver bullet for getting them out of political jail. They clung to this hope even as the evidence internationally mounted that Covid vaccines did not work.

In a piece called "The Idiot's Guide to Discrimination", Collits wrote: "In these enlightened times, we are seemingly about to enter an age of novel and unprecedented othering. The othering of the unvaccinated.

"Yes, we in the West, despite the courageous protests by people who actually are no more or less selfish than the next person, and despite all the analysis by the informed Covid and vaccine dissidents on the world wide web – those who haven't been silenced by Big Tech on behalf of Big Pharma – are about to create the Vaccine State. And my, won't it be a deep State.

"And despite all the human rights commissions in every damned state and territory, and all of the international rights treaties to which we are a signatory, this new Vaccine State will be government run. That this whole new architecture of conformism will be built on the very thing – discrimination – that we as a nation have been trying so hard, and through so many silly mechanisms, to eliminate, should be a cause of knowing smiles as to its utter irony."

There were plenty of other ironies about the vaccine apartheid being implemented nationwide. One being that it was already well recognised from overseas experience that the vaccines did not stop infection or transmission, making vaccine passports utterly pointless.

But Australia's political class perpetrated this "demonically evil farce on steroids" nonetheless.

"Australia faces a crisis of governance that is, well, dare one say it, unprecedented. The threats to our freedom, rights, economy and civil society posed by Covid-related policies – lockdowns, international border closures, interstate border lockouts, the sinister QR code tracking of citizens, mask mandates and now, vaccine passports – go far beyond anything we as a people have previously experienced, outside world wars. All because politicians, in an act so disgraceful that it is now cliched to call it out, have chosen their own welfare over ours. If ever there was a hill to die on, it is, surely, this one."

Politicians were calling for ever higher fines and harsher jail terms for Covid dissent, and sticking your protesting head above the parapet was simply asking for trouble. Protesters everywhere were being labelled selfish and stupid. There was no escape from the hectoring, the lecturing, the othering of non-conformists, the government infomercials, the Covid propaganda. Spirits ebbed.

In a piece titled "Scotty from Astrazeneca", a reference to the Prime Minister Scott Morrison's enthusiastic promotion of vaccines, which now had multimillion dollar advertising budgets thanks to the taxpayer, Paul Collits wrote: "The gloves are now off in the vaccine wars, with almost daily attacks on the non-vaccinated and threats of vaccine apartheid. These attacks are without precedent in this liberal democracy of ours, and constitute the greatest attack on personal freedom in our history.

"As reported, businesses such as cafes and pubs should be allowed to open to fully-vaccinated patrons only, Prime Minister Scott Morrison has said, as companies around the world bring in compulsory vaccination for workers.

"We'd have to have more restrictions on people who are unvaccinated because they're a danger to themselves and others," he said.

"If you're not vaccinated you present a greater health risk to yourself and to others than people who are vaccinated, and public health decisions will have to be made on that basis."

"In other words, Prime Minister, medical apartheid. Crushing the right to a normal life of those who, quite reasonably, question the efficacy of, and the need for, a non-vaccine whose dangers are untested yet clearly real, as even a cursory reading of the international scene reveals. There is substantial evidence that the vaccines shamelessly promoted by politicians cause documented, substantial, harmful impacts on many who take the jab."

Demonstrating that indeed totalitarianism comes from within the population itself, that the destruction of individuality is inherent in the human condition, there had been 15,000 calls to Crime Stoppers as the public was urged to dob in their neighbours, their friends, their relatives, anyone they spotted defying Covid edicts.

Stasi Australia.

Everyone was a spy.

"I never predicted that my own country would lose its sanity, its spine and its morality."

SEVEN
THE RIVER RUSHES BY

Totalitarian government, like all tyrannies, certainly could not exist without destroying the public realm of life, that is, without destroying, by isolating men, their political capacities. But totalitarian domination as a form of government is new in that it is not content with this isolation and destroys private life as well. It bases itself on loneliness, on the experience of not belonging to the world at all, which is among the most radical and desperate experiences of man.

Hannah Arendt. *The Origins of Totalitarianism.*

As AUSTRALIA EMERGED from that long Winter of Discontent in 2021, an inverse of the normal order in the realm, the country was now entrenched in the world's imagination for all the wrong reasons; as a warning of where Covid mania could lead.

To live through it was bewildering, and frightening, for to the average news averse poorly educated citizen there was no other story but the official story; the fury on independent media non-existent, and who had time to cruise the foreign news sites?

Our leaders knew what they were doing. They told us so. Who were we to question doctors and epidemiologists, a word many people would struggle even to spell. The scientific and medical experts; dare to question them and you were regarded as arrogant beyond belief.

No wonder Australia was chosen as a place where it would be easy to herd the entire population into mass vaccination; and get away with it.

Old Alex put together a piece for his magazine titled "Australia becomes the Laughing Stock of the World".

He wrote: "Australia's political and social derangement grows worse with every passing day. With thousands of businesses having been destroyed, with millions of people still in lockdown under the harshest and most truly insane Covid response on the globe, overseas news outlets and commentators are looking on with savage disbelief. How is this even possible?

"Two centuries ago Australia was the harshest and most remote penal colony in the world.

"Now the country has returned to form, locking up its own citizens, issuing hundreds of fines every day, blanketing suburbs with military and police, with a daily blitz of confusing information or disinformation, for without context much of the scare campaign over Covid is meaningless, and every day the country inches closer and closer to a complete social and political collapse."

Extreme isolation settled into all their lives. Anyone could read what the world press was saying about Australia, but few did. And even if they did, the cafes and bars were closed, there was nowhere to share views; and the question of vaccination and compliance with the blizzard of diktats had so deeply divided the community, there was no common ground.

Australians remained loyal to their country, even as their leaders became demonstrably insane; mad with their own power, drunk in a Covid frenzy.

***

In that long, cold valley, it hadn't stopped raining in months. The terror of isolation, of lockdowns, of the military helicopters overhead, of an all spreading evil, soiled everybody's soul.

Old Alex felt like he was a soldier alone in a remote military outpost. He renamed the house, from "Conway Gentlemen's Club" to "The Shepherd's Hut", for no other reason than the spirits told him to. The world's richest man Elon Musk, with his dreams of a neural interface and making humans an interplanetary species, was already planning to build his planetary wide "hive mind" on the foundation of Twitter, the ubiquitous messaging app which was then at the height of its censorial reign, censoring anyone who dared to disagree with Big Pharma's Covid narrative.

The collusion between pharmaceutical companies, government and social media was already an open scandal; the fraudulent had already been exposed, they just acted brazenly, as if they hadn't already been sprung, just like a drug dealer who continues to deliver his illegal wares knowing full well the police are watching him.

For the same reason: The money's too good.

***

Australian governments state and federal were spending vast amounts of money imprisoning their own populations; and the true, incomprehensible madness of it all, the population shut down, shut off, and burrowing into their own points of safety spread like a stain through everyday life; for the world was a dangerous place.

Highly credentialed experts locally and internationally had been warning that lockdowns and curfews would not work, but Australia's apparatchiks paid no heed.

In an article titled "Australia's insane COVID rules are a warning to the rest of the Free World" journalist Rich Lowry wrote at the time in the *New York Post*: "The 18th-century English philosopher Jeremy Bentham came up with the idea of the panopticon, a prison designed to allow all the prisoners to be observed by one guard.

"What even Bentham couldn't conceive of, despite his creative musings about schemes of perpetual surveillance, was a society like contemporary Australia.

"Once an honourable member of the Free World, Australia has lurched into a bizarre and disturbing netherworld of bureaucratic oppression in the name of public health.

"Lockdowns have cut a swath through the norms and conventions of an advanced Western democracy, from the suspension of a state-level parliament, to the banning of protests, to military enforcement of the COVID rules.

"With the Delta surge, more than half of Australians are locked down, often in response to a tiny number of cases."

Health advice. Health advice. Health advice. That was the justification politicians used time and time again to justify the destruction of Australia's traditional freedoms. Health advice that was strongly influenced by massive funding from the pharmaceutical companies.

"Australian authorities don't fool around," Rich continued. "State premiers have vast powers, and use them. In Melbourne, located in the state of Victoria, a curfew is in place, and limits apply to people leaving their homes. There are hefty fines for non-compliance.

"The spirit of the lockdowns was perfectly captured a few months ago by the chief health officer of the state of New South Wales, who warned, 'Whilst it is in human nature to engage in conversation with others, to be friendly, unfortunately this is not the time to do that.'

"Ah yes, the public health threat of over-chattiness.

"The Australian news media might as well be an arm of the public health bureaucracy. It produces stilted and hysterical reports about lockdown violators worthy of some dystopian future."

***

Afghanistan had fallen, and it did indeed mark the End of American Empire, just as assuredly did the collapse of the Covid narrative, and the blatant fraud and corruption involved in the raking of vast wealth, hundreds of billions of dollars in the currency of the day, off the world's population for a vaccine which did not work.

After all their fantastically expensive, utterly failed military exploits of the last half century or more, of the untold millions killed by American bombs and American military might, the next time they declared war, the world would laugh, surely. Another Saigon? Another Kabul. Another world where the greatest military power on Earth is humbled by the peasants? Where the feudal lords win despite all their advanced munitions.

But another foolish war did come along. Just not yet.

Most of the population, at this point in time, had never even heard of a country called Ukraine.

In Australia the same thing was happening, on a more domestic or subterranean level, the government had overstepped the mark, had failed to recognise the terrain or understand the enemy, had become blinded by their own power, and had locked up the entire state. Millions of people who had to show just cause as to why they were outside their own homes.

***

"We are asking industry to dust off their COVID safety plans, get the QR Codes in check, and we're also working on an App in NSW that will allow you to sign into a venue but also have proof of your vax all in one to make it as simple as possible, and we'll have more to say on that in the coming weeks," the New South Wales Premier Gladys Berejiklian declared as a frigid winter turned into an equally frigid spring.

One Sydney based writer, Mark Powell, managed to catch the spirit of the times as well as anyone, in a piece titled Is The NSW Government Becoming a Hobessian Leviathan?

"Gladys Berejiklian, the Premier of New South Wales, announced at her most recent press conference that the government is working on a 'proof of vaccination app'. This will in effect take the place of the current QR Code by supplementing it with an affirmation that the individual has also been vaccinated.

"Over the course of the COVID-19 pandemic, the state has assumed more and more control. Shutting churches made the celebration of a weddings illegal, closing down construction sites and small businesses, introduced a nightly curfew in affected local government areas, with police using rubber bullets to control civilian protests, and now the announcement of mandatory vaccinations for those in teaching, all in the name of public health and safety.

"In a significant display of political overreach, a church in western Sydney was not only fined approximately $50,000 for physically meeting, but was also banned from operating for seven days. This has the effect of preventing the church from meeting in any form, either physically or online. Clearly, the Berejiklian government has surreptitiously assumed sovereign control of both the ecclesiastical and civil spheres."

NSW Police Deputy Commissioner Gary Worboys said: "I can reassure the community that there is every effort going into those particular church services that are coming up on streaming, and pieces of information that are saying other church services are going to occur."

***

Old Alex's state of mind was an inconvenience of loneliness and isolation. There were much greater, more intensely human, more poignant and far more tragic inconveniences happening in real time all around him. Not least at the various state borders; Queensland to New South Wales, South Australia to the Northern Territory, Western Australia to the rest of the country.

While Australian bureaucrats and politicians proved extremely, deceitfully slow to admit fault, choosing instead to stonewall criticism and the gathering wave of evidence incriminating them in the greatest fiasco of modern Australian history, one who was not so hesitant was Victorian Ombudswoman Deborah Glass.

Her report Investigation into decision making under the Victorian Border Crossing Permit Directions was a sterling piece of work, exposing the human drama behind the hard statistics and the heavy makeup of television presenters.

Her report opened with the words of one respondent: "I feel anxious, stressed and depressed every day at the thought of being stuck in NSW, away from my parents and family back home in Melbourne. I am scared, alone and losing all motivation to live. Please, Please, Please, allow me to come back home."

Another: "We just want an exemption to be with our dying daughter. She is terminal, palliative and end of life. We are being treated inhumanly. A decision taking weeks we don't have."

In the end 2,649 exemption applications to attend funeral or end of life were received by Victorian authorities between early July and early September of 2021. Of them only 877 granted, leaving another 1,772 heart wrenching stories for which the authorities showed zero empathy. Zero. They were too busy grandstanding in front of their daily press conferences.

In the same period there were 10,812 exemption applications to return home for health, wellbeing, care and compassionate reasons. Of those only 895 were granted, leaving 9,917 disappointed applicants, some in perilous circumstances; that is, people who could not return to their own homes in their own country.

No wonder, as protestors stormed through the streets, anger was growing by the day.

The Ombudswoman stated: "Everyone in Victoria now knows about lockdowns; we have all had our freedoms limited since the start of the COVID-19 pandemic in March 2020. We even got used to border controls: for almost two years, Australian states and territories have imposed them, often on a few hours' notice, in response to spikes in cases.

"Countless plans have been upended by lockdowns and closures, or the prospect of isolation and quarantine. Since January 2021, Victoria has operated a traffic light system, where every person wishing to enter the State required a permit, based on the latest health advice.

"But the closure of Victoria's borders in July 2021 impacted thousands of Victorians in ways few, if any, could ever have contemplated."

Many of these complaints were heartbreaking.

On 20 July 2021, Victorian residents in red zones were given 12 hours to cross the border – an impossibility for many, especially the elderly or those with young children in remote parts of New South Wales.

Then on 23 July 2021 the lockout hit, retrospectively applied, so no-one could enter unless they had an exemption.

Overnight, thousands of Victorians were locked out of their own State. For the first time in over 100 years, the Victorian and New South Wales border, defined largely by the Murray River, was closed.

People could request an exemption for a number of specified reasons, including end of life events or returning home for health, wellbeing, care or compassionate reasons.

Thousands of people were stranded. People who had travelled to visit ill or elderly relatives, or who needed to return to care for them. People unable to return to care for their animals. People who had moved for jobs or study whose circumstances had been upended by the pandemic, who were homeless because their homes were in Victoria. People paying double rent with no job. Pensioners paying out money they could not afford.

This was not merely a problem of the volume of requests. With almost 8,000 exemption applications open in early August, the Domestic Exemptions Team was scaled up from 20 staff in early July to 285 by early September.

Decision-makers were given detailed guidance on when to approve. The evidence required was extensive. It included statutory declarations, proof of residence or ownership of animals, letters from medical professionals, financial statements, and statements of relationship to people who were dying.

The ability to respond was inherently problematic for people in caravans or temporary accommodation; or people unfamiliar with technology, the internet or without access to it.

One complainant told the Ombudswoman: "I had to constantly book online appointments with our doctors to get more and more paperwork vouching for the severity of our mental health. It was so dehumanising and humiliating."

Another complainant needed to travel to help care for her sister with an intellectual disability and terminal cancer, who was living with their elderly mother. She was asked for evidence of her sister's cancer diagnosis, treatment and life expectancy; her birth, marriage, divorce certificates and driver's licence; and a statutory declaration from her 86-year-old mother explaining why it was difficult for her to continue looking after her daughter.

It was hard not to agree with the complainant that such requests were "beyond unreasonable, very intrusive and unkind, inhuman actually".

One woman from regional Victoria, who needed to care for her animals, who was worried about having her flock put down because the department had asked for further information they claimed she did not provide, said: "I cannot fathom the cruelty of this process and their decision. Surrendering our animals has broken my heart, my spirit and my faith in our state government and the humanity of the people that make such decisions based on fear and not at all on human rights, compassion or justice."

The Ombudswoman recorded: "Other people felt caught up in a bureaucratic nightmare that bordered on inhumane: people whose applications were not processed because they had not submitted a COVID test in time, when they could not plan travel until the exemption was approved; people refused exemptions with no reasons or review process, being told simply to apply again.

"Applications were closed as expired when they were not processed before the intended travel date had passed, leaving people with no choice but to start the process again. Between 9 July and 14 September 2021, the Department received 33,252 exemption applications, of which only 8 per cent were granted.

"The overwhelming majority were not specifically rejected but closed for other reasons – the impact was the same as a rejection. They could not cross the border.

"People were not given reasons for the refusals or an avenue of appeal. It appeared to us that the department put significant resources into keeping people out rather than helping them find safe ways to get home. The whole scheme failed to comprehend the very real need for many people to come and go across the border for a whole range of reasons, even in the face of official warnings.

"How much could have been spared if more compassion had been shown. The effect of a complex and constrained bureaucracy meant some outcomes were downright unjust, even inhumane. We cannot let this happen again."

***

Australia was making headlines around the world for all the wrong reasons.

'Up to now one of Earth's freest societies, Australia has become a hermit continent. How long can a country maintain emergency restrictions on its citizens' lives while still calling itself a liberal democracy?' – The Atlantic.

'Heretofore an honourable member of the Free World, Australia has lurched into a bizarre and disturbing netherworld of bureaucratic oppression in the name of public health' – National Review.

Australia is 'hollowing out entrenched practices, principles and institutions of democracy and parochial state premiers have heavily diluted Australia as one nation, fragmenting it into several different states and territories that have frequently closed off their borders to other Australians' – Japan Times.

'What's the point of Australia?' – UnHerd.

'How has it come to the point that Australia needs to call up the military to eradicate a virus that is now endemic in the world?' – The Daily Telegraph (UK).

'Canberra plans to send its military personnel to help enforce social lockdown' – Global Times (China).

'If there is one nation that has gone insane with COVID, it's Australia. It's scary because their lockdown protocols mirror what Dr Anthony Fauci and other COVID panic porn manufacturers want to do here' in the USA – Townhall.

'The risks to Australia's democracy' – Brookings Institution.

'The authoritarian takeover of Australia' – Spiked.

***

If Old Alex read the tea leaves right, even the intelligence operatives felt the ancient pull to the future, and infinity brushed through them all. Ayahuasca. Carlos Castenada. All the methods of mind expansion they thought of merely as tools.

There was then, on the temple mount, the temple dogs barking the warnings that had frightened and impressed generations of primitives, those before the world transformed, the species transformed, before all was split asunder, before the ravishing, before the country which called Australia destroyed itself, before it became a prison island, before the peasants starved to death on the roads of disaster; before all that, when the ancient technologies and ancient life forms merged to create a new kind of divinity.

While the physical world might look much the same on the surface, Covid proved an epoch changing event in many ways.

It was a different realm. A different way of seeing. A different kind of human. A different walk in The Garden of Good and Evil. A different style of caring, when the humans of old became a kind of humus to a new species, when they looked back at the humans of the pre-21st Century as they in turn had looked back on Neanderthals, as some primitive link to a future not yet born, bearing, still, traces of their DNA.

They would, or could, live side by side. There was no need for the cruelty birthed at that time. Compassion was not their forte, but there was no reason for slaughter, no need for cruelty.

These blood stained histories would puzzle the historians of the future; why were they so damned cruel to each other, why did they care so little for each other.

The fear mongering, the psychosis, the anxiety and derangement driven into the populace by the feeble overlords and their ridiculous, incompetent bureaucratic edifices, was actively turning Australians against Australians.

And those old carriers of truth, journalists, failed in their jobs, failed in their hearts, held no integrity in the face of the greatest crisis the country had ever encountered, and Old Alex, upset by the dereliction of the profession he had once so loved, watched as his former colleagues ignored all warnings, watched the betrayal of the people by the ruling elites, watched as the empire built its own destruction, and wished he cared not.

On an average day Old Alex encountered few pro-vaxxers. And while their theories may or may not have been insane, The Mark of the Beast, "they're culling us", "there's bio-genetic tracers in the corporate poison", whatever they said, it was all an indication of the intense level of distrust the government was creating.

New South Wales, his state, was leading the way in the creation of medical apartheid, vaccine passports, and there would be plenty of trouble to come.

Plenty.

Sad they could not see their way to the light. Or to a peaceful co-existence. Or just to a fruitful, happy and productive life.

The disillusion, the anger, the disgust, the confusion, day by day it all settled well into the heart of the population.

And they would all pay dearly for the reckless power drunk insanity of their ruling classes. And cry: Why Did No One Stand Up?

But, of course, more and more people were standing up. Each to their own capacity.

***

As previously recorded, there was one Australian writer who stayed pretty much in the Red Zone throughout this period, and that was Paul Collits.

"Gladys Berejiklian is not running a Liberal government in the sense that anyone would understand it to be. The Premier and her health minister deceive us every single day.

"This woman is no friend of liberty.

"You and your mates in the political class have mandated the crushing of families, communities, economies and hopes, on a political whim and a political gamble."

"Australian politicians and our media are, relentlessly and without shame, creating Covid hate figures out of innocent people whose crime is simply getting on with their lives. They are doing this to deflect and to feint. And to cover up their own, wicked Covid crimes.

"Creating enemies that either do not exist at all or whose characteristics and attributed crimes are wildly exaggerated at best, or made up at worst, is the oldest trick in the Pol Sci 101 manual. It has been on display all around us during the Covid fiasco.

"It is employed by premiers, by their cheer squads in the media, by curtain-twitching cadres with first names like Karen, by politically correct writers intent on signalling virtue to their adoring hordes, by police commissioners acting well beyond their brief, by out-of-their-depth public health officials.

"Pity they aren't following the science.

"Vaccines do not work, as ever mounting overseas evidence shows, if the objective is to prevent transmission of the Covid virus. This vaccine is not, actually, a vaccine;

"There are tens of thousands of cases, only a small minority of them reported, of Covid vaccines causing great harm to those who take them. Why, then, in God's name are they doing all this?"

***

One of Old Alex's favourite writers of the era, Sonia Hickey, detailed the latest events in a story on that first day of Spring, 1 September, 2021. These weren't a group of disaffected miscreants, as the government would like the populace to think.

"It was common knowledge that truck drivers across the state were planning a protest on 31 August, and it was one of the incidents the New South Wales Police Force had been both warning against and preparing for.

"And while that protest turned out to be relatively modest, police were busy shutting down 79 separate demonstrations across the state, during which they arrested more than 150 people and issued nearly 600 fines.

"Police say the demonstrations were in contravention of the latest Public Health Order, whereby the entire state is locked down.

"In defiance of the current lockdown, which is in its tenth week, protesters gathered in a range of locations in Greater Sydney including outside State Parliament in Sydney, in Waverley, Fairfield, Campbelltown, Blacktown Sutherland, as well as in Cessnock and Lake Macquarie.

"Rallies were also held in regional New South Wales including outside Byron Shire Council Chambers in Mullumbimby, in front of the Lismore City Council chambers, in Wagga Wagga, Orange and Dubbo.

"Many of the 153 people arrested were released soon after their identity was established, but others were charged with a range of offences including contravening a public health order, assaulting police and resisting arrest.

"The Police Force has once again made clear that Strikeforce Seasoned will continue to investigate those believed to be involved in conduct that contravenes public health orders, even after the protests themselves."

Public health orders!!!!! As time would tell, this had nothing to do with public health, but a miasma of corporate interests, government malfeasance and disordered public policy infested by charlatans. The nation's politicians had become no better than snake oil salesmen. If only everyone had eyes to see.

These movements can be seen as the beginning of the massive Convoy to Canberra six months later, and mirrored the development of the internationally renowned Canadian Freedom Convoy.

***

In a separate piece for the Sydney Criminal Lawyers Blog, Sonia Hickey reported on the motives of the truckies: "The nation is polarised over whether protests should occur during COVID-19 lockdowns.

"Those against these protests see them as an unjustified intrusion on the civil liberties of others, namely the right against being infected by the virus. They label protesters as irresponsible, 'covidiots' and 'super-spreaders', expressing the view that protesting leads to a rise in infections. They assert that protesting is counter-productive to the objectives of protesters in so far as it is likely to cause the extension of lockdowns.

"Those in favour point to the democratic right to protest against actions by government. They see lockdowns as an unjustified intrusion on civil liberties, asserting that the mental, financial and economic harm caused by lockdowns outweighs any potential harm from the virus. They argue that public demonstrations are the only viable way of voicing their views in a way which will be heard. They argue that there is little or no evidence of community transmission in public, viewing assertions to the contrary as unfounded.

"The situation has led to a great deal of division, sometimes to the point of animosity, between groups, work colleagues, friends and even family members."

Truckies, however, are a breed apart. By their nature, they aren't easily bullied. They are traditionally sceptical of government messaging, and essentially immune to government propaganda. And what's more, they talk constantly between themselves.

"Hundreds of these critical workers have vowed to block every major highway in the nation, taking a stance against the closure of road-side truck stops and prohibitions against entering states without a vaccination which, they fear, could lead to blood clots and other serious problems given the nature of their jobs.

"Last month, a convoy of trucks drove through Sydney, blocking traffic and blaring their horns, to protest against the temporary closure of construction sites.

"Many truck drivers are concerned about the vaccination, in particular their documented range of potential side-effects. The AstraZeneca vaccine has been associated with blood clotting, and because most truck drivers sit for long periods of time, they fear this potential side effect could be seriously detrimental to their health.

"Right now we have state leaders using Emergency Powers to make rules that are arbitrary and rushed, which don't involve cooperation with other states, which are discriminatory and in direct contrast to personal freedom of choice."

Already, It would be right to note, serious concerns about the safety and efficacy of the vaccines, potential conflicts of interest and the process of "regulatory capture", which was rife in Australia.

For instance, Australia's Therapeutic Goods Administration, responsible for approving the vaccines, is heavily funded by pharmaceutical companies, a clear case of conflict of interest. The Australian authorities should have seen the warning signs, that there were multiple concerns over the administration of the vaccines and the profiteering of vaccine manufacturers. They chose to turn a blind eye. While all around, and in the months ahead, the scandal would simply snowball to the point where it became commonly accepted wisdom: We had all been conned.

***

There was a string of appalling examples of grotesque government overreach and the savage consequences on the lives of families and individuals.

That early Spring of 2021 the Queensland government hit a new low when it refused to let a family with a four-month-old sick child suffering from Spinal Muscular Atrophy drive home from Sydney to quarantine at their isolated rural property, 250 kilometres west of Brisbane.

Jessie Evans, her partner Billy Blacker, and their four-month-old son Rocka, drove to Sydney in August of 2021 for the child's treatment at Sydney Children's Hospital in Randwick, one of the country's leading paediatric institutions.

Trying to get home, the family were told by Queensland Border officials that they could not return by car. They must fly to Brisbane and undertake two weeks of quarantine in the city, despite an offer from charitable medical emergency service Angel Flight to take them on a private, sterile aircraft from Sydney to an airstrip near their home, avoiding exposure risks.

Queensland Health rarely granted exemptions to their grid of restrictions because the situation "presents an unacceptable risk with the potential of stopping along the way, for example, for fuel".

Border officials told the family that Jessie and Rocka could fly to Brisbane and then isolate at a hospital while father Billy stayed in hotel quarantine, at the family's expense. This would separate the family, and given Rocka's condition, for which there was no cure, robbed them of precious time together.

The family had all tested negative to Covid, and Rocka was immunocompromised. The longer the family had to stay in Sydney or travel through airports and other public spaces, the greater the health risks were for Rocka.

The family made an emotional plea to the nation's media and got widespread coverage.

"We're Queensland residents, we're not going there for a holiday and we didn't come here for a holiday," mother Jessie said. "We're just trying to do the best by our family and our child and just go home - it's as simple as that."

Not everyone has the capacity to make emotional appeals to the nation's media. Not everyone presents as a nice, good looking young country couple clearly desperately concerned for their four month old child, and most of these stories were ignored by a corrupted media.

This age of deceit, the subterfuge which was the public square, was mere film across a darker country.

There were countless other stories of this senseless overkill, the cruelty of politicians and their herd animal apparatchiks, their own Banality of Evil writ large across the human face of the country. Most suffered in silence; unable or unwilling to approach news organisations which, in any case, paid for by the government to spin the Covid message, could not see or would not tell the thousands of human stories staring them in the face.

Prime Minister Scott Morrison even made it into *The New York Times* for his particularly loathsome style. He used government planes to take the 55 minute flight from Canberra to Sydney where, ensconced in a publicly funded mansion with spectacular views of Sydney Harbour, he could catch up with his father on Father's Day, which in Australia falls on the first Sunday of September.

Meanwhile, purportedly to "protect the vulnerable", a litany of heart breaking stories, of families separated from their children, of elderly patients in aged care facilities dying shockingly lonely deaths without being able to see their loved ones, of families gathering at border crossings to wave to each other across a line of ballards, enveloped the country.

The litany became, in a sense, a liturgy of grief.

And all this suffering, as would later become accepted wisdom, was in order that pharmaceutical companies in league with governments and lunar right elements of the intelligence agencies could herd terrified populations into accepting mass vaccination, making the companies hundreds billions of dollars and entrenching power into the hands of governments and elites.

As of 2021, the average life expectancy in Australia was 82.8. The most recent figures available suggested the average age of death from Covid in Australia was 85 and the median age at death 86.

***

Came the first day of Spring in The Land Down Under, and one of the best known figures of Australia's Freedom Movement, Monica Smit of Reignite Democracy, was mouldering in jail after being arrested on incitement charges.

The democratic right to protest had been abolished in Australia, with brutal scenes of suppression and violent clashes between police and demonstrators now part of daily life.

The brutality of the state was there for all to see.

And with the mainstream media co-opted as nothing but a tool for the worst government in the nation's history, it fell to the outliers to tell the story.

Activist Monica Smit proved herself to be one of the most indefatigable active journalists in this blighted era, time and again putting herself front and centre of the conflict between protestors and police.

She filmed her own arrest, which subsequently had thousands of views on the web, and was later charged with two counts of incitement and three of breaching the Chief Health Officer's directions.

She spent 22 days in solitary confinement after refusing to sign bail conditions. A magistrate ruled on the first day of that cold wet Spring that if Ms Smit was to get bail she had to abide by a 7pm curfew, follow the Chief Health Officer's directions and not encourage anyone to breach those directions or publish anything that might incite breaches.

Ms Smit was also told to remove any material previously published online that might incite people, to not attend protests and to wear a mask unless she had a medical exemption.

Monica refused to comply, instead choosing prison.

Prosecutor Anthony Albore said Ms Smit used the messaging app Telegram to encourage people to attend the protests.

Court documents stated that in the lead-up to a protest on the August 11 protest, Ms Smit posted that "lockdowns take lives" and urged people to demonstrate.

She also posted numerous messages before the August 21 protest, the documents alleged, including: "The more they lock us up, the more people will have nothing left to lose … and that's when Australia stands up!"

The police also argued for Reignite Democracy Australia's website to be shut down and sought an order which would remove all online debate about lockdowns.

Those who had ignited this conflict watched from their mansions as the streets turned violent and sullen.

In sneering tones, demonstrating exactly why Australia's legacy media was failing, Rupert Murdoch's News Limited recorded: "A reality TV wannabe who has emerged as Victoria's most high profile anti-lockdown campaigner has livestreamed what she claims was her own arrest."

In reality, Monica Smit was one of the most charismatic and courageous figures to emerge from this era. And far from quashing Australia's Freedom Movement, all the authorities' efforts simply compounded a gathering storm.

After 22 days in solitary confinement, Monica Smit was released after an appeal to the Supreme Court, where Justice Elixabeth Hollingworth found the requirements to abide by a curfew and to remove online material were onerous.

Her lawyer, Queens Council Peter Chadwick argued to the court: "The reasonable view is that the Bail Act provisions are being used to effectively silence Ms Smit."

Needless to say, most of the victims of Australia's authoritarian derangement did not have access to expensive lawyers, had no chance of appealing their case to the Supreme Courts of their various states, and lacked any public profile to make it all possible.

***

There was, or so it seemed at the time, no end to it all.

The public were repeatedly told that the only way of this morass, out of the imprisonment in which much of the population was now marooned, was to roll up their sleeves and "get the jab".

The National Cabinet, as it was called, was a device the then Prime Minister Scott Morrison came up with after the abrogation of parliament, a "Cabinet" so-called consisting of the Prime Minister and the State Premiers.

All of this was treated with great import by the hostage media, hostage to their funding source, the government, which was pouring out tens of millions of dollars in tax write offs to tell their side of the story.

It was hard to find words to describe this farcical debacle, as the country wheeled into a cold, wet, tormented spring.

***

What was clear was that mass vaccination of the population was front and centre of the government's agenda; caution and public health be damned.

There had been a week of intensifying debate about the vaccination thresholds in the national plan for reopening the nation.

As Stephen Duckett and Anika Stobart of the Grattan Institute wrote, in a story headlined National Cabinet Leaves Us in the Dark About Reopening the Nation, that the so-called National Plan to return to normal civilian life was hazy, confusing and represented a complex of competing interests.

"While expectations for the meeting were high, there was no showdown – at least as far as we know.

"The current plan is vague, with words such as 'may occur' and only subject to 'in principle' agreement."

"Deferring the day of reckoning has papered over the cracks. National Cabinet is holding tight for another week and awaiting further modelling."

That was modelling from a government favourite, The Peter Doherty Institute for Infection and Immunity. Also supported with funds from China and the Bill and Melinda Gates Foundation. It didn't seem to matter that some of their modelling was wildly off the mark.

In the end, on one estimate at the time, 93 percent of the population received at least one dose of a Covid-19 vaccine; with more than 58 million doses administered.

As time evolved, and the consequences became clear, this became seen as a shocking, appalling record. The needle and the damage done.

At the same time the Australian Technical Advisory Group on Immunisation, another organisation whose reputation history would be quickly trashed, recommended vaccination for 12 to 15-year-olds, to begin on September 13 of 2021.

In what would later come to be seen as a crime against the indigenous people of the country, ATAGI recommended the vaccination of all Aboriginal and Torres Strait Island children.

What an absolute mess. Bucket loads of money disappeared into this chaos; this, as it turned out, utterly corrupt web of maladministration, malfeasance and outright lies.

***

The entirety of Australia had been turned into a prison island. The dismal mismanagement of the Coronavirus had destroyed the country, while a privileged class of politicians and bureaucrats enjoyed ever greater financial rewards.

They knew not what they did.

They destroyed themselves.

The country was already at boiling point. Old Alex could only take the temperature from where he stood, and he detected a gathering malaise, despondency, despair and disempowerment in the population, and much like any other prison, there were about to be riots in the prison yard.

Like so many others in that blighted time, he had switched off from the mainstream news, tired of the daily hysteria and grandstanding of the nation's fourth rate politicians and their fawning acolytes, their mad financial illiteracy, their utter contempt for those they ruled, their cruelty and indifference to their fellows, their snivelling, truly disgusting gorging at the public trough. Tell us what you really think.

He wasn't privy to all their purposes, much of it lay beyond his comprehension, why sometimes some things worked and were remarkably successful, while others crawled through space and time to wither on a barren rock.

Without form.

Made of many.

Cruel. Indifferent. Capable of love or at least kindness. Capable of blessing an entire area with abundance. All at once. These things were beyond explanation; outside time, why some humans were culled and others thrived, why the natives had been allowed to die out, despite their millennia on these lands, why an evil spirit had settled in the corridors of power, why the people complied with what was clearly a derangement.

It was The End of Empire.

For the previous weeks most of his news he picked up from what were now rare encounters with people; borders closed, schools closed, the daily absurd press conferences of a truly absurd political class, the forced vaccination of a population which had much to lose. The official death toll from the vaccines was now nine, making those very politicians pushing the agendas of Big Pharma murderers in their own right. The unofficial toll lay in the hundreds. Whatever your source. Believe what you want.

An incompetent, dishonest, and yes, in any normal sense of the word corrupt government edifice, in league with the worst corporations modern capitalism had ever birthed, were forcing a medical treatment on the population for which, by very definition, they had no way of knowing the long term effects.

The more they pushed, the more the population pushed back.

It was turning into chaos, utter chaos, one step at a time.

All that was left was to document the train wreck. Because out of this chaotic debacle, another truth would come.

And not the happy clappy truth beloved by some of the nation's most senior politicians, crawling and fawning as they were to a god they did not understand; but to something else entirely.

EIGHT
THE SHRINE OF REMEMBRANCE

> Service is but Magic
> Moving through the world
> And mind itself is Magic
> Coursing through the flesh
> And flesh itself is Magic
> Dancing on a clock
> And time itself the magic length of God
>
> Buffy St Marie. *God Is Alive, Magic is Afoot.*

THE ESCALATION OF protests in Australia and the state sponsored violence to crush it began, in a sense, with the little things, before running straight out of control. The blizzard of regulations and restrictions reached one of its more insane peaks when the Victorian State Government made the directive that food and drink could no longer be consumed indoors on construction sites, thereby shutting down the hallowed tearoom, a place to relax and recuperate between long hours of intense physical work.

On Friday the 17th of September, 2021 defiant construction workers set up their smoko and tea break areas on the streets of Melbourne, thereby creating massive traffic jams. Impromptu "tea rooms" began popping up across the city. Plastic chairs littered the streets at Lonsdale, Swanston, Spencer, and Sydney Road, with trams partially cancelled.

Covid Commander Jeroen Weimar was not impressed, calling the protest "dangerous" and insisting that the gatherings would be a place for the virus to spread. "It's probably where we drop masks to eat and drink and where we see people," he said.

Construction sites were already under heavy restrictions with plans for mandatory vaccinations, check-ins, on the spot inspections, and worker shift bubbles. Each site was required to have a CovidSafe marshal overseeing health and safety operations.

"We have seen too many cases in construction," said the Premier.

Daniel Andrews imposed a 25% workforce cap in place for Victoria and warned the construction industry that if they wished to remain part of the 'cap' they would have to comply with the new order.

"If they want to work and be part of that 25%, they need to be vaccinated with one dose by midnight next Thursday. If they're not, they won't be able to come on site," said a frustrated Andrews. "That's keeping them open. The other thing would be to close them down to zero."

The protest came to a natural end after the smoko break was finished.

But the race was now on. Until this point, construction workers and tradies had been largely uninvolved in the repeated protests which had racked Melbourne. Now, they were front and centre. And they were a very different breed.

***

The days preceding the fabled Shrine of Remembrance protest were highly dramatic, with the shutdown of the $22 billion construction industry spurring massive protests on a daily basis.

The moves sent 300,000 workers into unemployment; often unable to pay their bills or care for their families. The government was demanding compulsory vaccinations before workers could return.

As would later be revealed under Freedom of Information requests to the disgraced Therapeutic Goods Administration, the regulatory body which approved and promoted the "vaccines", the government already knew that the experimental medications were poorly tested, had multiple side effects, and their effectiveness, if any, lasted only a few weeks.

But never mind the facts; when it came to Australia's grandstanding politicians Covid tyranny and their daily press conferences were all they appeared to care about. Bugger the welfare of the population.

On Monday, 21 September, 2021, Australian Associated Press reported that riot police had moved in to disperse crowds at the Melbourne headquarters of the union, the CFMEU, after a protest turned ugly, with the union blaming "outside extremists" for the violence.

Police used pepper spray and rubber bullets to move the crowd, which took over the intersection outside the Queen Victoria Market.

Bottles were thrown at the already smashed glass entrance doors to the building in Melbourne's city centre as those protecting the entry sought refuge indoors just before 4pm.

AAP reported that there also appeared to be some conflict between protesters, with a number of small fights breaking out within the crowd of bright orange and yellow "high vis" vests.

The union released a statement just after 4pm, saying it has always supported freedom of choice regarding vaccination.

"We are not going to be intimidated by outside extremists attempting to intimidate the union, by spreading misinformation and lies about the union's position," the statement said. "The CFMEU will always advocate for safety, jobs, and freedom of choice."

Earlier on Monday, hundreds of construction stormed the building, protesting against new mandatory vaccination rules for the building industry and chanting "f*** the jab".

The protest escalated when two union officials, including Victorian construction branch secretary John Sekta, came outside the Elizabeth Street office to speak to protesters just before midday. Setka was met with boos and insults from the crowd, while some protesters hurled bottles.

"Please calm down. Can you at least give me the respect to talk? We're not the enemy, I don't know what you have heard," he said to protesters in a video posted to social media. "I have never, ever said I support mandatory vaccination."

By 1pm the protest had swelled to fill both sides of Elizabeth Street, with union delegates standing at the front of the building to stop protesters from entering.

Rain and hail did not deter the protesters, with calls for Mr Setka to come back outside and march with them.

Premier Daniel Andrews told reporters in Melbourne during his daily coronavirus update the protests were "not smart, they are not safe".

"Protests don't work. Getting vaccinated works, following the rules works. That's how you stay open, that's how you get open," Mr Andrews said.

The claim that the vaccines worked was an outright political lie by the Premier of Victoria, the by now internationally notorious Daniel Andrews.

***

There was scene after scene which simply defied belief. Nothing to do with the Australia most of its citizens had grown up in, and which most of the world had come to accept, a friendly, unsophisticated, freedom loving nation.

The following day, Saturday, saw wild melees on the streets of Melbourne, as police in large gangs aggressively pepper sprayed protestors at every opportunity.

Public transport into the city, including trams and buses, was suspended, leaving the streets eerily quiet, with nothing but the sound of helicopters overhead.

More than 2000 police gathered in the city to confront protestors.

More than 230 people were arrested and 10 police officers injured after hundreds of protestors converged on the inner-city. Most of the arrests were for breaching directions of the Chief Health Officer.

One image which became emblematic of the whole rotten edifice of Covid repression was that of a 70-year-old grandmother being pushed to the ground by police and lying helpless on the ground while she was pepper sprayed directly in the face, an experience which could well give an elderly person a heart attack. The striking image was replicated on posters and t-shirts and in myriad online posts.

One voiceover on footage filmed by Marty Focker, a protester arrested 17 times over the course of the protests, recorded: "You can see a group of three police officers approaching her. And then one of them has pushed her to the ground. She has fallen backwards, hit her head on the tarmac, been concussed, and then had her face doused in pepper spray. This is an extremely shocking act of violence and it's very sad to see.

"This could have killed her and it could have killed anybody regardless of their age."

There was so much pepper spray in the air at some points during the protests that it looked like snow. Lines of police and protestors faced off against each other, before police advanced with their canisters in hand.

Multiple disturbing images emerged from the day, including police pouring pepper spray onto protestors from overhangs along the side of a highway.

There were plenty more such scenes; a passionate young worker who had his face smashed in so badly by the police he was lucky to live; a construction worker given his notice who simply walked off the side of the building, committing suicide.

This was all over a vaccine which, as history soon proved, was neither safe nor effective, should never have been approved for mass consumption and for which multiple experts around the world were already expressing outright scepticism.

And all allegedly for the protection of a population fed up to the back teeth with the destruction of their lives and livelihoods after more than 200 days in lockdown, yet another of the Australian government's measures which did not work against the most over-hyped disease in history.

While numerous police quit in disgust, not one of the political perpetrators behind this brutal and unnecessary farce ever apologised.

The slavish devotion of Australia's politicians to the vaccine narrative raised serious questions about the corruption of Australia's regulatory bodies, and the politicians themselves.

In retrospect their repeated urging of the population to vaccinate, amplified through government owned or manipulated media and the crushing of both real world and online dissent, appears not just misguided or irresponsible, but patently criminal.

Follow the money?

***

Over this period Melbourne officially became the most locked down city in the world.

As numerous experts around the world had been warning since the beginning, lockdowns don't work, but Australia's political class ignored all the warnings.

The result of these deranged public policies led to the unprecedented scenes of violence on the streets.

And with construction workers now caught up in the protests, for the first time Australian academics, and many of the nation's middle class social justice warriors, saw people they know nothing about: Australia's working class.

The sight of Victoria's Premier Daniel Andrews and Australia's Prime Minister Scott Morrison, both unfit, unathletic men, condemning the behaviour of construction workers, that is those who did hard physical labour for a living, was sickening to behold.

Neither would survive a single day working on the nation's tough as nails building sites. But they were happy to condemn those who did.

Australia undeniably had the worst response to COVID of any nation on Earth bar China. Clear for all to see.

***

The day before the unforgettable scenes at the Shrine of Remembrance, Tuesday 21 September, "We built this city!" pro-choice tradies brought Melbourne to a standstill.

Demonstrators began gathering early in the centre of Melbourne, chanting "freedom" and "F**k Dan Andrews", as the crowd slowly grew.

At the same time, police formed a line in front of the construction union's CFMEU headquarters.

While crowds were gathering that morning, Bill Shorten, a former Opposition leader and well known Labor figure, appeared on television dressed in an expensive black jacket, white shirt and mauve tie, stoking a fiasco entirely created by his fellow politicians, his comrades in arms.

The fact that the political class pretended that the protestors did not have genuine grievances repeatedly illustrated just how far the Labor Party had drifted from its working class base.

"I never thought I would see a scene where you have people who call themselves Nazis, using encrypted message systems to bring a rent-a-crowd. I mean, some of these people in the crowd were, I am reliably informed, fake-tradies. They had been down to the Reject Shop and got themselves a $2 high-vis hoodie so they could pretend they were construction.

"There is a network of hard right manbaby Nazis, you know, just people who just want to cause trouble. These man babies, they want to complain about the vaccination, and they deserve to get the full force of everything that's coming their way.

"The fact they were coming after the union because the union has actually been showing leadership and saying we want to have a safe workforce and we want to have safe worksites and we want a safe population.

"The union was targeted because it wasn't following the extremist ideology of a few troublemakers."

The protestors weren't Nazis or "manbabies", and Shorten's garbage comments did nothing but illustrate how out of touch a politician can become when they spend their entire professional life on the public tit. Elected to serve, elected to represent, these people did nothing of the kind. One more failure of Australian democracy on the road to hell.

***

Photography from the day shows the streets jam packed with protestors. As always in a modern day Australian crowd, there were all sorts of people from all sorts of backgrounds, Sikhs, Maoris, Islanders, many of whom worked in the construction industry.

As the crowd grew near the CFMEU headquarters police began firing tear gas at protesters.

Some in the crowd put their hands up, chanting "don't shoot". The sea of yellow and orange safety vests and the bright orange smoke of flares made for dramatic footage.

The group, even larger than the day before, began marching through the city to Parliament House, now lined with a wall of heavily armed police with riot shields, behind them a line of police on horseback. The crowd chanted: "Every day, every day".

Along the march Channel Seven reporter Paul Dowsley was hit in the back of the head by a can. He claimed he had had urine tipped on him and his throat grabbed. There was plenty of faux outrage about the incident.

But the media's own violence towards the citizenry by continually denigrating legitimate protest, by acting as agents for the authorities and by ignoring or failing to report some of the most brutal police excesses ever witnessed in Australia could not be ignored.

By failing to hold the government to account and ceaselessly promoting government hysteria, Australia's mainstream media became entirely complicit in creating a kind of psychosis in the entire population; an irrational fear which ultimately led to millions of adults and children being persuaded to allow themselves to be injected with an entirely unsafe "vaccine".

Their own abject failure to report the story correctly throughout the Covid era ensured that mainstream journalists were hated by protestors, and drove the shift to alternative news sources.

Frustrated by the walls of police at Parliament House the crowd returned to the union headquarters. Once again, police were waiting for the crowd, so they took a different approach, heading towards the busiest section of the Melbourne freeway, the famous ten lane West Gate Bridge.

The crowd easily blocked the bridge, shutting down traffic in both directions.

"No job, no freeway" was one slogan. Lines of protestors could be seen as far as the road stretched. This was no small protest.

For a brief window in time, protesters crowding onto the bridge began chanting and dancing in what could almost be seen as a ritual conquest, exhibiting a celebratory joy after the misery of extended lockdowns.

Riot police arrived on the highway and began firing, with protestors soon dispersing off the highway. After seven hours of action, most protestors were calling it a day.

Police said 62 protesters were arrested and three police officers were injured. Victoria's Chief Commissioner of Police Shane Patton said officers used pepper balls, foam baton rounds, smoke bombs and stinger grenades which deployed rubber pellets.

"These crowd control equipment munitions were necessary because we can't allow this type of conduct to go on," he told reporters later in the day. "We will stop this protest. We will then step back and investigate and hold those to account who need to be held to account. The message is clear – you can't come in and break the law. We will hold you to account. Crowds like this are for cowards."

Patton said police had "intelligence" that protests were planned again for the following day and he implored people to stay at home.

"No one benefits from this type of conduct, we will be out in force again, I can assure you of that," he told reporters. "I won't disclose what our tactics will be tomorrow, but they will be different. Please just stay home, we do not want a confrontation."

Premier Daniel Andrews also issued a statement late in the day: "There is no excuse for the terrible behaviour we have seen in our city over the last two days.

"Acts of violence and disruption won't result in one less case of Covid – in fact it only helps the virus to spread. Thank you to the brave men and women of Victoria Police for their work today – and every day – to keep our community safe.

"We know vaccinations are our only ticket out of this pandemic. There is no other way. For those who think violence is the answer, I ask that you think of your fellow Victorians – doing the right thing over many months, following the advice of our health experts.

"We have come too far to turn back now.

"Please spare a thought for our healthcare workers who are working such long hours looking after patients, many of whom are struggling to breathe.

"The more of us who get vaccinated, the fewer us who will end up in hospital.

"It's as simple as that."

A Premier who was using the state funded police as a virtual private paramilitary force to crush all dissent, a Premier whose direct orders were leading to unparalleled scenes of violence on the streets of Melbourne, a Premier who was lying about the efficacy of vaccines.

***

There were people who would look back on the 22 September, 2021, and say that was the day, the moment, when they became radicalised, that was when they faced the brutality of the State and realised it was not there to protect them. There are few days so packed with drama down here in the Great Southern Land.

Once again, some of the best coverage came from the nation's burgeoning independent media. TOTT News, quick to awake to the significance of events, recorded it all in detail, as did many other vloggers, bloggers, pretty well everybody wanted to have a say. Here they set the frame.

The Date: 22 September, 2021.

"For the third straight day, protesters have descended upon Melbourne to exercise their fundamental right to have their voices heard, in a day that will go down in Australian history.

"The police rolled out the counter-terrorism unit early in the morning, chasing the group through the Melbourne CBD, before a standoff occurred at The Shrine of Remembrance.

"Both the beginning and the end of the day witnessed scenes of heavily militarised police firing non-lethal projectiles on unarmed Australian citizens."

Freedom demonstrators, many of whom were tradies, once again headed to the city at around 10am. Unlike the previous day, police were not prepared to simply let peaceful individuals march through the city.

All of this police action was the result of direct orders from the Premier of Victoria Daniel Andrews, with the vociferous approval of the Prime Minister Scott Morrison and the flag waving support of a corrupted media, just as willing to betray the citizens as their political and corporate overlords.

As quickly as protesters arrived, riot police descended on Melbourne's Central Business District to confront them.

"To be clear, once again, the protest is about choosing what to inject into your body. This is the reaction of the state.

"One protester ran past the mainstream media, claiming 'we can't feed our families' while holding a sign for medical freedom. He was soon chased by police, before narrowly escaping."

After a cat and mouse game through the city, the group were funnelled to the outskirts of the Business District. Thus, as a direct result of police action, a sizeable group of protestors ended up marching to the Shrine of Remembrance, thereby creating one of the most symbolic scenes of modern Australian history.

At this time, the mainstream media were describing the standoff at the Shrine of Remembrance, a revered place established to honour fallen soldiers, as "targeted", "disgusting" and "disrespectful".

As if all those young men, farmboys and children of the working class, those soldiers who had died in foreign wars at the behest of Australia's oligarchs of the day, would have approved of firing on unarmed civilians. As if they too hadn't, in all their naive and courageous ways, themselves fought for freedom.

***

The government's propaganda wing, the Australian Broadcasting Corporation, ran innuendo after innuendo claiming the protestors were being infiltrated by "neo-fascists" and right wing groups.

What, people who dared to exercise their democratic right to protest were now neo-fascists?

Yep, that's the one.

The slur of being fascist had been repeatedly used for years against groups which dared to exercise their democratic rights and disagree with government funded narratives, be it climate change, multiculturalism, mass immigration or gay marriage.

The Sydney Morning Herald, Old Alex's alma mater, was quick into the fray with the headline: "Violent protests show the far right are capable recruiters and have found fertile ground thanks to COVID."

Academic Josh Roose proceeded: "Far-right nationalists, anti-vaxxers, libertarians and conspiracy theorists have come together over COVID, and capitalised on the anger and uncertainty simmering in some sections of the community.

"They appear to have found fertile ground particularly among men who feel alienated, fearful about their employment and who spend a lot of time at home scrolling social media and encrypted messaging apps.

"The far right are a lot more capable of recruitment than we give them credit for. They have found an audience who are angry, frustrated and looking for someone to blame.

"This is particularly the case among young men who are increasingly attracted to right-wing nationalism and make up the majority of protesters. Victoria Police Commissioner Shane Patton has said the majority of protesters at the Saturday protest were men aged 25-40, who came with violent intent.

"Many of these groups share similar ideas: that there is a cabal of politicians and elites who are oppressing you. That freedom is at risk, that one must stand up for liberty, that there is a wealthy and unelected ruling class controlling you."

Really? You don't say!!

Elise Thomas at the Australian Strategic Policy Institute provided a more nuanced view: "Over the past week there has been a great deal of debate about who exactly has been storming through Melbourne's streets. It's been repeatedly claimed, including by union leaders, that the protests, which started over mandatory Covid-19 vaccinations and restrictions on the construction industry, have been 'infiltrated', 'orchestrated' or otherwise organised by far-right actors.

"So far, the allegations of far-right manipulation have been vague and unspecific. No one has yet identified any actual far-right figures involved in organising the protests, given any evidence of what they've done or even been clear about what exactly they mean by 'far right'.

"Thus far, there is little indication of meaningful involvement by known far-right groups or actors in organising the protests. Indeed, as anyone who has been watching them would know, the protests have barely been 'organised' at all. Meeting points are sent out over Telegram and individuals share them across their own social media accounts on other platforms like Facebook and Instagram. Beyond those meeting points, however, there really hasn't been much organisation in the protests to date.

"The use of 'far right' as a generic label slapped onto every anti-lockdown protest dilutes the meaning of the term, hinders understanding of what's actually going on, and can be actively counterproductive.

"We cannot combat conspiracy theories with our own search for invisible bogeymen."

***

One of the most compelling of all the voices to emerge from this era was that of Michael Gray Griffith, one of the driving forces behind the activist group Cafe Locked Out. He gives an insider account of that day. Here is his story.

"Stop making me do this," he said as he pounded my head into the ground with his plastic shield. "Stop making me do this."

"I'm not making you do it," I said, though I don't know if he heard me above all the yelling and screaming.

Next to me, Giuseppe Grasso, an Italian man, short and stocky was being pounded too. On the steps of the shrine we had interlinked arms as the police, dressed like storm troopers, finally came in. But Giuseppe was strong, and he refused to let my arm go, forcing the officers to wrench us apart.

Finally, our link broken, I was thrown to the ground and cuffed, which felt like I'd always thought it would feel. Briefly, as they did this, I had a knee pinned against my upper back, making it very difficult to breath and allowing me to briefly experience what George Floyd must have felt.

I actually wondered if this was where I would die, for there was nothing I could do as I heard them ask, "Are you happy now? Aye, are you happy?"

Finally I was dragged up and led to a grassy area where they sat me on the ground and took my details before finally setting me free, with the warning that if I came back I would be jailed.

"This isn't personal," one officer kept telling me. "This isn't personal."

"Well it feels personal," I told him, despite knowing I was not meant to speak.

"Yeah, well think about your kids huh," he said. "Think about your kids."

"I am, that's why I'm here. That's why we are all here."

Even those of us too young to have children had been saying all day, that if we don't try to beat this tyranny now how will we hold our heads up in the future when our children are living under it.

After that the officer chilled out and asked me what I did, like he was actually interested. When he found out I was a playwright, he looked shocked. When he asked if I'd written anything he might know, I told him about Marooned; a suicide prevention play that the army had once toured to its barracks for they believed it had the ability to stop men killing themselves.

"Men like you," I said.

That was the last thing he asked me. After that he uncuffed me and left me in the care of other officers. And there were lots to choose from. This may sound dramatic and even scripted but it's all true.

But the moment that saved the soul of the police for me was as we were walking away. I was now with another man, Joel, a young well-built father who in the struggle, had taken a punch to the face. Joel wanted to ask if it was ok to wait for his brother. As we waited I asked the officer, also a father, why the police had to be so violent?

He claimed that it wasn't him. He hadn't been there. He had been here, guarding this road block. Then he lowered his mask and said, clearly frightened as he said it, "To be honest guys, I admire what you're doing. I'm on your side."

***

The Civil Aviation Safety Authority declared Melbourne's Central Business District airspace a no-fly zone that afternoon at the request of Victoria Police to prevent media drones and helicopters from capturing aerial vision of the anti-lockdown protests.

According to the CASA directive, nothing but police helicopters could fly within three nautical miles of Melbourne.

The police lost a court appeal by media organisations the following day.

Police claimed protesters were using the live aerial footage to learn their location and media were ordered to delay any broadcasts for 60 minutes so as not to endanger ongoing operations.

Protesters outside The Shrine were holding anti-lockdown signs, flags and singing the national anthem as riot police gathered around them and footage of arrests started to appear on social media.

Voice for Victoria observed: "The new police tactic is to not try & diffuse or control things. They now rush & open fire at unsuspecting crowds to scatter them." News organisations would have to apply to the police force to be permitted to fly their helicopters inside 250km, and a blanket ban was originally placed on live broadcasts."

Mike Amor at Seven News tweeted: "I have been lucky enough to report extensively around the world and the attempt by @VictoriaPolice to dictate what can and can't be covered by the media, by restricting the use of helicopter vision, is a move that doesn't belong in a democracy. Where does it end.."

Media helicopters were not the only ones being blocked. As TOTT News reported: "If you were looking for a reliable live stream today, you were not alone. Traditional live streaming personalities were nowhere to be seen – not even recording emptiness in the city – while those that were attempting to film were mysteriously disappearing.

A number of comments on the TOTT News Facebook page also raised these concerns.

"Where is the coverage?", "Why can't we see anything?" – both common questions.

Citizen journalist Melbourne Detective also claimed to have had his page removed.

In addition there were major problems with all normal telecommunications systems. Maps from Telstra showed network issues across in the middle of Melbourne. Vodofone showed a total blackout.

***

The mainstream media covered the protests in often sniffy tones.

Fortunately or unfortunately, those who were protesting paid little or no attention to traditional news sources, except to lament their dishonesty.

Melbourne's *The Age*, which had run a breathless non-critical pro-vaccine pro-lockdown line throughout, reported under a headline "Stand-off at Shrine ends in cloud of tear gas and hail of police rounds": "Melbourne endured a third day of anti-vaccine anarchy on Wednesday as protesters chanted 'freedom' on the steps of one of the city's most sacred landmarks, the Shrine of Remembrance, only to be blasted off late in the crackdown as the protesters were being cornered.

"The Shrine, which was built in 1934 and commemorates those who served and died in Australia's wars, was left with its lawns littered with rubbish, including a full can of chickpeas, tear gas canisters and leftover 'bean' rounds. One decorated veteran stood by with his head in his hands.

"The hours-long stand-off between police and several hundred protesters came at the end of another meandering march through the city. Once the demonstrators had occupied the steps of the Shrine and were sitting around the eternal flame, they chanted a mix of anti-vaccine slogans and invective at Premier Daniel Andrews, as well as singing the national anthem and holding a minute's silence for people who had died by suicide during the pandemic."

Shrine chairman Captain Stephen Bowater decried the protest as "disgraceful and disrespectful. The Shrine of Remembrance is sacred. It is not a place of protest." he said. RSL Victoria said the protesters were "

"The protests began on Monday with construction workers angry about a vaccine mandate in the sector and other health orders, but have grown to include those opposed to vaccinations and coronavirus lockdowns. The number of construction workers appears to have diminished.

"More than 200 people had been arrested by about 8pm Wednesday evening."

Victoria Police Deputy Commissioner of Public Safety and Security, Ross Guenther, said all those arrested would be issued with fines and some had been charged with more serious offences. Mr Guenther also decried the use of the Shrine steps in the protest.

"My observation is that it was completely disrespectful that the crowd ended up at the Shrine, which is such a hallowed ground in this great city."

Among the chants of "freedom" came the chorus of John Farnham's unofficial Australian anthem You're the Voice:

> We have the chance to turn the pages over
>
> We can write what we want to write
>
> We gotta make ends meet, before we get much older
>
> We're all someone's daughter
>
> We're all someone's son
>
> How long can we look at each other
>
> Down the barrel of a gun?
>
> You're the voice, try and understand it
>
> Make a noise and make it clear
>
> We're not gonna sit in silence
>
> We're not gonna live with fear

The government called the protesters criminals, but they didn't look like criminals. They looked like any normal Australian crowd, a genuine mix of people of all ages and social backgrounds, people who faced life with sincerity and were rarely driven to protest.

***

The ever bolshie Caitlin Johnstone, one of Australia's few independent journalists with an international reputation able to make a decent living out of her work, wrote: "A lot has changed for Victorians since the lockdowns started. Our lifestyles. Our waist sizes. The kinds of things we see as normal.

"And a lot has changed in Victoria itself since we've been in lockdown as well. For example, have you seen our police lately? They're acting differently too. They're firing on protesters with rubber bullets and other projectile weapons with alarming frequency in order to end demonstrations against government shutdowns, lockdowns and vaccine mandates, frequently for no other reason than because the demonstrators are disobeying them.

"Use of force by Victorian police is officially required to be 'reasonable, necessary and proportionate to the threat posed by an incident.' When you see a video clip of Melbourne protesters just standing around the Remembrance Shrine begin fleeing to escape harm and being fired upon with less-lethal weapons as they retreat, for example, does that seem reasonable, necessary and proportionate to you?

"Okay, if you don't want to oppose police brutality on principle without making it about the supposed ideological positions of its victims then that's your right. But surely you don't think the normalisation of this kind of violence is something that's only going to affect people you disagree with politically going forward, do you?

"Surely you're not naive and narcissistic enough to believe the many dramatic deviations from normal policing protocol we've been experiencing during these protests will be rolled back when you personally no longer deem them necessary?

"The way police are dealing with protesters today is the way they're going to deal with them from now on, unless we do something. And in order for that something to be done we're going to first have to collectively ask ourselves, is this the kind of country we want to live in from now on?

"Do we want to live in a country where protesters are fired upon by dangerous projectile weapons if the police decide it's time for them to leave? Where protests are violently quashed if the government, the only so-called democracy in the world without any kind of statute or bill of rights, mind you, decides they don't have permission to protest? Where armoured stormtroopers patrol the streets? Where people are apprehended simply for filming police? Where police show up at your doorstep to interrogate you on whether you're planning to attend any protests or know of anyone who is?"

***

There is a lot of theory and entire courses at police academies on the dissolution of protest, and one of the strategies is to present false or misleading alternatives, thereby creating confusion and division.

There were reports the police had said to protesters that they could leave peacefully if they wished, however, the group was split on what to do. Tensions soon rose as police moved closer.

Police said protesters could leave through St. Kilda Rd, to which protesters responded they wanted to leave the way they came. They suspected the suggested way was a trap.

However, the negotiations soon stopped, as police moved in, firing on people and arresting who they could. From this point, police began chasing protesters out of the park, continuing to stalk and fire.

One distressing video showed the force chasing an unarmed group and firing from behind. One man in a yellow shirt can be seen putting his hands up and surrendering, before police shoot him down with rubber bullets anyway and pounce on him.

One user commented on Facebook: "It's like something out of a horror movie. Firing at a peaceful protest. The one good thing I saw was the person (supposedly a policeman) with the round shield, pulled another 'officer' back when he went forward aggressively yelling at the crowd. The protesters didn't do anything to warrant the way these terrorists/mercenaries/hired thugs, dressed in riot gear pretending to be police doing what they did, who are in service to the public... who are these people??"

One man, after being shot, simply described it all as "unbelievable".

***

The Prime Minister of Australia Scott Morrison was off in Washington hobnobbing with the President of the United States of America Joe Biden; while democracy died on their watch.

As part of what could only be hoped was a valedictory tour, Morrison announced a $90 billion nuclear submarine deal; military spending having escalated during the Covid era. Those whose sweat paid for these massively expensive contracts, such as the construction workers of Melbourne, were unlikely to see any benefit from these outlays for themselves or the nation during their lifetime.

Speaking from the US Capital, the Australian Prime Minister said the Shrine was a sacred site and not a place of protest. "The conduct was disgraceful," he said. "It was disrespectful and it dishonoured those Australians who have made the ultimate sacrifice and I would hope any and all who were in that should be ashamed."

Another media event saw the following exchange.

Journalist: "There are horrendous videos coming out of Melbourne of police brutality and they're going viral in America. Americans are talking about Australia, and they've been doing this for some months, as an authoritarian dystopia, what do you say to them about Australia? Are you running an authoritarian dystopia, a gulag?"

Prime Minister: "Of course not. Australia is a country that has seen over 30,000 lives saved, through COVID successfully. That has seen our economy come through COVID, arguably better than almost any other developed country in the world. We've worked together to produce these outcomes for the benefit of Australians."

Meanwhile outside the surreal world of Washington canapes and diplomatic glad-handing, Morrison's own country burned.

***

The question of why protestors had ended up at the Shrine of Remembrance became critical in interpreting the event.

Again it was up to Matthew Martin Gray to give the inside running.

"In the morning the place we'd been told to meet was surrounded by police and with no other protestors to be seen it looked like it was going to be a fizzler. So, despondent, we prepared to go home. But then we came across a few construction workers and joined them in a search for the larger group.

"It was now as we crossed a park that a black armoured vehicle, known as a bear cat, stopped suddenly and officers dressed like a swat team leapt off its side and started firing rubber bullets and these other things, I'm not sure what they are.

"Terrified, we ran.

"Once clear, and still astonished, instead of heading home we decided to head back to the city in search of the main group, our rattled party led by three young women who were determined to be heard. I'm not sure why we followed, for it was clear we didn't stand much of a chance, but then all that was waiting at home was compliance.

"A short time later, on a city street, with a slightly bigger group, the bearcat returned and again started firing, indiscriminately. I was shot in the hand, a ricochet I think, but it hurt and still does, and my live feed grabbed this image. The man closing in leapt onto the back of the man next to me, and so I walked, waiting for the same thing to happen to me, but it didn't.

"And so once again we ran off but this time our dispersed group met a few others and then these numbers grew until we reached Flinders Street where we found a major group.

"And that was it, because we'd reached the centre of the city in numbers this big, and I'm not sure how many there were, they stopped firing. Instead, they blocked all the side streets as we, like the day before, began walking around the city picking up numbers as we went. Displaying, as we walked, our injuries to each other, and many people had them. One young man was bleeding from the back of his head.

"Finally, even though it was on the other side of the city to where we were, someone who had a loudspeaker suggested the Shrine.

"As they said this, it felt like a perfect idea.

"Remarkably, we reached it without further incident. I was expecting the police, who had the numbers and the weapons and that armoured car, to block us. But they didn't.

"Did they want us to go there? Was the person who suggested it working for the police?

"Whatever the case was, we knew, as we sat on the hallowed steps of the Shrine that we finally had, as powerless people, a little bit of power. For as the police encircled us it was clear to both sides that despite all their weapons and armour they had a problem, their souls.

"Despite all the mass media on their side, who effortlessly were portraying us as the bad guys, rioters, we knew they couldn't find a way to shoot us here, like they'd been shooting us in the city streets all morning.

"It was a moment none of us saw coming, where we, looking like a group of Aussies at the cricket, belted out our chants for freedom, and then sung the national anthem with the gusto of prisoners who were momentarily free. And them pondering what to do.

"Every now and again the line of police came a few steps closer. In all their black and behind all their shields and black face masks, it was difficult to remember that they were Australian and not an invading force. But this intimidating tactic didn't work for we'd already been assaulted and terrorised in the streets, and instead of going home, we'd constantly regrouped until what was left had made it here.

"And we weren't here because we thought we were Anzacs. We were here because this place was unmistakably good. A symbol of freedom, where we hoped that the ghosts of our country's ancestors, the ones this shrine was dedicated to, the ones who sacrificed their lives fighting tyranny in other lands, would protect us.

"We knew we would get arrested. We knew we were finished. But if we got arrested alone on the streets, or later at home, the world's media wouldn't hear about it or care, but if they had to arrest us here, as we sat together, peacefully demanding freedom on a monument built to celebrate freedom, then maybe, just maybe the footage might leak out past all these black storm trooper uniforms, like a bright ray of truth."

Michael Gray Griffith concludes: "Stop making me do this," the officer growled as he and others repeatedly banged the shield against my head.

"I'm not making you do it," I replied, knowing all we could hope for was that someone would hear.

NINE
WE WEEP FOR YOU AND YOU ARE NOT YET BORN

For we are not alone, it seems
So many riders in the sky
The winds of longing in their sails
Searching for the other side
And if we rise my love
Oh, my darling, precious one
We'll stand and watch the galleon ships
Circle around the morning sun

Nick Cave. *Galleon Ship*.

A YEAR BEFORE The Shrine of Remembrance imprinted itself on the nation's soul with some of the most violent policing ever seen, one brave officer put his name to what many of his work colleagues were already feeling, that the authoritarian derangement in the Covid era was going against all that they believed in. With a new breed of officers proud to protect and serve, the paramilitary roles they were being asked to adopt went strongly against their instincts.

Many hundreds of police followed in Cooney's footsteps, abandoning the service they had dedicated their lives to.

In the year that had passed since Constable Andrew Cooney of the Grafton local command put himself forward as the public face of a group calling itself Cops for Covid Truth, Australia had become unrecognisable.

If a lowly Constable in a regional town could see through the farce that was the Covid fiasco, why couldn't Canberra's grotesquely well paid politicians and bureaucrats?

When, exactly, did Australia's public health system become so utterly corrupted by the influence of American vaccine manufacturers?

Could anyone have once ever imagined a scene like this, of police officers pepper spraying a defenceless 70-year-old grandmother straight in the face?

But so it had come to pass, with scenes of police brutality now occurring across the nation on a regular basis.

And Australia had become not just the laughing stock of the world for its authoritarian overreach, but one of the saddest countries on Earth.

Millions remained in lockdown, essentially under house arrest.

And their misery deepened by the day.

For the first time since putting his job on the line, and subsequently leaving the force, Andrew Cooney spoke out in a new video. This is what he had to say.

***

My name is Andrew Cooney. For the last 12 years I have been working as a police officer for the NSW Police Force.

In that time I have always done extra to my duties. I did the recruit show. I always did extra roles. I would run extra operations for the police. I am really pro-police. We want police. We need police.

And that is why I'm here today.

To let police know that we need them. I have had a lot of police come to me worried about what they are being asked to do at the moment.

Unfortunately no one within the police can actually speak. And that's my role. I'm here to speak for them.

In October of last year I wrote a letter to the Police Commissioner because I was worried that what we were doing was unjustified and unlawful and it was eroding the police relationship with the community. We are becoming divided. We are becoming police versus citizens. People are more frightened of getting a fine than they are of an alleged virus.

That was an evidence based letter I wrote. It showed that what we were enforcing was not justified. Covid is not what we've been told it is. On top of that we were breaching laws.

Covid is not about health it is about control.

Health is about connecting, it is about being outside, about your interaction. It's not about isolation.

So I felt someone within the police needed to bring that up. No one had. I waited a long time before I released that letter.

I was waiting, waiting, waiting and basically it got to the point where I couldn't sleep at night not doing anything.

I approached Advocate Me with what I had and asked for their assistance to help get a letter together. We came up with a plan that we would do an Open Letter and make it public because they believed it would be suppressed internally.

With that we have literally had people come up crying, saying thank you. I thought there was no hope.

It hit a point where I had so many police come to me, not knowing what to do, feeling someone should say something. And I was stuck basically under non-disclosure agreements or gag orders. I couldn't move on. I couldn't talk to these police. I couldn't talk to members of the community. And I couldn't do anything publicly because of these orders.

So I made the decision to resign from the Police Force so I could speak for the police who were still serving.

I couldn't show up as a police officer and force this tyranny onto the population knowing what was behind it. What we are enforcing on the community is unjustified. We're breaching laws imposing these things on the community, these rules.

It was unjustifiable and unlawful.

The police are being used as a tool by government for political and other background agendas.

I felt someone needed to be the tip of the spear, to break that ice. All I wanted to do was to plant the seed.

The problem with the police, and the problems I see and the phone calls I'm getting from police, they don't want to enforce this stuff.

They are part of a community, so enforcing this on the community, they are enforcing it on themselves.

If they're going to enforce this stuff they are removing their own freedoms. Most of the police now understand Covid is not what we've been told it is. They are frustrated with it.

They're over it. A lot of them actually want to leave. But again, they're in a situation where they might have a mortgage or something.

There's a lot of scared police out there at the moment, fearful of where we are headed. Fearful of what they are being asked to do. Not wanting to do it. It is not why they joined the police. They joined to help the community, to be there for members of the community. The government is just creating a divide. The police themselves are feeling isolated.

They're really struggling with it. So many are on stress leave since Covid. It's clear what is happening to them. I have been aware for a long time and so are a lot of police that what is being displayed in mainstream media is false.

It's being able to read mainstream media and say, what are they trying to get up?

Looking deep, they are pushing Covid so hard on the population, I looked the other way. And what I found was a whole world of doctors and scientists, thousands and thousands of them, who are putting forward facts that are being ignored.

Mainstream media have a lot to answer for. They are pushing this agenda. They are a tool. They call it programming. There's a reason they call it programming.

***

New South Wales police were obliged to get vaccinated by the 30th September of 2021 or face the sack. Across the country, major institutions from aged care to the police were facing massive administrative disruption as hundreds of their members said no to "the jab".

As history would very quickly prove, this was for a "vaccine" which should never have been given regulatory approval in the first place.

In Queensland all police officers and staff members will be required to have their first dose of a COVID-19 vaccine by October 4, 2021 and their second dose by January 23, 2022.

More than 1200 Queensland police were just saying no to a mandated medical intervention about which they had little or no confidence, and which by stint of the rapidity of its development no one could possibly know the long term consequences.

The authorities made it clear that those 1200 officers would simply be replaced with more compliant officers; or those uncaring enough to take the risk with their own health. No problem. We're all fine with that, too. Decades of experience; decades of service; and they were all expendable.

***

Aftermaths, like ruins and leaders in defeat, are always evocative; and so it proved to be. There was a whole of government, whole of security agencies effort to silence the protestors who, as time would soon reveal, were not just on the right side of history, but had every right to protest the draconian and useless measures being dished out to them by a government which had lost all its ethical moorings.

September 23rd was a very strange day for Melbourne. A number of red flags suggested there was an intentional blackout of the city, as familiar scenes of thousands marching through the city were nowhere to be seen.

Media organisations were banned by Victoria Police from broadcasting live aerial footage, and spent the whole day contesting the decision in court.

Livestreams on-the-ground were reportedly interrupted and deleted, while telecommunications was experiencing outages across the board.

Familiar independent media personalities were nowhere to be seen, before a range of conspiracy theories began running wild when some finally checked in to report 'no activity' for the day.

This corroborated mainstream media reports of a 'non-event' on September 23, despite Victoria Police stating in their afternoon report that 92 individuals were arrested during the day.

TOTT News asked: "What really happened during this blackout? Why was there a blackout of everything happening in Melbourne on this day? Why do none of the stories align with one another? Did police use their new found powers to infiltrate and/or take over the movement/personalities during this time?"

Everyone awaited the following day, now with media restrictions lifted, to see what had occurred.

Joel Gilmour, one of the main livestreamers from the Shrine, recorded: "People were a bit more secretive about location and the planning of how it went ahead. We know there are plenty of infiltrators watching to give away where we are. That is why the few you might see streaming went off. So we didn't actually get together in large numbers. There were definitely small groups spread out everywhere, but we were being very cautious in our chats not to have the police come and attend straight to us. I am aware that there were some live streams that were stopped and some people couldn't stream.

"They definitely did interfere with mobile towers. They did also remove, I experienced it yesterday, they removed the live button, so I could start a live Facebook. The police will say they've scared us off, but that definitely is not the case. We'll be back again tomorrow."

And in the aftermath Old Alex had one recurring thought: "If they could do it once, they could do it again."

That is, destroy any semblance of democracy, and any right to protest.

***

Deliberately created chaos and division amid the ranks of the protestors, false rumours and false leads, infiltrators, computer experts, media massaging and manipulation of public opinion, political barnstorming, that is a massively expensive operation to destroy a spontaneous protest from people with a genuine grievance.

As Melbourne emerged from a communication blackout things already appeared to look very different for campaigners on the ground. From the beginning of the day, several different locations were suspiciously leaked on communication channels of the movement, to which leading figures said they were infiltrated."

First the confusion. Multiple different gathering points were broadcast. At the same time, some supporters of the protests were receiving knocks on their door from the police.

Really, someone should make a Museum of all this. There is so much material; and no coordinating body to record it.

Whatever operations that were undertaken by authorities during the blackout, protesters now found themselves divided, and trapped in the suburbs in the face of police.

After several locations were suspiciously leaked on that Friday, September 24, 2021, police began to stalk small groups of freedom protesters trying to join together in the inner-city suburb of Northcote. Authorities moved in quickly, surrounding Northcote Plaza with a large number of officers.

Riot police also arrived on the scene, forcing bystanders back into the shopping plaza and preventing them from leaving the local area.

Police not only surrounded the plaza, but began to storm through in search of activists. Some arrests were made early – both on protesters and bystanders who didn't follow directions. Scenes never before seen in the uneventful suburbs of Melbourne.

The only livestreamer on the ground, broadcast by Joel Gilmour, whose enthusiastic coverage won him a legion of fans, showed the protest group subsequently retreating to the park and outer suburb streets while being stalked by walls of police.

Police swarmed the park, advancing closer and making arrests in the process.

As the group attempted to escape through the suburban streets, Joel successfully passed back through the police lines. His freedom was short-lived. Heavily militarised riot squad members confronted him. He was arrested shortly afterwards and his livestream taken down.

The clips which remain on line, and form part of a valuable historical record, were captured by those who managed to save copies.

TOTT News concluded: "These scenes painted a very concerning picture about Melbourne's freedom efforts. Gone were previous days of turning up to the city in great numbers and marching. Now, we see a group intentionally divided and stalked in the suburbs – before they even made it to the city.

"No violence, no incitement towards the police – just a group trying to leave their local area.

"They couldn't even get off the ground. Not to mention that hundreds had already been arrested during the week so far, being fired at by police with non-lethal projectiles on multiple occasions.

"Concerns of a blackout conspiracy had become the dominant talking point at this point. Thousands could have emerged on the 24th after the blackout had ended, ending all suspicions about a major operation that had smashed the movement. However, this didn't happen."

The movement had been smashed.

The Australian Broadcasting Corporation reported: "Victoria Police arrested 31 people at a shopping complex in Melbourne's inner north, with hundreds more arrested across the city as protesters attempted to continue this week's anti-lockdown protests.

"In total, 215 people will be fined for breaching public health orders across Melbourne, with a number of other people to be charged with criminal offences including deception, theft and drug offences.

"There was a heavy police presence in inner Melbourne throughout the morning, with protesters mostly found in smaller groups scattered across the city and nearby suburbs. Anyone who did not have a legitimate reason to be in the CBD was either moved on or arrested."

***

Then came Saturday, the Millions March, with events around the country.

Infuriated Old Alex wrote: Black clad police firing into unarmed crowds. Feelings ran strong. Somehow we're all fine with it.

Two police standing over an unarmed 70-year-old grandmother pepper spraying her in the face. Somehow we're all fine with it.

Genuine protest was an unfamiliar sight in Australia after the orchestrated public displays around climate change and Black Lives Matter and for almost two years of recent history, gay marriage. All of them were narratives backed by bucket loads of taxpayer money. But a genuine, working class revolt: brutally crushed. No chance.

And we're somehow all fine with that, too.

We're fine with the mainstream media blatantly lying about the violent displays of authoritarian abuse seen on the streets of Melbourne.

The blindly abusive, deranged scenes of police punching protesters, slamming their heads into the ground, never before seen, never before witnessed in the Great Southern Land, taxpayer funded military style police literally assaulting the citizenry; and somehow we were all fine with that, too.

It was a terrible thing.

It was a terrible moment.

***

As journalist Paul Gregoire wrote in the cutting edge Sydney Criminal Lawyers Blog: Australia watched on in disbelief as the violence on Melbourne streets escalated, with hordes of heavily armed police officers clashing with members of the public protesting against extended lockdowns and vaccination mandates.

The mainstream media has focused heavily on violence and offensive acts allegedly committed by protesters, largely overlooking the many instances of police brutality – whereby officers used excessive force to perform arrests and engaged in conduct amounting to dangerous assaults against members of the public.

Gregoire asked, how did we go from pandemic to such escalating violence on the streets?

The severity and longevity of Melbourne's lockdowns are well documented. As are the psychological effects: loneliness, increased domestic violence, emotional instability, depression, anxiety.

It's only recently that psychologists have begun to talk about the pent up frustration, otherwise known as "lockdown rage".

And it's not just spilling onto the streets in Victoria, it's spilling out all over Australia – into social media, into conversations over backyard fences and into supermarkets queues.

And there's plenty to be angry about: protesters, lockdowns, Covid denialists, masks versus no masks, vaccine mandates, QR check-ins, harsh fines and the slow rollout of vaccinations.

The social division across the nation is palpable.

Our national solidarity is perhaps the greatest casualty of the pandemic.

In industries and institutions across Australia individuals now face the same diabolical choice: get jabbed or join the dungeons of the unemployed. Distrustful of their politicians, distrustful of the multinational corporations which have created the vaccines, and extremely distrustful of the government's aggressive push to get the entire population vaccinated, a significant minority of the population are just saying no, and opting to leave their industries rather than comply.

This alone will create massive societal and industrial disruption in the coming weeks and months.

So-called "anti-vaxxers" are not the fringe dwelling conspiracy ridden lunatics the government is so desperately trying to paint them. They're perfectly decent ordinary citizens concerned about the direction the country is taking, and who feel deeply that the violation of personal sovereignty involved in mandated vaccination routines is a step too far.

***

The lioness, the world's top predator in the lexicon of imagery of animal spirits, was hunting now through Old Alex's dreams.

She didn't need the falcons. She didn't need the invisible machines manipulating time. Their hyper-intelligence. Their uncanny abilities.

She could already see whichever way the rivers ran.

In the valleys of the future.

"I wouldn't talk much about that."

Old Alex shrugged.

At least in his imagination he came from a different history, a time when it was impossible to lie, so interconnected was the future of the species.

And in any case, nobody would believe it anyway.

Everything about this situation was hard to believe.

Aiding in a catastrophe, all these hidden hands. He was uncertain how to proceed. There were so many elements at play. Secret intimidations. Coercion. Games. Soldiers, fallen soldiers. Men who no longer believed in what they were asked to do. A desecration, a desolation, at the heart of the state. A polity gone not just sour, but deranged. A violence that had crept through everyday life. A terrible sin. A cry in the stain that was once called Australia.

Compliments of the chef, those who cooked up these circumstances, as if there was a mist of psilocybin or some other hallucinogen in the air.

These derangements took on tiny forms, and were nationwide. Everyone felt it. Sad, downcast eyes. Human interaction kept to a minimum unless the truth, their sorrow, their disbelief, would creep out and have them arrested, or jumped on by the herd; their fellows they had once assumed were decent human beings. No longer.

They became frightened of each other.

Frightened of the authorities.

Frightened of the state.

Frightened to go outside.

Old Alex could hear one officer, forced to seek out a lie, complain constantly of what a waste of time it all was.

He held a crucible in his hand; he heard the ancient warrior spirits swarming through forests; he knew that all, now was on the march. That at these points in history greater forces were at play. We are all mere instruments in a cosmic drama, they might once have said. But now these forces were better understood; and remained just as dismal in their impacts on individuals, and now on entire populations. And just as frightening in their inexplicability. And just as awful in their consequence.

If there was one truth, we would never have come in these incarnations.

As it was, those ones who had, for so many weeks extending into months simply groomed their feathers as they watched over him, or the lioness playfully biffed him as if he was a cub, or the soldiers who settled into the valley as if they were the armies of old, pre-industrial, making shift in the higher reaches, settling in to protect an old king.

All these things were gone now.

This was a time of extreme crisis.

There was a violent derangement on the streets.

An entire population was being destroyed.

And the future the spirit emissaries sought to preserve? The one they saw being destroyed in front of their eyes every single day; they were outside time, nothing that happened here could harm them. It was not a kindness they sought to do, but something more magnificent, breathing across generations, uplifting entire populations, bringing to the fore all that should have been done, and while the people surrendered to their own worst instincts, and the evil that possessed their administrations, these entities sought, and found, a higher beauty.

***

As the first month of spring turned into the second, there was one piece of news that buoyed the spirits of many. As the bitter Covid lockdowns continued, Premier of NSW Gladys Berejiklian, with every passing day, became an ever more divisive and deeply despised figure. Until one glorious day, the extremely powerful Independent Commission Against Corruption brought her down.

The NSW corruption watchdog announced it would investigate whether she breached public trust or encouraged the occurrence of corrupt conduct during her secret relationship with disgraced former Member of Parliament Daryl Maguire.

And as far as Old Alex was concerned, glorious joy was spreading through the millions of households enduring some of the worst lockdowns in the world, characterised by grotesque levels of over policing, helicopters overhead and military on the streets.

Each day's mandatory press conference provided a full case study of state incompetence, the arrests, the hundreds of daily fines, the increasingly angry population, it all just grew worse. And worse. And worse.

If anyone wanted to see where her policies were leading, they only had to look across the southern border to Victoria, where the sight of police pepper spraying defenceless citizens and bashing anyone who dared to protest had become the new Covid Normal.

The New South Wales Government was threatening jail time for unvaccinated people who attempted to enter venues in breach of forthcoming public health orders, which would limit entry to vaccinated persons only.

NSW Customer Service Minister Victor Dominello, tasked with overseeing the development of the digital vaccination passports due to be rolled out in the coming weeks, warned businesses they would be required to immediately report to police, or face legal consequences, any instance of an unvaccinated person attempting to gain entry.

How much was all this costing? The country was haemorrhaging money at every turn, and tens of billions of dollars were being raked off Australia's working poor and poured into the coffers of vaccine manufacturers.

The government's new system planned to link Covid vaccination status with QR Code check-ins at venues across the state, such as shops, restaurants, bars and pubs, gyms and sporting and other entertainment venues.

In a statement the Minister declared: "Businesses and customers have a shared responsibility to comply with the rules and keep the public safe. People who create and use fake vaccine certificates will face the full force of the law and could face jail time.

"Fraud is a very serious matter and won't be tolerated. My message is clear – put the community first and get vaccinated."

***

The latest insanity perpetrated by the power brokers in Macquarie Street, the location of the NSW Parliament in Sydney's Central Business District, was the "no jab no job" mandates creating havoc across multiple industries. Like the general public, many government workers were suspicious of the high level of bullying and intimidation involved in enforcing vaccinations.

Thousands of teachers, police officers and many others faced the sack in the coming days as "no jab no job" campaigns ramped up.

The group National Education United held successful Reclaim the Line protests around the country on that first full weekend of October, with many wearing t-shirts emblazoned with their profession and years of service.

An open letter with from the legal groups Advocate Me and Human Rights Advocates read in part: "As if forced home detention under arbitrary stay at home orders were not enough, Australian governments state and federal have stepped into the abyss, introducing vaccine passports and a medical apartheid, only allowing those who are fully vaccinated certain freedoms.

"It has been brought to our attention that all NSW on-site school staff are being exposed to egregious conduct for exercising their right to decline the COVID-19 injection.

"This is a significant population of over 5000 individuals, employees including Principals, Assistant Principals, executive staff, teachers, administration staff, counsellors, school learning support officers and maintenance staff."

"Mandatory medical interventions are a breach of basic human rights and medical freedoms. We all should have the right to go about our everyday life without being forced or coerced into being injected with a drug, especially an experimental one using new technology.

"You are reminded that even though you might be the executive departmental staff; you are still only a public servant and not a qualified medical practitioner. You do not have the right to segregate education staff in the knowledge that the science does not substantiate such a decision; nor do you have the right to instil fear in education department employees, who are now unsure of what roles and duties they will be permitted to perform as trained and qualified individuals."

All the while it was overseeing extreme lockdowns and mass vaccination campaigns, the NSW government refused to release the medical advice on which they were acting.

One intrepid reporter, Callum Foote at Michael West Media, sought the medical advice for the lockdowns through a Freedom of Information request. His conclusion: "An old toilet roll would be more useful than the information which you have provided, completely useless information for which you charged hundreds of dollars."

***

Those opening days of October saw Reclaim the Line demonstrations around the country for a Group, held to support workers including teachers, police, paramedics, aged-care workers, health care workers, firefighters, construction workers, airline staff, miners, truck drivers and more. Filled with professional ranks, the protests were less rambunctious than some of the others the country was seeing. Locations included Sydney, Melbourne, Brisbane, Canberra, Perth, Newcastle and many other regional centres.

Placards included: "COVID-19 just tested positive for Fraud", "One has a moral responsibility to disobey unjust laws", "United We Stand", "My Body My Choice", "4 Years Paramedic. 6+ Years Community Mental Health, Years of Dedication, Now Unemployed.", "Teaching Principal, 33 Years", Pro Choice Pro Voice, No Covid Jabs 4 Kids", "Paramedic 13 Years, Saving Lives Yesterday, Stood Down Today", "No Forced Jabs", "Tradies Body, Tradies Choice", "Reclaim Humanity Compassion and Common Sense" and "Coercion is not Consent".

After almost half a month of straight protests, Australians were back at it again.

It was now official: Australia has had the worst response of any nation on Earth to Covid-19, with some of the world's longest and most draconian lockdowns, the Federation destroyed with most internal borders shut, millions of people under house arrest, thousands of businesses destroyed, military on the street, and in recent days some of the most violent crackdowns of protesters ever seen.

With a subjugated people no longer coping, the "no jab no job" mandates became the latest flashpoint. Australia was now unrecognisable from the country it was only 20 months before.

Workers from multiple sectors across Australia went on strike that Friday, 1 October, as the clock ticked towards compulsory vaccination.

The collective strike was organised by National Education United, a newly created and fast-growing alliance of more than 18,000 teachers and workers from multiple industries who were fighting state government mandates.

Spokesman Christian Marchegiani aka Mack said the strike represented a show of support for anyone facing medical discrimination and the threat of losing their jobs.

"At no other time in living history have ordinary Australians faced such an unimaginable threat to their freedoms – freedoms that until now, we have taken for granted," Mack said.

"No Jab, No Job policies are being implemented through coercion, manipulation or 'incentives', and everyday Aussies are losing their rights to work.

"There is also a frightening danger of Australia seeing vaccination passports for the first time. Is this really the type of society we want to live in? Each of us has to decide where we draw our line in the sand and to take relevant action, with courage and heart."

With zero ethical political leadership, and with violent scenes of protest now a regular feature of life in Australia's major cities, Australia appeared well on the descent into a totalitarian hell.

All the warnings, all the pleas for common sense, had been ignored.

Just as many observers both in Australia and around the world were already doing, future historians would look back at this period of Australian history and shake their heads in bewilderment.

How could this be?

***

Participants were encouraged to wear white shirts with the words #ReclaimTheLine on the front and their years of professional service on the back.

"On October 1 we reclaim the line that was taken from us. Freedom, liberty, and our right to choose if we take the vaccine," the NEU announced on Sept. 25. "This will be our defining moment in history. This is the line in the sand. The hill we stand on. We will do this in silence and wearing white. We will come peacefully and respectfully. We will show the authorities we are united as one country and that they have no need to be violent with us."

The protest at Shellharbour, a peaceful family oriented seaside village two hours south of Sydney, was typical.

Reliving his glory days as one of Sydney's best known news reporters, Old Alex bought a couple of reporter pads and headed off down to what was now his local beach.

At its peak, around 90 people gathered along the foreshore dressed in white. There were no loud chants, no shouted slogans, no speeches, nothing but a quiet assembly, dominated by school teachers and health care workers, all of whom faced the sack if they continued with their refusal to have "the jab".

Without a visible police presence, there was no confrontation of any kind. The protestors gathered peacefully and departed peacefully.

One woman, Genevieve McKenzie, said she had just been stood down.

"I work in a hospital setting," she said. "Due to the government mandate I have been stood down without pay as of today. I thought I had freedom of choice."

Ms McKenzie cannot return to work unless she has the mandated vaccine.

"The necessity of an income is a concern, however the last two months have been riddled with stress and anxiety, knowing how this was going to be handled."

One teacher with 14 years of service said: "You have to stand for your truth."

She relayed a story of a nurse who died after the "second jab".

Whether apocryphal or not, there was now an abundance of these stories; against a backdrop of intense official propaganda and a haphazard, lacklustre government which had lost control of the narrative.

Another teacher, with 17 years experience, said: "Stop this madness!! If I say any more it will be profanities!!"

Another, with 40 years experience, said: "We are here to stand up for our basic human rights. We want body autonomy. We want to make choices about what we put in our body.

"And we want to continue the work we love without being coerced into taking an untested, and more than likely dangerous inoculation."

Another teacher, who brought her two children to the protest and now faced the sack, said the best thing the government had done was confine her to her home during the lockdowns, because it had allowed her time to do research on the internet, and Covid had woken her up.

"Have you woken up?" she asked. "We want to keep democracy open in our country. We want to protect our children. My body my choice. I have to provide for my children. To feed and house them I have to have a job. I resent being forced to make that choice, to have an experimental jab which is not even fully approved. It is terrible."

***

"It happens but once in a lifetime," one of the Watchers on the Watch observed, and he silenced them, and showed them something few could, or should, ever see.

And so it was, we came to these imperilled times.

As far as old Alex was concerned, the country was being bludgeoned into submission. Caution was thrown to the wind and the spirits were combat ready, those that gathered in his waking dreams in the valley below. Another spring of protest. The protests that began in their hundreds a year before now numbered in their thousands. The vast expenditure on policing showed a cruelty beyond all reckoning; an imagining that would not just haunt the victims being wrestled to the ground; but the soul of a nation destroyed.

They curled, he listened, they cupped his chin and stared google eyed straight into his heart; and the majesty built, the perimeters set, the sky a deep haze, the murmuring unconquered. We came to you. If there was anything to be learnt from this: no one needs the pretenders. He remained silent in face of all their evils. The course was already set. It mattered little, their murmurings and pretensions.

No amount of threats would rid him of their pestilence. In the scheme of these things, in ancient temples and temples yet to be, in the waft of air on skin and perfumed rooms, in loves lost, so many loves lost, no, it would not be possible, he said, to show strength, courage, determination. These things were gifts. A weak man made strong. Show respect.

Ancient forests and courses of human action; and they came now.

Over the previous year Australia had witnessed some of the most violent protests and largest mass arrests in its history. Now the sullen indifference of a hoodwinked population had turned to something else. Compliance? Connivance? Obedience?

Old Alex noticed it in old friends; they had been wild in the day, now they bought the government lies, hook, line and sinker.

That same generation whose most transformative experiences had been the anti-Vietnam protests of the 1970s.

For just as we still did, back then Australia signed up to America's endless wars, and danced a dance signed on the dotted line of truly massive defence contracts.

These crises were spelt out in blood, manufactured out of thin air, the money raked off an impoverished people.

And while taxpayer funded academics still blathered on about climate change, the people themselves had lost all their liberties.

This day, another day of protest, thousands of police and military personnel would line the streets.

And this day, just as they done a year before, outliers, brave souls, his souls, their souls, would face certain arrest against the phalanxes of black wrapped police officers, and the credibility of the country, the credibility of the authorities, the stability of the country, its now increasingly uncertain, tendentious, contentious future, would all be borne aloft, imprinted permanently into the nation's history.

***

The very public Tania de Jong, awarded an Order of Australia, was a soprano singer, speaker and award-winning social entrepreneur and philanthropist, and had been outspoken on the loss of liberties from the beginning. In a piece originally published by *Spectator Australia* and which Old Alex republished in his magazine, she wrote: "Our politicians and public servants need to find a new way of dealing with the pandemic which empowers rather than disempowers Australians.

"With premiers around the country demanding zero cases before they open borders and remove their draconian lockdowns, it is not surprising that people around the nation (and the world) wonder if Australia can ever get out of the mess our governments have created.

"One moment we are getting some of our freedoms and a little of the joy of life returning, and in the next we are ruthlessly pushed back into our boxes by our fear-peddling premiers hiding behind their overwhelmed health officers. Under the pretext of protecting and saving us from our terrible fates they misrepresent, misinform, obfuscate, coerce, bully, intimidate and play political one-upmanship and it is time we, the public, wake up.

"Enormous anger and frustration echoes across our communities accompanied by sorrow, despair and loss of hope. We are lonely, isolated, imprisoned, scared and sick.

"Scared of what this nation is becoming and sick of the premiers' daily posturing. Our hopes, dreams, milestones, rites of passage, businesses, relationships are being trampled on. We are simply pawns in the political games of heartless leaders who only care about the next election. They defend all of this with the catchcry of saving lives when what is really happening is the destruction and diminishing of lives and livelihoods.

"Please stop the fear-mongering and start sharing information and solutions about how people can protect themselves and their loved ones. We did not elect our premiers to be our mothers and fathers. They need to back off and allow us to look after our beloved Mums and Dads, children and loved ones without their intimidating interference."

***

Protests in Melbourne continued, producing some of the most unbelievable footage as protestors ran screaming from walls of police, or were aggressively wrestled to the ground and handcuffed.

There was extremely heavy policing across the centre of the city as protesters once more faced walls of heavily armed police.

A deadpan Australian Associated Press reported on 2 October, 2021: "The group marched past the National Gallery of Victoria and the ABC's Melbourne headquarters, blocking roads and local traffic. Initially greeted with a minimal police presence, officers and mounted police began to move in close to the group just after 1:30pm, breaking them up into smaller groups, before they began to make arrests.

"By 2pm, much of the anti-lockdown crowd had dispersed among the parklands."

When asked about the day's protest by reporters, COVID-19 commander Jeroen Weimar expressed his frustration at their actions. "Why? Really, I mean, we get it. We get the fact that people are frustrated, we get the fact that we're upset. You're not helping yourself, you're not helping anybody," he said.

"At best, you run the risk of generating more transmission. At worst, you know you're creating, you're fuelling a bonfire, that's already on fire. I just think it's a really unhelpful thing to do."

The protests were the largest in size since protesters occupied the Shrine of Remembrance for hours on Wednesday 22 September, which had been broken up by Victoria Police with tear gas and rubber bullets.

The scene on the ground was equally chaotic, with sirens screaming, the sound of helicopters thrumming overhead and panicked crowds running before lines of police advancing on foot and on horseback.

Footage showed groups of police running along the side of the Yarra River with a number of protesters being aggressively swarmed to the ground by heavily armed officers. The dramatic pursuits, arrests and extreme policing in Melbourne's Royal Botanic Gardens that first Saturday in October, 2021, were all recorded and broadcast across social media.

Some of the best footage was filmed by Rukshan Fernando who streamed as The Real Rukshan. He had established a significant and enthusiastic following due to his calm and honourable focus on the action. The sound of helicopters flying low overhead added to the sense of threat. Umbrellas were painted with the words: "Coercion is not Consent". Chants included "What do we want? Freedom!" and "My Body My Choice".

"Shame on you Victoria Police" was one of the more polite epithets thrown at police as they aggressively swooped on protestors, arresting who they could.

"I'm scared for my kids," said one fleeing mother with a bloodied face. "The coppers were chasing me from behind. I don't want the jab. I'm for medical freedom."

In an interview with Rukshan Sky News host Rita Panahi said: "We have seen the rise of citizen journalists because much of the media has failed so abysmally to cover what is really happening. There's a reason why Melbourne will become the most locked down city in the world. The media's complicity in creating an environment where that is possible cannot be overlooked. Too many have been preoccupied with being propagandists for the government and the police. Craziness has been normalised.

"Maybe he is attracting millions of views because he is showing what is really happening and allowing people to explain why they're so upset rather than just demonising any anti-government dissent as some anti-vaxxer, neo-Nazi-inspired conspiracy."

***

On 5 October, 2021, Australian flags flew in New York City, as demonstrators chanted "Save Australia" in solidarity with The Land Down Under. The large crowd gathered outside the Australian consulate for speeches.

The march began in Brooklyn outside Department of Education headquarters earlier in the day, as anti-mandate advocates gathered to hear speeches.

The march mobilised and moved across the Brooklyn Bridge and into Manhattan, with chants of "Wake up, New York," and "We, the people, will not comply."

Importantly, at least for Australia, the march showed solidarity for Australians facing vaccine mandates for employment, the introduction of Covid-19 passports and the shocking excesses of the police state once known as Victoria.

A prominent banner at the head of the parade read: "No Medical Mandates Health Freedom".

"What's going on in Australia is not just going to be Australia. And when it shows up on our doorsteps, we're gonna punch it right in the f***ing teeth," one speaker said.

"We're holding the line for Australia, we support Australia!", said another.

"Australia, fight, fight, fight, tyranny!" one woman waving an Australian flag shouted.

Much of the world's population knew absolutely nothing about Australia beyond the koalas and kangaroos. Now Australia's Covid dystopia was international news.

TEN
THE IMPERIAL BATTLESHIP HAS LANDED

They don't know me
And they don't own me
Oh God help us all
Look what we've become
Oh God help us all
And fix what we have done
See no evil
Bow to the needle
Didn't we turn out great?
Sick is the new health
Poor is the new wealth
Truth is whatever they say

Five Times August. *God Help Us All.*

THAT SPRING OF 2021 Ron DeSantis, Florida's Governor and American Presidential hopeful, said at a press conference: "Look what's going on in Australia right now. After a year and a half they are still enforcing lockdowns by the military. That's not a free country. It's not a free country at all, in fact, I mean, I wonder why we would still have the same diplomatic relationships when they are doing that. Is Australia freer than China – communist China – right now? I don't know, but the fact that that's even a question tells you something has gone dramatically off the rails."

Spectator Australia editorialised: "Off the rails is putting it mildly. For those who didn't see the images on social media (the majority of the mainstream media avoided showing them), the approach by the Mussolini-style, black-clad Victorian Police forces included bludgeoning a man on the ground with a rifle butt, tackling numerous unsuspecting individuals onto concrete surfaces, shooting people with rubber pellets, throwing a 70-year-old woman to the ground and then spraying her in the face with capsicum spray and other such grotesque human rights abuses almost too numerous to mention.

"These images are now sweeping the globe and are fast becoming the new face of Australia. Nyunggai Warren Mundine recalls how Covid restrictions are eerily reminiscent of the same brutal authoritarian overreach which Indigenous Australians endured for decades.

"Already one Victorian police officer has been suspended but a full investigation is needed and criminal charges must be laid where police brutality has occurred. Shamefully, not a single political leader has so far addressed these potential crimes, preferring instead to demonise the protesters and hide behind the Orwellian shield of 'public health': 'We are smashing you in the face, shooting you, throwing you on the ground, kicking you in the kidneys and spraying a toxic substance in your face in order to protect your health'."

***

Paul Gregoire of the Sydney Criminal Lawyers Blog, perhaps a little prematurely, wrote: "Soon the lockdowns will end. The disparities in the enforcement of public health measures will disappear. Most who have been forced to stay at home will return to work. The vaccination drive will end. And there will be no more anti-lockdown protests.

"But, as life in the community begins to take on a semblance of what it was like before the pandemic, it will never be entirely the same again. And one aspect to the COVID-19 period that will likely remain is the shift in policing methods that has occurred whilst the virus was lurking.

"As NSW Police Commissioner Mick Fuller has made clear, this state's law enforcement approach to COVID-19 has been to treat the virus itself as a criminal.

"So, considering that the nature of pandemic policing is preemptive – and the impossibility of on-the-beat officers actually capturing COVID-19 and locking it up – this approach has meant that all potential carriers of the virus have been treated as crime suspects.

"Meanwhile, down in Melbourne, Victoria police found the recent anti vaccination mandate protests an opportune time to whip out its non-lethal weaponry and use it upon the citizenry, which was a first – but likely not a last. Indeed, in the coming months, public health fines, and demonstrations aimed at lockdown restrictions and vaccine requirements will fade, but the police overreach that has occurred won't.

"The approach to the global public health crisis in NSW, as elsewhere, has been one that relied on measures to curb the virus, coupled with a heavy-handed policing approach to enforce them.

"However, health measures don't seem reasonable while they're administered via point of gun."

Commissioner Fuller was placed in charge of the NSW COVID response right from its onset at the end of March, 2020. This, again, sent a confused message to citizens going through extreme shock after just having been locked down for the first time in their lives.

"Isolating and mask wearing are designed to stop the transmission of an airborne virus, yet the lockdown and restrictions on behaviour were implemented when public distrust in government institutions was at an all-time high, so, therefore, the ground was fertile for conspiracies.

"In the early days of Covid there were absurd stories about a man being fined for eating a kebab on a bench, then came a Victoria police officer assaulting a woman over not wearing a mask, which was later followed by the recent seizure approach taken to southwest and western Sydney."

A Policing Biosecurity Report found that once NSW police stopped a person over a suspected COVID breach, 45 percent of individuals were then searched. And this was not for having the virus.

Gregoire concluded that the use of weapons against the public set an alarming precedent.

"The weapons were bought as part of the Victorian government's 2016 Public Safety Package, with the official reasoning for acquiring them being the so-called African gang crime wave, and heated protests that saw the alt-right and the left facing off.

"Heavily clad Victoria police officers aimed and fired VKS 175 shot pepper ball semi-automatic rifles at unarmed protesters, as well as using Oleoresin capsicum spray, which is trigger released from a canister. And while these types of weapons may be 'non-lethal', they can blind and maim.

"The use of these weapons on civilians is perhaps the most detrimental shift in policing tactics that's occurred over the last 18 months. And while 'freedom' protesters are likely to become a thing of the past, a precedent has been set whereby police can use such arsenal on public protests."

***

Outside the wall of "academic for hire" university professors promoting the vaccines and thereby protecting their own funding sources, a serious corruption of the public narrative in and of itself, the discontent brewing among the nation's intellectual class was becoming increasingly obvious.

Chief Editor at On Line Opinion Graham Young wrote: "Mandating or coercing COVID vaccination is one of the most important civil liberties issues of my lifetime. It's a fundamental breach of human rights allegedly guaranteed by a number of international conventions and Australian law, as well as our long tradition of liberal democracy.

"Nowhere is the legal case against put more clearly than in a judgement of the Fair Work Commission. It says, in a dissenting judgement, that because the vaccines are part of a clinical trial, coercing someone to take them breaches The Nuremberg Code, the Universal Declaration of Human Rights, the Declaration of Helsinki, and the Siracusa Principles.

"The judgement also holds that vaccine mandates also breach Australian law as the Australian Human Right Commission Act 1986 (Cth) gives effect to Australia's obligations under the International Covenant on Civil and Political Rights Article 7 which provides that no one shall be subjected without his free consent to medical or scientific experimentation.

"Another way of measuring the severity is to ask what individual Australians will put at risk to avoid the vax.

"The answer to that is that thousands have protested on the streets, risking fines in the thousands, and others are about to protest silently by losing their jobs and livelihoods, a price greater than any of the current fines.

"In the end, the individual will is more important than the legalities. Conscription didn't end because it was a breach of human rights, it ended because the public pressure was just too much.

"So how much civil disobedience must there be before a government breaks?"

The discontent within the police was obvious to anyone who was paying attention. A 16-year veteran of the Victoria Police gave a blockbuster interview claiming the authoritarian abuses now making headlines around the world had left many police disturbed about the actions they were being asked to take.

Acting Senior Sergeant Krystle Mitchell was interviewed on a podcast called Discernable on Friday the 9th of October, 2021. She wore her full uniform during the interview and announced that she would be officially resigning from the force at the end.

Sergeant Mitchell came across as highly credible, a very decent human being who, not so long before, had been a proud member of the Victorian Police Force.

The interview sparked considerable public support. "Total respect to this woman who chose not to ignore her natural human instinct of humility and empathy over the corrupt government directives," read one of many messages. "This fine lady won't be the only one who stood up to speak out against Chairman Dan, she will be the first one," read another.

Acting Sergeant Mitchell said she had watched the relationship deteriorate between the community and police officers while Melbourne was stuck in the longest and toughest lockdowns in the world.

"I have a medical exemption and I don't wear a mask. My partner and I were out walking during our two hours of exercise on the weekend and there were police everywhere.

"These aren't just police doing their 'reassurance patrols'. They're not 'reassurance patrols'. You're not reassuring anybody in the community. You're scaring people that there are that many police in the community.'

"I'm choosing to quit because I can't remedy in my soul any more the way in which the organisation I love to work for is being used and the damage that it's causing to the reputation of Victoria Police and the damage it is causing the community.

"All of my friends that are police officers, that are working on the front line, are suffering every day enforcing CHO directions that the vast majority, or certainly a great majority, don't believe in and don't want to enforce."

Sergeant Mitchell cites ethical conflicts as the reason for speaking publicly. She said she had talked to over 300 fellow police officers, and the majority felt the same way.

"How I see my organisation being used during this pandemic troubled me greatly. The stories that they tell me, and the stories that they share privately on our union Facebook page about their experiences in dealing with the community during the pandemic. It's really tough on them.

"In part, the reason that I wanted to do this whilst still serving and wearing the uniform today is so that the community can see that it isn't all police that are against them, and for police to see that it isn't all protesters that are coming there to fight with you. It's a minority, there's a minority on both sides.

"The way in which we police now has completely changed, and a vast majority of the focus of policing is on Chief Health Officer directions that you know are infringements on your everyday liberties.

"I hate this divisive language that is being used. Calling protests 'illegal' I just think is ridiculous. The only reason that protests are illegal is because Victorian Premier Daniel Andrews made it so.

"By Daniel Andrews making protests illegal, he is responsible for the increase in violence that has occurred as a result from police and from protesters. By making it illegal, Daniel Andrews, in my opinion, has escalated the violence."

Victoria Police said Ms Mitchell's comments in no way reflected the views of the Force and would be the subject of a professional standards command investigation.

Sergeant Mitchell resigned her commission at the end of the interview.

**

The Assyrians were a book or a literature obsessed culture, some of who regarded the written word as so magical it must be a God sign; and if the beginning was the Word then these spirits or entities were sustained or brought to life through that mechanism; the chants, the obsessions, the all encompassing nature of it all derived from that one source. In the beginning the Word.

Perhaps that's why it felt to Old Alex as if Ishtar, the cruel Assyrian God of love and war, had passed through that valley.

One minute the Generals, the next a Mesopotamian richness overlaying those frozen fields. Australia itself, in a sense, had become frozen; the mean spirited overlords, the absolute disconnect of the bureaucratic caste, the divorce from all that was real.

The spirits mustered for another attempt at communication. "We Come At The End of Empire" they whispered once again, time and again..

In this case, the American Empire.

"It's ectoplasmic," Old Alex said, when the spirit realm came up for discussion at the local tavern.

"All is connected," the former army officer said in a reflective moment down at the Lakeview; and what was once the domain of philosophers and fantasists was now, with the rapid evolution of the technologies, provable, capable of being understood. Odd what blokes talked about in these different times. The spirits are prayed into life, whispered into life, they function out of the souls of millions; their power real, their visitations realer still.

And so it was. And so it will be.

There had been an upbeat mood in the country's mood after the departure of the much reviled Pentecostal Scott Morrison and his replacement by Anthony Albanese.

All that praying, showering with riches, prosperity theology, looked pretty damn grubby about now.

Like a garden springing back to life after a fence has flattened it.

Your false gods, your feeble hands, your abuse of the citizenry, your pillaging of the public purse. You and your ilk.

An old journalist muttered darkly. Almost everyone felt powerless, the most frightening thing of all in that frightening time, the behaviour of the mob.

Around the world people heard the same voices of the spirits: "We are gathering strength. We are in your realm. We come from afar and near."

In times of crisis. At the end of Empire. And here, now, in these ordinary streets, where people went blithely about their lives, entirely unaware that some of the cruellest and most arrogant people on the planet were playing God. And destroying what they saw as "surplus men".

The fissures everywhere. It was a small thing; but there was a five week delay on Death Certificates, the Funeral Home had told them when the family were arranging the funeral of his mother. When did that happen?

The fervour was gone. The insipid had arrived. The streets were quiet. And everywhere empty; the gasp of the raw, the dawning of the realisation, we've all been deceived.

In gilded dreams in a frozen place absolutely the same message rang through him time and time again: "It is not up to them to play God."

***

Welcome to 'Freedom Day'. Monday 11th October, 2021. As Sonia Hickey recorded in the Sydney Criminal Lawyers Blog, it was freedom day for and some and discrimination day for others. She wrote as follows.

It's the day for which many residents of Greater Sydney have been waiting for more than 15 weeks – 107 days to be precise.

Non-essential businesses are permitted to accept those who are fully vaccinated – a class of residents who are also permitted to travel more than five kilometres from their homes.

Long-awaited catch-ups with family and friends are being scheduled by the over 70% of residents who are fully vaccinated, and there's a sense of optimism for many as the state marks the first step on the path to fully opening after the Delta outbreak.

The return of freedoms to the fully vaccinated include being able to enter bars, pubs, restaurants, gyms, hairdressers, beauty salons and other "non essential business", as well as attend entertainment and sporting events, and be included in higher caps on weddings and funerals.

But, rather ironically, 'freedom day' also marks the start of a period of discrimination against those who are unvaccinated – what some see as a 'subclass' who will remain 'locked out' until 1 December 2021.

Some of these people are waiting for the existing preliminary approval to be made final. Others are concerned about the ever-changing directions regarding the appropriate age groups for respective vaccines. Some want more information about short-term and/or potential long-term side effects, pointing to suspensions of vaccines in other countries, and simply wish to wait, while others take issue with the efficacy of the drugs – given that those who receive them can both contract and spread the virus.

Still others are taking a stance on the integrity of their own bodies, while there are many who resent the government's pressure to inject drugs for which it has given pharmaceutical companies immunity from claims, and for which the Australian government has neglected, unlike many other countries, to introduce a compensation scheme for those adversely affected.

The only places the unvaccinated can enter are 'essential businesses', like supermarkets and pharmacies. People who are fully vaccinated need to use the Medicare app on their phones to show vaccination status, or a printed certificate.

In some venues, children under 16 will have to be accompanied by a fully vaccinated member of their household to enter. This includes hospitality venues, non-critical retail stores, personal services, sporting, recreation and entertainment facilities and events.

On the spot fines of $5,000 may apply to businesses for not complying with the Public Health Order vaccination requirements. Individuals who don't comply, or use fraudulent evidence of vaccination or check-in could be fined $1,000.

***

Sandy Barrett at the Advocate Me Blog wrote as follows.

When I read that New South Wales was celebrating "Freedom Day", I couldn't help but laugh at the absurdity of it all, because what now exists there is the antithesis of freedom. How anyone can celebrate slavery is beyond me.

Those "freedoms" have so many conditions attached to them, one can only compare it to a dog that has had its leash temporarily extended. But this is the insanity of the world today. Only the propaganda machine can stretch the imagination far enough to tell you that moving from lockdown to lockout is freedom.

It was the American journalist and war correspondent Edward R Murrow who said that "A nation of sheep will soon have a government of wolves." He knew a thing or two about how tyrannical governments operate. Unfortunately, Australians are only just beginning to learn.

When locking people up repeatedly fails, isn't it clear that those measures don't work? And isn't that the ideal time to start considering alternatives? Instead, like gambling addicts, our governments have doubled down and enlisted police and military to enforce their draconian measures.

The experts that our premiers and their Chief Health Officers hide behind are committees inside committees inside committees, with compromised bureaucrats tied to global corporations, which include Big Pharma and their pandemic modelling.

***

Coincidentally, perhaps, Freedom Day was also the day Amnesty International chose to release their report, dated 11 October, 2021, The Policing of the 2021 NSW Lockdown. It read in part as follows.

During the COVID-19 pandemic, and particularly during periods of lockdown, police in Australia have been given unprecedented and extraordinary powers to enforce COVID-19 restrictions.

From 25 June 2021, when Greater Sydney, the Blue Mountains, the Central Coast and Wollongong went into lockdown, NSW police have too often taken a heavy-handed approach to enforcing COVID-19 Public Health Orders. These Orders were frequently modified, often with a days' notice and without sustained processes to clearly and accessibly communicate their content to relevant communities. The final version of the Public Health Order runs to 56 pages.

Since the lockdown began, dozens of people have experienced concerning interactions with police, including being incorrectly issued fines and being stopped and searched under the pretext of the COVID-19 restrictions. The confusing nature of the Orders and the impunity given to NSW Police in relation to incorrect issuing of fines early in the lockdown were key contributors to this haphazard and overly punitive approach.

The Public Health Orders during the 2021 lockdown did not contain any specific provisions relating to protests or human rights-related activities, effectively making protest a prohibited activity during the NSW lockdown. The policing of the few COVID-safe protests that happened during the lockdown was heavy handed, and resulted in peaceful protesters and legal observers being fined tens of thousands of dollars

Many of the concerns reported to the COVID policing website involved police not using discretion when issuing fines, police misunderstanding the COVID-19 Public Health Orders, or mistakenly issuing fines to those not breaching restrictions.

On numerous occasions reported to the COVID policing website, police did not appear to be aware of the content of their powers under the COVID-19 restrictions and mistakenly issued 'move on' orders or fined people who were not breaching Public Health Orders.

Incidents included police fining people $1000 for breaches related to undertaking 'outdoor recreation' despite the activity taking place in Local Government Areas where outdoor recreation was allowed for households or up to two people from different households.

***

One story Old Alex did run in his magazine that October, by a talented not all that young writer Jeremy Aitkin, who had written a series of entertaining pieces on his adventures in the job market. This piece was called Covid Line.

It is 7.00am Wednesday morning in early Spring. It is hot under an almost transparent clear blue sky; the tarmac is already starting to radiate heat and is steadily becoming hotter. A large white marquee has been set up in a suburban commuter train car park, in it a police wagon with two young detectives is waiting.

The detective on the driver's side is filming his mate. A student nurse, dressed in full personal protective equipment, walks up to the passenger and slides a thin white swab stick into his nostril, deep, looks at the detective in the driver's side, smiles and twists the swab around. The police officer is connected to the nurse like an umbilical cord. She pulls the swab stick out, places the sample in the vial, as the testers start to cheer, I clap.

The constable who has been tested has both his hands on his forehead as tears roll from his wet red eyes down his cheeks, a common response from the swab.

The detective in the driver's side smiles, waves to the nurse, and drives off into the day. It is going to be a great day!

We are deep in lockdown and the new mandatory requirements mean that essential workers must test every three days. Today will see between three to four thousand tests being done.

Heat is beginning to rise from the tarmac and is mixing with car fumes and as the sun reflects off the car windows it's really hard to see and write the patient's details on the vials.

A car comes and I lean in and record the details on the vial and then ask, "Close contact, anything I should know?" I say.

"Yes, my husband," she says.

"When?"

"Yesterday," she says.

I step as far away from the car as I can and take the swab, call over a nurse who tells me to write Urgent, Close Contact on the vial. The driver is worried and asks the nurse what she should do. The nurse tells her to go home and isolate. I then ask the nurse what I should do.

"Nothing, you've probably had a few close contacts already."

***

As Greater Sydney started to open up and a range of new public health orders came into force across the state, some businesses refused to discriminate against the unvaccinated.

A Sydney barber shop closed its doors just hours after reopening, after someone reported to CrimeStoppers that it was allowing entry to unvaccinated customers. A nation of dobbers. Stasi Australia.

On its Facebook page, Walkabout Barber Enterprises in Warners Bay on the South Coast of New South Wales said that when police attended the premises, they gave the owner and staff an ultimatum – either serve vaccinated customers only, or close their doors until 1 December 2021 when all Australians, vaccinated or not, would be able to attend.

In a heartfelt social media post, the business owner explained his desire not to discriminate and chose the latter, saying "If you don't stand for something, you will fall for anything." His story was widely supported.

A number of other already-struggling small businesses followed suit, despite the financial impact.

***

Dr Michael Tomlinson, an expert on universities in the Asia-Pacific region, found himself sharing an experience with thousands of others, including Old Alex, whose short tempered exasperation with the blizzard of regulations and the panic attacks brought on by the masks meant that he essentially tried to avoid entering any commercial premises at all.

"During my weekend shopping in Melbourne, Australia, I was turned away from my favourite café and not allowed to sit even at an outside table by order of my master, the Chief Health Officer of Victoria. Later, I was told off for recklessly entering a food store to order a takeaway burger and muffin, a food store which I was allowed to enter last week but not this week.

"And then I blundered into the bakery, forgetting that only two people are allowed in at a time. Any business owner who might be confused by the fast-changing rules can consult the 47 pages of detailed formulations in the Chief Health Officer's 'Open Premises Directions (No 2)' or seek help from their legal advisor. They are supposed to station a Covid Marshal at each entrance of the premises to turn away the infidel but this is not happening.

"None of this obsessive micromanagement will make any difference to the course of the pandemic, but it puts relentless pressure on us all to get vaccinated, contributing to the State Government's targets. It will declare victory over the pandemic when these targets are met and case numbers go down over the summer. Next August they may well go up again, and there will be renewed pressure to lock us all up, vaccinated or not.

"I was denied entry to these premises because I am one of the unclean, yet to be vaccinated, and so a danger to public health, even more so than last week, apparently.

"Under new pandemic laws introduced into the State legislature this week I could be sent to jail for two years for disobeying a health order.

"Of all the unprecedented violations of human rights and individual liberty that have been inflicted on populations during the Covid-19 pandemic, the most intrusive has been the relentless campaign to coerce every last individual to be vaccinated."

***

A number of police officers left moving testimonials which could be readily accessed through the Cops for Covid Truth Telegram site. Senior Constable Craig Blackman of Victoria Police joined the growing number of police resigning their positions. The mainstream media ignored them all, adding with every fatal misstep their complicity in an historic period of criminality.

Blackman became a prominent speaker at a number of protests. He wrote as follows.

I heard the Premier of Victoria declare that "unvaccinated people" will lose their right to employment and would be "locked out" of both the Economy and the Healthcare System, due to the decision not to take an injection with unknown long term side effects being considered "high risk behaviour".

I was so disgusted by this blatant demonising and discrimination against a section of the Public that I made the decision that I could no longer be a part of any organisation that would be party to such blatant and deliberate breaching of Human Rights and creation of a "two-tiered" and segregated society.

Let me ask you, if "high risk" behaviour justifies being denied medical treatment, where does that ideology end? Should a person who overdosed on illicit substances be denied treatment and left to die because of the choices they made? How about people who ride motorcycles? Cyclists who ride on the road and get hit by a car?

How about smokers, or people who drink too much alcohol, or get diabetes from an unhealthy lifestyle or go on dates with strangers through dating apps and get sexually assaulted? How about rock climbers or Surfers or Racing Car Drivers or Jockeys or people who play contact sport?

Should we also deny medical treatment to these people and leave them to die because of their life choices?

Of course not, because that would be inhumane and disgusting in a society that values Human Rights, Freedom of choice and respect for each other as individuals.

The Premier didn't stop there. Daniel Andrews went on to mandate that all "authorised workers" must be injected with a drug (that has been repeatedly referred to as a vaccine, which it is NOT) that has a poor short term safety record and no long term safety record at all, if they want to retain their Human Right to employment.

So now, two weeks to slow the spread back in early 2020 has become "show me your papers or no soup for you"!

If this situation wasn't so dire it would be comical!

The ability to earn a living, to put a roof over your and your families heads, to put food on the table, to provide basic needs for yourself and your dependents is now being removed from people unless they comply with the Government's demands. Is this Australia? Is this Democracy at work or something quite the opposite?

The stress, anxiety and pure mental anguish that these "mandates" are causing is immeasurable. I shudder at the thought of what these people must be feeling at this point, faced with a choice between starvation and homelessness for their whole family OR participate in a medical trial that has in fact, killed thousands of people around the world.

My disillusionment with the organisation is not only due to the tactics used to Police this Pandemic response, but what I believe to be an abject failure in our ability, as professional investigators, to not see that the narrative used by the Government, did not and does not match the evidence on the ground and from around the world, and therefore further investigation was required.

***

Red is for danger. Red is for distance. Red is for the vast reaches of space and the origin of everything.

"The imperial battleship has landed," Old Alex said at one small gathering, apropos of precisely nothing. Except that that was the way it felt; as if the story was beginning all over again, as if these creatures outside of time were settling here, in a giant, awe inspiring swirl as they settled in this time and place. In a technology definitely not of Earth, and most definitely not of this time.

With the same questions repeating over and over inside his skull: "Why here, why now?"

And the same lines repeating over and over: "We stood for you on a distant shore."

And time and again, almost a thrum: "You are blessed. You are blessed. Blessed art thou."

And so these mad swirls ran through his head in this most ordinary of places; Oak Flats; and on the ground, a kind of distancing, or increased parochialism, as the country became increasingly divided, as bureaucrats talked of following the medical advice and keeping Australians safe, while in reality nobody could make head nor tail of the constantly shifting rules, regulations, diktats, ceaseless and often contradictory announcements, and the government's repeated refusal to release any of the medical advice on which this tyranny was based.

The head of the national COVID Vaccine rollout, Lieutenant General John Frewen, claimed only one or two percent of the population remained unvaxxed, but on the South Coast of New South Wales Old Alex encountered few people who were vaxxed, and among those who were some were resentful that they had been obliged to do so for work, as Omicron raged across the country making everyone ask: "What were the last two years about? Why were we locked in virtual house arrest in our own homes; and our neighbours urged to dob us in if we spent more than two hours out. Why? Why? Why?"

And why was a "vaccine" which didn't stop anyone being infected being so obsessively pushed on the population.

The contradictions ran wide and deep, and there would be no resolution this day.

Except for one thing: the crimes committed here today would live on in infamy; would resonate down the corridors of history; and as people look back on these strangest of times, wonder, how could it be? How could this have happened?

"I don't make the rules," yet another freshly empowered idiot declared as she insisted he wear the useless masks.

"Every little fascist in the country has been unleashed," Old Alex spat back.

While snake oil salesmen, vaccine peddlers once known as politicians, pushed the product more and more aggressively onto the civilian population, at the same time as the counter narrative, a rich tapestry of outrage, grew stronger, more diverse and more alarming by the day.

Health bureaucrats took away our personal sovereignty. They took away our rights. They treated us all with utter and complete contempt. They refused to treat with courtesy and respect anyone who dared to disagree with the government narrative. And Old Alex was convinced that through "consultancy fees" and other forms of backdoor funding from Pfizer and Moderna they were being very well paid to act the way they did.

While the contradictory narratives coming in from all around the world daily blew their idiot narrative apart.

Yet all the time Australia's politicians and bureaucrats pretended it wasn't happening, that they hadn't already been exposed for the liars they were.

How stupid were these humans, that they thought they could play God?

***

Stuck there in that strange aerie, deep on the south coast where a cold, wet spring had turned into an equally cold, wet summer, it seemed to Old Alex as if the destruction of Australia was simply an afterthought; a consequence, of a massively corrupt global edifice; with Australia's politicians and technocrats all bought off, their willingness to betray their fellow countrymen sheer insanity.

It was against this backdrop, that the release of Robert Kennedy Jr's book *The Real Anthony Fauci: Bill Gates, Big Pharma, and the Global War on Democracy and Public Health* meant so much to him.

Almost everyone suffered from the effects of long term isolation during those interminable lockdowns, and for anyone on the outside looking in, little common ground or camaraderie; the like minded had all fled online because there were no legal gathering points. Banned and abandoned.

Riveted, he read the 800 page heavily footnoted tome across several days, and published a couple of extracts in his magazine, all of which confirmed his own view that Australia, despite the absolute level of damage being inflicted on the country, was only a small part of a larger play.

Below are a couple of extracts, confirming all his worst fears, and in a book already on the bestseller lists, despite the lack of a single mainstream review.

Firstly:

In July 2021, one year and four months into the misery of the global lock down, the Federal Aviation Administration had to divert air traffic over a section of the country stretching from the west coast to Michigan to make room for the fleet of private jets converging on Sun Valley, Idaho, for the 38th annual meeting of the world's most exclusive Enclave, sometimes called the summer camp for billionaires, or mogul fest. The 2021 meeting included Bill Gates, Apple CEO Tim Cook, Mark Zuckerberg, Amazon founder Jeff Bezos, Mike Bloomberg, Google founders Larry Price and Sergey Brin, Warren Buffett, Netflix CEO Reed Hastings, Disney Chair Robert Iger, Via com/CBS chair Shari Redstone, and one of the lockdown's most influential propagandists, Anderson Cooper, who has acknowledged that he responded to a CIA recruitment poster while attending Yale and worked an indeterminate number of Summer's thereafter in Langley.

All the discussions at the event were as usual, closely guarded, but participants acknowledged conversing about cryptocurrency and artificial intelligence. This year the robber barons hosted, as their guests of honour, CIA director William Joseph Burns, and by all reports, the mood among the titans was bullish. By that time, US billionaires were well on their way to increasing their collective wealth by $3.8 trillion in a single year, while obliterating the American middle class, which permanently lost about the same amount. These tech and media magnates, who had magnified their billions from the lockdown, were the same men who would use their media and social media platforms to censor complaints about the lockdown, even as it filled their coffers past the bursting point.

Each of these fat cats had helped grease the skids for the calamitous collapse of America's exemplary constitutional democracy. The Bill of Rights was, by then, indefinitely suspended. The participants of that event had privatised the public square and then obstructed the free flow of information and open debate – the oxygen and sunlight of democracy. Their censorship allowed their allies in the technocracy to affect the most extraordinary curtailment of American constitutional rights in history: closing churches across the country, shuttering a million businesses without due process or just compensation, suspending jury trials for corporate malefactors, passing regulations without constitution and guaranteed transparency, public hearings or comment, violating privacy through warrantless searches, and track and trace surveillance and abolishing the right to assembly and association.

After 20 years of modelling exercises, the CIA – working with medical technologists like Anthony Fauci and billionaire internet tycoons – had pulled off the ultimate coup d'etat: some 250 years after America's historic revolt against entrenched oligarchy and authoritarian rule, the American experiment with self-government was over. The oligarchy was restored, and these gentlemen and their spymasters had equipped the rising technocracy with new tools of control unimaginable to King George or to any other tyrant in history.

And you could damn well bet that if the CIA was involved, Australia's agencies would be joined at the hip. But why, that was the question that kept recycling through Old Alex's brain, why were the intelligence agencies so closely involved in what should have been a straightforward public health issue?

Surely they must have known the massively destructive impact they were having on millions of Australians, and on the nation as a whole. Surely if he could see, if the tens of thousands of people demonstrating in the streets could see the horrific damage they were doing to a once proud nation, so could the government apparatchiks.

If you were paid enough, would you personally betray your fellow countrymen?

Secondly, from *The Real Anthony Fauci*:

"This should be a medical and not be a military operation," Holocaust survivor and medical ethics advocate Vera Sharav told me. "It's a public health problem. Why are the military and the CIA so heavily involved? Why is everything a secret? Why can't we know the ingredients of these products, which the taxpayers financed? Why are all their emails redacted? Why can't we see the contracts with vaccine manufacturers? Why are we mandating a treatment with an experimental technology with minimal testing? Since COVID-19 harms fewer than 1 percent, what is the justification for putting 100 percent of the population at risk? We need to recognise that this is a vast human experiment on all of mankind, with an unproven technology, conducted by spies and generals primarily trained to kill and not to save lives."

Well, no better way to control a population than to instil a kill switch, Old Alex thought, apropos of nothing but general suspicion.

Robert Kennedy Jr concluded: "Covid-19 is not the problem; it is a problem, one largely solvable with early treatments that are safe, effective, and inexpensive. The problem is endemic corruption in the medical-industrial complex, currently supported at every turn by mass-media companies. This cartel's coup d'etat has already syphoned billions from taxpayers, has already vacuumed up trillions from the global middle class, and created the excuse for massive propaganda, censorship and control worldwide. Along with the captured regulators, this cartel has ushered in the global war on freedom and democracy."

Australian government apparatchiks ignored the obvious: that once the world's oligarchs had made their hundreds of billions off the back of the Covid scam they would cash in their shares, move blithely onto the next money making opportunity, and leave the health bureaucrats and politicians who had peddled this garbage on their behalf betrayed, holding the bag and facing an angry public, angry police, angry military, and an extremely angry public service, all of whose personnel had been lied to and their good intentions exploited; all of whom were now seeing the suffering and the damage inflicted on their friends and colleagues.

And many of whom had seen their own children suffer severe health consequences as a result. Not one of those apparatchiks who had so frantically promoted lockdowns and vaccines were able to explain why they had so willingly and dishonestly betrayed their fellow Australians. And almost all of them would retire before they could be dragged before a Nuremberg style inquiry.

ELEVEN
PARTIAL TO THAT PARTIAL LIGHT

> Beyond the human realm, there is the growing abashed understanding that other forms of intelligence exist, capable of comprehending and navigating the world in ways wildly different from ours, no less successful and no less poetic. One measure of our own intelligence may be the degree of our openness to these other ways of being – the breadth of mind and generosity of spirit with which we recognise and regard otherness.
>
> Maria Popova.

JUST AS ELSEWHERE, Covid became massively politicised in Australia. Exactly why the left embraced lockdowns and mass vaccination, despite the lack of evidence that either strategy actually worked, always seemed odd to Old Alex, one of those strange, inexplicable things in an era when many things made little or no sense. Unleash havoc upon the world.

Wasn't the left meant to stand up for the rights of the individual against the brutality of the state?

Most journalists of his generation lent left in the small "l" liberal sense; they genuinely wanted to leave the world a better place. It was those monstrous to the point of mythically evil figures on the right who were destroying humanity. People would honestly say, in those denizens of inner-city Sydney: "I couldn't possibly sleep with a conservative." Now it was those same supposedly arch villains, painted as such in our youthful, gouache enthusiasms, speaking up about the blizzard of never-ending diktats, the loss of personal liberties, the futility of lockdowns and the increasingly questionable performance of the vaccines.

Questions that were at the forefront of the complex and foreboding dystopia most Australians were living through at that exact point in time.

Bella D'Abrera of the conservative think tank Institute of Public Affairs, publishing in the equally "conservative" leaning *Spectator Australia*, wrote: "Australians are currently being subjected to hitherto unprecedented control over, and incursions into, our lives by the State.

"We have been subjected to a seemingly inexhaustible and constantly changing supply of confusing, dehumanising and arbitrary edicts which are daily issued by a cabal of unelected health bureaucrats and their politician handlers. Our police forces have successfully cowed the citizenry into unquestioning obedience.

"Even more remarkable has been the willingness of many to become accessories to this political overreach by 'ratting out' our friends, families and neighbours.

"The speed at which the state has assumed this power has been astonishing, and many Australians are naturally asking how we got here.

"We have seen the state dramatically increase both its extractive and coercive powers over Australians, whose acquiescence has been astounding. So too has the willingness with which Australians have unquestionably handed over their freedoms and human rights.

"The country has been reshaped to such an extent that the rest of the world is having trouble recognising Australians as the freedom-loving 'larrikins' they imagined us to be. Some mainstream media commentators in the US are now asking if Australia can still legitimately continue to call itself a liberal democracy. I think the answer is no. We have been disciplined into authoritarianism. This may take decades to undo."

***

We awaken in times of need, the spirits told Old Alex in that haunted valley. Corpus Christi. As if a Second Coming.

Here in the boondocks, far from the world's capitals.

The perimeters were being established. Indeed it was remarkable, filtered, as almost everybody's experiences were at this time, through an electronic medium, the number of apparently sane commentators talking about the spirit realm, spirituality, the gods, or God.

Still the ancients moved upon the waters, and implanted images, as they had done for millennia, amongst primitive peoples; what, the unvaccinated? A population and a psyche haunted by the millennial, End of Days rhetoric of the major faiths.

Australia had not just gone mad, as he kept muttering to himself, there was an evil afoot. The perversion, as far as Old Alex was concerned, of Christianity practised by the Prime Minister was a terrible affront, not just to the common people and the various disciples of all those disciplines; but to common decency. A great believer in Prosperity Theology, the notion that God rewards the faithful with riches, Morrison most certainly saw the enrichment of his mates, quadrupling the national debt to almost a trillion dollars while billions of dollars of taxpayer funds were funnelled to his mates, some of the richest people in the country.

Perhaps the End of Days, or the End Times were indeed a kind of end, with the forced and rapid evolution of man into something else; but there was no need to be cruel, just as there was no need to be cruel to the trees, the last common genetic link between human and vegetable being some 700 million years ago.

All from a seed, an extraordinary seed.

They could treat their ancestors with a grace, dignity, magnanimity, with a kindness for life and a kindness for the struggle for survival common to all species, or they could be as cruel and indifferent, indeed as brutal as some of their own kind were to each other; to this very day; in these blood soaked wars, in his refusal to step back from the brink of societal wide destruction.

Yes, humanity had reached a point.

Yes, the prophets had, it appeared to many, pointed to this time.

"We can only see a fraction of what is there," a strange man said down the beach; by the pool, where the same outbreaks of disagreement between the pro and anti government forces, between the vaxxed and the unvaxxed, the convinced and the sceptical, had broken out amongst people normally entirely indifferent to the immediacy of politics.

Be gone from this place, he told the evil that stalked, as if it could possibly be as simple as that.

Magisterial. Magisterium.

And all had been corrupted.

And the blind would wither on the vine. And no longer would the blind lead the blinded. They had courted disaster, and would themselves be destroyed. And Australia, the Great Southern Land, would never be the same again.

***

Australian governments were at the height of their efforts to vaccinate the entire population.

From the Prime Minister on down, through phalanxes of health bureaucrats to armies of television presenters, there was one relentless message – get vaccinated to protect yourself, your family and your community.

Yet surely the protagonists must have already known that the vaccines did not work as advertised, did not prevent infection or transmission, and indeed were proving counterproductive.

All you had to do was follow the international data to know that what the Australian authorities were peddling to the Australian people was rubbish; that all their dangerous bullshit was at best a heist, a multi-billion dollar theft from naive taxpayers, at worst deeply socially irresponsible public health messaging which would lead to excess deaths and massive distress, as parents were persuaded to vaccinate their children with an experimental product for which the long term consequences were entirely unknown, and the short term safety signals alarming.

Early that November of 2021, why wait to begin coraling the herd, the Queensland government announced a series of easing of restrictions, for the vaccinated only. And that these liberties would come into force just days before Christmas. No coincidence there.

People just wanted to go back to their old lives, to meet up with friends, go to concerts and sporting events, mingle in public, for a certain percentage, just so they could go to the pub.

Queensland Premier Anastacia Palaszczuk announced a range of measures that promised to see a return to normal for vaccinated Queenslanders while protecting the most vulnerable.

Pubs, clubs, nightclubs and music venues would be freed of all restrictions provided all patrons and staff were fully vaccinated.

The measures were to take effect from December 17th or once the State reached 80% of eligible Queenslanders fully vaccinated, whichever came first and affected everyone 16 years and older.

The Premier said these measures were a reward for vaccinated Queenslanders, who deserved their lives to be returned to normal. "This pandemic has been a long, hard road," she said. "Soon our borders will open and COVID will be in our communities. This is about keeping our freedoms."

From December 17th events at all Queensland government hospitality venues including pubs, clubs, hotels, bars, restaurants and cafes would be open only to vaccinated staff and patrons Ditto entertainment venues, ditto art galleries, museums and libraries.

Police would be required to enforce the new rule.

The government lied. The vaccines protected nobody. They did not prevent infection, transmission, hospitalisation or death.

Tourism and Sport Minister Stirling Hinchliffe said making sure spectators were fully vaccinated was critical to keeping all Queenslanders safe from Covid-19.

"If you want to see sporting spectacles you need to be vaccinated," Mr Hinchliffe said. "Without double vaccination you won't make it past the turnstiles."

All for nothing.

They all lied. The vaccines were worse than useless, and many of those perpetuating the lie must have known this was the case; that in terrifying and mandating the population, and filling their heads with false promises of escape, they were doing far more harm than good.

Surely these people, with all their resources, their education, their handsome salaries, must have already known that their magic vaccine bullet was a dud, that their claims were false.

***

For her determined efforts to get the Queensland population vaccinated and for ignoring all the warning signs coming from well credentialed international experts the state's then Chief Health Officer Jeanette Young was rewarded with the plum job of Governor of Queensland.

In a public statement issued on 31 October, 2021, the day before she took up her new post as Governor, Young expressed no regrets over her disastrous Covid mismanagement, ignored the massive protests which had become a regular characteristic of her state, the many dissenting and cautionary voices both in Australia and around the world, and yet again fervently pushed the by now extremely controversial Covid vaccines.

And expressed not one single word of sympathy for the thousands of people who had lost their jobs for refusing to take it.

Australians have an outsized respect for the medical profession, and most particularly for doctors. Unfortunately, in this case they listened. "Covid-19 has commanded my attention day and night for almost two years now and I am certainly proud of the way we have weathered this crisis," Young declared after a long self-approving list of her own achievements. "As I write this, more than 61 per cent of Queenslanders aged 16 and over are fully vaccinated and more than 75 percent have received their first dose.

"These two shots are as close as we'll get to a silver bullet to this virus. I urge you – one last time as Chief Health Officer – to get vaccinated if you have not already done so.

"If you plan not to, please reconsider.

"At the very least, I encourage you to speak with a medical professional, someone qualified to provide advice."

That is, the same doctors who faced deregistration if they dared to speak out publicly against the vaccines.

A year on, excess deaths in Australia were oscillating somewhere between 15 and 17 percent above the long term average according to the Australian Bureau of Statistics; mirroring the disaster being visited on other jurisdictions which pushed lockdowns and mass vaccination.

And as Young also declared in the same statement: "When you're the Chief Health Officer of Queensland, you're not just doing a job; you're taking responsibility for the health and wellbeing of a state. You have more than 5.5 million patients and you care deeply for each and every one of them."

***

To add salt to the wound, Young was married to microbiologist Graeme Nimmo, who was Queensland Health's state director of microbiology before retiring. He had previously served on advisory boards for Pfizer and other drug companies Novartis and bioMerieux. In 2021 Novartis announced a deal to produce the Pfizer-BioNTech vaccine to help meet worldwide demand.

News Limited reported that documents showed Pfizer and Novartis paid Professor Nimmo's travel and accommodation costs to attend the 2011 Antimicrobial Resistance Summit in Sydney in 2011. A health source said Professor Nimmo was also believed to have performed work for a company which merged with AstraZeneca.

In an interview with The Courier Mail in 2020 Dr Young said Professor Nimmo's advice had been "critical" during the pandemic. "He's my sounding board. He's always very, very wise. He's exceptional. He is the perfect person to be married to when you've got a pandemic, or you're a chief health officer who doesn't know anything about pathology and infectious diseases."

How could these people, so well connected, so close to the action, not have known the consequences of what they were doing?

Or it didn't really matter? Bill Gates was, as it turned out, running Australia's Covid response through his proxies, his loyal lieutenants, his capture of Australia's regulatory bodies, and his web of academics, researchers and politicians, minions dancing on the string of his billions.

In February of 2021, Dr Young said Pfizer and AstraZeneca were "both fantastic vaccines".

She certainly did everything in her power to promote the defective and poorly tested products, including the implementation of what soon came to be seen as monstrously immoral vaccine mandates.

Like her fellow Chief Health Officers further south, Kerry Chant in New South Wales and Brett Sutton in Victoria, Young earnt the contempt not just of other medical professionals, but of the thousands of people who lost their jobs as a result of her conduct.

How would you describe their behaviour, if not as malfeasance?

***

Senior Australian Clinical Trial and Drug Regulatory Affairs Consultant Dr Phillip M. Altman spoke for many within his profession when he said: "The assumption that COVID vaccines are safe is a fairy tale.

"Vaccines usually take about 10 years to develop. Many vaccines fail basic safety testing along the development pathway. More than a dozen approved conventional vaccines have been withdrawn due to serious safety issues. But these experimental gene-based so-called COVID vaccines have proven to be the most dangerous in history. The very thought of giving these vaccines to infants, children and pregnant women and healthy individuals who are at extremely little to virtually no risk of COVID without any long term safety studies is reckless and probably criminal in my opinion.

"Inappropriately defining the gene-based COVID-19 jabs as 'vaccines' was a masterstroke both in terms of marketing, public acceptance, avoidance of legal exposure for damages and expedited drug regulatory approval. Unlike conventional vaccines, these so-called "vaccines" did not prevent infection and they did not prevent transmission of infection. This was clearly stated by the original emergency authorisation for use by the US FDA. It was in plain sight.

"The claim that this was a pandemic of the unvaccinated was an outright lie told by our most senior health bureaucrats to convince people to take a gene-based drug which had grossly inadequate short-term safety data and no long-term safety data.

"Anyone with any relevant formal scientific training should have known there was never any clinical evidence to support vaccine mandates. This has been known from the beginning.

"Industry and labour organisations destroyed careers, businesses, families and imposed financial stress and mental anguish across Australia for nothing. It is still going on in hospitals and companies like Telstra, AGL and Qantas.

"It is all for nothing.

"Those so-called health experts, advisors and industry leaders who advocated and ruthlessly imposed the draconian and totally useless vaccine mandates, if they had a modicum of self-respect and integrity remaining, should apologise, compensate those damaged and then resign. Ignorance is not an excuse. But those to blame have not admitted their mistakes, not apologised and still have their jobs."

And Jeanette Young was promoted to one of the best jobs in the land, Governor of Queensland.

***

Where else to go but inward; under virtual house arrest, still, where else was there to go but inward? Apart from receiving his instructions in the heart of the forest, "just work, just work, finish the task in hand", there had been few images, or visions flooding Old Alex's normally cluttered imagination in the previous weeks.

The interminable, infernal rain never ceased. His house, like other houses in the area, was infected with a dangerous black mould, another lifeform creeping through his lungs and his psyche.

The time channels were so turbulent he just sat and watched from his aerie as they manifested in long, streaming, churning clouds running down that long valley from the sandstone escarpment.

He understood little of it, least of all the reason behind his instructions. Why him? Why now? Why here?

There was something about this time that was for all time. And they spoke through those they could. The role of scribe even in these turbulent times when billions of words flooded across the globe every day, philosopher kings jostled for attention and new technologies rendered the written word, and the very books one could hold in your hand, obsolete. An arcane artform.

A lone sentinel, or scout, a standard bearer, would appear on a hill opposite; on horseback, gazing at the scene, his yellow and red flag flying. He would watch the scene for some time, wheel his steed around and disappear.

What it meant he did not know; whether the first scout of an army which lay beyond, a warning, simply a watching, he could not divine.

Beyond the turbulent, roiling clouds streaming past, there lay little else. No animal spirits, no manifestations, no lioness stalking the savanna lands, no time machines, little more than beauty of place, the flight of birds, the breath of wind through the shrubs, the interminable rain, the distributed intelligence of trees. As if God was everywhere and nowhere; spirit drenched and forsaken. As if mystery cloaked them all.

If this was about time, a messaging from afar, then indeed the times were riven, the nation's fortune squandered. And this became, then, a time for all time; when the scholars, sages and seers of the future would attempt to understand what had happened; and why. How it was possible. How humans could treat each other the way they did in the centuries that would follow from this point in time.

A time for all time.
A time which carried a warning for us all.

***

There were widespread protests around the country throughout that blighted month of November, 2021, the final month of Spring in The Land Down Under.

They were different in nature to anything the country had seen before, joyful, spirited, determined, organic; and the policing response to these protests was also different to anything Australians had ever experienced, more violent, more extreme, more militaristic.

Demonstrators were focused on vaccine mandates, continuing restrictions, particularly for those who were not double vaccinated, state border closures and difficulties with international travel, all public policies enforced by a new authoritarianism.

The problem with covering ongoing campaigns, protests, disruptions or attempts to overthrow any of the country's numerous social injustices is that from a reporter's and news editor's point of view they become repetitive. Papers cover them when it suits the agendas of their owners or that of governments and readers they wish to please or appease, witness climate and race. But this wasn't a case of boredom, or compassion fatigue.

That Australia's historically significant freedom protests were so poorly covered, frameworked in what in an unbiased light was one of the most compelling stories the country had ever lived through, was testament to the corrupting influence of government and money on the nation's media.

***

One of the greatest Australian traditions is Melbourne Cup Day, one of the world's most famous horse races. The entire country does, basically, come to a standstill.

It is held on the first Tuesday of each November. By midday of that year, 2021, a sizeable group of anti-lockdown protesters had gathered outside the home of the Cup, Flemington Racecourse, calling on Victorian Premier Daniel Andrews to stand down.

They shouted, "save our children", "free Victoria" and "sack Dan Andrews".

One large yellow and black banner read: "Make Victoria Great Again".

News Limited reporter Brooke Rolfe wrote: "The group was protesting against the new pandemic legislation presented to parliament last week, using the tagline 'kill the bill'.

"Someone speculated that at one point, there were more people gathered outside the venue than inside."

As the marchers arrived in their hundreds at Flemington Race Course they chanted "No Vaccine Passports".

The proposed laws gifted the Victorian Premier with the power to declare a pandemic for three months at a time without the approval of the Chief Health Officer. Victorians could face huge fines of $90,870 for breaking the rules by taking off their masks or leaving homes for a non-authorised reason, with heftier fines for more serious offences.

The crowd chanted "Save our Children, Save our Future". As had come to characterise these events, there were spontaneous displays of camaraderie as people who had been isolated for long periods found other likeminded people. The event was family friendly, with some people bringing their kids and their dogs.

Homemade placards included "I love Melbourne No to Segregation" and "We'll Break the System if the System Isn't for Us".

***

It was with sickened heart, in the brutal regimes of the time, in the deepest hypocrisy of their public statements as the streets of the Victorian capital were stricken with violent confrontations and a terrible yearning for the abyss.

As wind whipped through their glacial forms; and any pretence at good intent vanished.

Democracy was over.

Common decency was over.

The brutalist regimes of the future were already in the present.

The cosy familiarity of a country called Australia was gone.

All much of the world had ever known about the country, thanks to populists documentaries, was that we had the most dangerous animals on Earth.

Poisonous spiders, venomous snakes, giant crocodiles, and a friendly, unsophisticated population.

Now people, still naïve enough to believe their politicians, talked of Freedom Day, how good it would be, but freedom day never came. There were a myriad of excuses for locking people in their own homes, that is, imprisoning entire populations.

Information control. Information management. Information mismanagement. The perpetrators did their best to conceal their crimes.

What was the term for attacks against an entire population?

People were homeschooling their children. Demoralised, defeated, he noticed it in almost all his encounters now, that there could hardly be a more vicious or more dishonest, more incompetent way of dealing with an issue.

Not just Australian against Australian. But government against the people.

You lock them up and throw away the key, you destroy their livelihoods and give them no hope.

Never had there been a more incompetent government.

Never had there been more violent displays on the street.

The governments state and Federal were virulently pushing vaccines, as if they were the cure to this terrible impasse. You can have these freedoms back when we get to 70%, 80%. The problem was, people in lockdown have plenty of time on their hands. They can look up all the latest studies and analysis for themselves, all of which raised many questions about Australia's mass vaccination campaign.

Who were these people to hold such sway?

***

The Melbourne Cup protest was just the prelude for a month of unrest.

Avi Yemini at Rebel News Australia, which grew dramatically in popularity on the back of his energetic coverage of the protests, reported on the activities of the following day: "Police in Melbourne trapped, pepper-sprayed, beat, arrested and fined anyone who dared exercise their fundamental human right to protest The hundreds who attended the organised rally outside the State Parliament from noon were met with brute force.

"Protesters were demanding an end to all remaining lockdown restrictions. Many were also calling for premier Daniel Andrews to resign.

"Today's protest comes as the state recorded its fourth consecutive days of no new Coronavirus cases. The rolling 14-day average of new COVID cases in Victoria is only 1.9 cases."

Powerful footage showed protestors surrounded by armed police pouring pepper spray onto the front line of protestors. Officers operating in groups then adopted a tactic of surrounding and arresting protestors one by one and dragging or escorting them behind a line of police to be processed in a makeshift police station.

To camera Yemini said: "Today the response was heavy handed, as we have seen at every other lockdown protest till now. Pepper spray is being used. But the one question I have is why, why when there are zero cases. Police are moving in on what is a peaceful protest of five or six hundred people. I'm not sure how this protects anyone.

"Some passersby found themselves accidentally trapped and unable to leave."

One middle aged man says: "I heard this lady speaking and I chose to stop and listen to what she was saying, she seemed a fairly sensible, conservative, peaceful person. Now I find myself surrounded by Victorian police who are rapidly moving in on me, and I find this very distressing."

A young woman says of the arrest of a fellow protestor: "Four police walked up behind that man, he had no idea they were coming, and they grabbed him around the neck. This is a disgrace. This is an absolute disgrace."

Many protesters were presented with punitive $1652 fines. One man was unsure why he had copped a $4,957 fine, and shrugged, "because I'm special".

One man with grazed shins, hands and face said: "I just got tackled to the ground and kneed in the back. All that sort of stuff. A few scratches. I guess I'll be alright. It is a clear priority for them to shut this thing down, and I think it's because we're speaking out against the government. That's the truth."

Victoria Police said 404 people were arrested and 395 penalty notices were issued. A female senior sergeant was taken to a hospital with a suspected broken arm following an arrest. Protesters were alleged to have shown "disregard for the safety of the broader community and the directions of the Chief Health Officer".

Some were fined for not wearing a mask, others for breaching public gathering directions and still others for assaulting police or failing to provide their name and address. Six people were taken into custody.

All of the others were arrested, fined and released.

***

There were protests around the country across both the Saturday and Sunday of that first weekend in November.

With much of the country still in lockdown, or only cautiously moving out of lockdown, there was a sense it was all happening far, far away; a surreal feeling that this couldn't be happening in Australia, heightened by the lack of mainstream media coverage, the lack of congregation, the lack of any serious debate in all locations except the carved out region of independent media.

Both Sydney and Melbourne had exited their strict lockdowns, but many restrictions remained for the unvaccinated, fuelling yet further anger and division.

Old Alex's home state of New South Wales exited a total lockdown, that is house arrest for most of the civilian population, on so-called Freedom Day, 11 October, 2021. But if anything, that seemed to fuel the fury; people could travel more easily, and were less certain to be arrested.

And with a sense of outrage driving so many, protests were a good place to vent and to meet like-minded Australians. There was no coherent line through any of this morass. Characters emerged and disappeared; partly as a result of the organic nature of the protests there was no one single charismatic leader reflecting the nation's story back to it.

***

Replacing the widely ridiculed and to her critics deeply hysterical Gladys Berejiklian as Premier was Dominc Perrottet, a Catholic with seven children and a man ostensibly less enmeshed in the corrupt culture of NSW politics.

In a sense it was he who undid the Gordian knot, declaring "We cannot live here in a hermit kingdom on the other side of the world. We need to re-join every other country globally and do that in a sensible and measured way."

Until then the entire state had been under the dictatorial insanity of the Chief Health Officer Kerry Chant and her loyal codependent Health Minister Brad Hazzard.

Meanwhile, down south, Melbourne, now officially the most locked down city in the world, exited total lockdown ten days later.

Those who listened to the government propaganda emanating from the Australian Broadcasting Corporation and the mainstream news channels in turn flooded social media with insults towards lockdown sceptics and anti vaxxers, every panicked fool unleashed. Perrottet held firm.

Western Australia was still cut off from the rest of the country, while Melbourne remained Ground Zero for the disintegration of Australia as a functioning country. Victorians protesters repeatedly flocked to Melbourne's Central Business District to oppose mandatory vaccination requirements and new permanent pandemic laws.

State border closures and difficulties with international travel remained, particularly for those who were not double vaccinated. Australia's plunge into totalitarianism was praised by the world's globalists, most particularly Bill Gates, while on the ground the country erupted.

***

Video footage showed mainstream media being cheered, jeered, and forced to film from behind police lines.

As a print journalist in a country which barely read newspapers, Old Alex knew perfectly well the normal crowd reaction to television cameras: they loved them. It didn't matter how great the personal or public tragedy, once the television crews showed up the public was almost always more than willing to talk.

As for him, armed with nothing but a reporter's pad and a biro, they had no understanding of who he was or why he was asking such detailed questions. But a television camera, they would tell them all, and with a little luck be able to watch themselves on television the same night.

Print journalists often envy the handsome salaries and easy jobs of television reporters. To see them ducking behind police lines to avoid the anger of the crowd, that was a sight for sore eyes; for it was the television channels, now heavily funded by government, which had been directly responsible for creating panic and misinforming the public.

"Tell the truth you maggots," shouted one Melbourne protestor as the roaring crowd set up a chant. "Tell the Truth, Tell the Truth".

Melbourne saw one of the largest demonstrations since the beginning of the Covid conflagration. One large banner read, "Where there's risk, there must be choice".

It should have been obvious to even the most naive of observers that the heavy manipulation of the public narrative and the algorithmic downplaying of these protests at the behest of government was doing more harm than good, that Australia has never been so divided.

Even on the pages of the august but now barely read newspapers where Old Alex once worked, all too often all he could see was former colleagues fawning over health bureaucrats, and relaying the Covid hysteria the government so clearly wanted to perpetuate. To do otherwise, they apparently believed, would be to damage the government's public health messaging, and would therefore be deeply irresponsible.

Shortly thereafter, in what was barely even a wrinkle in time, they were all proven wrong, and in their callous disregard for the truth, themselves deeply irresponsible.

The public's loss of faith in the mainstream media was one of the reasons why this was such a significant turning point in Australian history, as whole swathes of the population turned to independent media as a more reliable source of information.

***

There were elements about it all, there had been from the very beginning, of "the greatest story ever told"; a spiritual dimension beyond the realm.

Perhaps it was this element, certainly some of the protestors believed it to be so, that divine inspiration or the eternal spirits came not just to individuals but to crowds, thanks to the social nature of the species, inspiring the unique nature of the protests. As if they had all been infected by a divine light.

The poster for the fifth bimonthly Worldwide Rally for Freedom, kangaroos hopping across an outback landscape coloured by a setting sun, declared: "Together, We Are Free".

On that Saturday, 20 November, 2021, there were protests in Australia's capitals, from Darwin to Perth to Sydney, as well as regional centres including Mt Gambier, Warrnabool and Bundaberg, Queensland's famous home of the potent and popular Bundaberg whisky.

That the government, an apparatus wedded to global and corporate interests, continued to ignore or demonise these passionate and widespread protests, defied immediate comprehension.

A climate change or black lives matter rally, echoing bureaucratic agendas, attracted maximum mainstream coverage. As powerful as they were, these protests attracted virtually none.

The Australian government, just like their counterparts in Canada, New Zealand, America and the UK, had destroyed the traditional impulses of the Fourth Estate with bucket loads of money. He who pays the piper calls the tune.

In this case Australian governments, through their tame media hounds, were perpetrating one of the most destructive agendas in human history thanks to the millions from the likes of Bill Gates and Pfizer, while the Gates funded World Health Organisation framed the narrative.

One thing was for sure: Australians had had enough.

While crowd numbers are notoriously difficult to estimate, organisers across the country claimed numbers in the thousands, even in a far flung town like Mackay in Queensland; along with hundreds of thousands in the nation's capitals.

Even the traditionally hostile mainstream media acknowledged protestors in the tens of thousands; despite dismal weather across much of the eastern seaboard.

***

20 November, 2021 will go down as the date for some of the largest scenes of mass protest ever witnessed in Australia.

To be blunt, it takes a lot to get Australians out into the streets. Some of the world's most over-the-top draconian enforcement of Covid regulations had provoked a major and perhaps predictable backlash as millions had seen and indeed continued to see their lives disrupted or destroyed by the nation's out of control authorities.

These protests were now not just a movement, but a phenomenon.

Placards held jubilantly, defiantly above the thronging crowds in Melbourne included: "Freedom Comes from God, Not Government",

"The Further a Government Drifts from Truth, the More it will Hate those who Speak it", "We are the Great Reset", "Shadow Ban Dictator Dan, We Vote Against Government Corruption" and the by now ubiquitous "Do No Harm" and "Leave Our Children Alone".

One speaker, addressing a jam packed crowd, declared: "Remember these four words: Not On Our Watch. Are we going to let them experiment on our kids? Is that going to happen?"

And the crowd roars back: "No".

"Are they going to track you wherever you go? Is that going to happen?"

And the crowd begins to chant: "We say no. We say no."

One of the organisers declared: "We have been assaulted by police many times. Let us live our lives as we please. What a crowd! Freedom! As we know the police have acted disgracefully during the lockdowns which never needed to happen."

"Are you getting high on this or what?"

"I am, you are, we are Australian. We are one, but we are many, and from all the lands on Earth we come."

The live stream by The Real Rukshan, whose video record of the demonstrations provided an invaluable documentation of these historic events, was viewed more than 400,000 times, shared more than 16,000 times and liked more than 33,000 times on one platform alone.

One online comment amongst the more than 10,000 others declared: "From America to the people of Australia God bless you as long as we all keep fighting for our rights we're gonna win stay strong and don't give up God bless us all."

That word again, as if God was everywhere in these demonstrations. It was uncanny.

As had become characteristic of these rolling demonstrations, there were impromptu concerts displaying a quite remarkable showcase of talent and high spirits amongst younger generations of Australians, the so-called baby boomers and Generation X who had visited this horror upon their fellow countrymen retreating towards their graves, clutching their public service salaries and their worthless certitudes while the Millennials and Generation Z, those born after 1980, took to the stage.

"Music is free!!"

After one spirited performance the singers lead the entire crowd in fist pumping the air and chanting: "We Will Rise. We Will Rise."

Another speaker, Matthew Lawson, declared from the makeshift podium, essentially just a piece of cleared concrete in the middle of a park: "I am so proud of the people of Victoria. We have gone through the harshest lockdowns in the world. We have been locked down. We have been criminalised. We have been hurt. Mental health is going through the roof. People are hurting everywhere. Yet we are here in numbers, in hope and in love. And we are never going to be silenced.

"The human spirit can push through anything. The government is afraid. They control us through division, fear and despair. But now we are no longer afraid. We are courageous. We are strong. We are united. If the government will not stand for us we will stand for ourselves. The power has always been with the people. Now we are awake. For the people here with kids. We are fighting for you. We are fighting everyday and we will not stop.

"They call us extremists because they are scared. The only things we have that are extreme are extreme care, extreme compassion, extreme kindness and extreme love. Never doubt the power of love."

***

The Millions March posters trumpeting the protests organised for the following weekend, midday on Saturday 27 November, 2021, read. ' Standing for – Human Rights – Medical Freedom – Informed Consent – Truth & Transparency – Freedom of Speech – Peaceful & Family Friendly".

The long list of locations indicated the spreading power of the movement, for which a bewildered, inept, out of touch government had no answer but their weaponry, the police and the military. Their spackle in shoring up their fake, dishonest narrative was their complete manipulation of the mainstream media. Concurrently, the real world swarmed with stories of vaccine injuries, the gross damage of lockdowns, the futility of their measures, and, already, the utter callous corruption of Big Pharma and the Bill Gates funded institutions which had engineered this nightmare.

There were protests in the sundrenched state of Queensland, including at the tourist destinations of Hervey Bay, the Sunshine Coast, the Gold

Coast and the old beef and sugar cane town of Toowoomba further inland. There were protests in the northern retirement town of Ballina in New South Wales, the country music capital Tamworth, at the now sparklingly renovated Foreshore Park in the once gritty steel town of Newcastle, at Sydney's central Hyde Park, Glebe Park in the public servant town of Canberra, in Victoria's capital of Melbourne, outside the television station Channel 7 in the South Australian capital of Adelaide, in Launceston in the island state of Tasmania, in the West Australian capital Perth, now cut off from the rest of the country. And so it went.

Old Alex wrote: With a number of books now emerging about the Covid era, including most recently Robert F Kennedy's *The Real Anthony Fauci: Bill Gates, Big Pharma, and the Global War on Democracy and Public Health* and Alex Berenson's *Pandemia: How Coronavirus Hysteria Took Over Our Government, Rights and Lives*, it has become clear that military and intelligence agencies have been closely involved from the beginning.

"In this vein, it has long been claimed, in what at first seemed like a pure conspiracy theory at the time, that Australia, with its small population, was the testing ground for techno-fascism.

"While the Australian authorities have fallen obediently into line, the political, medical and media establishment all working to provoke fear and confusion, destroying businesses and lives in the name of keeping Australians safe, the people themselves are proving far less malleable.

"The country is being ripped apart by the very people and agencies the public had come to trust: and the originally brutal, violent suppression of dissent is now morphing into nationwide protests. The weekend's dismal weather across much of the eastern seaboard did nothing to quell protests.

"This unprecedented period of Australian history has also birthed or propelled independent media, with legacy media looking more and more irrelevant, and dishonest."

While the mainstream media, as it had done since the beginning, like the nation's politicians hostage to profit motive of corrupt pharmaceutical companies, was doing its best to ignore or demonise the protests, nothing could hide the size of the protests in an increasingly interconnected world.

***

Image after image told a truth the authorities could no longer hide. That these weren't a bunch of mad, radical conspiracy theorists, but regular Australian citizens from all walks of life.

At one protest after another demonstrators in Sydney met phalanxes of masked and armed police as they chanted "Hold the line, hold the line" and "Shame on you, shame on you."

At one point the protest descended into violence, with traumatic scenes of screaming women and children.

It was no wonder, faced with having to do this very dirty work, that in the coming months many hundreds of police across the country would quit their jobs.

Placards in Adelaide, often regarded as the most civilised capital in Australia because historically the state had never a penal colony, read: "Leave Our Kids Alone", "When Injustice Becomes Law Resistance Becomes Duty" and "It's not Science if you're not allowed to Question It."

***

Down in Oak Flats it was as if people were emerging from their caves and tunnels, as if they had been living in darkness and were now standing blinking in the sunlight, bewildered, unsure. Down at the local shopping mall, it was obvious, nobody had been outside for a very long time. There was a ginger testing of the limits; as if even to be near someone else was in itself a danger. The human bonds were broken. Despite all their sociability, this was a very cruel species.

So it was that the tempers darkened and deepened, so it was that the world they entered became a remote outpost of where they had once been. Australia, far far from anywhere, far far from the centres of power, yet now transfigured by the fibre like darkness which grew like reed beds across the surface.

Compelled into silence, for all was danger, for there was no simple, ordinary conversation or exchange of views, for Old Alex a kaleidoscope of images kept demanding attention, and he kept trying to blot them out. Drinking heavily was one way to do it, except that act alone added another layer of insanity to bewildering times.

Once again a powerful empath was in the area, and because of his long-born belief, trust no one, he tried every mental trick he could to avoid contact; and left them exhausted and disappointed, before, finally, the cogs clicked into place.

Down at the shopping centre in Oak Flats, a small string of unassuming shops lining what was called Central Avenue, although there was nothing grand about it, Old Alex ran into an old acquaintance from the beer garden down at the Lakeview.

They quickly established that neither of them, as the new pariahs of Australian society, were down at their local watering hole, "Church" as it was jokingly called, because neither of them were double vaxxed. It was easy enough to get fraudulent papers to suggest that in fact you were vaccinated, but sometimes fraud is not the best way to go.

There in that rushed encounter, for no one dwelt long together anymore, his drinking buddy, normally a jovial figure with beer in hand, quickly told a story of a friend's wife who had died after having "the jab", blood clot, and they blamed a broken leg from six months before.

It wasn't exactly hard to find horror stories. There were thousands of them, if truth be known, tens of thousands of them. You didn't even have to go on the web. An injured population was a major source of income for the pharmaceutical companies, a self-reliant, beer swilling labourer, not so much.

By now every Australian had heard these stories; and still the government mandated the vaccines, forcing the population to have a vaccine they did not want, or face a life of poverty and disenfranchisement.

***

The remote outback town of Katharine in the Northern Territory was now in lockdown.

On the streets of Shellharbour, from what Old Alex could gauge from his odd interactions, people were by now extremely fed up with the ongoing, dystopian regulation; masks, social distancing, travel restrictions and all the rest of the debacle visited upon them, supposedly to keep them safe, in reality social devices used to herd the population into mass vaccination.

This was not an area of dancing prima donnas spitting out "how dare you", but a working class area where teachers and doctors were still respected. These same people who had a naive faith in their betters had all been betrayed. Politicians, of course, bureaucracies, of course, media, most particularly the media, academe, medical authorities; all of their protestations of professional competence amounted to a pile of beans.

Protests grew louder. Suspicion spread. But in one grey beam of light, an interminably cold wet spring finally looked like it might be breaking, just in time for summer.

***

The imperial battleship was here, the ladders spilling down to the planet's surface.

"We come at the End of Empire," the spirits explained time and again to Old Alex, whose waking visions had grown more and more intense with every extended day of lockdowns. Always there were those same phrases through those receptors of the infinite which we as humans are born with in order to communicate with the ancient spirits, born from evocation, born from this cold and sometimes extremely beautiful place. We were all prisoners. But anyone who dared to listen could hear an explanation for what was happening, that indeed empires collapse; tectonic shifts in the human psyche do occur; and those who contemplated immortality and dared to assume the power of life and death over the people, time captures all.

What made it make sense was the utter irrationality which had swept over all of them because it was all of a piece; the utter madness of the political class, the Covid hysteria which engulfed them all, as the hyper-connectivity of the era was exploited by the worst of the worst.

Humans did this to other humans. Australians did this to their fellow Australians.

The most singular echo of that era was societal wide cruelty and indifference, an absolute lack of care. An abandonment of all civil practices. An absolute contempt for those who dared to disagree with government, or corporate messaging, for those who dared to question the response.

As many had commented, there was a dark feel behind it all, as if new technologies, developed with in depth studies of the herd behaviour of wildebeest and flocks of birds and crowds of humans; hence the whole hyena thing, panic the herd, pick of the outliers, you can channel the herd in any direction you like simply through fear; and all this dark intent came flying down to the present day.

And we looked on bewildered at the behaviour of ordinary people; as they lined up to be injected with an experimental technology, and then lined up to inject their children.

It was frightening, bewildering; and every day the spirits settled further into place, the wheeling from above, the strange carrion cries as they wheeled above the history of this time; the funnelling, the strangeness, the darkness, the very great darkness of these times.

And so it was, we called to you.

And so it was that Empire, the utterly corrupt and failed American Empire, ended. That one civilization collapsed and another began. That one form of humanity ended, and another began.

> "If I could sail a galleon ship
> A long, lonely rider across the sky
> Seek out mysteries while you sleep
> And treasures money cannot buy."

TWELVE
SHATTERED GROUND

In my youth the heart of dawn was in my heart, and the songs of April were in my ears.
But my soul was sad unto death, and I knew not why.
Even unto this day I know not why I was sad.
But now, though I am with eventide, my heart is still veiling dawn,
And though I am with autumn, my ears still echo the songs of spring.
But my sadness has turned into awe, and I stand in the presence of life and life's daily miracles.

Walt Whitman.

THE SPIRITS AND the ancient gods were here, speaking so loudly, for a reason.

As magisterial as they could be, these were frightening times. The behaviour of the perpetrators was absolutely chilling, no regret, no apology, no sympathy.

The world was looking at the greatest crime against humanity in history; that seemed the only explanation for what Old Alex knew to be true. That they didn't come in ordinary times. That they rarely intervened; that indeed they rarely spoke, content to be where they were and what they were; magisterial, vast. "I am here, and you are where you are".

But now was different. And the same explanations, or messaging, that he had been receiving for months there in that remote aerie on the south coast said it simply: "We are here to preserve a future."

This staggering thing, the scale of this disaster, the destruction of Australia, his country, just incidental in a wholesale global destruction of traditional society; no apology, no explanation came from billionaires and oligarchs who had perpetrated this crime against ordinary citizens; arrogant, aloof, cold beyond cold.

For Alex it was as if his own eyes had been appropriated by entities not even remotely human.

And amidst this manifest tragedy; there were those, the perpetrators, the blind leading the blinded, their magnificent salaries, all of it in distended waves and short choppy thoughts; this sadness for the fate of the humans, on a scale that was almost impossible to grasp; and so it was that these seemingly insane thoughts went round and round in him, as the spirits crawled and crept and swirled on a planet surface and expressed a sadness for the shared fate of humans as their history was stolen from them, as entire societies rearranged and self-destructed, and still it seemed the humans cared so little for each other, or knew so little about their own destinies.

"We come at times of trouble, we come at the End of Empire, we come to thread our way to the future, outside of time."

The beauty of it, the searing, frightening beauty of it; the death of hope, the ignorance of the population, the savage arrogance of the corrupt leaders, the oligarchs who had perpetrated this destruction of the country; all of it would survive in a record; and be destroyed in a future collapse; when they sensed that the key to their survival would be lost, unless they found it here.

***

There was a very good reason why the likes of Bill Gates funded journals and newspapers around the world, they crafted the narrative to promote their financial interests. Ditto the vast funding of academics, both by corporate interests and government. They also shape the narrative, their papers and reports filtering down to the street via uncritical news reports. In Australia, amidst so many other things, the Bill and Melinda Gates Foundation funded not just the regulatory bodies but both the academic journal *The Conversation* and the interminably woke vaccine and climate change promoter *Guardian Australia,* along with the thinktank The Lowy Institute.

The proverbial "two clicks to get to the Bill and Melinda Gates Foundation" principle ran across Australia's entire Covid response,

Australia was not a culture which valued academic endeavour, but nonetheless the reaction on the streets to the political insanities of Covid hysteria was mirrored at a "higher level", with a few brave souls, academics, doctors, community leaders, standing up against the tide of groupthink, that distinctive behaviour of a panicked mob.

It's tempting to wonder if a better educated population would have been so easily lulled into one of history's greatest deceptions. But it did not suit the Australian government to have a well educated population.

Since early 2020 most Australian academics sang true to their government and vaccine funding sources. They produced a string of articles for public consumption singing the praises of the vaccines, including the benefits for children, a vaccine for which they, like any normal citizen, had no idea what the long term consequences might be and for which the short term safety signals were absolutely alarming.

Few citizens were equipped to detect the falsehood.

The Land of the Long Weekend had been steadily dropping down the global education rankings for years; and this was mirrored in the lack of inquiry and the gullibility the broader population displayed during the entire Covid era.

***

One of the very few Australian academics to show any independence of thought or to speak out against the multiple Covid insanities inflicted upon the population was Gigi Foster, a Professor with the School of Economics at the University of New South Wales.

As the government deliberately stirred up hatred against the unvaccinated, so, too, Gigi Foster endured the same isolation and scorn in the academic corridors as the freedom warriors were facing in the deepest of suburban byways.

"I've got people who absolutely hate my guts. Won't go on to debate with me. I've had multiple appearances where the host tries to find someone who will be there with me and kind of provide a counterpoint and nobody will do it. They ask multiple people, they won't do it. People hate me. People see me as literally the devil."

Gigi Foster was the co-author of *The Great Covid Panic*, which the esteemed Martin Kulldorff of the Harvard Medical School described as: "A tour-de-force on how the pandemic response was driven by fear, crowd thinking, big business and a desire for control, rather than sound public health measures. This is bound to be a classic."

Well, a classic if anyone read books anymore.

In a piece called Australia: Champion Covidiot for the Brownstone Institute Gigi Foster wrote: "No, Australia's trust in institutions has not served it well during this period. What has happened is that we have seen how corrupt and/or incompetent the people in charge of our institutions really are, and – to our horror – how our misplaced trust in those institutions has led to an abject failure of our systems of democratic oversight and accountability.

"Our tendency towards 'mateship' and our pro-social nature caused us to obey rules they and others in positions of power sold to us as for the greater good that in fact delivered horrific losses to our country that will cripple us for a generation.

"Few in Australia publicly questioned these policies in 2020 and 2021, in part because when they did, speaking from personal experience, they were vilified in the public square of social media as granny-killing Trumpkinaut death cult warriors and pieces of human excrement.

"In short, the trusting Australian people have been had. Australia has been shown to have produced some of the most docile, authority-loving, uncritical people in the developed world: people ripe for brainwashing and manipulation. Unlike our COVID results, our sheepish national culture cannot be explained by our geographic location, our high levels of sunshine, or our demography."

***

It was the behaviour of other people, of Australians against Australians, which took Old Alex most by surprise. Trapped throughout lockdown in what felt like house arrest, he became fascinated by the political concept of totalitarianism, reading Hannah Arendt's classic *The Origins of Totalitarianism* and *Eichmann in Jerusalem: A Study of the Banality of Evil*; along with the more recent Michel Dismet's *The Psychology of Totalitarianism*.

There was essentially no one to talk to in Oak Flats about any of this, his attempt to join a book club at the local library quashed by his unvaccinated status, and he was still legally unable to go to the local pub where he could at least vent.

So it was a comfort, if any comfort could be found in any of this, in the repeated confirmation of "man's inhumanity to man", the innate cruelty of humans and more broadly, of the struggle for life itself, to come across people like Gigi Foster.

She wrote, in a piece titled We Can All Be Evil and the Germans Were Nothing Special: "For more than two years, the world has been swept up in covid mania. Ordinary people of almost every nationality have accepted the covid 'story', applauding as strong men and women have assumed dictatorial powers, suspended normal human rights and political processes, pretended that covid deaths were the only ones that mattered, closed schools, closed businesses, prevented people from earning livelihoods, and caused mass misery, poverty, and starvation.

"The more these strong men and women did these things, the louder the applause, and the greater the disapprobation and abuse levelled at those who decried such actions. Police bullying of those speaking out against the covid story was cheered on by populations keen to see the naysayers brought to justice.

"The past two years have proved that the Germans of the National Socialist period were really nothing special.

"The West refused to learn, or by now has forgotten, the central lesson of the Nazi period (1930-1945) despite the plethora of eyewitness voices in post-WWII art and science that made it abundantly clear what had happened…The key point made by the top intellectuals writing about the Nazi period was that anyone could become a Nazi: there was absolutely nothing odd about the Germans who became Nazis. They simply got seduced by a story and swept off their feet and out of their minds by the herd, making up their reasons as they went along.

"The brutal lesson that the intellectuals of that era wanted to pass on was that pretty much everyone would have done the same under the circumstances. Evil, in a word, is banal."

***

The lies mounted daily: the most egregious of them being the oft repeated phrase "Keeping Australians safe".

The authorities were doing nothing of the kind. They were pandering to some of the most corrupt corporate entities on Earth. Either they didn't know, or they didn't care. Or the money was just too damn good.

Here in this place known as Oak Flats there was nothing to do unless you already had your networks. The only community gathering place was the pub, and it was basically empty.

Another cold, wet and windy summer made the place even more insular than usual; the second year in a row when summer never happened.

A carrion carryover, a dredge that should have evinced or extinguished all hope, a crawling extinguishment of all enthusiasm, a place of loneliness and counting days, of dying friendships and a cast of herd behaviour; panic the herd, pick off the outliers, and you can move them in any direction you like. There was no point trying to talk to anybody about anything, and nobody did. A trip to the shops, with all the masks, QR coding and social distancing, had become a deeply unpleasant experience.

All was lost, lost, is that what you wanted to say?

Well, it was hardly a cause for celebration, to watch your own country being destroyed.

But he didn't back down, he didn't go quiet, he rallied from an exhausted and tormented place, and watched as time wheels tumbled in turbulent clouds in the valley below, and if all was lost for these people, it was not lost for all people.

The man who had destroyed Australia, the truly odious Scott Morrison, the only Pentecostal Prime Minister on the planet, was seeking re-election.

Peculiarly, it was this place, this ordinary place, which would birth a prosperity spilling down the generations, ultimately leading to one of the most spectacularly beautiful civilisations ever witnessed on Earth.

And beyond that, they would call to him. What happened? What happened here? How could it possibly be? How could an entire country destroy itself? How could a once prosperous place, providing security and work for its serfs, throw millions of people into such shocking poverty?

How could a country with so many spectacular natural gifts destroy itself? How was it possible? How was the soul of the country destroyed?

The crimes committed here today will reverberate down through all time.

The nature of man revealed.

And the criminal thugs, those government thugs who destroyed this place would slide into acrimony and concealment, would slip beyond the river of history. And disappear.

But to understand the future of history, you had to understand the present.

The crimes committed here, today.

****

A time for all time, that's what made this period so strategic, so pivotal in the daisy chain of heightened experiences which strung down through history.

In a piece called What Covid Containment Has Done to Our Children Gigi Foster wrote: "For the past two years, what Western governments have done to the next generation – all in the name of keeping them safe, of course – has been calamitous. Instead of trying to ameliorate problems for our children that were already clear, well-documented and steadily worsening over time, in March 2020 the authorities began to perform particularly gruesome social experiments on them. What kind of generation will result?

"A 2021 Lancet paper gives us a grim picture of the result, based on data from 204 countries. The key finding was a spectacular increase of more than 25% in both anxiety and depression disorders. Those just entering adulthood (ages 15-25) and women were the hardest hit.

"IQ and cognitive functioning develop based on investments in early life and are then generally thought to recede beyond early adulthood. What do we see as the harvest of covid mania for our kids in this area?

"Researchers already knew the West was in big trouble on this score before the pandemic, with the best data coming from a study of army conscripts in Norway and showing a 5-point IQ drop between the cohort born in 1975 and the one born in 1990, with the drop after 1975 undoing the gains made after WWII.

"The finding of a large IQ drop pre-2010 holds also for the UK and the US. While we don't know why for sure, the front-running explanation is that this decline is the product of the mental distractions introduced into society by mobile phones and the internet, which have increasingly damaged the ability of their users to focus and to hold complex abstractions in their heads. Thinking hard has become passé.

"Data suggests that two years of covid madness has inflicted severe, long-term damage on our children."

Foster wrote that a school closure was effectively a year of education lost, at least for children from poor backgrounds. That is on top of the large IQ declines already occurring before 2020. The data are consistent with the rise of a generation of permanently cognitively damaged children.

"Can it get worse than this – a generation depressed, anxious, obese, and operating at cognitive levels thought to be long extinct? We are afraid it can get much worse.

"The West is raising a crippled generation. People born in the past five to 25 years are more obese, less intelligent, more depressed, less happy, more conflicted, more prone to drug abuse, less proud of their country, and less encouraged by the authorities than those born even 10 years prior.

"A monstrous generation, ideologically besieged by what external observers looking for our weaknesses call a 'bizarre horde of savages', is currently being shaped by our schools, media, and propagandists. Our youth have been taught to hate themselves, their own culture, and their own history. Their weak intellectual ability means they will struggle to decipher what has happened to them or who they are. Relative to generations as recent as Generation X, our youth are unhealthy, anxious, socially shy, prone to flee towards online gaming and offline drugs, stuck in victimhood narratives, angry at the world, and lonely."

"Today's children will be tomorrow's monsters because our societies are raising them, right now, to be monsters. A generation taught to take pleasure in draconian, bureaucratic rules oriented toward face-saving, with no regard to victims. A generation used to propaganda and make-believe certainty. A generation blind to millions of deaths, whether at home or abroad. A truly frightening generation – not only crippled itself, but ready to cripple others – is on its way out of the blocks."

***

They were partial to that partial light of the forest, those ethereal manifestations of the ancient spirits which swarmed through Old Alex's imagination, coating every surface, spreading, spreading.

The population was as confused, anxious, terrified even, as they had ever been. The supply chains were breaking down.

Two years into this social derangement the blizzard of government diktats grew ever worse, more strangulating, more confusing.

As Naomi Wolf put it so concisely in her magnificent book *The Bodies of Others*: "Nominally directed at public health, the behavioural checks on citizens of the formerly free West, its restrictions multiplying dizzyingly, left people flailing, tossed about by strange unknowable currents. Like the afflictions streaming from Pandora's box, they bore great ill and endless new harms.

"So what were these 'restrictions' really for? Why were they proliferating and shape shifting day by day and week by week?

"The true reason is that, in the elites' war against Western humanism, 'restrictions', had become the weapon of choice. Why? Because historically restrictions disempower the restricted and leave them open to the theft of their lands and assets. 'Restrictions' endow the ruling class with unlimited power and reduce ordinary people's power to that of medieval vassals."

That is, not the creation of an industrious, productive and proud population, but the creation of a new slave class.

***

Western Australia remained cut off from the rest of the country; already an island nation, Australia itself was more deeply divided than ever before, each state was already well on the way to becoming its own principality.

The vaxxed, the unvaxxed, the believers, the sceptics; the supreme arrogance and indifference of those who had completely stuffed the country, those who swore blind across our benighted country that they were acting for the common good. .

Class riven. Ethnically riven. Nothing the government did was of any assistance to the ordinary person; and ultimately a government which does nothing but generate complexity and difficulty in the lives of the citizenry will collapse.

Partial to that partial light, as Nick Cave had put it in that evocation of the spirits, his album Ghosteen, there were times when he could feel them moving around him, and others when he ignored him, or they were far off. The warship had landed on this remarkably complex battlefield. Everything was circular. Everything was crying out.

While the Watchers on the Watch wavered between self righteousness, curiosity, boredom and self-interest, Old Alex too wavered on the precipice of enlightenment or flinging himself determinedly into the mud; never to be seen again, never to be haunted, never to fulfil his destiny, to die early and unhealthy; or to live a long, productive, and what was left of it, happy life.

Tired, tormented if you will, by the social isolation, Old Alex stepped out on to a different field, and moved graciously amongst the trees, and murmured in the half light, the glow worms lining the banks along the dirt road; there in the beautiful, staggeringly beautiful upper reaches of the Kangaroo Valley River, there amid the ancient forests, truly, ancient and calm, of a different type of distributed intelligence.

He'd never done anything like it before, camping out like that with Jackie and her friends, his numerous adventures being largely confined to cheap hotels, and it felt perfectly natural, and fun, and a revelation in itself after that long period of isolation.

Humans are social animals. "We become persons amongst persons" as the Peruvian saying went.

The natural spirit of the people had been crushed. They wore their masks; and when he went to arrange a birthday for his son, where he could once again express his pride and say, "nobody could ever ask for a nicer son", he realised all were guilty, that it would not be possible because of vaccination status; once again the whole vaccine passport routine for cafes, restaurants, clubs and pubs had been re-imposed, he heard. He, like so many others, had simply given up listening to the news. Everyone had already decided which hill to die on.

**

While Australia's left leaning media emote constantly over the nation's indigenous population, there was not a word of protest as the Army rounded up First Nations people and left them no choice but to get vaccinated. That freezing Spring ended with one of the greatest scandals ever to be perpetuated against that same cohort of the population every social justice warrior in the country wrapped their virtue signalling in; comfortably assuaging their communal guilt while oozing fake empathy for "elders past, present and emerging".

As in other Western countries, the question of race became a modern day minefield. Under most circumstances it was easier and simpler just not to go there.

At the time Old Alex wrote: "The remote Northern Territory areas of Katherine, Binjari and Rockhole have been placed into a hard lockdown, with an operation underway that includes transferring positive cases and close contacts, that is entire remote communities, from their sacred homelands.

"In Australia's heavily manipulated media environment, TOTT News is one of the very few outlets in the country following this story critically and in depth.

"And yet this is one of the most truly outrageous, and most important stories, this country has ever seen, with repercussions stretching well beyond the alleged forced vaccination of sovereign peoples against their will. And on their own homelands.

"The Covid narrative is unravelling worldwide. It should be called out."

Few Australians have ever been to these remote aboriginal settlements, and access is severely restricted. A reporter can't just hop in a company car and decide to go and investigate what is happening.

While ignored by the mainstream the moves attracted vicious headlines in some smaller outlets: "Aboriginals Hunted by Military, Kids Jabbed by Force" and "Australia Begins Covid Ethnic Cleansing Military Round Ups of Indigenous People".

American radio host Stew Peters declared: "I just saw this video which shook me to the core. There are all kinds of reports all over the internet of aboriginal people being hunted, chased down like wild animals by their own government, by their military,

"Kids are being chased by the military personnel, tackled to the ground, pinned down and force jabbed with syringes."

While quickly scrubbed from major platforms including Facebook, the powerful appeal for international intervention could still be found on anti-censorship platforms.

Standing in front of a large aboriginal flag and flanked by First Nations people a spokesman declares: "We are part of the original Tribal Sovereign

Federation. We are standing here united to make an international call for assistance. We need international attention focused on what is happening here in our communities.

"We have the Northern Territory government force vaccinating our people, pressuring them using military, using foreign military, foreign police officers, and local military and local police officers to pressure our people to take this bioweapon. They are not informing the people. They are lining them up. They are telling them they can't eat in the shops, they can't leave the community, they can't go shopping elsewhere.

"Those who are fleeing to get food or fleeing to avoid this forced vaccination are being fined $5000. So this is martial law. This is a war crime. This is a crime against humanity. We are the guinea pigs. We are the dry run for everything, for the rest of the country and the rest of the world. They are trialling it on us.

"What they are doing now is they are forcing this genocidal weapon on to us, through coercion, through force, through pressure, through the relief of getting a feed or food or getting money. They are pressuring us in every way. And now they are going in with the military. They are locking down entire communities. They are not letting people in or out.

"They are protecting their crime by shutting everybody out. Our people are scared. Our people are frightened. Our people are terrorised out there. This is torture. Do not be mistaken. We are calling out to the international community to bring this to the attention of the world. This is genocide against the oldest living culture in the world.

"Our culture is your culture. Our law is your law. We hold all seven DNAs."

Injecting Australia's indigenous population with a gene based "therapy" which could potentially alter their DNA posed a particular trauma. Part of the massive resistance to vaccination amongst Australia's indigenous was due to the widespread belief that their blood, their DNA, was different to that of Europeans, unique, ancient and strong, in itself sacred.

Whatever the case, this was paternalism of the very worst kind.

Members of the tribal group making the plea were reported to have subsequently attended a freedom march in the Northern Territory capital of Darwin, where police used pepper spray to arrest and disperse demonstrators.

The Land of the Long Weekend enters The Great Australian Stupor during the summer months of December and January. Armed with barbeques, tents and sunscreen, much of the population heads to the beach or their nearest waterway.

Summers in the Australian Outback are hot, often very hot. That didn't stop the Australian government locking down the indigenous in their humble often unairconditioned homes.

Wheeling into 2022, and the Labor Chief Minister Michael Gunner, peddling one falsehood after another as justification for locking down people in crippling heat, announced that unvaccinated citizens in remote communities would no longer be able to leave their homes for work or exercise.

No normal Australian suburbanite or city dweller can really grasp just how isolated these communities are. Yuendumu, for example, which came under the draconian lockdowns, is in the Tanami Desert 293 kilometres North West of Alice Springs, and is one of the largest of the remote settlements, with a population of 750.

Much of the surrounding landscape is of intense spiritual significance, and the region is known for producing some of the most sought after and beautiful Aboriginal art found anywhere on the continent.

With no respect, no respect whatsoever, the white authorities stomped over these lands and coerced the population into receiving a "jab" they did not want, an experimental gene "therapy" which was neither safe nor effective and was already causing outrage and consternation around the globe. With zero reason to trust the white colonisers, they feared the destruction of the precious heritage of their ancestors which ran through them as blood.

***

Nowhere was the conduct of Australian authorities, readily reminiscent of totalitarian societies, more stark than in the impoverished settlements of the Northern Territory. Australian Defence Force personnel were deployed in army trucks to "assist" with a reported Covid outbreak in remote indigenous areas. And when we say remote, we mean perhaps 50 houses hundreds of kilometres from the nearest neighbouring settlement.

The remote pastoral and government town community of Katherine and surrounding areas of Binjari and Rockhole were placed into a hard lockdown, with Chief Minister Michael Gunner telling reporters at a Sunday morning press conference on 21 November, 2021, that an operation began overnight that included a coordinated removal of positive cases out of the community.

"It's highly likely that more residents will be transferred to Howard Springs today, either as positive cases or close contacts. We have already identified 38 close contacts from Binjari, but that number will go up. Those 38 are being transferred now."

At the 2016 census Binjari had a population of 190.

Temperatures were soaring into the 40s, and people locked inside their stifling, crowded homes endured as long as they could. The poor suffer as they must. Some households went without power for days.

Mask mandates were introduced across the region, including Miniyera, population 600, the old mission town of Ngukkur, population 200, and Kalkarindji, population 330.

Gunner announced that the "residents of Binjari and Rockhole no longer had the previously existing five reasons to leave their homes," which had included buying food and supplies, exercising for up to two hours, care or caregiving, work, or education.

These restrictions were tightened until members of the community got vaccinated.

"They can only leave for medical treatment, in an emergency, or as required by law."

The measures were the toughest actions deployed in the Northern Territory.

That is, indigenous people living on their own sacred homelands could not leave their homes, even as they watched their neighbours being carted off to a quarantine station, otherwise known as a National Resilience Centre. Or to critics, a concentration camp. You couldn't make this shit up.

***

The Chief Minister said that he had contacted the then Prime Minister Scott Morrison to express his gratitude for the "support" of Defence Force personnel, and the army trucks being used to remove allegedly positive cases.

A rapid assessment team of some 30 personnel hit the ground to begin contact tracing and were deployed from Darwin and Alice Springs to, in the official jargon, "assist residents".

In announcing the Binjari crackdown, Gunner took the opportunity to unleash against those who objected to vaccine mandates and the increased focus on indigenous communities, in a truly stunning display during questions with reporters, in a tirade which attracted attention for all the wrong reasons.

He labelled anyone who disagreed with mandatory vaccination as an "anti-vaxxer".

"If you are anti-mandate, you are absolutely anti-vax. I don't care what your personal vaccination status is. If you support, champion, give a green light, give comfort to, or support anybody who argues against the vaccine – you are an anti-vaxxer. Absolutely. Your personal vaccination status is utterly irrelevant."

Gunner also denounced 'misinformation' from "tinfoil hat wearing tossers". As it turned out, the tinfoil hat wearing tossers were 100% correct.

Gunner's actions created immense fear, confusion and distress across these small communities.

A few short months later, in May of 2022, Michael Gunner, after having played such a vivid role in Australia's Covid derangement, resigned unexpectedly, claiming his heart was no longer in the job and that after the birth of his second child he wanted to spend more time with his family. Maybe, just maybe, he realised the true horror of what he had done.

THIRTEEN
SOS AUSTRALIA:
THE NEW WORLD ORDER

In times of crisis, we summon up our strength. Then, if we are lucky, we are able to call every resource, every forgotten image that can leap to our quickening, every memory that can make us know our power. In this moment when we face horizons and conflicts wider than ever before, we want our resources, the ways of strength. We look again to the human wish, its faiths, the means by which the imagination leads us to surpass ourselves.

Muriel Rukeyser.

The first Saturday of that benighted summer demonstrations were held around the globe under the tagline SOS From Australia.

In a powerful and well produced video Monica Smit of Reignite Democracy Australia says: "Let me paint you a picture. Australia. Once known as one of the safest and freest countries in the world. A land of spirit and ceremony. A land of opportunity, where the hopeful came for a new start, so their children could be free and prosperous. Where the battler had a chance and poor men made good. A land where you were free to explore your surroundings. A land with room to spread your wings.

"A land of brotherhood, celebration and connection. A land where you came to visit and didn't want to leave. A land of privacy rights and medical rights, freedom of speech, freedom of movement, freedom to protest. Freedom to worship.

"But something happened."

Voiceover: "Today is the first day of the New World Order."

Footage. New South Wales Health Minister Brad Hazzard: "We've got to accept that this is the New World Order."

Footage: New South Wales Chief Medical Officer Kerry Chant: "The New World Order."

Back to Monica: "The Australia we once knew is no more."

Footage: Channel 10: "Lockdown Six was announced on August 5."

Monica: "It is no longer the land of the young and free. It is now a land of division, blackmail, coercion, discrimination and medical apartheid. A land where movement, speech, religion and opinion are no longer free. Protesting is illegal. Police must enforce corrupt policies to keep their jobs."

Footage, Krystle Mitchell, Former Acting Senior Sergeant who blew the whistle on the level of discontent within the Victorian Police: "And I won't be a police officer after the end of this interview. "

Monica: "Police shoot protesters in the back while they are running away. Doctors and nurses cannot speak. They will lose their licence."

Footage: Dr Carolyn Bosak, General Practitioner: "I can't really talk about that."

Monica: "People have lost their jobs because they don't want the injection. Children are missing school and attempting suicide at a high rate. We need to show our papers to go shopping."

Footage: David Koch, Seven's Sunrise Breakfast show: "If you want freedom, get the jab."

"We can't travel across state borders unless we apply for permission. Members of parliament are censored and defamed."

Footage: Member of Parliament Craig Kelly: "100% of those studies…" David Koch: "It's a conspiracy theory."

Monica: "Pregnant women are arrested for a social media post."

Footage: Police: "Search warrant." Zoe Buhler: "Search warrant for what?"

Monica: "Activists who fight for democracy are imprisoned."

Footage: Police: "You are under arrest for incitement."

Monica: Our human rights are gone. Our human rights are GONE."

Footage: Member of Parliament George Christensen: "It's time we took off the Covid blinkers and look at what's happened to our once great and free country."

Monica: "Australia can no longer fight for itself. We have been silenced, assaulted, blackmailed and psychologically damaged. We tried to fight this battle alone. The government has instilled so much fear that we have lost our vigour to fight. We are a broken nation. And although we will never give up we need your help to continue our fight.

"We need help from our international friends. We are seeking your support to apply political and economic pressure on our leaders to change the destructive path that we are on. That is why we are organising a worldwide protest in support of our plight for freedom. This is an official SOS from my beautiful country. We plead with you to hear our cries for help."

The flyer read: "S.O.S. from Australia. Protest on our behalf at your nearest Australian Embassy or Consulate. #SOSfromAustralia."

***

That same weekend the Bill Gates funded and to all appearances aligned *Guardian Australia* reported the government's announcement that Covid vaccines could soon be rolled out for children as young as five.

"If all goes well, the doses will be rolled out from January," the paper declared.

At the same time, the streets swarmed, and supportive demonstrations were held around the world, including in Helsinki in Finland, Lisbon in Portugal and Frankfurt in Germany. At a protest in New York a large sign read: "You Are Not Alone Australia".

There were also protests around Australia.

Incensed, upset, stirred and disturbed you could say, Old Alex wrote in A Sense of Place Magazine: As Australia disintegrates before our eyes, one extraordinary event follows another with extreme rapidity. What was once a slow motion train wreck is now a collision with destiny at lightning speed.

Australia has become an international pariah for its absurd mismanagement of the Covid scare and the outrageous abuse of its own citizens, who have been fined, bashed, bullied, imprisoned and pilloried by taxpayer funded functionaries.

The past ten days have in themselves been extraordinary.

Protests have been held around the world under the banner SOS Australia in support of the nation's increasingly powerful freedom movement.

While the nation's political leaders look more and more ridiculous with every passing hour, thousands of people across the country, teachers, nurses, police, health workers and many others are being sacked for not being double vaccinated; as well sourced stories about thousands of vaccine deaths and hundreds of thousands of vaccine injuries spread like wildfire across the internet, ensuring many people are a damn sight more frightened of the vaccine than the virus.

The Premier of Victoria Daniel Andrews, the man responsible for pepper spraying grandmothers in the street, arresting pregnant women in their own homes and instituting the longest and most destructive lockdowns in the world, has granted himself dictatorial powers.

In the Northern Territory the indigenous are being removed from their homelands and placed in quarantine camps, while Premiers around the country, not content with the rampant destruction of people's lives and businesses over the last two years, are now making hay with the Omicron Variant.

But if you listen to the majority of the nation's politicians, or to its execrable mainstream media, you would have no idea. As many commentators have noted, the single most frightening aspect of recent times is not "the virus", but the willingness of the population to accept the destruction of their own liberties.

What is equally frightening is the shocking dishonesty of the mainstream media and their "journalists".

As hundreds upon hundreds of thousands of people had demonstrated across the country in recent months, and were now sparking sympathetic rallies around the globe, the national newspaper *The Australian*, where Old Alex worked for 15 long years, entirely misrepresented the situation. Once proudly regarding itself as a paper of record, it preposterously and dishonestly claimed in a caption for a contradictory photograph that the number of demonstrators were confined to a courageous few. There was only one plausible reason: the millions of dollars being funded to the media by the Australian government under the cover of Covid was distorting its coverage.

The newspaper had always been a schizophrenic beast, sometimes good, sometimes bad, but the caption on a contradictory picture of a street jam-packed with protestors took the cake. It read: "A rare freedom protest in Sydney at which a few brave souls stood up to authoritarian overreach."

The freedom protests were not rare, and the brave souls were not few.

Their sheer blatant dishonesty during the Covid era entirely discredited the legacy media, and led to a rise in independent media.

Everywhere in the mycelium of the age, social media, the channels thronged with images of Australia self-destructing.

***

Dreams, were they really dreams, swirled through his consciousness, there in the reaches of that remote south coast. If in time there was a place like this, if in time we were all born into a Garden of Eden, if in time there was a placement, overwhelmed and overwhelming, the scale of the tragedy now being visited upon them was too much for any one person to bear, and he walked free, but it was not about his freedom. He was as shocked, stunned might be a better word, by what was unfolding as anybody else. You didn't have to fast forward very far to see a Biblical time of tribulation.

In some senses Old Alex was more comfortable in his own skin than at any other time in his life, but it was not about him. It was about a scale of a tragedy, it was about an extremity of human experience, it was about the blind leading the blinded and the enormous consequence of it all; as death rates began to soar, as the cold, hard reality began to seep through the bones of those who had been hoodwinked, who had thought they were doing the right thing.

He watched in disbelief as old newspaper colleagues, people he had thought intelligent, progressive, the pushers of boundaries, congratulated each other on getting their booster and poured scorn on the unvaxxed; the outliers they would once have supported; people outside the swim.

The quiet was terrifying; that was true, the silence of the suburbs, but this, now, was a more imperilled quiet, as if the corruption of the polity spread though the mainstream media he had once been so proud to be part of. Regrets, that bout of shame, guilt, regret and remorse so familiar to the dissolute, figured through his own life after another bender, and he, in a dismally bewildered fashion, puzzled over the rank stupidity of it all. The public queued, queued, to get vaccinated and tested. They drove across town to vaccinate their own children.

They shouldered a responsibility, those active members of a rising, contradictory, dissident storm, and while the mainstream media continued to be loyal to their funding source, the government, and continued to peddle a narrative with less and less credibility, his own disbelief compounded. How could it be? How could this be possible?

It was a scorn, they poured, on their fellows. But more and more the scorn ran both ways.

Prime Minister Scott Morrison's polling plunged. The election had to be held by the 21st of May, 2022, the very last thing he wanted to face.

Leader of the Opposition Anthony Albanese might be as bad or worse; as ludicrous, preposterous, out of touch and ignorant, deliberately ignorant, but you had to get rid of one before you got rid of the other.

The country was becoming increasingly ungovernable; had been heading that way for many years; with its creaking bureaucracies and extravagant wastes of public money, disconnected from the people public officials were meant to serve.

We come at the End of Empire. We are partial to that partial light. We have always been and will always be.

And in the awe of it, the magisterial awe of it, from Old Alex's end there was no doubt the imperial warship had arrived. If anything, he prayed for courage. The ravishing, in a sense, that same social and geo-spatial phenomenon they once called The Coming of Christ. These elementors had begun their evolution long before humans. And they were now a lateral lightning across the planet.

***

Responding to the SOS call from Reignited Democracy Australia, Christine Anderson, a Member of the European Parliament, said: "I will do whatever I can to make it known to the world that your once free and liberal democracy has been transformed into a totalitarian regime which tramples on human rights, civil liberties and the rule of law."

Anderson was one of the most single mindedly courageous and outspoken Members of the European Parliament on the malfeasance which characterised the Covid Era.

In a clip widely distributed on Twitter and YouTube and across social and alternative media, Member of the European Parliament since 2019 Christine Anderson declared: "This message goes out to the people of Australia. I am a member of the European Parliament. And I am answering your

SOS call. I am imploring all of you around the world who still think your governments are looking out for your best interests. At no point in history have the people forcing others into compliance been the good guys.

"The welfare of humanity has always been the alibi of tyrants. Do you not realise that this vaccine does not protect you from Covid?

"It does, however, protect you from governmental oppression – for now, that is. But don't think for even a second that this is not going to change tomorrow.

"I'm a German, and we once asked our grandparents how they could have just stood by in silence, allowing a horrific, totalitarian regime to come about. Anyone could have known. All they had to do was open their eyes and take a look. The vast majority chose not to. So, what will you tell your grandchildren? Will you tell them you didn't know? Will you tell them you were just following orders?

"You need to understand this is not about breaking the fourth wave. It is all about breaking people.

"Australia does not need a 'No Covid' strategy. What Australia needs is a 'No Oppression strategy'.

"So I stand in support of Australia with your fight for freedom and democracy. We need to stop our governments from transforming our free and democratic societies into totalitarian regimes.

"We need to do it now. We need to stand up now."

***

Scandal after scandal enveloped Australia's quarantine centres over excessive costs, failed deadlines and poor utilisation.

Anyone who doubted this was a nationally coordinated whole of government fiasco didn't have to look very far.

There were now Quarantine Camps, in Orwellian Newspeak known as Resilience Centres, up and running around the country.

Christmas Island: North West Point Immigration Detention Centre, Phosphate Hill, Construction Camp Alternative Places of Detention (Alpha, Bravo, Charlie).

Northern Territory: National Resilience Centre (a.k.a., Manigurr-ma) and the Todd Facility (part of the Mercure Alice Springs Resort).

Queensland: Damascus Barracks (a.k.a., National Resilience Centre) and Queensland Regional Accommodation Centre.

Victoria: Alternative Quarantine Accommodation (a.k.a., National Resilience Centre, Mickleham).

Western Australia: Bullsbrook Training Area (a.k.a., National Resilience Centre).

Referring to his state's vaccination programme and health passport system, Victoria's Premier Daniel Andrews said: "Why would you have that thing up and running and then pull all the architecture that you have built, all the infrastructure that you have built, the culture that you have changed – why would you change that four, five weeks later? We will not do that."

Indeed, why would you spend hundreds of millions of dollars to build a string of ghost barracks?

Already the fear was abroad in the community: If they can do it once, they can do it again. They can imprison anyone they like. They can imprison everybody.

**

All the way into 2023 the Federal Finance Department carried the proud announcement: "The Australian Government is working cooperatively with all states and territories to implement measures to control the spread of COVID19 and to maintain a robust quarantine system that keeps all Australians safe.

"The Australian Government is partnering with state governments to deliver Centres for National Resilience in Melbourne, Brisbane and Perth – purpose-built quarantine facilities that will support overseas travel and ensure the safety of the Australian community. The Commonwealth has entered into Memoranda of Understanding with Victoria on 4 June 2021, Queensland on 16 August 2021, and Western Australia on 16 August 2021 for delivery of these Centres.

"The completion of the first beds at the Centre for National Resilience Melbourne is expected by the end of 2021.

"The first beds in Perth and in Brisbane are expected to be complete by the end of the first quarter 2022.

"The Commonwealth will fund the construction of the Centres and state governments will be responsible for the operation and management of the facilities following construction completion and for the duration of the COVID-19 pandemic.

"Following delivery of 1,000 beds in Melbourne, and 500 beds in each of Brisbane and Perth, the Commonwealth Government will review the capacity requirements to determine if additional capacity is required. The Centres will be able to expand quickly to meet future needs, with design and broad infrastructure requirements already determined to enable a fast ramp-up of any additional future capacity."

Much of what happened inside these camps, the ones already in existence, built or repurposed, was concealed from public view and immune to journalistic scrutiny, not that any of the nation's captive media were trying too hard.

While Old Alex hadn't personally tried, no doubt any working journalist would find getting access to these facilities and to the people detained within nigh on impossible; the bureaucratic processes involved about as easy to negotiate as the wall of obfuscation or point blank refusal one faced when trying to access the nation's prisons.

***

Tormented by isolation, in the predawn Old Alex found himself doing Buddhist exercises by the lake, while the same phrases kept repeating through his head, an insistent messaging from afar. They did not want him to be mistaken, to misunderstand his role, to fail in his duty, those spirits mixed into the eternal ether, those emanations from both afar near, entwined into his own sense of place.

It felt to him as if the rampant, uncoordinated and highly competitive development of artificial intelligence had been before, in the birth of angels and demons, gods and devils; even as the well established theory of The Big Bang, the beginning of everything, collapsed with the echo of far more ancient worlds. It had all happened before. In this case, the déjà vu was real. We were marooned in the infinite.

This remarkably fecund planet had been fought over for millennia, but now there was something different about it, something so blindingly insane, so evil, so indifferent to the people they harmed, so cold in their pursuit of power that it was beyond the reach of human intellect, in this frightening time when frightening entities stirring along the lake's edge.

Overhead, the imperial warship had arrived, and was settling above them into a time and place, a circular whirl, a vast movement. There was no one single intellect, no one single voice. They moved across the waters. Yes, they had been here before.

They were planning regicide, and we were all servants when it came to this kind of power, magisterial, beyond time and space, beyond anything commonly understood; and the country? The minutiae of hazard affected everybody, big and small.

His were only small concerns in contrast to the genuine crises inflicted on so many people. Nonetheless: When the vaccination requirements were lifted at the local library Old Alex made a failed attempt to join a book club, anything to improve his social life. They're lovely people, you'll fit right in, the council's book club officer told him.

At the only meeting he attended, sitting in the rather comfortable surrounds of a new council library, looking out across a half landscaped park, part of the procedure was to talk about the books you had read most recently. Old Alex had just read Robert F. Kennedy's *The Real Anthony Fauci*, and Alex Berenson's *Pandemia*, so he spoke about them.

Bristling, a retired school teacher said: "Do you mind if I ask? Are you vaccinated?"

"No," he replied.

"I won't be able to come back to the book club if there's someone unvaccinated here. I was one of the founding members."

When it became clear there could be no common ground, Alex made an attempt to be conciliatory. "They have certainly divided the country," he said.

She snapped straight back: "Who are they?"

"Bureaucrats, politicians."

It was the same everywhere. Friends. Families. Communities. All were divided on the question of vaccination, and who was inconsiderate enough, insane enough, not to get "the jab".

The diabolical nature of what had happened, of the perpetrators, the scale of the crime, it left him absent without leave; and his head kept covering the same ground over and over again.

"I keep forgetting to breathe," he had said to someone down at the local cafe.

"Don't they have air where you come from?" came the rejoinder.

"No," he replied.

Truthfully enough. They looked at him as if he was mad. "An out of body experience," one of the Watchers on the Watch explained to his younger colleague.

Think what you like. We live in a quantum world. And so it was, that terrible glitch in history, when time folded in upon itself and they were all helpless.

Had they planned to do this all along, those human oligarchs, the holders of the reigns of power over an entire species? It increasingly looked like it could be so.

***

The Australian authorities must have known, even as they were gaslighting the the Australian public, urging them to get vaccinated, even foisting it on the nation's schoolchildren, that alarm bells were going off all around the world; that increasing numbers of people believed the Covid story had already been exposed as fraudulent and that the "safe and effective" mantra was an outright lie perpetrated purely for the sake of profit.

One might think that even if they could ignore the massive disruption to Australian society and the hundreds of thousands of people marching in the streets, that the many tales of vaccine injuries and the suffering of children might have affected the stone cold hearts of Australia's bureaucrats. You'd be mistaken.

Early in the New Year of 2022 then Federal Health Minister Greg Hunt proudly announced that 73 percent of the nation's 12 to 15 year old children had been fully vaccinated. Children aged 5 to 11 could now come forward and "benefit from the protection a COVID-19 vaccination provides".

Children in that cohort, as had been widely documented around the world, were at virtually zero risk from Covid as their natural immunity simply shrugged it off. But there they were, Australia's Covidian class, vaccinating the nation's children with an experimental gene therapy which did not prevent infection, or transmission, and for which the safety data was alarming.

It was a sad madness. Beyond sad. A terrible, frightening lunacy.

Internet censorship and manipulation by Google and Facebook at the behest of their military, government and Big Pharma clients made it difficult for the average punter to find out the truth of what was going on, to discover that there was another very alarming and highly credible narrative.

The injecting of billions of people required massive manipulation of social and legacy media; and a full out effort to discredit anyone who dared to disagree with the narrative of Pfizer and Bill Gates in particular.

Nonetheless, it is in the coverup that the story almost always comes undone. And so it was in this case. Why, if it was not a scam, would such heavy censorship, suppression of alternative views and media manipulation be required; not to drown out a few nutjob conspiracy theorists, but some of the most highly educated and intelligent people on the planet?

***

The fact that the vaccines were ever approved much less promoted in Australia would later become a head shaking tongue clicking bewilderment; and even now there was so much evidence out there for the case against mass vaccination, including the nation's children, it should clearly have been given active consideration. There was no excuse for ignorance.

Just as one example, it is to this day hard to imagine why Australia's health bureaucrats and politicians would ignore such a highly intelligent and well regarded man as Reiner Fuellmich, who had repeatedly warned that the Covid-19 story was a fraud. But ignore him they did; instead mandating vaccines and urging the population to get their boosters.

Dr Fuellmich is an international trial lawyer licensed to practise in Germany and California with 27 years of practice who specialises in corporate fraud and had successfully sued large corporations including Volkswagen and Deutsche Bank on behalf of the public.

In September of 2021, before the excoriating Grand Jury of Public Opinion began its forensic examination the following year, the Berlin-based Corona Investigation Committee of which Fuellmich was a leading figure released a report alleging what many already feared, that the Covid-19 "pandemic" was planned, that the virus was man-made, and that the heavily manipulated government and media hysteria had the sole aim of funnelling people into vaccination.

The story made no sense until one realised the vaccine was not made for the virus, but the virus for the vaccine.

According to Dr Fuellmich, a second Nuremberg trial was on the cards, to prosecute all who were complicit in this unprecedented crime against humanity. Already at street demonstrations across Australia t-shirts and placards read "Nuremberg 2.0."

Fuellmich spoke in a measured, lawyerly tone:

"Our hearings prove the following results beyond a reasonable doubt.

"The Covid measures were never about health. We don't have a pandemic. We have a virus circulating that any human with an intact immune system can fight just as well as the flu. Our governments, at least almost all European governments as well as that of the US, are not acting in the best interests of their people but are largely under the control of global corporations and NGOs."

In the months ahead Fuellmich would flesh out the Committee's findings of deliberate fraud, unreliable PCR tests and dangerous vaccines from a string of highly credible witnesses into an event badged the Grand Jury of the Court of Public Opinion.

Fuellmich said that at the conclusion of the case and after all the evidence was submitted, he was confident that participants would recommend indictments for crimes against humanity against all six putative figurehead defendants: German virologist Professor Christian Drosten; Chief White House medical advisor Anthony Fauci; World Health Organization Director-General Tedros Adhanom Ghebreyesus; Microsoft founder and vaccinology philanthropist Bill Gates; COVID vaccine manufacturer Pfizer and multinational investment management corporation BlackRock.

"They are using the mainstream media and our governments, both of which they literally own, to convey their panic propaganda 24/7. Since July 10, 2020, we have consulted with about 150 distinguished scientists and experts from all around the world. If someone had told me a year and a half ago that the outcome of the Corona Committee's work to date would be this, I would have told them to take their pills and see their doctor."

All this evidence was available to any Australian authority who cared to look. They chose to look the other way, to where the money lay.

Crimes against humanity. Even in his windswept valley, Old Alex played his tiny role. Others played theirs.

Pin pricks in history. You had to believe it mattered; not just because of the scale of it, the billions who were impacted; but beyond that.

A time for all time. An extremity of the human experience which would become a case study of horror and malfeasance in the years to come; no matter the evolution of the species.

The inescapable conclusion is that the Australian authorities must have known, even as they supported the bashing and pepper spraying of protestors, that there were serious ethical, moral, judicial, and medical issues surrounding the vaccines; as they pushed on with vaccinating millions of Australians, including school children. A vaccine which had already demonstrably damaged large numbers of people, and had truly appalling safety signals.

***

That was then and this was now.

The Earthlings, those primitives, were trying to manipulate the time flow. That was the only reason they were interested in him.

Isolated, depressed, drinking way too heavily, like, one could easily say, so many others in that period, in Old Alex's inflamed imagination a lone standard bearer appeared on the hilltop opposite, repeatedly, coming to see if he was still there, if he was receptive to their messaging, if, as they loved him from afar, he could hear them. Not him as a person. But as a message stone in the flow of history.

The Shepherd's Hut, the Beginning of Empire, was only slowly beginning to be established.

Time flowed over all of us, yet it was here, in this place, at this point, that we found ourselves, "time itself, the magic length of God"; in this crucible of an era. At the End of Empire, the American empire, the rule of corrupt oligarchs.

***

Australia was wheeling into an election year, the politicians gearing into election mood, and the blatant falsity, it rang across an already suppressed and tawdry cultural landscape, full of tin and plastic and sheets of superficial falsity; a deadpan plastic dystopia being born here today; with a sleeping populace, amidst the trees, the surveillance bothering him, as it was meant to do, yet again.

These false warriors gathered at these times, their shallow, callow, brutal, sadistic intent. They served their masters. He served his, not the time lords, but something else.

The sage from four centuries hence, waxed once more into existence; that desperate plea, that desperate search, there in the ruins of their floating cities, there amidst the collapsing polity and the frightening slums of the future, there when they saw another period of a broken history, when they tried to speak outside of time, when they tried to rescue their own broken polity and another cruelty which had just been unleashed, just as was happening here, in the early 2020s.

The incense from that sacred temple, and all around them the starving people, this cruelty and collapse which spoke across time. Be kind to your people. Be kind to your livestock. That was one message that stretched across time.

Or as Hannah Arendt had put it, those who "feel down centuries, soar across continents". Or as Nick Cave repeatedly put it, "we are not alone".

These profundities, they were of little help to the humans of that era, this era, when the blind led the blinded, when all means of public discourse had been corrupted, when communications were not believed, when bully headed military operatives poured scorn upon the divine, when the dimensions beyond everything were dismissed as fantasy, when conflicting agents and agencies created unnecessary storms; and he struggled to focus under the weight of whisky, and quite frankly, despair.

This was what was brought to him. This was what mattered. The battle had been lost.

More and more the people were awakening. And more and more people of conscience were saying: "My God!! What have we done?"

But it was too late to save them.

It was only time to be born anew.

That was the sadness, the overwhelming sadness, of it all; as someone equally as emblematic, from an equally distressed time, signalled to him for understanding, signalled to be free, messaged in despair, desperately tried to save his brothers, hopelessly sought for understanding, and urgently told him how it was that he could leave a message across those interlinking centuries.

The Imperial Warship stood above all this.

It was not for us to divine their reasoning; it was for us to do our duty, each of us in our allotted time.

To be honoured thus.

For Old Alex, these wild fantasies rang true in his heart.

***

Predictably, as state governments issued thousands upon thousands of fines against citizens for going about their usual business or breaching one of the many constantly changing diktats which had turned the country into a living, suffering misery, the country's courts were clogged with cases. Every last person who was issued one of those punitive fines felt they had been unfairly treated and were inclined to dispute them. .

Sophie Hickey of the Sydney Criminal Lawyers Blog, one of Old Alex's favourite writers of the period, wrote that in New South Wales alone more than 7,000 people had sought reviews of Covid fines and most have failed, with only one in ten of the reviews lodged with Revenue NSW, rebranded from the pretty much universally loathed State Debt Recovery Office, succeeding.

"Freedom of Information documents revealed there were 50,905 pandemic fines issued from 1 July 1 to 10 October of 2021, a critical period when Sydney was dealing with a significant outbreak of the Delta variant. At the time, NSW Police launched an enforcement blitz.

"On 9 July, NSW police deployed 100 extra officers to Sydney's south-west with the aim of patrolling the streets to ensure the largely migrant population is abiding by lockdown restrictions, such as having a reasonable excuse to be out.

"In August this year, the NSW emergency cabinet adopted regulations drafted by NSW Police – which included increased police presence in all areas, including specialised command officers, riot squad police and 1400 members of the NSW highway patrol.

Additionally, 500 members of the Australian Defence Force joined police operations.

"According to reports, a woman breastfeeding her baby in a park, an elderly man obtaining urgent medical attention, grandmothers looking after their children in the playground and people sitting alone in their car are amongst those people challenging fines.

"The NSW Government has failed to put its trust in the public to make their own decisions and do the right thing by themselves individually, and for their families.

"Instead, we've endured heavy-handed law-enforcement, coercion and the tyranny of vaccination mandates all of which have completely undermined the principles of individual freedom of choice and other principles of democracy as well as contributed to deep social divisions which will take a lot of time to repair."

All of this, as time would soon demonstrate, was for nothing. All this garbage rained down upon the population prevented not one case, saved not one life, and did nothing but cause additional suffering.

That chant among demonstrators, faced with walls of heavily armed police, "You Serve Us", was nothing but a flash of optimism, dismally out of touch. They were the rulers, we were the ruled.

***

Old Alex tried to warn a friend from down the Lakeview who had young children, please don't vaccinate your children. You will come to regret it. He and his wife ignored him. Fast forward a year and guilt, horror and panic ran behind everybody's eyes. You did this to your own children?

Meanwhile doubt was spreading like wildfire, both among health professions and the general public.

The only way through this morass, as many were discovering, was to build alternative systems, an alternative to the much pilloried World Health Organisation, an alternative to the dystopian visions of the World Economic Forum, and in Australia alternatives to the discredited professional bodies, including the Australian Medical Association.

Just as on the street, professional dissidents, with experience and qualifications on their side, gained traction.

The newly formed and almost instantly a significant player, the Australian Medical Professionals Society, joined with the Nurses Professional Association of Australia to pen an open letter to the nation's leaders.

The letter urged the Australian Government and the Therapeutic Goods Administration to take immediate action to prevent harm to Australian children in light of the most recent disclosures of the risks from Pfizer vaccines.

"It came as a huge surprise recently to discover evidence that Pfizer knew about a whole range of adverse events likely connected to their product; a novel gene-based vaccine that departs radically from all prior vaccine technologies. This arose from a freedom of information request to the Food and Drug Administration, which resulted in a court determining the immediate release of the information was in the public interest.

"This new information has particular implications for the roll-out of the gene-based, experimental, investigational, provisionally registered vaccines to preteen children from 10 January 2022.

"It appears the reported adverse events predate the vaccine roll-out in Australia. The report itself was finalised by Pfizer on 30 April 2021, a couple of months after the Australian roll-out commenced.

"This report reveals that Pfizer were well aware of a vast array of previously unknown vaccine adverse events, including 1200+ deaths compiled in a period of only 10 weeks. Pfizer conceded this is a large increase in adverse event reports and it is apparent this significant volume of adverse events is not the full story. Over 100+ conditions are listed, many of which are very serious.

"These medical conditions include cardiac diseases, haematological conditions, renal conditions, autoimmune disorders and neurological conditions.

"There is strong evidence to suggest that Pfizer has withheld vital information from Australian governments and the broader international community.

"The risk/benefit ratio in children, which was not in favour of Covid-19 vaccination originally, is now very likely to be very negative by any reasonable assessment.

"In the light of this new Pfizer data, it appears not to be contentious to say that Australian children will be harmed by this product.

"We request that you suspend the availability of these gene-based vaccines for all children immediately."

The letter was ignored.

The country had already entered its own Heart of Darkness.

***

Australia's high handed apparatchiks ignored not just their own doctors, nurses, academics and the hundreds of thousands marching on the streets, but the daily flood of international evidence putting the lie to the Australian government's utterly irresponsible fear mongering.

As one of Australia's most distinguished, experienced and insightful journalists, Rebecca Weisser wrote in *Spectator Australia*, the Israeli predicament, equally pertinent to her own country, was sparking an outbreak of truth telling. Israel, in common with Australia, was in the process of becoming one of the most highly vaccinated countries on Earth.

"It must be galling for Australia's political leaders and health advisers that, having bludgeoned and bullied almost every Australian into getting vaccinated, the country is second only to Israel, which this week broke the global record for daily Covid cases.

"Morrison is desperate to point out that it's not his fault. There has been no policy to let Covid 'rip'. Regulations are still in place enforcing masks, distancing, density limits, isolation, testing and vaccination. What is painfully obvious is that they are not working.

"NSW and Victoria have announced that booster shots can now be given every three months in a desperate attempt to stem the tide of infections. Good luck with that. A clinical trial in Israel has found that a fourth dose of the Pfizer vaccine doesn't prevent infection by Omicron any more than did the third."

Professor Ehud Qimron, head of the Department of Microbiology and Immunology at Tel Aviv University and one of the leading Israeli immunologists, wrote: "In the end, the truth will always be revealed. When the destructive concepts collapse one by one, there is nothing left but to tell the experts who led the management of the pandemic – we told you so.

"Two years late, you finally realise that a respiratory virus cannot be defeated. You have failed miserably in almost all of your actions, and even the media is already having a hard time covering your shame.

"You have not set up an effective system for reporting side effects from the vaccines, and reports on side effects have even been deleted from your Facebook page.

"You slandered colleagues who did not surrender to you, you turned the people against each other, divided society and polarised the discourse. You branded, without any scientific basis, people who chose not to get vaccinated as enemies of the public and as spreaders of disease.

"The truth is that you have brought the public's trust in you to an unprecedented low, and you have eroded your status as a source of authority. The truth is that you have burned hundreds of billions of shekels to no avail – for publishing intimidation, for ineffective tests, for destructive lockdowns and for disrupting the routine of life in the last two years."

***

If you didn't feel sad about this era of Australian history, you weren't sentient.

The human part of Old Alex was gripped by lucid dreams; the part which felt saddened by the clear totalitarian creep, which simply could not believe what was happening all around him, a deeper, darker undertow that was making the country unrecognisable. Outrage after authoritarian outrage just became accepted as the norm, while above the ancient spirits, a slow wing above us all, sometimes as if an ethereal stingray soared through the skies above, a million years nothing to it, and here we were, making all the mistakes of little men.

It was the same imagery that had haunted him since the beginning of this crisis, this civilisational collapse, where the spirits of earth and sky washed and lapped from distant shores and soared over this place as the imperial warship settled above. For the gods were roiled. And their time was now.

Viewed from the future, one would have expected the population to be in revolutionary ferment. But instead the suburbs still slept, and the matrons tutted, and the warlords strutted, and the dismal political class tried repeatedly to lie themselves out of trouble, and when all was lost, well not lost, destroyed, when their moment in the sun, this species, how beautiful this planet had been, he could yet but marvel at how dismal, viewed from inside their cultural torment, this situation had become.

His own swarm began signalling death in other times, those who would torment him, for time would do more harm to these people than he could ever do. But he was dangerous now, "in the pastures of the Lord", and would brook no more the intelligence operatives ridicule and idiot setups and moronic castigating of sexuality or difference, these crimes on two legs who should have long been abolished. In a different time and position of power, he would have ordered their throats slit in a second, for yes, the likes of him were born of fire and conflict and adversity. He could sense them now, whenever they were near, and the words would flash: "Hostile".

And he would say to them: "Beware."

But the time for warnings was over.

What would happen here today, what would happen in this place, would fold over into that linking point of the future, where the sages and seers and the unconnected would join. You think we produce billions of seeds because we were born in a comfortable place? You think the lifeforms you see today produce billions of seeds because we did not overcome extreme adversity?

He had drunk too much away, that was true. But in a sense it didn't matter anymore, there was only one task.

The human part of him would watch, compartmentalised, but that didn't matter much anymore either, the idiocy of surveillance which was the Covid state and which he endured personally. The jeers. The scorn. The lashes. The brutality visited upon ordinary people. These increasingly harsh times.

How could one not care?

But they did not care; these humans he watched with an increasing sense of detachment.

"No shortage of tyrants, no shortage of fools."

Well now, you just watch history on the turn.

And you will be forgotten.

But not this anointed task.

***

There was a flurry of incidents bridging into 2022, protests, arrests, a simmering, brewing defiance, and a terrible seeping despair at the madness of it all.

Some of the largest demonstrations were held around the country on the 22nd of January marking a Worldwide Freedom Rally.

On the west coast, following a decision by Premier Mark McGowan to yet again backflip on opening the Western Australian borders after more than 600 days of isolation from the rest of the country, protesters returned to the Central Business District of the state capital Perth. Despite the 40C heat they waved banners, including a placard of McGowan in Nazi uniform, listened to speeches and surged through the streets urging people to "wake up" and "take down the government".

Melbourne once again saw large crowds and a heavy police presence. Signs with slogans such as "my body my choice", "save our children", "free Victoria", "fake news", "be fab stop the jab" and "unvaxxed sperm is the next bitcoin" dominated the streetscape.

Sydney also saw massive crowds; with some protestors wearing bright yellow-t-shirts blazoned with the words: "I stand for freedom."

Protesters were spotted with signs that said "wake up Australia", "we don't need no vaccination", and "stop medical apartheid".

Brisbane also saw large crowds, with music, speeches and a wild enthusiasm marking the rally.

Adelaide, despite wet weather, also saw significant crowds. One banner read: "Faith Courage and Love Over Fear" and "Freedom Freedom Freedom Freedom Forever".

None of this deep stirring of the nation made it into the legacy media where Old Alex had worked much of his life. Now manipulated or taken over by government and corporate interests, the Fourth Estate could no longer be relied on to tell the truth. They sang true to their funding sources, that is government and corporate interests, including pharmaceutical companies, and damaged the country deeply as they pelted forth their falsehoods.

Journalism, as the old saying goes, is the First Draft of History.

Throughout this deeply troubled period of Australian history it was the independent news sites and the newly empowered citizen journalists who became the only true contemporary historians of the weekly protests which transformed Australian cities at the same time as almost all normal civilian life collapsed.

Many, many hundreds of thousands of people had taken to the streets in the previous months, in utterly unprecedented displays of protest which were either ignored or demonised by the nation's bought and sold mainstream media. The abrogation of their civic responsibilities by the nation's journalists, as their outlets have turned into vehicles of government propaganda, was for Old Alex one of the saddest aspects of these times.

One of the only Australian politicians to stand up against the Covid hysteria, Senator Alex Antic of South Australia, wrote: "Almost all of

Australia's big media outlets repeat the same politically correct mantras about every major issue, and those who hold contrary views are often ignored, dismissed, ridiculed, or regarded as dangerous.

"This disturbing trend has never been more apparent than over the past two years, in which the legacy media has manipulated the public into a state of perpetual anxiety over something that is not dangerous to most people.

"One example of this is their ubiquitous support for vaccine mandates, which many Australians oppose for a variety of reasons that must be taken seriously. People who think critically about vaccine mandates realise that they raise a plethora of complex questions that require sound reasoning to navigate and involve moral judgments.

"What role should government play in our personal medical decisions? What authority does the government have to vaccinate children against their parents' will? What right does the government have to restrict the movements and career prospects of people who don't want to be vaccinated? What sort of precedents are being established by this authoritarian creep, and where will it lead? These questions require thoughtful answers, but almost all journalists in legacy media corporations refuse to ask them.

"Instead, they busy themselves with ridiculing so-called 'anti-vaxxers', provoking fear about every death associated with Covid, and continuing to tout the vaccines at every possible moment despite their lack of efficacy in preventing transmission. This is not journalism or honest, facts-based reporting – it is propaganda, and many people who are familiar with the media of communist regimes sense the similarities with our major networks given their uniformity and demonising of dissenters. It doesn't take an epidemiologist to work out that the edicts of our unelected health bureaucrats are arbitrary, oppressive and nonsensical."

***

Part of every Australian summer, in between families with young children filling the public pools and the nation's famous beaches, the infinite feel of hot, gusty wind, is the Australian Open, when the world's most famous tennis players descend on Melbourne Park, and whichever station has managed to procure the broadcasting rights beams the two week tournament into the nation's lounge rooms.

Old ladies tut over the length of dresses or the alleged rudeness of one of the male players, and the psychodrama of competition, the sound of television commentators and the whack of tennis balls, weaves into the summer air.

That year Melbourne Park had an extra piece of psychodrama, as Australian politicians, most particularly the Prime Minister Scott Morrison, seized the opportunity to make an example of Novak Djokovic, the worst of the worst, an unvaccinated person who refused to bow.

The absolute frenzy of the nation's politicians in urging the masses to get vaccinated had nothing to do with their health. Even the most cursory survey of the emerging literature demonstrated that there were serious concerns about the Covid vaccines. It was all about political theatre; consolidating power, and money. Bucketloads of money courtesy of some of the largest pharmaceutical companies on Earth.

Scott Morrison had to face the electorate by May, four short months away, and as the world's only Pentecostal leader, a man who believed God lived and breathed within him, fully expected the divine presence would deliver him another poll defying victory.

And on his path to victory God had delivered unto him the world's most famous tennis player.

Playing to the cheap seats, he was good at that, Morrison declared: 'Rules are rules. To enter Australia you either have to be vaccinated or you have to have a valid medical exemption and show evidence of it. It's as simple as that."

The humiliation of Novak Djokovic and his deportation from Australia provided all the television footage Morrison so desperately craved.

***

Taking to Twitter, back then, as critics attested, little more than a messaging board for American intelligence agencies, Morrison declared: "Mr Djokovic's visa has been cancelled. Rules are rules, especially when it comes to our borders. No one is above these rules. Our strong border policies have been critical to Australia having one of the lowest death rates in the world from COVID, we are continuing to be vigilant."

Soon enough Australia would have one of the highest death rates in the world, but no politician and no bureaucrat put up their hand to take responsibility for that. Success has many fathers, failure none.

Everything the Australian government did during the entire era backfired, destroying the country madness by madness, diktat by diktat, and "Novax Djokovic" became an instant hero to freedom fighters across the land.

The Australian government deliberately stirred the mob, and got exactly what they wanted, with commentators and fellow tennis players flinging their derision at the Serb.

***

Many words were spilled on the saga of Djokovic's deportation, and some of the best were from Kit Knightly at the quirky British magazine *Off Guardian*: "Getting to leave Australia is an odd thing to be considered any kind of punishment these days. Actually it would be an absolute blessing, if any of us could escape.

"Australia has fallen. Peace, prosperity and freedom have been sacrificed on the altar of 'safety', and Covid 'vaccination' has become a quasi-religious rite in their country, even more so than the rest of the world.

"As such, the unvaccinated are slandered, punished, threatened and othered at every turn. Locked down, locked up and locked out.

"Can you only imagine what could happen if people found out it was all for nothing? Or that the heaven-sent vaccines aren't the magical solution to all that ails us?

"In this kind of political climate they simply can't afford to have an 'anti-vaxxer' on national television, healthy and athletic and winning championships against a field of vaccinated rivals."

***

In a piece called Prison Island: I Wish To Be Deported, the ever on fire Paul Collits wrote: "I have spent endless hours trying to think of a way of leaving this God-awful place. A country that is now almost impossible to leave. Just like North Korea and Cuba. The big three liberal democracies. It is as if Hotel California was written for us, now. At the time people thought it was about hell. "You can check out any time you like, but you can never leave." These days, Australia passes as a reasonable simulacrum for the place down below. Down under, perhaps.

"Why leave Australia? Well, post-Djokovic, clearly I and countless others who are guilty of thought crimes and modern-day leprosy are no longer welcome here. Immigration Minister Alex Hawke said so. He and his boss fear a tennis player becoming a lightning rod for an emerging protest movement. A protest movement potentially with electoral consequences. There is no way that anyone remotely sentient believes that Novak Djokovic is a health threat to anyone. Are these people serious?

"A Liberal Government condemning someone, actually fearing someone, who would stand up for liberty and against the infringement of basic individual rights. Wow. No wonder people of principle, independence of thought, backbone and conscience, don't want a bar of the place any more."

As the sentiment went: what had become problematic in modern Australia was not that we were descended from convicts, but that we are descended from prison guards. The officers who volunteered for duty in Australia back in colonial times seemed to be driven by exceptional sadism. Even small violations of the rules could result in a punishment of 100 lashes by the cat o'nine tails. It was said that blood was usually drawn after five lashes and convicts ended up walking home in boots filled with their own blood – that is, if they were able to walk.

As one of Old Alex's favourite writers of the period, Professor Ramesh Thakur of the Australian National University wrote: "The international humiliation inflicted so publicly on Djokovic in pursuit of vaccine apartheid was morally corrupt. It lacked both scientific justification and hard data in support. It indulged a government's every illiberal instinct to control information and bully people into compliance. Djokovic's deportation was petty, vindictive and an example of medical tyranny.

"The claim that 'No-vax' Djokovic poses a threat to others' health is risible. Djokovic had to be kept out of Australia not because he could infect other people, but because he is a visible reminder of vaccine failure. The government was terrified that a twice-infected but unvaccinated Djokovic, flaunting his athletic prowess on the pitch for a record 21st Major triumph, could end the constant escalation of COVID terror.

"The capacity of authorities and governments to stubbornly – even cussedly – ignore facts, data, and evidence throughout the pandemic has been awe-inspiring."

***

On the final day of January 2022, as people around the country began their preparations to descend on the nation's capital for the historic Canberra Convoy, Old Alex, as editor, ran in *A Sense of Place Magazine* a piece called First We Must Grieve, by social worker Julie Birky. Because he could. She wrote as follows.

To move forward in a healthy way, society needs to mourn the many losses of the past two years; the loss of those who have died with Covid, and from Covid, and those who have died having nothing to do with Covid.

We need to mourn a missed cancer diagnosis, a new struggle with addiction, and our child's newly diagnosed mental illness.

We need time and space to mourn the loss of hope we had and plans we made, of businesses closed, of church groups no longer meeting, of relationships with co-workers we won't get back, of trust in institutions, and of our previous understanding of health. Parents, grandparents, children, teens, and community members all need time to grieve for childhoods halted, rites of passage cancelled, and celebrations skipped.

We should not be ashamed or afraid to lament the sadness that comes with moving away from homes we loved, parks and theatres we won't visit again, careers we said goodbye to, and travel plans postponed so many times we simply cancelled them. We must allow ourselves to feel sadness at the loss of time we simply cannot get back, at much anticipated experiences that were instead spent in isolation and loneliness.

It is healthy to feel the sorrow of goodbyes only said in our hearts, of weddings had in a room with one stranger instead of filled with loved-ones, and of lonely funerals with covered faces where masks were the only things that soaked up our tears.

It is time to set aside our Covid divisions and grieve.

I encourage you to come together in your homes, churches, libraries or schools and invite anyone who has lost something over the past two years to mourn together; begin to remake connections through shared losses and grieve with one another. Collective grief can build the empathy and connection lost since pandemic restrictions began. You can make this connection with just one person or with a large gathering of people. When we give ourselves time and space to grieve together, our shared feeling becomes the first stitch that binds society back together.

There will be a time for demanding answers and seeking justice. But first, we must grieve.

Margaret Mead once said: "Never doubt that a small group of thoughtful, committed citizens can change the world; indeed, it's the only thing that ever has."

FOURTEEN
CONVOY TO CANBERRA

Make a stand
While you can
For your lucky land
Raise your flag, fight for your rights
It's in your hands
Make a stand, while you can, for your lucky land
The fight for freedom is never over
If you're locked Down Under

Dusty Starr.

IT'S HARD TO overstate the crushed, hermetic, demonic feel that had settled across the Australian psyche after two years of lockdowns, border closures, social distancing, mask wearing, mass vaccination and mass psychological operations perpetrated on the people. Old Alex felt it keenly, stranded there in that long valley, a prisoner of himself as much as a prisoner of the authorities.

Thus it was that he came to be present at one of the largest and most politically charged gatherings in Australian history, the Convoy to Canberra.

Although as the editor of A Sense of Place Magazine he had republished plenty of material on the anti-lockdown, anti-mandate demonstrations which had been building across the country over the previous two years, for him it had been as if they were happening somewhere else. He had never actually been to one himself. His role was at the keyboards, so he thought; to flail there in the flesh, well that was for the young and the bold.

Emerging from those lonely windswept days, he was down at his local cafe, the Village Fix, enjoying a moment of camaraderie with the regulars over coffee when, one blessed morning, he encountered a man who had been down at the gathering protests in Canberra, and was talking enthusiastically about how wonderful it was. He was only back in Shellharbour to grab a change of clothes and sort a couple of things, and then was going straight back.

Like so many others during that period of extended lockdowns, Old Alex had become more or less a hermit. It was as if his own life as a city reporter and a fully fledged, sociable human being, caught in the midst of the hurly burly of life, was at an end, extinguished.

Intrigued by the tales of the Canberra protest he asked, how hard it was to get there and where one might stay.

And he heard for the first time the words, Camp Epic. Sleep in the car. Park anywhere. Everybody will help you.

So he went home, packed up his car, and headed to Canberra.

Like so many others, called to be there.

***

The humanitarian crimes committed by Australian authorities against their own citizens, beginning in early 2020, would live on in infamy, but it is the people themselves who create a nation's history.

On the 12th of February 2022, one of the largest gatherings of Australians in the nation's history marched on the National Parliament in Canberra to protest the totalitarianism of the Australian Government, chanting "Sack Them All, Sack Them All".

Crowd numbers are notoriously difficult to calculate and prone to distortion. Estimates varied between demonstrably incorrect official figures of 4-10,000, up to three million. Many estimates settled around the 1.4 million figure.

At the very least it's fair to say, and demonstrably correct, that many hundreds of thousands of Australians, having lost all faith in their government, descended on the national capital.

Whatever the exact number no politician, intelligence agency, police force or political strategist in Australia failed to notice that a massive number of people marched on the nation's capital, with a remarkable amount of good cheer, jubilance and camaraderie; character traits which the nation's leaders had failed to show in the previous two years of authoritarian derangement.

Between 2020 and 2022 Australia was gripped by a madness which was spiritual, administrative, political, social and judicial in its dimensions.

Sentenced to the role of scribe, his humble record could do only a little to document this profound turning point in Australian history.

In the preceding two years many thousands of Australians had stood up against the rising tide of tyranny, only to find themselves pepper sprayed, bashed by police in repressive, dictatorial abuses which made headlines around the world, imprisoned, fined, thrown out of their jobs, socially marginalised and ridiculed in the mainstream media.

Across the preceding two years there had been one remarkable demonstration after another, attracting at first tens, then hundreds, then thousands, then hundreds of thousands of participants.

But if the nation's government manipulated mainstream media was to be believed, they numbered only a few, and all were either nut jobs or conspiracy theorists.

Nothing could have been further from the truth; but the protestors, from all walks of life, were given no credit and no voice – until they found their own.

There is an odd resonance to events of this era, as if the destruction of Australia was only an afterthought; that all the millions of people's lives destroyed by megalomaniacal politicians, Pfizer or Bill and Melinda Gates funded academics and lunatic, over-paid, self-aggrandising health bureaucrats barely even rated a mention in the power centres of the globe.

Australia's democracy proved virus thin.

Those who claimed Australia was merely a testing ground for technofascism gained a new credibility.

A nation which once prided itself on its laissez faire approach to life and the friendly, easy going nature of its population lay besmirched by a descent into totalitarianism.

All the systems Australians had come to rely on failed them at their time of greatest need; every last one of them.

The mainstream media, the social media platforms, the legal profession, the courts, the politicians, the bureaucrats, the medical profession, the police, the military, and not least of all the universities, with their filthy hordes of snake oil peddlers and intellectual traitors loyal to their government and vaccine manufacturer funding sources.

***

The drive from Shellharbour to Canberra is nigh on three hours. From that imperilled valley, printed with ill will from the agencies, messages from afar and his own sense of dread, he made the trip without incident.

Old Alex found Camp Epic, on the outskirts of Canberra without difficulty, operating at other times as the city's Showgrounds, and joined the line of cars and passed the gates without being checked. There were smiling people everywhere as he entered what seemed like a city of tents and caravans, yet again that mediaeval feeling of a great gathering, a preparation for battle.

Everywhere he looked people had already established their camps, or were in the process of erecting tents. He asked where he could find a spot, and was directed up the road to a small secondary showground.

He found a vacant spot next to the perimeter fence and parked. He had never been a camper, more the colourful life of cheap hotels for the likes of him, but never mind. An improvised canteen had gone up, feeding hundreds of people with donated supplies, and he grabbed a cup of tea and a sandwich. Everyone he met was friendly and delighted to be there, everyone had something to say.

He asked his way down to the administration of the Convoy, and presented himself at the door of a building beneath a set of large stands looking out over the main showground. He presented the "doorman" with a copy of *Unfolding Catastrophe: Australia*, told him he was a retired journalist and was wondering if he could be of any use.

He was welcomed in and directed to an impromptu media desk set up in the corner, where already established was Perry from Reignite Democracy Australia, Damo, a professional photographer from far north Queensland, and a good deal of coming and going from other parties. He set up his laptop, and began writing daily stories for his magazine. Just like that, he was slapbang in the middle of things, again. He couldn't have been happier.

There has always been one truly great thing about the sometimes freewheeling and not always rewarding profession of journalism; it gives you every excuse to observe events at close quarters, to ask anybody anything, and to look down and across both sides of a fence.

***

Churches and places of worship had been closed for two years, and these congregations of believers denied a fundamental aspect of their humanity. Equally, for the secular, those who saw their pubs, clubs and beer gardens as their "churches", had been denied an essential part of being human, getting pissed with their mates.

A fundamental part of the spiritual experience is the realisation that we are not alone; and whether or not that awakening is of the spirit, or simply to the communality of the human experience, significant numbers of participants believed the divine was at hand.

The long periods of government imposed isolation and absence from all normal forms of communality added to the joy and triumphal nature of the event.

Spiritual wars all have epicentres, and a large number of people, whether of religious or spiritual bent or not, spoke of the spiritual nature of the event.

Many of the individuals Old Alex interviewed expressed almost identical sentiments: "I was compelled to be here. I was drawn here. I just knew I had to be here; I couldn't not be here. I woke up and God was in my head, and told me I had to go to Canberra. I just got in my car and drove."

***

It was at this very juncture in history that citizen journalists and independent outlets displaced "legacy" media as a primary source of information for millions of Australians.

Streamers, bloggers, essentially anyone with a smartphone, pumped out stories and footage in a tsunami of alternative information which well and truly dwarfed the legacy media's increasingly poorly performing "news" outlets.

Mainstream media, always the subject of government manipulation, became a primary source of disinformation and fear mongering.

The government offered backdoor funding and tax concessions to newspapers and television stations to peddle their Covid messaging. Loyal to their funding sources, trapped by their failing business models and declining revenue streams, the media lost all impartiality, and thereby credibility.

You lie by commission or omission; and throughout the period beginning in 2020 the mainstream media lied constantly. Australia became a profoundly dishonest country.

With the death toll from suicides, broken businesses, broken lives and vaccine injuries mounting by the day, the nation's journalists literally helped the nation's politicians get away with murder.

Tell a younger generation that journalism used to be a respected reputation, and they look at you like you're from Mars.

In the parallel universe of government manipulated media and taxpayer funded academia it was as if nothing was happening, as mainstream journalists continued to ignore one of the biggest stories of their lifetimes, Australia's independent media was on fire.

***

David Oneeg, an impassioned singlet wearing Australian with an enthusiastic following the size of which would be the envy of many a mainstream journalist, became a classic of the new genre of citizen journalism with his podcast Aussie Chat.

Fired up by the Prime Minister Scott Morrison's claim that Australia would stand up to authoritarians in the Russia Ukraine conflict, he declared: "Australia always stands up to bullies!!! Might I remind you Scott Morrison, you opened up the door and rolled out the red carpet for a host of bullies who came here and screwed this country and screwed over regular Australian families. You rolled out the carpet for the World Economic Forum, the World Health Organisation, the United Nations and Big Pharma to lead Australia into medical apartheid, and it has been fucking catastrophic.

"They have trodden down Australia for the past two years. They have bullied, coerced, and manipulated Australians into this unscientific, untested, unjustifiable injection, on your watch.

"I know so many of you are so frikin' angry about what has happened in our country over the past two years. Many of us have been so angry seeing our country destroyed and torn apart right in front of our eyes. The will of the people has to be expressed.

"When will an Australian politician rise to the top and defend us, the Australian people?

"Our teen and youth suicide rates are at levels never seen before because of this bullying. Don't you dare say you stand up to bullies, because you don't. You have aided the destruction of this country. And I hope I've put another nail in your political coffin."

Your average Canberra bureaucrat would never meet a person like David Oneeg, yet here he was, on their doorstep with many tens of thousands of others just like him; completely outraged at the destruction of their lives and livelihoods.

Canberrans had been remarkably compliant throughout the period, claiming the mantle as one of the world's most vaccinated cities. In the streets, well dressed public servants religiously wore their masks; while the city's main newspaper and radio station ran a hostile line towards anyone who doubted the Covid narrative. Local Canberrans, on their public service salaries, had grown comfortable on the sweat, toil and taxes of the rest of the country and were entirely confronted by this gathering of ordinary, good hearted Australians, the citizens the nation's capital was built to serve.

One might have thought all those apparatchiks who had rained terror and ceaseless restrictions on their fellow Australians, bashing, fining, jailing and marginalising them could deny the truth no longer. But while the majority of Canberra's taxpayer funded elites sniffed and condemned the members of the working class now on their doorsteps as "bogans"; many others found it in their hearts to deliver supplies, rolling up with boxes of fruit and vegetables, trays of sausages, steaks, legs of ham; and massive amount of supplies, including shampoo, soap, toothbrushes and toilet paper.

**

The movement was essentially organic, and spontaneous, meaning that it was at times rudderless, without clear leadership or administrative structures.

The protests were both chaotic and glorious, and the burgeoning campsites, first outside the National Parliament and then at the showgrounds on the outskirts of Canberra which became known as Camp Freedom or Camp Epic, daily demonstrated a remarkable cohesion and goodwill amongst people from disparate backgrounds.

While political infighting, personality conflicts and conflicting views on the way forward were on clear display among the putative leaders, out in the makeshift tent cities which sprang up around Canberra the level of good cheer, cooperation and mutual support brought many people to tears.

Everyone there had been through a terrible time, courtesy of their own government.

All great social movements are born of chaos and extremity, just like life itself.

Thus it proved in Australia's national capital.

There were frictions and personality clashes; but there were also repeated and heart warming displays of kindness, cooperation and camaraderie.

Together they changed history.

People who had been essentially placed under house arrest for the previous two years embraced each other like long lost friends. Australia became Australia once again; a friendly, open, hard working and decent place.

One of the tongue-in-cheek signs read: "Make Australia Average Again".

And what a joyful celebration it was.

***

The Canberra Convoy started out as literally a few people being inspired by the truck convoy in Canada and thinking "why don't we do that"?

In early 2022 the blockading of the Canadian Parliament and the massive country wide support for the truck convoy were provoked by Prime Minister Justin Trudeau introducing poorly thought out vaccine mandates for truckers frequently crossing the Canadian US border. Just as in Australia, they came after a two year blizzard of liberty destroying health diktats.

The vaccine mandates were a step too far; with the backlash threatening to destroy the entire Covid narrative.

At this point in history, only the illiterate or the deliberately ignorant could possibly be unaware of the controversy enveloping vaccine rollouts worldwide.

The wave of protests across the globe occurred at exactly the same time as study after study demonstrated the Covid-19 vaccines to be useless at stopping the spread of the disease while producing multiple serious side effects up to and including death, and on a population wide basis producing negative efficacy.

The brutal crackdown on the truckers in Canada, including the freezing of bank accounts and multiple violent arrests, inspired and outraged millions around the world, including in Australia and New Zealand.

The Australian authorities, with their power and credibility fading by the hour, threw everything they could at ordinary people with entirely legitimate grievances, and they ultimately failed for one simple reason: In the end, the truth will out.

***

Australia's convoy was different in nature to other countries, attracting vast numbers of supporters across all sections of society; from disabled children in wheelchairs to the elderly, from the young and wildly enthusiastic to thousands of professionals, from members of Australia's rough and ready working classes to a very strong indigenous presence.

For everyone who showed up in person in Canberra, there were thousands of others lending their support.

Australians are a phlegmatic people; it takes a lot to make them protest. The country's youth may be drawn to convenient government generated narratives such as climate change or racism; but a genuine uprising was always considered impossible in the Land Down Under simply because Australians just wouldn't be in it, too lackadaisical and too satisfied within the confines of their suburban lives to put themselves out.

Two years of false promises and fake news courtesy of the government and their puppets in the mainstream media changed all that; with the mood rapidly turning sour across the country.

Two weeks to "flatten the curve" had turned into a two year blizzard of ever changing rules and regulations, making running a business or creating any semblance of a normal life virtually impossible.

Thus it was that when asked how long they were going to stay, many of those in the Freedom movement replied tongue in cheek: "I'm just staying two weeks to flatten the curve."

***

Australians, due to their geographical isolation, have long been among the world's great travellers. Now their homeland was a Prison Island, with many of its residents unable to leave the country due to some of the worst travel restrictions in the world, akin to North Korea.

Equally thousands of Australians were stranded overseas, unable to return home; while internally the state borders opened and shut on the whim of power-drunk Premiers, creating utter chaos for businesses and producing many heart wrenching scenes of divided families.

Even as Australia became one of the most heavily vaccinated countries on Earth, the promise of mass vaccination as the path out of Covid restrictions proved entirely illusory.

How insane it all was.

Everywhere the country was grinding to a stop, and everywhere individuals of independent mind began shouting out: "Enough is enough."

And so people, a significant number with no homes and no jobs to go back to, having lost everything as a result of the government's deranged mishandling of the Covid scare, got on their bikes, piled into their cars, packed up their trailers and their vans, and headed to Australia's national capital.

As poet Bill Massie put it:

> Oh Canberra here we come, here we come here we come
> Lookout Canberra here we come,
> we come from far and wide
> Millions of Aussies can't be wrong
> We are young, old, free and strong
>
> Truckers, Farmers, Teachers, Plumbers, Doctors, Nurses and all the Drummers
> We cannot be wrong
> We cannot be wrong
> We cannot be wrong
>
> Lookout Canberra here we come, here we come, here we come
> Mums and Dads Babes in gowns
> Heading to Canberra to see the clowns
> They are the clowns who have let us down
> Let us down, let us down
> Lookout Canberra We've arrived.

***

The excitement, and let's be frank, the astonishment, gathered like a rolling storm. The preceding days had taken everybody by surprise.

No one, not even the most optimistic of activists, predicted the size, strength, power and popular support for this spontaneous uprising.

Australians converged from all parts of the country, some footage showing mini-convoys barreling down country roads. Everywhere was the same; blaring horns, waving flags, triumphal shouts.

As the convoy gathered strength on the many roads leading to Canberra, crowds of locals assembled on overpasses and roadsides, waving flags and cheering them on.

These scenes and the rising tide of excitement were utterly unprecedented in the Australian experience. Day after day, images and footage of cheerful scenes at truck stops and campsites across Australia flooded across social media streams.

One participant, with an Instagram feed labelled Drain the Billabong, described himself as just a dude who loves everything to do with sport and works his ass off. He said of one of the impromptu roadside scenes at Wyong on the NSW Central Coast: "This is the Australia I remember and LOVE."

They hadn't even got to Canberra, yet on full display was a huge level of cooperation as trestle tables went up, BBQs were lit, food handed out, flags waved and t-shirts proudly worn, "I Stand For Freedom".

One professionally signed utility read: "Communist Australia. You Masked For This."

***

At Camp Epic thousands of people, not one of them wearing a mask, were clearly in a celebratory mood; busily exchanging experiences and making new friends. Their dogs, which had also spent two years in the extreme isolation of Australia's draconian lockdowns, mingled freely amongst the crowd.

Signs were erected: "Our Teachers Have Been Fired Because They Support Choice"; "The Threat of Unemployment Is Not Consent"; "Thousands of Workers Sacked"; "Help End Vaccine Mandates".

Along the highways, long queues of cars festooned with flags and makeshift signs tooted their horns while drivers and passengers shouted cries of victory out their windows.

There was much to be angry about; but perhaps what was most striking about these spontaneous displays was the festive atmosphere.

In just one of the many scenes across the country, massive lines of trucks and cars descend on Pheasant's Nest, normally a rather boring service centre on the road to Canberra; again the flags, the shouts, the horns, the spontaneous gatherings as people embraced each other, or engaged in earnest conversations as they shared their horror experiences of the previous two years.

It slowly dawned on everybody that they were not alone; that they were not in fact cranks and outliers flying against "the science" and the overarching wisdom of "the medical advice", as their power-drunk political leaders had repeatedly told them was the justification for the destruction of all normal community life.

Their views were now mainstream; their longing for a return to the nation's traditional freedoms, for the right to go about their normal ordinary lives, the lives they loved, was mirrored in everyone they encountered and embraced.

***

Families on the Pacific Highway leading to Canberra manned overpass bridges, waving flags and signs saying "Thank You". As the multiple convoys converging on Canberra grew in size, so did the crowds applauding them.

Michael Gray Griffith of Cafe Locked Out fame recalled his own experience on the road: "On Sunday morning I left Melbourne in a convoy of fifteen vehicles, several of which only came for a section of the journey, to offer us support and see us off. Still, the next morning, by the time we reached Wodonga we had grown to over 170 vehicles.

"All through the night people kept arriving at the makeshift camp, established on the side of the road opposite a service station.

"It was a camp that had an electricity running through it. The kind of electricity that attracts. Most people didn't know each other. Most had never done anything like this before, and no one had any idea what would happen next. All we knew was that we had come too far and now there was no going back. We were on a quest to save our country from tyranny, and we were all one people. We could all feel that too. Two years of division was bonding us into a tribe.

"One of the most remarkable things was that on nearly every car was an Australian flag. A lot of people were also wearing it like a cape. And mostly it was the blue flag, and yet despite their clear pride for their country, their country had ostracised them."

New arrivals into the Canberra campsites were greeted with cheers and waving flags.

"This is it, folks," popular Aussie Chat streamer David Oneeg declared to camera on the main avenue leading to the national parliament, the sound of horns blasting in the distance. "We've been hearing rumours that this convoy approaching is about 25 to 30 kilometres long, maybe longer.

"This is the moment we've all been waiting for. Here they come. This is beautiful. I've got goosebumps. Aussie pride is back. This is the real deal."

And then a most remarkable sight heaved into view on the normally sedate boulevard leading to Parliament House; a wall of trucks, cars and four-wheel-drives, Australian flags waving and horns tooting.

***

Messages of support from across the country and around the world streamed across Oneeg's feed: "So proud of you of all you freedom fighters", "Awesome", "Ohhh, so beautiful!", "My eyes are tearing", "Stick together, stay strong, make us proud", "Go you amazing people", "The Aussie spirit has woken up."

"Convoy for Freedom" reads the banner on one of the two lead trucks, the other reading, perhaps appropriately, "Over Size", as the camera panned to a seemingly endless line of vehicles.

"HANDS OFF OUR KIDS" read a banner along the side of one massive lorry.

Another truck was bannered with the words: "Maskerade Over".

Yet another was signed across its rear: "End Tyranny Free Australia".

"Come on Aussies," Oneeg continues, almost jumping out of his skin with excitement. "This is people from all over Australia."

A young family on the side of the road waved makeshift placards, "Freedom", "Stop Mandates".

From the very first moments the protests were remarkably good spirited, as jubilant protestors waved and shouted out their car windows and Oneeg joyfully shouted back: "Heh, how you doing? You're Live on Facebook!"

***

Country music performer Dusty Starr put it thus in his song Locked Down Under:

> One thing about history
> It helps you see how tomorrow could be
> And if you think we've learnt from our mistakes
> They're just reruns, old repeats
> Denying freedom of speech
> Propaganda machines
> Clearing the way for a new regime
> And when they call in the dogs
> To herd all the sheep
> It's time to hit the streets
> And make a stand
> While you can
> For your lucky land
> The one thing we know that is true
> This is a time of change.

There was not a mask or a QR code in sight; and zero social distancing. The nation's Chief Medical Officers, the same self-important bureaucrats who had been preening in front of the cameras month after tortuous month, suddenly appeared like the out of touch fools they were.

These grotesquely privileged apparatchiks, paid more than ten times the average wage of the workers they were attempting to control, mesmerised by their own self-importance as they became household names, were so damn clever none of them realised you cannot save a society by destroying it.

For the first time in a very long time ordinary people, the ones without university degrees and fabulous salaries, felt vindicated; the feeling they had clung to that they were on the right side of history confirmed at last. Their days of isolation, of being ridiculed by politicians, bureaucrats, media pundits and their double vaxxed neighbours, were finally over.

This was not a few isolated crazies; this was a country which from coast to coast was declaring its disgust at the bureaucratic and authoritarian overreach which had been visited upon ordinary, decent people; the police bashings, the pepper spraying, the hi-tech weaponry used for crowd control; and the disgraceful deceits of the nation's political class.

Hashtags blossomed across the internet, #convoytocanberra, #convoytocanberra2022, #Convoy2Canberra.

Observer and life coach David Nieuwenhoven wrote: "There had been a lot of talk in various groups about heading to Canberra and making a stand of some sort in a non-violent way to let those know in power that we are well and truly over this absolute nonsense, mandates, fear mongering and more and many good people including nurses, doctors, fireman, teachers and essential workers just want their jobs back!

"Let's face it, pretty much every person in Australia has been affected in some way in the last two years. Many people lost everything; including loved ones to suicide, jobs, friends, family and more.'

One young tradie spoke for many when at a parallel protest in Perth he shouted at the Premier of Western Australia Mark McGowan: "Give Us Our Jobs Back Ya Dog."

It was all many people wanted; the right to work, the right to live their lives without the government in every corner of their lives.

The rich had grown massively richer, the public sector had expanded significantly, and the politicians ate up television time putting themselves front and centre of everybody's lives; all, in the end, for what?

The only people who hadn't had their lives and livelihoods destroyed or savagely impacted were the privileged political class, bureaucrats and the already ultra-rich, who were more than satisfied with the historic transfer of wealth upwards from the middle and working classes.

What started out as a "road trip" for a few dedicated activists desperate to reach out from the isolation of their own bunkers rapidly became something much bigger. The meme "Let's go to Canberra" turned into a widespread and joyful chant, "Everyone's going to Canberra", spreading across social media and through the thousands upon thousands of individuals, families and groups coming from all corners of the country.

**

Social media platforms like Telegram and even Facebook, which had played such an invidious censorship role throughout the Covid era, suddenly had thousands of people saying they wanted to go too, then tens of thousands, all focused on the sole idea of getting people to the capital whatever way they could; to be seen and heard, to at long last take meaningful action against the tyranny which had been crushing them and their families for far too long.

Trucks were out of the question for many, because most truckies in Australia do not own their own trucks.

So, people organised buses, carpooling, caravans and trailers were loaded, and people just decided they would get there however possible, by train, by bus, by plane.

Soon tens of thousands; then hundreds of thousands over a very short period felt compelled to head to the capital, every last person with a powerful and intensely human story to tell.

Many, without even the petrol money to return home, declared: "We're not leaving until this is over!"

As one protestor observed: "Everybody here is on the verge of losing everything."

There is an old saying: "Grace is more likely to be found in crisis than in comfort."

And perhaps that was part of the reason for the wildly festive atmosphere; not a dance macabre in the face of death, but a breathtaking act of defiance, a triumph of the human spirit.

***

Canberra's Parliament House, an elegant 4,700 room building designed as a symbol of national unity, was opened in 1988 by Queen Elisabeth II and cost what was then regarded as a wildly extravagant $1.1 billion. The front forecourts are normally a sedate tourist zone, characterised by tour operators and the comings and goings of sleek white Commonwealth cars.

The Prime Minister in 1988 was Bob Hawke of the Labor Party, the last Prime Minister to have any genuine connection to Australia's working classes.

Hawke passed away in 2019, and we will never know what he would have made of the nation's great unwashed, that is its citizens, showing up on the doorsteps of the national parliament.

The current residents of Canberra sniffed, turned the other way, or unleashed the hounds; their supreme arrogance and indifference intact.

Although to be fair not all of them behaved that way, with donations of food, clothing, toiletries and bottled water pouring into the camps.

The first members of the Convoy to show up on that Monday, 31st of January, 2022, all expressed themselves frightened, exhilarated, overwhelmed, both moved to tears and very much out on a limb; a few brave souls determined to protest in the face of the grinding, heartless and massive machinery of an authoritarian government.

By 2pm the normally sedate forecourts of the parliament were packed with hundreds of protestors waving the white, red and blue Australian national flag, the Australian Red Ensign flag, traditionally associated with military service and thereby national pride, the Aboriginal flag with its bold red, orange and black colouring, and the blue and white Southern Cross Eureka flag, historically associated with worker revolts.

And thus the biggest story in Modern Australian history began.

Early footage showed campers parking on the lawns outside Parliament House, while police looked on helplessly.

Stories emerged in the following days, whether apocryphal or not Old Alex could not confirm, of numerous police in Canberra quitting their jobs rather than acting against their fellow Australians; or bursting into tears and throwing their badges on the ground; or of passing out ear plugs to protestors to help protect them against the hi-tech weapons their fellow officers were using to target the crowds.

What could be easily confirmed was that hundreds of police officers quit their jobs rather than comply with vaccine mandates, an estimated 1200 in Queensland alone, while many senior police who resigned provided moving online testimony of their absolute disgust with the authoritarian abuses against their fellow Australians they had been expected to execute.

Some of the nation's most senior police condemned in no uncertain terms the politicians and health bureaucrats who had destroyed the lives of so many of the citizenry.

This particularly telling response by those expected to act as the front-line enforcers for the diktats of the nation's politicians and bureaucrats is well documented on a Telegram Channel called Cops for Covid Truth.

***

The mainstream media were notable for their almost total absence from the protests; for their blatant lying about crowd numbers, and in any case were decidedly unwelcome when they did show up.

One piece of footage shows a middle aged woman giving a television cameraman such an earful he made the professional mistake of arguing back. She is unrepentant: "Bloody disgraceful. I asked him which station he worked for and he wouldn't tell me. That's not doing his job. Other people in this country don't have a job right now. Why should he have one?"

The mainstream media might have stayed away; but citizen journalists did not. One of the most prominent, Janaya Markwell, who posted under the tag Convoy Roller Girl, was exuberant when asked by celebrity streamer The Real Rukshan what she thought: "It's absolutely incredible. I love every minute here. The energy here, electric, beautiful. Everyone is coming together, so excited, loving it. Seen the food tents? Locals are constantly dropping off supplies, food and water. It's so exciting. Everyone is having the best time."

There were impromptu concerts; drums, clapsticks, didgeridoos.

The massed, masked up and heavily armed police offered a sad contrast to the joyful attitude of the protestors themselves.

By midday of that first exhilarating day, vehicle after vehicle was being welcomed onto the lawns in front of Parliament House by their fellow Convoy members. Police found themselves surrounded by a chanting, flag waving crowd every time they tried to intervene or block a vehicle from entering: "Let them go. Let them go. Let them go, you dogs. You dogs. You're outnumbered today."

It's not that often in Australian life you see the indigenous fighting with one voice alongside their white brethren, but today they did, with the Aboriginal flag everywhere to be seen.

"Wake Up Rise Up Australia" read just one of the handmade signs being waved in a sea of flags.

Police attempts to block entry to the parliamentary lawns failed.

As Michael Gray Griffith wrote of the exhilaration of those opening hours: "Our culture has been raped, and now, within the trauma, turmoil and the shame of that, is a new future forming? A future never more visible than within the camp growing outside the front of the national library in Canberra.

"It is a camp forming from people who are arriving here from all over the country. Many are coming in waves of convoys, like the one I arrived in, others are turning up alone, some after driving for hours. One unemployed gardener I met came with his daughter from Mt Gambier, after racing out to buy a campervan. Another woman told me she drove all the way down from Cairns. It was a long way she said, a long way.

"And down here the police, at least on the first day, were trying various tactics to move us on. But on to where? The reason most of us had nowhere to go was the reason we were here.

"I believe that what is happening now is something that will not have been seen before. It is an ongoing explosion of courage, that will keep exploding all over the country, as those who have had enough will go fuck it, if not now, then when?

"For thousands of years people have awaited the second coming, and without question, most people in the resistance see this as a spiritual war, a war between good and evil. Well what if, under the darkening shadow of evil, this is the second coming? Except that what is good, call it God or call it whatever you like, is arriving within all of us. Forming within the conjoined souls, who, after still refusing to comply, are coming together and forming, organically, and without even knowing it, the womb of our new world."

Greeted like conquering heroes after what was inevitably a long drive, new arrivals were grinning from ear to ear.

***

By midday the protestors were gathering around the front of Parliament House, the mood a surprising mix because nobody knew what to expect, nobody knew what was about to happen, and the initial confrontations with police attempting to stop the campers from setting up on the most public and symbolic lawns in the country had already set a sour tone of conflict and confrontation.

Just to add to the atmosphere, a violent storm appeared, with dark clouds hovering over the nation's seat of government.

By half past one the chants outside the doors of Parliament had begun. "Sack them all. Sack them all."

A spokesman for the group Informed Medical Options said the "Sack Them All" chant exemplified the frustration many people were feeling.

"They feel they are not being heard," he said. "And they are not being heard. The mainstream media will probably label us as crackpots. That there is something wrong with us. No. No. It is well past time when they can hide out in this house and ignore the people of Australia."

The atmosphere was defiant, but the hundreds of thousands of people who had marched in towns and cities had done nothing to change the incompetence and the cruelty which had characterised the state and federal government Covid responses to date.

Most protests, however noisy, fall flat; with a few hundred chanting, placard waving civilians unlikely to change an aloof and unresponsive government, either its politicians or its phalanxes of bureaucrats. There may have been plenty of bravado, but at this point in time nobody realised that they were about to be bolstered by many hundreds of thousands of supporters in the largest spontaneous uprising the country had ever seen.

> Truckers of the world unite
> This is a battle we all have to fight
> Hitch up your rig, trailers & gates
> Go fight this battle with all your trucking mates
>
> Start up your rig throw it into gear
> This is the battle of the year
> Politicians have let us down
> Time to throw them out of town
> We the people must take control
> No more mandates no more jabs
> No more lockdowns by these scabs
>
> Without our truckers we'd be lost
> You carry the country through sun hail ice & frost
> Honk your horns loud & clear.
>
> Bill Massie.

***

Even as protestors wore their "Real Men Don't Wear Masks" t-shirts and waved "Hands Off Our Kids" placards, and thousands more continued to pour into Canberra, their vehicles festooned with variations on the "My Kids Are Not Lab Rats" theme, came the news that GoFundMe had frozen access to more than $160,000 in funds raised by supporters.

The action followed a similar move in Canada, where more than $5 million in funds had been frozen.

And then the heavens opened up and poured rain upon the protestors; with dogs and children and flag draped protestors splashing cheerfully through the environs of the national parliament.

From the very beginning the politics of the freedom movement were remarkably confused, with various factions among the protesters competing for their points of view to be heard.

While there was a remarkable atmosphere of collaboration and good will between the protestors at large, there were deep political divisions between sections of the movement on clear display; both personality clashes and political differences. The divisions ran along the lines of those who wished to work within the system to reform the policies they disliked, such as lockdowns and vaccine mandates, and those who wished to dissolve parliament altogether and establish a new kind of polity.

Not that any of it mattered. Australia's political system had failed everybody. Professional politicians were not welcome. This was a people's uprising.

In the end the reality was clear: both sides of Australia's Tweedledum Tweedledee politics of left and right had ramped up Covid hysteria to ridiculous levels, abrogated previously unheard of powers to themselves, destroyed the liberties and freedoms of Australians and betrayed the people they were meant to serve.

One figure who enjoyed some community respect was avowed Christian and former Qantas pilot Graham Hood who said that on his journey there he had spent the previous night at Pheasants Nest. "I saw hundreds of people in tears, not because they were sad but because they finally realised they were part of something that was worth being part of. They are proud and they are alive and they are part of Australia. We have allowed this country to degenerate into something that sucks.

"The last time Australia mobilised like this was during the Wars. They rode to enlist on horses, motorbikes, they caught trains, they walked. They went because they wanted to defend and protect this country. That is what we have done."

Another polarising figure to emerge was former SAS officer Riccardo Bossi, who repeatedly and passionately called for the dissolving of Parliament and fresh elections: "This is a moment in history. We either win or lose. Those bastards up there are already killing our kids. What do you think they've got in store for us next? We have to end this here and now. This is it."

***

Somehow in this entire melee the conflicting personalities and agendas were of no great import; it was clear, Australians had had enough.

As one of the many flags declared: "The People's Revolution".

There were no camping permits, there was no coordinated plan, there was no administrative structure or elected leaders, but most startling of all was that after the vicious idiocy which had destroyed all semblance of community life over the previous two years, the prevailing atmosphere was one of enormous good cheer.

One participant amongst those first campers, Simon Hunt, who spent three nights between Old Parliament House and New Parliament House and outside the columned edifices of the National Library, described the atmosphere thus: "We rolled in. There were so many people there; and they just kept on coming. The atmosphere was incredible. Families and dogs, and wherever you went everybody was engaged in conversation.

"Above all it was very welcoming, like finding yourself in a crowd of old friends after getting out of a two year stint in prison.

"So many people came with nothing. Many came by themselves. But everyone was on the same page.

"Australians are reticent on the whole; but everyone was friendly, supportive. Food tents started up. Kitchens were organised.

"All the people who came with no money got fed. There was so much good will and camaraderie, it was incredible.

"Then the police started hassling us."

***

As the inventor of the mystery story Edgar Allan Poe, himself prone to waking dreams and bouts of mysticism, had put it two centuries before lucid dreaming began to spread across the planet:

> In visions of the dark night
> I have dreamed of joy departed—

But a waking dream of life and light
Hath left me broken-hearted.

Ah! what is not a dream by day
To him whose eyes are cast
On things around him with a ray
Turned back upon the past?

That holy dream—that holy dream,
While all the world were chiding,
Hath cheered me as a lovely beam
A lonely spirit guiding.

Well, they cuddled into their tiny part of history. And it was hard to find a single person who did not think there was a spiritual element to it all.

At first Old Alex had no idea why this period was so significant, why it felt as if the ancient gods had conjoined with the souls of the day, why they were even here.

It was glorious, of course, but frightening.

As for the country, it was a bloody mess.

***

One young woman wearing a halter top with the word LOVEDOWN pencilled across her breasts pretty much summed it up. She held high above her head a sign which read: "We're not from the Left or Right, We're from the Bottom and We're Coming for those on Top!"

Many hundreds of thousands of Australians had been protesting for months on the streets of the state capitals. But this time around the deceptive conduct of mainstream journalists and the government apparatchiks pulling their strings no longer mattered; every single abuse by the authorities was streamed multiple times live to the internet; every last detail of this historic event was recorded and uploaded in real time.

People had travelled from all over Australia to be part of the Convoy; and it was now crystal clear that the government had entirely lost control of their Covid narrative of fear, hysteria and oppression.

A government which had lied constantly, which had destroyed the country and betrayed the people, now had a fomenting revolution on its hands.

Destroying millions of people's livelihoods, careers, dignity and bodily integrity, as the Australian authorities had done, was always going to end only one way; with protesters in the streets.

Every day in the lead up to the major march there were demonstrations at various institutions around Canberra, including the High Court of Australia.

As luck would have it, on that first full day, as the town began to fill with demonstrators, Australian Prime Minister Scott Morrison was scheduled to speak at the National Press Club.

Morrison's shameless lust for power had landed him in a job he was not intellectually or temperamentally equipped to fill. And made him the most despised person in the country; loathed not just by the millions of people whose lives he had destroyed under the cover of Covid-19, with his totalitarian instincts and his ever repeating lie that he and his ilk were "keeping Australians safe"; but by his own party, many of whom were just as aware as the public of the massive amount of harm this Prime Minister had done to the country and to his countrymen.

Not to mention their chances of re-election.

While the numbers were disputed, it appeared to Old Alex that at a reasonable guess well over a million people had descended on the hotels and camping grounds of Canberra. There was no privacy; and here is just one telling vignette.

Sitting in adjacent cubicles in the toilets, one excitable lad shouts to his mate, "I'm doing a ScoMo, I'm doing a ScoMo."

You know you've lost the public when your name becomes synonymous with the act of defecation.

Scott Morrison had shown not one single shred of sympathy for the hundreds of people who had died or been injured as a result of the vaccines he so ardently promoted, nor a shred of sympathy for the thousands of adverse events, including miscarriages and permanent disablement.

He had shown no sympathy whatsoever for the many protestors bashed in the cities, locked in their homes, fined and imprisoned; and not a single shred of empathy for the thousands of people who had lost their jobs for refusing to submit to the vaccine, or the tens of thousands of business owners who had seen their livelihoods destroyed by the government's totally over-the-top response to Covid. And no sympathy whatsoever for the hundreds of thousands of families separated from their loved ones thanks to the dramatic, and utterly pointless, shutting of state and national borders.

The country broke apart under Scott Morrison's watch; and now he was being forced to confront the people's whose lives he had trampled on.

All in an election year.

***

If he was trying to keep up the pretence that the protestors descending on the capital were of little import; Scott Morrison had to do even more dodging and weaving than usual as he was confronted by a loud, proud and angry crowd at the National Press Club, normally a rather sedate venue where politicians are given undue reverence as they unveil their various plans, their speeches ritualistically followed by softball questions from corporate journalists.

As the Prime Minister spoke the platitudinous words of his well prepared speech, a typical mélange of homilies mixed with a list of supposed public service achievements, his words were broadcast over the PA system to those who could not make it into the comfortable and exclusive rooms of the National Press Club. The crowd outside were having none of it.

Each mention of the virus and each self-congratulatory justification for the ruin his government had visited upon the country were greeted with groans and jeers.

"The past three years have been some of the most extraordinary that our nation has ever experienced," the Prime Minister intoned. "Younger generations have never known anything like it.

"The succession of natural disasters from drought to flood, fires, pestilence, a once in a century global pandemic, the recession it caused, has pushed our country to the very limits.

"It has been tough raising your family, keeping your job, doing your job - especially for those health and aged care workers, who we thank for their tremendous service.

"It's been tough keeping your small business or your farm going.

"It's been tough keeping your children's education up, caring for elderly relatives, those with a disability, and it's been very tough on them too.

"Our way of life has been completely turned upside down.

"For so many Australians it has been exhausting – financially, physically, emotionally.

"And I don't doubt many have stayed awake at night after telling their kids or those they care for, or those they employ that it's all going to be OK, but wondering to themselves, in the quiet of that night, whether it really will be."

It would be one of the last times Morrison would publicly attempt to put a positive spin on his and his government's abject mishandling of Covid before he realised he was not on a winner.

Members of the crowd were colourfully and casually dressed; standing on the roofs of their cars, waving flags and placards including "In A World Of Propaganda Truth Is Always A Conspiracy", and generally making their views clear.

The scene inside the National Press Club was also more lively than usual, with prominent political commentator Peter Van Onselen confronting the PM with a leaked text exchange between the then NSW Premier Gladys Berejiklian and a member of his own Cabinet where he was described as "a horrible, horrible person", a "fraud" and a "complete psycho" more concerned with politics than people, a Gotcha moment which added memorably to the public humiliation of the occasion.

The expression on the Prime Minister's face when asked for his response to this critique from his own side of politics was what Australians would describe as "whacked over the head by a mullet".

As the senior politicians who had shown up to support their leader departed in their chauffeur driven Commonwealth cars, they were greeted with cries of "Shame On You, Shame On You".

The Prime Minister's car, with an apparently dumbfounded Morrison inside, was pursued by protestors shouting "You Dog, You Dog".

For Morrison haters, of whom there were many, it was a truly splendid day. For a frustrated crowd, it was all great fun, and would have been funny if it had not been so serious, the damage wrecked on Australian society so complete.

***

Day three of the Convoy to Canberra was a cooler day, but only weather wise.

Hourly the police entered the campsite in Canberra's parliamentary zone and did a walk through. All of them were masked up and initially polite. As they passed through the growing camp they were surrounded by protesters, who were trying to convince the officers to come over to their side.

Matthew Gray of Café Lockdown wrote: "These were angry people. People who had driven here from all over the land in a search for simple things: The right to work, the right to socialise, and the right to choose what went into their bodies. But as the tension continued to rise near the main entrance, where more and more police were arriving, the rear of the camp was open.

"I went there with a few others to wait. It didn't take long. Suddenly, four unmarked, four wheel drives with darkened glass pulled up in a line and with their engines running, they sat in a line like a modern day cavalry charge waiting for their order to charge.

"I live streamed this, and with my good friend, the photographer Daniel, a Mauri in his late sixties, we sat on the grass before them. Soon other freedom seekers, for the word fighters is wrong, sat next to us.

"We believed that despite the clear intimidation that they wouldn't run us over. This was Australia.

"But then two of these four wheel drives reversed before driving off, at speed, into the camp, past young children who were playing cricket, and as they did this officers from a tactical branch burst out of these remaining four wheel drives and ran into the camp.

"We followed these men.

"By the time we reached the centre of the camp it was all a mess. The police were kettling themselves, as their colleagues were arresting someone, and the freedom seekers were surrounding these officers, our hands in the air, to show the world that we were unarmed, and all of us were chanting, 'You serve us, You serve us'."

The rest, as Michael Griffith put it, was a shit-fest.

The same police brutality Australians had seen time and time again on the streets of the nation's capitals, from the true psychopathology on Melbourne's streets to the military manning of the western suburbs of

Sydney while army helicopters and surveillance drones flying overhead, from police pepper spraying children in the suburbs of Brisbane to the utterly outrageous rounding up of indigenous peoples from their sacred homelands in Central Australia; all that had proved a national disgrace and international embarrassment for two long years, all of it was now in the nation's capital.

And all of it was being streamed multiple times by anyone with a smartphone; adding to the layers of shame that had accreted across the national psyche.

Heart wrenching footage emerged from the conflagration.

This is Australia? People were asking, and their voices were the voices of the broken hearted. This is Australia?

Gray continued: "One man hugged me because I was crying. He was crying too. Lots of people were. And not from the pepper spray or the fear. But from disbelief that these police officers, who should be our heroes, were now our oppressors.

"They were here to try to move us on because their masters knew lots more people were coming. Lots more. And they wanted the head of the forming snake cut off.

"These officers weren't protecting the public, they were, instead being used by the politicians to try and crush what we were.

"And over these few days, many of these officers have told us they are on our side, although that is hard to see sometimes.

"And their masters should be scared, for what we are is the counterbalance. These officers are doing this for a pay packet, while we have nothing to lose, because apart from our souls, it has all been taken away."

***

While authorities in Canberra tried to disband the burgeoning campsites around the city, multiple mini-convoys were still threading their way to the Australian Capital Territory along the highways and byways of the nation.

By now the ignition switch had been pressed, the fire lit, the contagion of wildly enthusiastic Convoy participants were being swept up in one of the most extraordinary events any of them were ever likely to experience; whatever cliché you wished to grasp for, none could suffice.

Multiple streamers, bloggers and independent news sites documented the gathering wave; the shouting, the waving, the tooting horns, the blaring trucks, the glory of it all.

One man, on his way down from the Gold Coast recorded: "The wet roads have not dampened the spirits of the second convoy wave headed to Canberra from Queensland. I have not experienced such a positive, friendly and supportive mood on a driving trip around Australia ever!

"The Commonwealth Games had a tremendous atmosphere and friendly banter but this is something different. It's more than just a celebration of an event. It's a journey of hope. The delight and comfort in knowing there are so many others on this journey. Others who feel like you do. They aren't strange.

"They yell support, they honk horns, they wave flags, and they stop and lend a hand to those stopped on the roadside.

"These people are giving life and hope to people who have been locked up, isolated, beaten down and treated as lesser citizens.

"The mood is changing. You can feel it. You can see it in the eyes of those in the convoy. You can certainly hear it; the hearts being kick-started and a throbbing of expectancy.

"I don't know what the days ahead will hold but if this gathering of souls on the road to Canberra is any indication this is the birth of something very special.

"History is being made."

***

To rely on his good work, for while podcasters, streamers and social media butterflies were everywhere, old fashioned writers and reporters were thin on the ground, Matthew Gray reporting from Ground Zero, so to speak, wrote: "I have been saying for a while, that we all been surfing an incoming wave of tyranny, well what we are now is the first rise of another wave, a growing tsunami of people, Australians wanting what people all over the world crave, freedom.

"Even as I write this, people are coming up to me and introducing themselves. They have come from everywhere. Two women who just arrived had driven down from Townsville. Two days of solid driving.

"This park is the line in the sand. You can feel it. We all can.

"Will we be the agents of change? Will our wave wash away their tyranny? Or will we be the last stand of everything that was beloved about our country? A fort crushed by officers trying to pay their mortgages; officers who, if that happens, will have to try to live in a house built upon and haunted by our ghosts."

On their website Café Lockdown recorded the voices of people the state had forgotten.

Janice Johnston told: "I lost my job in disability support because I won't get vaccinated but before I did I witnessed the company manipulating clients that could speak by telling them they wouldn't be able to go anywhere or socialise with others and also the ones with no voice were just given the jab, it was bloody heartbreaking."

Kylie Buxton also told Café Lockdown: "My son's story: Wish you had of gone into one of the surf clubs and asked them about mandates on their volunteers. Our 16 year old son forced to say goodbye to something he has been so passionate about. Last year Cameron received awards for Junior Lifesaver of the year also accumulated almost 300 hrs volunteering in 1 season. All his life I have taught him to make the right choices in life and you will be ok. Now he makes a choice to not put a trial drug in his body and he is punished for it. All he wants to do is serve his community, keep them safe

"I'm so proud of him.

"Shame on you NSW Surf Life Saving For Not standing up for your volunteers.

"How do we explain the logic to our kids that they can sit in a classroom with in Cameron's case 100 students but he can't be on the beach serving his community?"

***

One group calling itself OzTrucks to Canberra put out a poster: "You came for our Children. Now we're coming for You. Trucks, Buses, Motorhomes, Cars, Motorbikes, Pushbikes, Scooters and by Foot. Aussies are demanding our Freedom be restored."

>END ALL MANDATES
>
>END ALL COVID VACCINATIONS

END ALL MASK MANDATES

END ALL QR CODES

END MEDICAL APARTHEID

REMOVE ALL COVID STICKERS & POSTERS

REMOVE ALL PLEXIGLASS

REMOVE ALL BORDER RESTRICTIONS

***

With the government in election mode and the extreme discontent of the public on full display, the Convoy to Canberra became the biggest story in the country. There were escalating confrontations; and the by now familiar scenes of police gathering en masse to disband protestors.

"God help you, pieces of shit," one protester yelled at police as the pepper spraying, brutality and arrests began all over again.

One piece of footage shows two policemen, moving in on protestors, jubilantly clinking their pepper spray cans together as if they were beers; a collapse of moral authority within the police forces of which the many senior officers quitting their jobs had been warning for months.

This is what Australia had descended into. Nothing could have been more emblematic of this disgusting period of governance gone awry; of the tragedy which had consumed the nation, making it unrecognisable from the country it had been only two years before.

Three people were arrested that third day after officers, who had been patrolling the area all day, went to the campsite at the National Library of Australia at around 4pm. Written information was provided to demonstrators that they were parking and camping illegally and might be fined if they remained.

Footage showed more than 100 police massing for the confrontation.

A woman was charged with assaulting the police and two men were charged with obstruction for interfering in the woman's arrest.

Observers reported that the violent scenes which erupted around the campsite were as a direct result of the antagonising presence of the police; not of the actions of the protestors, who were almost universally peaceful.

It didn't matter what the authorities, the henchmen of the nation's politicians, did; people kept arriving on foot, by train, bus, bike and plane, in cars and trucks, some with large well equipped caravans, some with no equipment whatsoever. And almost all of them said the same thing: they had been called by God or the spirits. They didn't understand it, most weren't even religious, but they just had to be there.

FIFTEEN
A TIME FOR ALL TIME

We are living interludes, bookended between not yet and no more, each of us a random draw of the cosmic lottery, each allotted a sliver of spacetime in which to live out our lives as chance configurations of stardust suspended in time. There are times in life when the firmament of our being seems to collapse, taking all the light with it, swallowing all colour and sound into a silent scream of darkness. It rarely looks that way from the inside, but these are always times of profound transformation and recalibration — the darkness is not terminal but primordial; in it, a new self is being born, not with a Big Bang but with a whisper. Our task, then, is only to listen. What we hear becomes new light.

Maria Popova.

EVENTS ACCELERATED.

Australia was producing what looked very much like a national uprising.

Daily thousands upon thousands of people from all walks of life continued to stream into the capital. The stills and footage from that first week of February show joyous communality and good cheer among the protestors; while the fierce brutality of the crackdowns by police fully exemplified a deeper scandal.

By Saturday the 5th of February, 2022, there were already massive crowds in Canberra, all the more remarkable as protests had been effectively banned during the entire era of government generated Covid hysteria.

The march on Old Parliament House that day in itself made history, and while it acted in a sense as a precursor to the even more massive demonstration the following weekend was completely remarkable within itself.

The dismantling of the impromptu camp in the parliamentary precincts had begun in earnest the previous day. Authorities appeared early in the morning with warnings they would move camp equipment and "illegally parked" vehicles in the area, after issuing repeating similar warnings on the previous days.

Police located in a boat on Lake Burley Griffin issued warnings, through a loudspeaker darkly: "It is an offence for a person to camp on this land without a permit. It is an offence for persons to park a vehicle on this land without a permit. You are required to remove all vehicles, camping structures, tents and associated equipment from this location. You have one hour to comply with this request before police begin removing and taking custody of these items. Any person attempting to interfere with police in the course of their duties may be subject to arrest."

On social media, ACT Police issued a statement at 8am local time warning the campers of the operation.

Soon after, a large force descended on the park.

As one unfortunate tow truck driver hitched up a car, multiple cameras showed a police officer aggressively pushing a woman to the ground in front of her children, the same style of aggressive misconduct which had damaged the Force's reputation so badly over the previous two years.

Heavily armed police faced completely unarmed mums, dads, children and the elderly.

The atmosphere was fiery and increasingly outraged.

David Oneeg: "Tactical response teams, dog squads, riot police and the rubber bullet boys, all for people and families who just want to say no to the death jabs and go back to work. This is the battle of the ages, not just here but all over the world. Choose your side carefully. Satan and God are playing for keeps."

Sid, 73, who had travelled more than 1000 kilometres from Queensland. He was charged by police, who pepper sprayed him, causing temporary blindness. He had been standing alone in the protesters camp with his dog.

For every action there is an equal and opposite reaction, and he became a source of inspiration for many of the protestors.

Oneeg: "Police brutality is standard operating procedure now, and the people are no longer threatened by it – they become more determined. Like Sid – who returned to camp and vowed to fight on.

"It is not a democratic society when you are not only denied your freedom of expression including protesting but you are attacked and injured just for wanting to do it."

While the situation remained confused, some protesters complied with the police orders and began moving their cars. At least with an alternative campsite now organised at the Epic Showgrounds in the city's north, there was an alternative.

Extremely heavily armed police kitted out in full military gear, guns and gas canisters at the ready, dismantled camp gear and removed property from those who refused to move.

One portester, a former military officer, said the rubber bullets the police were using could kill if they hit the wrong spot. Australians may once have been unfamiliar with the damage rubber bullets can do, but now anyone with a social media account could view the devastating injuries these bullets were causing to protesters.

"And they have canisters of CS gas. Anyone who has been exposed to CS gas will tell you, don't do it today. It's not teargas and it's not capsicum spray. It burns everywhere. It is complete overkill. It is an absolute travesty of justice that this has been allowed to happen. I can't believe they can stand there in conscience facing women and children with those weapons."

***

The next day was an entirely different story; not of police brutality but of triumph.

While there were no reliable estimates of crowd numbers, footage shows tens of thousands of people turning up to protest, with a sea of flags along the bridges and boulevards leading up to Parliament House.

Former servicemen were well represented.

One woman holds up a large placard: "Breathing Working Travelling Hugging Loved Ones. Extremists?" Other messages include: "Vaccine Injuries Not Fake" and "Jesus Wins".

The crowd, jubilant, defiant, repeatedly sang:

We are one, but we are many
And from all the lands on earth we come
We'll share a dream and sing with one voice
I am, you are, we are Australian

The time was upon us all, the time when Australia finally stood up to tyranny and confronted the dark forces which had consumed the country for far too long. These were the people the government was meant to serve, and had instead attempted to crush. They weren't putting up with Australia's filthy descent into totalitarianism a second longer. These were the days when Australia changed forever, and a remote and ever more ludicrously out of touch government could pretend no longer.

The mainstream and social media platforms had utterly disgraced themselves over the previous two years; but what the authorities, the politicians, academics and media personnel, directly or indirectly beholden to their vaccine funding sources, failed to appreciate was that in this era of hyper-connectivity, the military mindset of command and control no longer worked.

One of Australia's new breed of young, passionate citizen journalists, Joel Gilmour, streamed just short of six hours of raw footage of the protests in Canberra, Australia's capital, straight to Facebook, with thousands of comments, shares and likes.

He and his fellow streamers easily outstripped the influence of traditional media outlets.

It was a day straight out of the history books; destined to resonate in the country's increasingly troubled history. There was strong participation from the indigenous and the nation's veterans, along with thousands of sacked nurses, teachers and police who, amongst so many others, had gotten in their trucks and cars and driven to Canberra.

With triumphant shouts, tooting horns and waving flags, assembled behind a giant banner condemning Covid-19 Vaccine Mandates, protesters assembled in central Canberra.

Numerous people were pushing their children in prams, attesting to the peaceful nature of the event.

"Sack them all. Sack them all. No more mandates."

"The turnout out here is absolutely incredible," Joel says to camera. "Wow! There's still more coming."

Yes, there most certainly were.

Exhibition Park in Canberra, otherwise known as Epic, lies on the northern outskirts of Canberra and is the site of the annual Canberra Show, which like other shows around the country exhibits the produce and achievements of local farmers and craftspeople, a festive occasion to delight the territory's children and the public at large.

It features a network of showgrounds and a racecourse, variously intended for horses, dogs, cattle and other events, and is equipped to deal with large numbers of people.

Which was just as well.

As the week progressed, numbers rose from the thousands into the tens of thousands, culminating in an estimated 200,000 people on this one campsite alone. Hotels, campsites and other forms of accommodation were full across Canberra.

With numbers rising daily, the atmosphere at the heart of Australia's Camp Freedom and the epicentre for the Convoy to Canberra was chaotic and glorious, jubilant, exultant; tinged with both exhilaration and fear.

There were plenty of smiles, musical performances, hugs were for free and kids played in between the tents or in organised activities; fire twirlers, opera singers, and impromptu artists added to the dizzying, joyful atmosphere, a kind of Woodstock without the drugs or the mud.

All participants said one thing: "This is history in the making."

Crowds lined the streets of the campsite cheering the arrival of every new truck and car. "Welcome, welcome," they shouted, whistling and cheering every last newcomer.

Country music celebrity Dusty Starr roamed the pavilions with his trusty guitar singing:

> Now we're from the right
> And we're shaking to the left
> We close our eyes
> Open wide
> And take the test
> We do a lock down turn around
> Jump up and scream.
> We're just waking up to Corona 19

There were signs everywhere calling for freedom and "Hands Off Our Kids". There were no mainstream journalists at the centre of the Epic Showgrounds, none daring to show their faces at one of the most singularly historic gatherings in the nation's history.

The role of Australia's heavily manipulated and controlled media in promoting panic and marginalising those who did not want to comply with government mandated vaccines would be the subject of introspection and reflection for years to come. But that was an argument for another time.

Nothing, no amount of whitewashing or rewriting of history by the authorities, could change the chaotic and glorious scenes which overwhelmed the nation's capital. More often described by outsiders as a "soulless shit box", joy and outrage overtook Canberra.

While in the centre of the city the nation's spoilt public servants, all masked up and socially distanced, added to the bizarre Stepford Wives feel of this artificially created city, at the campsite itself there were no masks, absolutely no social distancing, and certainly no QR codes.

This was myth busting at its best.

The hysteria visited upon the nation's capital, engineered by the most ruthless pharmaceutical companies on Earth in league with the Australian government was blown apart as hundreds of thousands of people joyfully celebrated a freedom that had been denied them through the previous two terrible years.

If large gatherings were really "superspreader events", as the authorities had been claiming they were as justification for shutting down everything from concerts to churches, then this was a superspreader event extraordinaire.

However there were no reports of Covid outbreaks as a result of the Convoy to Canberra.

As people celebrated their humanity won out at last, the high minded dictatorial lunacy of federal and state governments finally came to look exactly as it was: a criminal assault on the freedoms, the jobs and the bodily integrity of the populace.

There could be no going back to the days of house arrest and claims that gatherings of more than two people were a threat to public health, the days when if two people were talking outside their own home and a third person joined them that was regarded as a criminal offence and the neighbours encouraged to report them.

The game was up; the government perpetrated farce was over.

***

The Convoy to Canberra marked one of the greatest stirrings of national pride anyone had ever seen.

Daniel, 45, a farmer from Kempsey on the NSW mid-North Coast, expressed it thus: "Just the sheer magnitude of the gathering of the people, the smiles, the loves, the togetherness of everybody. Everyone helping each other.

"I came here; I just saw the inequality in everything around me and just knew in my soul that something was wrong and needed to be brought to light. That everyone needed to gather to put light on this.

"Everybody here wants freedom from the medical tyranny and segregation. They want to have elections that are untainted. And they need to stop jabbing kids, because of their level of natural immunity they don't need to be jabbed.

"You come together, and people are able to sit down and talk without the fear of being alienated, vilified, outcast from the group, because everybody is accepted."

***

Janaya Markwell, 25, Gold Coast, a very lively young woman who, armed with nothing but a smart phone and boundless energy, became one of the most significant documenters of the Freedom movement. She said: "To find the words to describe what I'm experiencing is quite difficult but I'll try my best. I've cried the most joyful tears from being so overwhelmed in the best way possible, the love and the energy is so beautifully electric. I feel at home here surrounded by like minded souls who have now become family. The community we've created continues to blow my mind as I've watched it all organically grow and come together.

"This is what they fear the most, from strategically dividing us for many many years to now we the people bringing everyone back together, restoring the love, compassion, empathy, connection, we the people have the power to create a new world for our generations to come."

***

Alison, 49, a former café manager from Brisbane, said she had left her job three months before, unable and unwilling to deal with or enforce the endless health diktats of masks, QR codes, social distancing, the final straw being vaccine mandates. She particularly objected to the idea that she was supposed to push vaccines onto her teenage staff. She now travels the country in her Woke Folk Coffee Van.

"We had the police come every other day," she said. "Each time they came they were inconsistent with their rules and said different things. Eventually I knew this wasn't the place for me to be.

"All the doors shut behind me, and another door opened.

"The people here at this campsite have been chosen to be here at the end of days. This is spiritual warfare. This is heavy stuff. I have three children. All non-vaxxed. I have been fighting this since my first was born.

"The Woke Folk Coffee Van came into my life and allows me to go places and talk to people. It belongs in the people's army. We need to push back. I aim to stay on the frontline, where all Australia needs to be right now."

***

Simon, from rural Australia, said he wanted to live in Camp Freedom forever with his pig called "Dude".

"I drove in here and I couldn't hold back the tears. I can truly now understand the meaning of the term 'tears of joy'. It's so beautiful. It's home. I don't want to go back.

"It's overwhelming. It's hard to put into words. I have never experienced anything like this. It's very healing.

"Dude brings so much joy, especially to the kids."

***

One young man told his story: "I had a franchise but because I refused to get jabbed I lost the whole business.

"My girlfriend is from the Philippines and she went back to her country, she was having trouble getting a visa here. She was pregnant.

"The $16,000 it was going to cost to have the baby here, we decided to put it into the business and I was going to go back to the Philippines for the birth.

"The lockdowns happened. 2020. I made no money from the business.

"Then they told me get the jab or lose my business.

"I just want to get back to my Baby Girl. And I want to see my girlfriend, I want to marry her."

And then he started to cry.

***

Brent, 34, who owned a construction business from Western Australia, described himself as a vaccine survivor.

"I spent 20 days in hospital and I was told the whole time it was anxiety," he says. "My wife and children are at home in WA.

"I want to go home as soon as possible. And that's when we achieve our goal.

"At this point in time I can't legally get home. I'm doing this for my kids, and if I didn't have the adverse reaction I wouldn't have woken up and my children would be vaccinated.

"When I left WA I was eligible to return because I was double vaxxed. As soon as you are due for your booster, you have to have it, which was the day I arrived in Canberra.

"My children will only be vaccinated over my dead-vaxxed body."

When last spotted, Brent was camping with a group of some 350 cars from WA, none of whom could return to their home state.

***

Peter, 50, a support disability worker who lost his job after being accused of talking negatively about Covid, said: "I am a single dad. I have to pay the mortgage. As soon as the people in my workplace discovered I was not double vaccinated, even though I had a medical exemption, they turned on me and went to management.

"I went to one of the large protests, and asked one of my fellow employees if they would cover me for an hour to allow me time to get back to work. I was accused of talking about Covid again, because I replied honestly when she asked if I was going to a rally.

"I was given a first and final warning; and after some bulldust had a fellow employee turn on me. That's what I'm dealing with. I was suspended. When I went to the Australian Services Union they told me to fall on my knees and beg for my job.

"It has been therapy for me, coming to Canberra, sharing my story with people in the same situation. It's been very sad meeting with other fathers, our role is to protect our children, and every father I have spoken to here have had children turn against them over this.

"It is heartbreaking for all of us."

***

The government dismissed these people at their peril.

One participant passionately argued that we should all learn from nature and Australia's stunning landscapes, that we should return the nation to its ancient spirits and rename the Constitution "The Land of Magnificent Trees".

There was a lot of that sort of thing. And it was very sincerely felt.

Entire suburbs of tents spread out from the showground's central pavilion, neatly lined in rows, with barbecues and beds and chairs. The atmosphere was invariably joyful.

Australians' love of camping and the outdoors was now serving them well.

For some it was an intensely spiritual event; as if an Imperial Warship inhabited by supranatural beings existing outside of time, those entities the humans call Gods, had settled in the sky above the campground; an airborne megalopolis, a giant and extraordinary swirl of out-of-this-world intelligences; as if there had been nothing like it since the Sermon on the Mount and the story of the Loaves and Fishes.

However various inflamed imaginations may have interpreted it; on the ground there was certainly a fair bit of loaves and fishes going on, as makeshift kitchens staffed with volunteers sprang up to feed thousands of people every day.

As if out of nowhere, the right people appeared at the right time, from chefs to dishwashers, kitchen assistants to food servers, while at the same time carload after carload appeared delivering supplies and donations, some travelling many miles to do so.

Michael Griffith of Café Lockdown again: "I stood at the front gates of Epic Park as vehicles kept arriving from all over Australia. These vehicles were flying Australian flags, both red and blue and many of these flags were upside down, and or their vehicles' windows were covered in slogans. Hands off our kids. End the mandates. Freedom.

"The day before the big march, this constant arrival of Australians became a tsunami. All day Epic Park's main winding road was a traffic jam of cars full of people who had come here, from every corner of the country, to demand that the government return their freedoms and leave their children alone.

"As soon as they passed through the gate, a crowd lining the avenues of Epic showground cheered and then the vehicle's occupants cheered back. They had made it. They were here, the Anti Vax Capital of Australia. The long, long drive had been well and truly worth it.

"Everyone who was here, these witnesses, kept stating that they had never experienced anything like this before. Many of them old people, and many of these were teary with joy, and assured us that nothing like this had ever happened before. Not in Australia.

"This was a Gathering of Guardians, the defenders of freedom. This organic, nationwide, communal protest was the birth of a new nation."

**

Kim Ward, 59, a former aged care worker from Redcliffe in Brisbane, had been at the camp since the first of the Convoy.

"It started about 10am. I just travelled down in a car with my girlfriend. There were about 60 of us outside the front of Parliament House, where we camped overnight.

"I thought, we're going to be screwed here. There's just not enough of us.

"Then they just started pouring in. We stayed in the car park the first night; the police moved a lot of us on. They weren't violent; but they were arrogant. You wouldn't want to approach them.

"The mood was great, even though there weren't many of us. There were people from all over.

"Now, there's probably more than 200,000 in this camp alone. It gives you hope. You don't feel so alone now, when you see how many people are fighting. I am amazed by the whole lot of it, these people fighting for their children. To be honest, I am so happy because we've made them nervous. We haven't seen much light."

***

Maria Pilar, 67, from Byron Bay in northern NSW, was part of the Convoy to Canberra from the very first day. She spent much of her time working out of a temporary office helping others.

"I am deeply concerned for the children," she said in her exuberant, heavy accent. "I come from an original sovereign tribe, the Mapuche from central Chile.

"We have never given away our sovereignty and our freedom.

"I was amazed from the beginning at the quality of the people I was with, the clarity and their skills. How well and how quickly we self organised. It is a spontaneous community.

"Now my heart is just full of joy to see so many people coming together in unity and cooperation."

***

Perry Thorp, 20, from Melbourne, the world's most locked down city, a Bible College student, found a purpose for his computer expertise helping with the social media campaign for Reignite Democracy Australia.

"Unity for a cause has brought me here," he said. "I feel deeply passionate to stand up for my generation and the ones to follow.

"I feel people my age aren't brave enough to step up, because they've been taught to respect society.

"That society has now betrayed them and their futures.

"I feel God is doing something here, in this nation, in the here and now."

***

Once inside Camp Freedom new arrivals set up their swags and tents, parked their caravans or set up beds in their cars. And they did this without anyone telling them where to park. Together they just figured it out, and then, instead of awkwardly talking about the footy or the weather, as was the Australian habit, they vigorously shook hands with each other then went "'fuck it" before embracing.

Then they asked each other if they needed anything. They shared food, beer and dope, and they laughed as much as they cried.

As one of the protesters declared: "The victory of this day was that we had answered the great question: 'What sort of future do Australians want? The answer was clear. The people want Freedom."

The Government, and its enabler, the propaganda machine known as the mainstream media, could never have compelled this many people to make their way to the Country's Capital, chanting "I want to take the booster."

Another observer said: "It appears, as always, courage is finally trumping fear. Sadly, we will probably have to play out the rest of the game, which could take a while, but it is only for show, for like I said, and somewhere in the halls of power they have figured this out too, that in this war, that was brought to the people, we, the people have already won."

***

"We should call this Australia Day," said one indigenous woman.

They came with their dogs. They came with their kids. They came with their hearts.

The 12th of February, 2022, was the Ground Zero of days; when the nation stood up and said no to the authoritarian derangement which had overtaken the country.

In one telling incident, in the early hours of the morning as hundreds of cars every hour continued to pour in, with queues backed up for miles, the police declared the Epic camp site to be full and blocked the entrance.

A crowd instantly gathered, chanting "Let them in, let them in".

An opera singer boomed out the national anthem from the chaos: "Australian sons let us rejoice, for we are young and free. Our land abounds in Nature's gifts, Of beauty rich and rare."

Within the hour, the police were forced into an ignominious retreat, and once again the cars, trucks and caravans, estimated at some 350 an hour, continued to arrive .

The atmosphere was absolutely electric; some said "spirit drenched".

One protestor said: "You will be telling your grandchildren you were here. They cannot take our freedom."

"This is a big victorious day, a great day," declared another.

***

Kath, 53, a delivery truck driver who lost her job due to the vaccine mandates, drove nearly 4000 kilometres from Darwin to be part of the rally.

"We've been protesting in Darwin for months, the group is called Free in the NT," she said. "It's for the children, basically. I am a new grandmother. I don't want the kids to grow up in this horrible world.

"We are standing up for human rights. And for choice. I've been made an alien in my own country. I can't work.

"Today was great. We are staying. Whatever it takes to change this rotten system. I've got nothing else to go back to; no job, no house. I was living in a Salvation Hostel before I came here.

"I just knew I had to come and stand up."

***

Charles, 59, from Gerringong, a teacher suspended without pay under the vaccine mandate regime, worked as a cameraman at the Australian Broadcasting Corporation on the day Parliament House opened, and can be clearly seen in historic footage as he films the Queen.

"I was there at the opening, and now I'm trying to close it down. It was great to see so many familiar faces as well as to meet so many new ones. The people are speaking with their feet against government overreach!!

"We the people are rewriting Australian history."

***

Billy Arnold, 42, from Wollongong was one of the many people who travelled from all over Australia to attend the day's extraordinary events.

And like so many others, his life has been entirely disrupted by Covid restrictions and mandates.

"It's the single largest collective event in Australian history of people coming together," he said. "Regardless of whether you are vaxxed or unvaxxed, there is not a single judgement from anyone. Everybody is equal no matter what demographic you are from.

"I arrived at Commonwealth Park, one kilometre from Parliament House, at 9am. I started filming while rollerblading on the main road as protestors arrived. Within one hour, off the top of my head I would say there was easily half a million people there.

"As the protest started to make its way from the park to Parliament House people were 20 wide on each side of the road and one kilometre long at least by the time they reached the House. And for two hours they were still making their way in droves.

"Never ever have I felt so alive and so welcomed by complete strangers. Words could not explain how I feel, except for the fact that everybody made comments about how great my smile was as I passed them, because it was from ear to ear the whole time."

***

Claire, 64, a finance broker from New South Wales, said: "I came because I wanted to take a stance for my grandchildren's right to choose their futures. I was actually crying. I was extremely moved. I couldn't believe how many people came together in one body for one common cause; to unite Australia for all our freedoms."

***

Nancy, 75, a natural therapist from Queensland, had been at Camp Freedom for the previous week.

"I drove down in my little car on my own. I got told by God I had to be here. I pushed against it for a couple of days, and then just got in the car with a mattress so I could sleep in the back.

"I felt compelled to be here. Many, many people are saying the same thing, they had a voice in their head, they just had to go.

"For me it was the mandates, because I didn't have a choice anymore. My three kids and two grandkids have all been vaxxed because of coercion for their jobs. I am absolutely frantic about babies being vaccinated. My stepson got inflammation of the heart and ended up in hospital after his vaccination. I have heard heaps of similar stories, particularly with young men. It is absolutely terrifying.

"That's what the grandparents I meet all say, what about our grandkids? We're old, we're going to be gone, but they've got a life to live."

***

Skeeta, 55, a homemaker from South Australia, one of the many people who would never normally be found anywhere near a demonstration, said she had been waiting for just this moment.

"I fight for the rights of all Australians," she said. "I came by plane yesterday. There were no police at the airport. I saw the camp from the air, and it amazed me how full it was.

"My husband has an auto-immune compromised system and is continuing to deteriorate. He has been mandated for his essential service job. He's not allowed back into Western Australia, where he flies month on month off.

"He's at home in South Australia. He's tired of fighting. And I've taken his role."

***

One of the warriors of that day called himself Spartan. He was a truck driver and a former military officer.

He had been arrested at protests several times over the previous two years.

He called the process "catch and release".

"I am here to reclaim freedom. I am here for the children. What made me fight now? I became a dad.

"I was one of the 300 Spartans against the Persians, and I am the Spartan against tyranny."

***

Louise, from North Queensland, is an immunisation nurse, the mother of seven and the grandmother of eight.

Now fully present, armed for duty with nothing but her presence.

She had received a number of awards, including the National Medal of Australia for her volunteering work with the State Emergency Service, and deeply regretted the bastardisation of her profession.

"I didn't do it for medals, it was to help people. I am here to help humanity. As an immunisation nurse we were taught you need informed consent, not to coerce, and that you must know the ingredients of what you are injecting.

"With all my years of service, for everything I have done and everything I can contribute, I have lost it all because I will not be jabbed."

***

Susan Pavan, a former mainstream journalist fully occupied taking care of four young children, nonetheless found time to play her role, interviewing and photographing participants. Old Alex was more than pleased to publish her work in his magazine.

"People were upset," she said of that historical day. "They expected something to change. There was a tsunami of freedom. People don't want to go back to their old lives. They want to stay. They want to start a new way, a new life.

"Everywhere you go people are smiling at you, hugging each other. After the last two years separated from normal society, people have found a new Australia here. They can't believe how wonderful it is.

"Everyone says they are doing it for the children I can't believe the energy. I was walking around at 1.30am, and people were still pouring in. It hasn't stopped.

***

One dad piggybacking his daughter on his shoulders wore a t-shirt with the message: "There's a future version of me who's proud. We are strong enough!"

Other members of the family, from Coffs Harbour in NSW, all wore messages blazoned on their outfits: "Mandate Medical Freedom", "Freedom Over Fear" and "My body, My choice, My Children."

"I have never seen anything like this, this is outstanding, it takes your breath away," he said. The energy is just incredible. It just blows you away. There are so many people thinking the same way."

And then he, too, started crying.

***

Julie from Queensland was in a wheelchair and wore a t-shirt blazoned "Be Kind". She had attended many of the rallies in Brisbane and on the Sunshine Coast.

"This is so big, amazing," she said. "I'm here for my grandchildren. I want their future to be free from the government telling them what to do.

"I want this country to be totally different to the way it's become."

***

A group of former police officers carried banners that read: "Police for Freedom: We are human beings serving and protecting other human beings."

Pavan observed: "I believe these are the frontline workers for freedom."

One placard for the activist group Cops for Covid Truth, which had played a telling role in changing the public narrative from the blizzard of deceptive conduct by the government, read: "Police are speaking out across Australia. Is Covid really about public health? On what side of history do you want to be?"

A former policeman of 41 years said: "I served in the police for four decades. We had a really good police force. I am really disgusted with the Victorian Police and the Union, at the brutality they showed. I am here to support my Australian brothers and sisters in their quest for freedom. I am not non-vaxxed. I want everyone to have a choice. I'm so glad I'm out of the police force."

***

Behind the human stories, there were also political ones, of course.

With the atmosphere absolutely electric, among the speakers was Monica Smit, one of the founders of and the public face for the group Reignite Democracy Australia. She went to prison after being charged with incitement for allegedly encouraging people to attend demonstrations after Melbourne went into its sixth lockdown.

At the time the clashes between police and protestors on the streets of Melbourne were attracting worldwide condemnation for the extremely repressive and often violent behaviour of police. Smit had been one of the most indefatigable citizen journalists in the thick of the action, and one of the most prolific activists.

She was charged with two counts of incitement for protests in August of 2021 and three counts of breaching the Chief Health Medical Officer's orders in September; and spent 22 days in jail after refusing to accede to strict bail conditions, including not posting to social media.

Fast forward to February, 2022 and she declared that the message from the freedom movement was straightforward: "We are coming. It's really simple, give us the rights that we already had, which by the way weren't yours to take away in the first place, give them back to us and we'll leave. It's that simple. If you don't give our rights back to us we're gonna keep coming.

"The message that we are sending to them is, we are absolutely determined. They have created us because of how badly they've treated us and they have created a monster. We will never ever go back to sleep.

"We have all been working tirelessly at home for the last two years but today we have all driven hours and days to come to our capital city and fight; not only fight but also celebrate our freedoms together.

"This is one of the most memorable days of all of our lives.

"On that note I want to give a massive, massive shout out to all the people that wish they were here that couldn't be here. We are your voice today.

"Look at us. Look around you. Two years ago we were running around like headless chickens trying to find a protest and now we have driven days to come to our capital city and stand up for our rights.

"It's just crazy. Could you imagine two years ago that you would be this person? Could you imagine that you would be the type of person that would never ever give up and never ever lay down and never ever get trampled on?

"That is you now; supporting each other.

"It takes effort but we've just got to do it because now whether you like it or not, we are family. And families never give up on each other and they always have each other's backs.

"It is far from over guys, but remember we are all fighting for the same thing. We just want the God-given rights that were already ours given back to us. We will get those rights back because good always prevails, truth always wins."

***

Jasmine, from Sydney, who took her dog to mingle with the demonstrators, said: "I'm here for the future generation. I am here for my children. I want to see all the systems crumble down."

Jared from the agricultural centre of Taree on the New South Wales Central Coast had just one strong message: "The mainstream media are liars."

Mark White, 69, from Ayr in North Queensland, rode a motorbike 2,448 kilometres down the inland route to Canberra.

"I came because I am furious and disgusted that the Australian government wants to kill me with the death injection. That's why I'm here. My agenda is to help dissolve the Australian government and have a fair society.

"The rally was absolutely magnificent, to be with so many people feeling the same way. I want to get behind a leader to help resolve this situation. I hope to stay in Canberra for as long as it takes.

"Many of the people I have met absolutely feel the same way. We are disgusted and furious. Join us or stand aside and watch. People think it can't be done, but it can. All we get is lies, day after day after day."

***

Lisa, 53, a sales assistant from Kingaroy in Queensland, wore a t-shirt blazoned with the words: "My body, My Choice, No Vaccine Mandate."

She has been attending an event held every Sunday in Kingaroy called A Stand in the Park.

"We stand for freedom, that's what it's about. But I'm not normally a person who would demonstrate. I have never been to a rally anything like what has happened in Canberra. It was inspirational, amazing, emotional, epic. It's just been brilliant, I love it. I came here to stand for freedom and to save the children, because what they're doing is wrong.

"My friend had the AstraZeneca and now she can't walk because she has blood clots and is in hospital. She can't work. She is a nurse and had to have it for work. What is happening is absolutely criminal.

"Another person I know had a heart attack after the jab.

"You hear horror stories all the time. It's absolutely criminal, wicked what they're doing, evil.

"And they just get away with it. They haven't lost a day's pay, and they've decimated millions. People have nowhere to live; they're living in their cars.

"I had a friend who crossed the Queensland/NSW border to visit his dying mother and couldn't come back. They were stuck in their car for three months.

"I had to be here. I came straight from work on Friday, and I had to come. It was in my heart, it's a 16 hour drive, but I just had to be here. I think this government is criminal and should be held accountable for what they are doing. Personally, I don't think they deserve to breathe the air we breathe."

***

Louise, 57, an administrative assistant from NSW, said: "I felt overwhelming pride to be taking part in an activity that can't be ignored by those in power. Without action nothing changes. Every person here today was doing their part in making a difference to stopping mandatory vaccinations. I came here for the opportunity to do something, rather than just watching it on the alternative news platforms. Just the opportunity to participate was motivation to get here."

***

Lyn, 67, a self-funded retiree from Melbourne, the world's most locked down city, said: "I have three married children, two of them who are teachers. I have six grandchildren.

"They were forced to have the third jab to go back to work and they jabbed my nine year old and seven year old grandchildren to go to school.

"My daughter said they basically jabbed them at the school on the first day it was available.

"I asked my daughter how it was at school and she said: 'Busy, because a lot of teachers are sick.' It's devastating for me because I know what's going on. I knew what was coming, the people have been coerced, lied to, brainwashed, we all know that.

"I was greatly encouraged at the rally by how many people came from all over Australia, and how passionate they were. Even the people who couldn't come, how encouraging they have been.

"I know I'm meant to be here. My first thought, I shouldn't go. Then I asked God, and I got the strong message to go. I don't mind camping even though I have a nice home.

"How wonderful it is that many of us have lost family and friends, but how supportive of each other everyone here is. We are all hurting. We have compassion and understanding for each other, we have found a new family."

***

Jim, 50, a chef from Canberra: "I say to the people of Australia. The people here are mothers, fathers, grandparents, doctors, lawyers, truck drivers and people from all walks of life. We are here with a sense of community, with only one aim: to make the government legislate against vaccine mandates and end lockdowns so that the people of Australia can go about their lives without the current division and hatred."

***

Julianne, 55, a retired police officer from Gladstone in Queensland, said: "I'm not able to articulate. I was just called to be here. Things reveal themselves after the fact. It's a spiritual thing. I feel like I am in the right place at the right time. My three adult daughters are watching me, and they are proud of me."

Marcus, 52, a builder from Sydney, said: "It was heartwarming and heartbreaking. Is this the new Australia Day? That's what it felt like."

Antony Pond, 44, an IT engineer from NSW, said: "Today was the beginning of the beginning of the creation of a new democratic Constitution, written by the people for the people. The atmosphere was compassionate, respectful and joyful."

Mother of five Elizabeth, 45, from NSW, said: "It is very personal for me. We need no politicians. We need some way of looking and solving issues from a new perspective; people who are dedicated members of society and have the ability to interact with other countries amicably to work together for our children for a better future.

"I felt compelled to come here. I am very moved. This is for our children's future. That's all there is to it."

***

That day notices went up around the Epic Showgrounds telling campers they must depart by midday of Sunday 13 February, 2022, that is, less than 24 hours after the march on Parliament House.

The notices claimed that the Canberra Show had been pre-booked 12 months ahead and the date could not be rescheduled. As almost every major event in the country had been cancelled for the previous two years, even church gatherings raided, the excuse was preposterous.

It was signed by the Australian Capital Territory Government, one of the worst perpetrators of Covid tyranny in the country.

That both the Epic showground administrators and the Show people themselves were reportedly supportive of the protestors and did not want them moved on was irrelevant to the authorities, who were determined to bust the demonstrators out of Canberra.

The thousands gathered at Epic were a political embarrassment to the nation's leaders and the political establishment which had foisted this debacle on their fellow Australians.

The authorities should not have betrayed the public in order to oblige the will of their political masters and their corporate backers, the overlords who had created this disaster in the first place, forging a protest movement which was not going to go away at their convenience, no matter how much gaslighting and propaganda they spewed from their comfortable offices.

The protestors should have been allowed to stay until their grievances were addressed; instead of being pushed out of the camp in the most brutal, authoritarian and deceptive manner possible.

This protest was a direct response to political and government overreach, a terrible and tragically demented tyranny which had lasted two long years, and the authorities had no right to attempt to destroy the voices of the people they were meant to serve.

Instead of choosing to protect the corporate thugs, political incompetents and grotesquely overpaid time serving bureaucrats infesting the halls of power, they should have moved to protect the public.

But to their eternal shame, they did not.

***

Twenty four hours after a jubilant atmosphere gripped Canberra, with one of the largest protest gatherings in Australian history, a deep anxiety afflicted the protestors.

The putative and publicly squabbling leadership of the movement at Camp Epic did nothing to dispel tensions. And all of them disappeared on the penultimate day, leading to yet more fear and confusion amongst the thousands who remained on the site itself, including a number with children who had no jobs and no homes to return to.

All the rhetoric from various members of the movement that they were there "until the job is done", or "until this is over", proved as substantial as smoke; leaving the diehards to face down the authorities on their own or roam the city streets, homeless and disorientated.

Tensions rose throughout the day, with many protestors leaving immediately after the rally. Others, lured out of Camp Freedom at the Epic Showgrounds to a rural property 40 kilometres outside by the false promise that they could set up their tents there, now had nowhere to go after police blocked the entrance.

Orders were broadcast by police ringing Camp Epic that protesters must leave the campsite by midnight or face arrest for trespassing.

The atmosphere was deeply chaotic; with many members of the freedom movement having no idea where they could go or what to do. There were reports that hundreds of groups were now camping along the sides of Canberra roads.

The grounds fell spookily empty, and those who remained were frightened, confused and anxious. Of those, many were families with children.

Significant numbers of the people Old Alex interviewed said they had nothing to go back to, they had lost their jobs and their homes and been made to feel like aliens in their own country. They wanted to stay in Camp Freedom, where they had found a new family and a new home. Some declared tearfully they wanted to stay there forever.

"Oh My God, this is a War," exclaimed one protestor amid the increasingly confused circumstance.

***

At an incendiary meeting of confused campers near Gate Seven of the showgrounds various speakers put their points of view.

Faced with imminent arrest, many were disappointed at the departed leadership.

One speaker shouted through the microphone: "If you care so much about your country and your people, where are you? We are the people holding the line. They are not believers. We are the people holding the ground here and now. We are the heroes."

Another speaker said: "People, do not be scared. I was there at the last eviction. Get your popcorn ready."

One speaker, wearing a t-shirt blazoned with the words I Do Not Comply, said: "If we walk away we might as well not have come here in the first place. The demons have done their work and 75% have left. But we are staying."

Another agitated camper declared: "They are all a fraud. The people are the authority."

Yet another declared: "The sheep have left, we are the fighters. We are going to win."

Another passionate speaker told the assembled crowd: "I was a builder earning $4000 a week. I lost my job to come down here. I have five kids. I am staying until this is done."

There were signs littering the increasingly sad and fraught site, along with messages blazoned on cars and t-shirts.

On cars: "We don't need no vaccination, we don't need no forced control."

On signage: "Protect The Children." "Leave My Kids Alone."

On t-shirts: "Unvaxxed Untested Unafraid." "After the Tribulation Let No Man Deceive You."

***

After the initial authoritarian abuses witnessed at the first camp site in the parliamentary precinct, the hands off policing approach which characterised Camp Epic for much of the week had been remarkably successful. The crowd was essentially self-policing, and there were no reports of violence, rapes, vandalism or all the other behaviours one might fairly expect with such a large and wildly diverse crowd.

That all ended on the 14th of February, 2022, two days after so many had marched on Parliament House in jubilant unity.

Camp Epic was already emptying rapidly on the final day when police moved in and aggressively moved every last protestor off the site.

In the inflammatory lead up, sowing yet more tension and confusion, protestors were initially told that they would have to move on by midnight.

One woman with two young children said people had come to her tent early in the evening and told her she would be bashed and arrested if she did not move on. The woman did not have a car and had no way of complying. The disturbing threats brought up visions of a distressed childhood. Interviewing her, Old Alex instinctively reached down to provide some comfort, but these people were beyond comfort.

The next rumour in this evolving drama was that campers had until 8am to comply.

As it turned out the police arrived in force at around 11am, repeatedly broadcasting the message: "Leave Now. You are trespassing. Leave immediately. If you do not leave you will be arrested."

Police, tolerating no resistance, spread out and worked their way through from the showgrounds from the top camping ground until every last protester had been evicted.

The irony of police aggressively moving demonstrators from the nation's capital, ostensibly the heart of Australian democracy, was lost on nobody.

As more than 98% percent of protestors had already left, and of the holdouts most were already packing up to leave, it was a largely pointless show of force.

In one of those all too human moments, one protester pleaded with the police: "Don't vax your kids."

One sign, emblematic of the passionate sincerity of protestors, read: "Touch Our Kids & It's War."

While from a policing point of view the dissolving of Camp Freedom may well have been deemed a success by the authorities, and even end up as a textbook model for policing in highly volatile crowd situations, it also left many questions over its inhumanity and deceptive nature.

Every last protester who was moved on had received the message: "The government is my enemy. I have no right to protest. This government would prefer I didn't exist at all."

**

Campers were told multiple conflicting stories.

One of those was that they could move to a large conference and adventure centre Caloola Farm, an hour outside of Canberra, provided free of charge by the sympathetic owner, also proved false.

Police blockaded the roads and refused to let protestors enter.

Owner Ralph Hurst-Meyers, closely aligned with the Australian Capital Territory's authorities, was known for his perhaps convenient community generosity. He said: "After consultation with the authorities, Caloola

Farm and the Hurst-Meyers Charity Limited will allow vulnerable people affected by recent events such as the elderly, the disabled, and the indigenous community, single mothers with children, vulnerable families with children, to temporarily stay at Caloola Farm free of charge while they make preparations to return home."

The problem with that, of course, was that many of the remaining protestors had no home to return to. The other issue was, these people didn't come to Canberra to set up a commune or a new Nimbin, they came to change the country and to restore their freedoms, most particularly the freedom to work.

The "hotheads", as they were described, that is the politically active and the outspoken who had been driven to action by the destruction of their lives, were not welcome.

Another rumour was that they would be welcome at another Council controlled camping ground at Cotter Creek half an hour away. That also proved false, with police aggressively moving protestors on from there as well, despite the fact that some of them had already made bookings and paid for their visit.

The final lie was that protesters would be safe and were welcome to stay on Ground Seven, at the top of the Epic showgrounds, because it was privately owned land.

In the dramatic unravelling, none of these stories, or deliberate falsehoods, turned out to be true.

The hundreds of people who moved up to Ground Seven on the understanding that as it was private property and the owner was sympathetic were easily kettled, or corralled, by police. They were given no choice but to leave after more than fifty heavily armed police entered the grounds; with backup forces standing armed behind them.

The protestations of the farmer who owned the land and had given his permission were ignored.

While many officers wore the standard uniforms of local police, there were other heavily armed special operatives wearing masks and holding leashed dogs, adding to the fear and panic already spreading through the crowd.

Amid these surreal and frightening scenes, as an old reporter who had covered demonstrations for decades, Old Alex thought it was obvious that a few of the officers were enjoying their role perhaps a little too much; but that many others were unhappy about the duties they were being asked to perform.

In the midst of this chaos, some of the younger officers in particular, were exceptionally polite, thanking the protestors for their cooperation.

They didn't like being involved in this shameful part of Australian history, and as the lockdowns and vaccine mandates had damaged them and their children as much as they had ordinary citizens, weren't entirely unsympathetic.

But as the many Australians refusing to accede to the government's vaccine mandates burnt through their savings and resources and new forms of government derangement came into force, the social chaos inflicted on Australia's working and middle classes by the Canberra elites would have serious ramifications for years to come.

Temporarily crushed and disbanded, next time around they were more likely to blockade the capital than politely march. The authorities succeeded in moving the protesters on this time around, but Australia's freedom movement was going nowhere but straight into the history books.

SIXTEEN
BLESSED ART THOU

To break a promise is to deny the reality of the past; therefore it is to deny the hope of a real future. If time and reason are functions of each other, if we are creatures of time, then we had better know it, and try to make the best of it. To act responsibly."

Ursula Le Guin. Author of *The Left Hand of Darkness*.

The world that the lockdowns and mandates, and all that is associated with them, unleashed is dark, corrupt, duplicitous, dishonest, dangerous, tribal, and pervaded with nihilism and a loss of moral clarity and a resulting criminality both public and private. How easy it turns out to be to shatter trust, to disable a functioning social order, to spread corruption from person to person, institution to institution, to the point that the centre no longer holds! I'm quite sure that very few among us knew that. We know now.

Jeffrey Tucker. Director. Brownstone Institute.

There was no point. The vacuity was complete. Back from the Canberra Convoy, drained not just by the event but suffering from the after effects of the hi-tech weapons beamed against the crowds by the authorities, Old Alex settled back into Oak Flats as if settling back into a part of history. We will come for you when we are ready. At the right time, in the right place. He was less impressed than ever with the heroic virtues of the common man. The mirror that had once been the mainstream media no longer reflected anything but the agendas of government, did nothing but coat the truth and create a parallel world where the voices of the devastated were unheard, thereby fully enabling what was already being called the biggest public health policy mistake in history; soon enough, in those echo chambers of the world's evolving hive mind, the biggest crime in history.

Much of the country had lost faith in their political leaders, but at the same time none of this was reflected back in the production and consumption of news.

This parallel, manufactured world, the end result of decades of media manipulation by governments and intelligence agencies, made it appear as if nothing was going on; that the routine rituals of the government, the eternally woke parrying over racism or sexism or climate change, were in fact the real world.

Which it most definitely was not.

The thing that struck Old Alex the most was the apparent lack of anger; at least in the immediate vicinity of Oak Flats, within the narrow circles he encountered, at least among the prosperous.

He couldn't understand it.

All around the echoes of lost worlds and greater kingdoms; of the original souls of transmutation and inheritance, those ancient precursors to transhumanism. We were born here and withered on the vine and were born again; we jumped species and races and times; we lived forever and were born again; we loved you and were indifferent. And were in no way even remotely human.

Against what angered the mortals, the few that were roused to care, what angered us the most was the destruction of beauty; and as they flew high over myriad circumstances; as the dire wolves circled the encampment, as the of light of disembodied wings, or spirits, settled in the valley, as the machines, those secrets beyond secrets, once more moved into view, as parallel, as complex, as extraordinary as anything on this complex globe.

All these voices ran through Old Alex's fevered imagination; and whether they were true or not, he simply could not tell.

The spirits would move into alignment, if and when it suited them. If and when they found the right portal in which to dock. That's what they told him; with that odd sense of déjà vu, as if these interferences in history, though rare, had all happened before; as mankind increasingly glimpsed the infinite nature of it all.

This population, their protests extinguished or ignored, was being paralysed or propelled into an entirely uncertain future; the destruction of their country, the destruction of good will, of sociability, of thirst and camaraderie and laughter, of the communal nature of their species, nesting with their families large and small.

On the other side of that divide of dreams and divination, they, those other lives so inexplicably connected to his own, swished down corridors in those floating hi-tech cities, or faced their final hour as mobs ransacked the temples. That was it. That was why we looked back on this era, the Covid era, not for sustenance but for fear, a warning of what could happen. For this truly was a frightening time.

***

The government is your enemy is an easy message to take out when you are being bashed, fined, pepper sprayed and imprisoned by police; when the army is on the street and military helicopters are flying overhead; and trust in government was unlikely to return any time soon.

What drilled home the reality of the totalitarian state which Australia had become was the controversy over the use of hi-tech weapons against a crowd of peaceful protestors, including the highly controversial LRADs, Long Range Acoustic Devices.

The truth of their use, or the use of similar devices, was difficult to establish, with the head of the Australian Federal Police Reece Kershaw, under questioning on the subject, telling a parliamentary committee: "That would be something that is with our police methodology which we would have to look at some type of public interest immunity claim."

There was ample photographic evidence of their presence in the precincts of both the Epic Showgrounds and at the National Parliament. There were also audio recordings which appeared to confirm their use.

With their science fiction look and surrounded by heavily armed police, the presence alone of such weaponry and crowd control technology added to the heightened fear and confusion.

What sort of person would use such weaponry against their fellow Australians?

There was also ample anecdotal evidence that these futuristic crowd control methods were used to disorient the protestors, professionals of all ages, adults and children, the elderly people, and both physically and mentally challenged Australians.

Many thousands of people, including Old Alex, reported symptoms which included unusually high levels of fatigue, mental clouding, disorientation, exhaustion, anxiety and nausea.

Others reported severe headaches and provided photographic evidence of extensive skin burns.

That the authorities were prepared to use sonic and microwave technology against their own citizens, and made an overt display of doing so, marked a step into the abyss.

***

The contrast between where he had been, surrounded by celebrating and protesting Australians, and where he was could not have been more extreme. Back in Oak Flats black ice, a kind of intersecting lattice, had crept across the sky and the same voice kept emerging: "We are not human." Because the gods were roiled and Old Alex felt as if he had to act.

But he knew that already.

Betrayed, exhausted in a sense, he bowed out of the cavalcade for a period. The human voices were different; a mix of radio messages and overheard conversations, even overheard intents.

Wolves circled the encampment, not to attack but to protect.

The politics had been as vile as the weather; the insanity of the moment perpetrated by self-absorbed politicians determined to save their own ugly necks, to perpetuate the myths they themselves had created around the efficacy of vaccines and the lethality of Covid-19, bludgeoning the population into acceptance while ignoring all alternative views, hammering the community into compliance.

It was a military insanity, a social insanity, a political madness.

It felt in those months as if they were, indeed, witnessing the breakup of the country once known as Australia.

That this had once been one country was a concept future historians might struggle to understand as they looked back in wonder at the shocking level of government malfeasance, the unforgettable, unforgivable squandering of public monies, the looting of the working class, as if their hi-tech whips flickering across broken backs of the nation's working class.

As summer dwindled into autumn, in Old Alex's state of New South Wales there was a passing return to normality, a brief cessation of the interminable rain which had characterised the previous two years, the horror of lockdowns disappearing in the rear view mirror.

An election had to be called.

After the ruling conservative party, known as the Liberals, were caught out branding the Covid vaccines with their own party logo the previous year, thereby creating quite a conniption in those desperate delusionary days when a dying government thought the vaccine rollout could save their political bacon. How quickly history changed it all; in those already seemingly far off days when the ruling elites thought mass vaccinating the population was an election winner. Instead, it very quickly came to look more like criminal malfeasance, a recklessly selfish disregard for the welfare of the population.

That both major parties in Australia were wedded to the aims of pharmaceutical companies demonstrated a corrupt nexus between government and Big Pharma which urgently needed to be unravelled.

The spirit manifests. The darkness dissolves. The gates were open, but none of the perpetrators would dare enter a realm where it was impossible to lie.

And so it seemed to Old Alex that the ancients were preparing the path for the next great step forward in human evolution. And those who destiny had chosen to play a role in this transformation went quietly about their duties.

And all was well; for now.

In a species with a tiny lifespan, another brief day when all was forgiven and nothing denied, when the swish of ancient aristocrats walking through stone colonnades rippled through the air around him, when once again he struggled with English and all was born anew.

***

Restrictions eased, the grip of totalitarianism pried from the psyche of the Australian population finger by finger. It was an election year; and at first it had seemed that the Convoy to Canberra, despite the exultant nature of the celebration, had achieved nothing. Because there was nothing else left, because the mainstream media through which he had once viewed the world had been drained of all vibrancy, and no longer bore any even remote relationship to reality. Because it rained constantly in that dismal year, he went back to work; publishing stories, struggling through the eerie swamps of the palaeolithic era, imagery which swam constantly through his overwhelmed imagination, "where the iguanas play", as Dory Previn had once put it.

The government, geniuses all, had finally worked out that the interminable population-wide lockdowns and restrictions of movement, the issuing of ceaseless freedom destroying diktats, that it all had a use by date. That the population were no longer impressed by their nation's tilt into totalitarianism. And that for the perpetrators, at least figuratively, lay the gallows in the village square.

On one account, the term "conspiracy theory" was invented by America's Central Intelligence Agency after the assassination of President John F. Kennedy to ridicule any idea that Kennedy's demise was more complex than the narrative which the CIA wished to fix in the public consciousness.

The coercion of public debate, the manipulation of the herd, if you will, or the nation-wide PsyOp operation, to use another frequently used expression, took Old Alex by surprise; dumb struck by the willingness of the mob to take on face value the word of politicians and bureaucrats whose word should always be treated with a dose of scepticism, for they have their own agendas; staying in power and maintaining their magnificent salaries for starters.

One thing decades of journalism had taught him. Do not trust politicians. Do not trust bureaucrats. They lie for a living.

By this time virtually every last conspiracy theory had come true.

Very early on, in February of 2020, author Anna Merlan, headlined a hit piece, "Anti-Vaxxers Are Terrified the Government Will 'Enforce' a Vaccine for Coronavirus". Well so it came to pass.

Fast forward to September of 2021 and the headline in *Daily Mail Australia* read: "No jab no pay policy will see thousands of Australians forced to get a Covid vaccine in sweeping new mandate from Scott Morrison."

Ditto anyone who suggested that vaccine passports would be introduced, that lockdowns wouldn't work, that many of the experts peddling Covid measures and Covid vaccines were financially compromised, that billions of dollars were being raked off working people in order to further enrich the world's oligarchs on the back of a vaccine that was clearly counterproductive.

Another so-called conspiracy theory was that surveillance would go into overdrive during the Covid era and the state's ability to control people's lives would be greatly enhanced. Well, so it came to pass. Another, that Covid-19 was being seized upon by a group of the world's oligarchs in league with a lunar right element within the intelligence agencies to cement their vision of a New World Order and to fundamentally remake the social order, and thereby the political contract. Well, so it came to pass.

As early as April of 2020 Australians were ordered to stay home or risk heavy on-the-spot fines, with police and drone patrols increased to enforce social distancing. Both the federal and NSW governments joined an emerging consensus across the world suggesting Covid restrictions would only be lifted when a vaccine had been developed.

That became the biggest conspiracy theory, or delusion, of all time.

With a poorly educated population, in Australia the charge of being a conspiracy theorist was a particularly successful marketing strategy, compartmentalising dissidents and silencing dissent. To park an opponent in the conspiracy camp was to have won the argument, akin to the charge of being a climate change denier, a men's rights activist or a racist.

A clever ideological ploy, it served to squash all rational debate. Until they were all proved wrong. And the establishment could deny the truth no longer, switching instead to filling the public square with war, climate change and the eternally fertile field of gender identity.

***

The Australian authorities hunted the freedom fighters and remnants of the Convoy to Canberra from every last camping site in the Australian Capital Territory. It was a costly exercise in more ways than one. Many of those remaining had lost their jobs because they refused to get vaccinated, and thereby had no way to pay their mortgage or their rent and were in the process of becoming homeless.

Hundreds gathered at the picaresque Warri Camping Ground set on the picturesque upper reaches of the Shoalhaven River. A few were still there a year later.

A significant number went home, sold up whatever assets they had, bought themselves vans, and became a new transient class on Australia's roads, a new generation of gipsies and itinerants. Old Alex never met anyone who regretted their decisions.

In memory of the spirit that had manifested and moved through Camp Epic, Michael Gray Griffith began what he labelled The Deplorables Epic Road Trip. He wrote: "When I headed off, I was thinking I might be heading into a war zone. But by my fourth day I now know I'm too late. The war has passed. This country, my country has been invaded and is now occupied, and its people have been subdued.

"But instead of soldiers patrolling the streets and intimidating any local who looks like they might resist, the soldiers are now residing in these peoples' souls, and the name of their controlling brigade is Fear. The truly conquered wear their masks properly. Their noses covered, their smiles hidden, their eyes like rabbits peering out of the burrows at the world that now frightens them.

"Often they are young, and they walk the streets or sit in the cafés, their heads up, proudly, displaying their joy of obedience via a personalised mask that they wear as if it was a swastika. There is no question as to whose side they are on. Maybe inside they have doubts, but externally they appear to be enjoying the new Authoritarian rule, the continuing evolution of the government's overreach.

"We are not just the unjabbed, our numbers now include the double jabbed who don't want the booster. They are our hope. And we need hope.

"Whilst the media bang on about the war in the Ukraine, they ignore, completely, the wounded and the dead left behind by this invasion of our culture.

"Myocarditis was once rare. Now our cardiologists are booked up for months. Now we have heart surgeons who are setting up to specialise solely to treat myocarditis.

"Instead of the people being outraged, and burning down the vaccination hubs, and arresting the doctors and politicians, they, as ordered by the soldiers occupying their souls, work obediently to secure and maintain the silence."

***

The country entered into election mode; in Australia an arcane triannual ritual the political detail of which bored even the participants, much less the public. Australians knew more about American politics than of their own colourless fare.

Legally the election had to be held by the end of May, 2022.

The Prime Minister Scott Morrison put it off for as long as he could.

Universally disliked even on his own side of politics, a bloated corpse flayed daily in the public square, Morrison was suffering dismal polling. A flurry of grift to party loyalists showed they were preparing for defeat. Nonetheless, somehow Morrison expected another miracle victory; believed that God was on his side and gave, as he put it, his prayer knees a good workout.

The divine don't like liars and those who connive with the rich, simple as that.

Curiously, after Covid restrictions and the ceaseless grandstanding of politicians had been front and centre of everybody's life for the previous two years, neither side of a two horse race wanted to mention Covid.

On the surface, and through the mediated lens of manipulated media, it might have appeared as if the Con to Canberra had achieved nothing. But indeed, the message had got through.

Both sides of politics, the once pro-small business conservatives the Liberals and the orthodox left known as Labor, were keen to disassociate themselves from the lunacies of the previous two years, at least during their respective campaigns.

Morrison was now so unpopular he couldn't campaign in many normally conservative seats, while his opponent, Anthony Albanese, had only one real asset: he wasn't Scott Morrison.

The few enjoyable highlights inevitably involved the public humiliation of the hapless Prime Minister, the stench of impending loss breaking through even Scott Morrison's encasing of supreme self-belief and religious conviction.

Morrison initially decided to go for a khaki election; that is to shamelessly politicise the nation's military. He had no other cards. The economy was a mess. The Covid response was an open sewer. He was personally disliked.

The khaki election promptly fell over when the Solomon Islands, traditionally within Australia's orbit, signed a security pact with China that would allow Beijing to deploy armed police and military personnel to the island.

Bluffing and puffing in front of the press, Morrison squirmed his way through yet another public failure.

Equally embarrassing on the khaki front, the Defence Forces were busted pretending to help clean up the streets of Lismore after a once in a hundred years flood. In reality it was nothing but a photo opportunity for Scott Morrison, and thereby a misuse both of the military and taxpayers funds.

On a mission to pick up a dog and by happenstance driving through the muddy, devastated streets of the town days later, with mounds of rubbish and rotting mattresses piled up outside thousands of homes, it was clear to Old Alex that most of the work was being done by volunteers; and the military, just like the Prime Minister, was Missing In Action.

The photo op backfired after the media discovered that the army was only putting on a show of helping locals. One report read: "Video and photos have emerged showing Australian Defence Force members clearly posing for staged social media Public Relations posts, while residents in the region continue to suffer with little to no support from authorities.

"One video shows almost a dozen ADF members standing around at a single property, passing rubbish to each other for the cameras, before soon dumping the debris on the road."

Online commentators went feral: "This is a big media stunt. Thanks for the reconfirmation that we cannot depend on current government structures – it is riddled with corruption from inside out."

Another day, another stuff up. Desperate to keep their man from any embarrassing encounters, Morrison's handlers avoided almost all the usual grin and grip opportunities of an election campaign, opting for endless, pointless stunts in front of the cameras to provide the media with their story of the day. Loathed by half the country and disliked by the other half, meeting an actual genuine voter rather than the sycophants, underlings, big end of town representatives and party loyalists who surrounded him was full of risk.

On the campaign trail, deluded by his own sense of self-worth, Morrison thought he could get away with going to the public bar at the Edgeworth Tavern in Newcastle, where the Liberal Party branch was holding an event.

He was promptly confronted by an irate pensioner. An old school man who, as the Australian expression went, "called a spade a bloody shovel".

A bored media, who also disliked Morrison to a man and woman, promptly seized on the event and away went another eddy of negative headlines.

The man said: "This is what you said when you got elected last time: We're going to help all those people that worked all their lives, paid their taxes and those that have a go, get a go. Well, I've had a go, mate, I've worked all my life and paid my taxes.

"You know another promise you made, you were going to have an integrity commission. It's the foxes in charge of the henhouse. You better fucking do something, I'm sick of your bullshit."

The Prime Minister walked away.

The next day's headlines strung around his neck like poisonous pearls, a thing of beauty to his many despisers.

***

There were internal and external narratives, as the country slowly drifted back to some sense of normality. The authorities, clearly, would have liked everyone to forget what had happened over the previous two years, and their culpability in the damage done to the country, but for many the consequences remained clear and ever present: the injuries, the deaths, the lost jobs, the impoverishment, the massive fines and complex court procedures, the ongoing health problems, and the absolute loss of faith in the public health system.

The thought kept running through Old Alex's head: "If they can do it once, they can do it again."

Finger by finger, step by step, the requirements for masks, social distancing, proof of vaccination, all of them drifted away. The apparatchiks and overpaid Chief Medical Officers kept trying to drum up relevance, but the population had moved on; and just wanted to bury the entire embarrassing saga. It was the exact same affliction, or silence, that settled over Germany after World War Two. As Hannah Arendt observed, ordinary Germans simply did not want to talk about, or confront, what had happened and their own complicity in it.

A silence marked the many graves.

Ditto in Australia, a silence masked a disaster.

The politics are as vile as the weather, Old Alex was wont to say, still largely isolated in that drenched, windswept valley. It hadn't stopped raining in Oak Flats in months during one of the coldest, wettest autumns in living memory; leaving Old Alex distracted and depressed by multiple discontents.

In his dank imagination the spirits were like birds settling in a flock. They didn't much like the interface, which was motivated by greed; by secrecy, by contempt for the average citizen, that is, the peasantry of old. Humble yourself before Your Lord, they declared, but all that imagery wasn't going to work this time around; the barking temple dogs, the belief in monotheism, the sacred, ancient beliefs of the primitives, the legends that were born and withered and died in a moment's breath, all of it now hung in the balance, a delicate thread like the snout of a cyclone swirling through millions of timelines. To find a place. Here, now, in the future, anchored to the past.

He was frightened for the future of his fellows, not his own; regretted the passing of the years in a field of jumbled imagery, welcomed a new embrace, found comfort in the arms of an old king, watched the water slide across the surface, shook his head in disbelief, marched in battle with his own belly split asunder, as he faced this terrible recognition of the fate of millions.

They moved then, across the water and the trees and the drenched, primordial landscape, "time itself the magic length of God", and built a signal post for those to come, and struggled with the organics, "Good Luck they muttered", and in those extraordinary carrion flights, in the sharpening of tools, in the breathtaking beauty of this remarkable place, of the times, the times, when they ran across open fields and were young again, when they climbed mountains and caught the wisp of a scent, when all that had been so cruelly obtained was washed away in the twinkling moment of a lifetime, a lifeform, as the flock settled in that ancient valley, soon to be a futuristic hub, and and the ancient guidance that he sought, the crippling indifference to the fate of humans, or individual humans, as they soared across time and civilisations and manufactured beauty to come to the heart of the matter; which remained exactly as it had been for months, despite all his indifference or attempts to avoid his own fate. Strange, in a sense, that it should be so hard.

What was most striking was the beauty of this place, as they crept back to a different kind of thought, and realised the terrible tragedy that had overcome this place.

There used to be a saying, rain is God's blessing on the Earth, but in this unseasonable season, when old codgers muttered to each other that they had never seen anything like it, when tens of thousands of people had been displaced by floods, when the washing machine surf of Bondi came to seem like a metaphor of the time, rapidly churning, utterly confused.

The country's politics really were as vile as the weather, that, at least, was true.

***

While the tidal wave of critical, well informed opinion was already rearing its way into a tsunami, Australia's health bureaucrats and their government puppets remained either illiterate or deliberately ill informed.

As always, Professor Ramesh Thakur, a statistical genius as far as Old Alex was concerned, remained right on the money, highlighting the fact that Australia was another country where Covid deaths had been far higher since the vaccine rollout.

Old Alex slugged the story: "Australia's Unmitigated Covid Fiasco".

"What does the Australian experience teach us about the efficacy of Covid vaccines? Why, for instance, have infections and Intensive Care Unit admissions been hugely higher after vaccination campaigns really got underway? Australia hit 50% of the population double-vaccinated (meaning a much higher percentage of the adult population) on October 10th 2021, and 70% in mid-November.

"On October 10th our total Covid-related deaths were 1,448. On February 15th 2022, with 79% of the total population fully vaccinated, the total number of deaths was 4,726. So the number who died with Covid after we hit 50% vaccination is 2.3 times higher than the number before that point.

"To come to the same conclusion from a slightly different angle, our previous highest Covid mortality rate was 0.85 daily new deaths per million people, on September 3rd, 2020. On that date, vaccines had not yet been developed anywhere in the world. The rate was exceeded on January 11th this year with 0.97 daily new deaths per million people, when we had 77.5% of the total population fully vaccinated. The rate peaked on January 30th at 3.39 daily new deaths per million people: four times higher than the pre-vaccination peak. At this time 78.3% of the population was fully vaccinated.

"Now let's look at ICU numbers, especially as this has been the most often cited public justification for encouraging and requiring vaccination. The pre-vaccines peak was on August 9th, 2020 with 2.17 ICU patients per million people. The highest rate of ICU daily occupancy was on January 18th this year, 16.44 ICU patients per million people.

"How can it possibly be justified to mandate universal vaccination on this data? This is simply not defensible on medical and ethical grounds. Globally and in Australia, hard data clearly show there is no discernible difference in transmissibility between vaccinated and unvaccinated of any significance to base policy on."

***

On the street, well attended protests with an increasing strength of pride continued throughout the first month of Autumn, March, 2022, with beating drums and whistles adding to the celebratory atmosphere, children in prams and street theatre, dismal weather notwithstanding.

In Melbourne placards included: "Democracy Needs No Free Thinkers"; "Will you really be happy when you own nothing? WAKE UP". In Perth: "Freedom Freedom Freedom".

In Adelaide: "The Truth Loves Liberty" and another with the image of Bill Gates and the words: "Wanted for Crimes Against Humanity No Poison Pricks For Our Children".

In Sydney: "Stop It Or Cop It. Nuremberg 2.0" and "TV is Fake News Do Not Comply"; "Lest We Forget" and "Mandates Stop The Lies Hands Off Our Kids We The People See You!!!".

On March 25, 2022 the Australian government announced that those considered most at risk of severe illness would be able to receive a fourth

COVID-19 vaccine heading into winter "following advice accepted by the Australian Government from leading immunisation experts".

On March 31, 2022, the Australian government announced: "Children aged 5 to 11 years are now eligible to receive a free COVID-19 vaccine. All vaccines are thoroughly tested before use, and reduce a child's chances of getting sick."

As was already well accepted, the vaccines were not thoroughly tested, children had almost no chance of getting sick from Covid and those so-called "immunisation experts" were almost invariably funded by Big Pharma.

The Australian government was lying, just as it had lied its way through the entire Covid era.

***

By mid-April Michael Gray Griffith of Café Locked Out fame was out on Australia's immense Nullabor Plains with his Deplorables Epic Road Trip. He wrote: "The people mover was new and the afternoon sun was deepening its maroon paint as the mother of these five children filled its boot with bags of shopping.

"Around the RV her young children, still in their school uniforms, were playing in this tiny wheat town's empty street, each one wearing their own personalised mask, and each mask firmly secured.

"As I entered the store I saw, amongst the other masked shoppers and staff, the ghost of the young man who approached us at the Nullabor roadhouse. Out there, in the middle of nowhere, the great plains only support a hand full of small distant anorexic trees, that's what Nullabor means, 'no trees,' and there, this man, who was wearing a worn black overcoat, with its collar up to shield his skinny neck and his chin with its three days of stubble from the desert's chilling wind, was shyly asking us what the banners on our truck were about.

"We told him we were touring the country, capturing the stories of Australians who had the courage to speak, and that the mainstream media ignored. We wanted to add their voices to the narrative, for we believed that presently our greatest weapons were our voices. We were interested to hear how they had been affected by the restrictions of the last two years, and what their thoughts were of the current state of the country and where it was heading. We were also wanting to challenge the West Australian border. That's where we were heading now."

The man replied that he was from Perth: "I'm trying to reach Brisbane. Do you think I'll get into South Australia? I tried to reach there a few months ago but they turned me back at Ceduna. I had to drive all the way back to Perth."

And his tone stated that he still couldn't believe this.

After checking that no one else could hear, he said, low, "I'm unvaccinated".

"Same" we replied.

But this didn't warm his spirit.

"It's the New World Order," he said. "I've always known it was coming. I've been telling people for ages, but I just never thought it would arrive."

Brisbane was where his elderly parents, Hungarian migrants, lived. Both in their eighties they were also unvaccinated and were calling what was happening in our country how they saw it; Communism.

"Together they had fled tyranny to offer their children a life where they could enjoy personal freedoms, and now here their son was a medical leper, a disenfranchised citizen on the run, from what he called a tyrannical state and unemployment, due to non-compliance, unsure if he could even reach them across heavily policed state borders."

***

Old Alex's imagination in riot mode, in his waking dreams he crept through the dark pages of history. We were assured our wishes would be fulfilled; but they always lied. If all war was deception, this lay somewhere underneath, in the detritus of the soul. The dishonesty, that's what got to him the most; how the nation's leaders lied so readily, how blindly ignorant the populace, how ignoble the blind acceptance of their fate. A lying leader, a corrupt polity, and out-of-touch bureaucracy fixed their fate.

Old Alex felt as if he was living inside a two way mirror, straddling the fate lines inside an inverse world, washed up against a fatal shore, as Australia was sometimes known, by a tide of destiny. The strangeness of it all was all laid out in the black treacle floods which leached across the sky; and across this time, this moment in time.

There was no use being angry about any of the country's putrid politics or shocking maladministration. A somnambulant population expressed no opposition. The soldiers took up camp on the valley slopes opposite. He gazed across the valley, watching those phantasmical soldiers as they made camp for the evening. Their realm, this realm, it was as if all of it had vanished and all he could see was the echo of their presence. Like everybody else, he struggled to make sense of the moment

Sometimes his mind just ran in cheap headlines, The Man Who Destroyed Australia Wants Your Vote. A political fight, a welcome relief from the derangement which had gripped the country.

The creeping, let's say galloping authoritarianism of the country grew ever more perilous every day; endangering the fates of so many, angering the spirits, and the few humans who could confront the truth, and cared, preferred to look the other way. .

The Prime Minister was claiming to have saved 40,000 lives during the pandemic, an arrogant, stupid and preposterous claim at best; a country which lay in ruins, whose national debt had been multiplied several times over, a country which was no longer free.

**

An election was about to be called. This day. 10 April, 2022. The last possible moment when it could be announced.

It was a ritualistic sham in a sham democracy; the country which had seen grandmothers pepper sprayed on the street, military on the streets, helicopters flying overhead. The public were waiting with brickbats, as the saying went, but where else to park your vote?

All the efforts of Reignite Democracy and all the other counter movements would come to nought, he believed, in a two-party preferred system which had been disastrous for any true representation of the sentiments of the populace for more than a century.

We soared overhead. We were indifferent. These human rituals.

The army gathered in the valley.

That lone sentinel, investigating whether he was still alive, as he knew now, their child, their children, the military dick wads who performed their scorn and couldn't wait for the end of their shifts, those arrogant useless fools who cluttered the ether and didn't believe a word of what they themselves were forced to say; a mind reader, a gossip, a collapsed polity, all of these things soared into a terrible destiny; these brief lifespans barely a moment.

Fireflies.

In his imagination Old Alex entered the magic arbour. He climbed a hill and could see beyond.

The media with which he had filled his life would now be filled with jousting politicians, false claims, counter claims, promises that would never be fulfilled as they garnished their own pockets. Instead of representing the voters, as they were paid today, the nation's politicians would plunder the public purse and a new lot of brigands would come to play havoc with the lives of ordinary people; those they neglected at their very great peril.

The ancients weren't angry. They only cared about one thing. A delicate thread to a time hence.

He was there to serve, amid the detritus of the race, the culture.

The country he had known was lost.

The parade of affectations was gone; and in its place would rise the great towers of the future, the soaring triumphs of architecture and science; and in here, somewhere, they would never forget.

Seer to seer. Voice to voice. One historical moment entwined with another.

What we do today depends very much on what we did yesterday, went the old rehab folk wisdom; and what we do here today, what this country was doing, was based on a bed of lies.

***

In the days before the May, 2022 elections the nation's freedom fighters still held the belief that they could make a difference, that all the marches and pamphleteering and placard waving would buy them a seat at the table; that democracy really did work.

No, it didn't.

This was a two party preferred system, two binaries of the same incompetence bestraddling a bureaucracy that held them transfixed. In the Australian system politicians were nothing but pimples atop a festering polity.

For an old newshound Alex, lost in the sepulchral hills that are part of us all, was strangely disinterested. It felt as if the change of administration was happening in a provincial capital far, far away, one we could only see in flying dreams. It had no relevance to the long term history of the place. One side of politics was as bad as the other. Each successive administration would prove as bad or worse than its predecessor. This longterm collapse employed multiple actors.

Naively, or so it seemed, at this point in the surrendering history the freedom fighters held hope that their increasingly numerous voices could no longer be ignored.

The obscene orgy, the pillaging of the public purse which had occurred under Prime Minister Scott Morrison, was already vanishing into the eternal now, as if there was no history, and the sullen outrage could be vanquished with the flourish of a pen, a change of government. The quadrupling of the national debt, the vast transfer of wealth from the middle to the upper classes, the billions of dollars dished out to Morrison's mates, "we look after our own", all of it suddenly seemed as nothing, something to be forgiven and forgotten, for both parties had been party to the authoritarian derangement which had seized the country under the cover of Covid, and which had already done such enormous damage.

At the same time as the global warming gang was seizing power an arctic blast enveloped the country; and there in that humble abode a dark wind whipped nearby trees and gusted around the house. Old Alex was cold, always cold, as if born for a warmer climate.

The army, that mythical army which assembled on the opposite slopes of the valley, was ready to be dispatched.

***

Whatever the future held, the hundreds of thousands of Australians who had taken to the streets over the past two years, many of them at great personal cost, signified a shift in the "temperature", if you will, of the national spirit.

The documentation of these demonstrations marked an historic record of one of the most tumultuous times in the nation's history, a prelude to what many people feared would be a dramatic decline in living standards and major social tumult, if not another Great Depression.

The mono-faced Covid disinformation and ridiculing of alternative views stemming from government and legacy media had the predictable impact of stimulating multiple independent news sites and determined bloggers, talented writers and social documenters who filled the void.

A fierce sense of injustice is a far greater driver than any wall of propaganda.

Susan Pavan was a mother with four kids Old Alex had first met at Camp Epic and who, both as a journalist and as a person, Old Alex took an immediate liking to. She went on the campaign trail. A piece he was particularly pleased to publish was titled The Giants Down Under: Australians Fighting Tyrannical Covid-19 Overreach during the final days of a Federal Election.

We have a thousand eyes. We are always out there. Talent steps to the fore at history's demand. Here's some of what she had to say.

"SACK THEM ALL"

A call for freedom from the two-party false paradigm.

Pavan wrote: "The 2022 Election represents the essential political conflict of our time – one between the corporate oligarchy and the beleaguered working classes.

"Less than a week remains until Australians head to the polls, and demonstrators have taken to the streets to let the establishment know what they think of them. A collective voice of rejection to their agenda.

"Australians will not forget the last two years."

So went the headline: "Federal Election In Australia Is Just Around The Corner And In One Last March Aussie's Fighting The Tyrannical Covid-19 Response Are Taking No Prisoners In Their Attempt To Make Political History."

The public's trust of the major parties was at an all time low. Even billions of dollars in campaigning can not buy trust.

Pavan wrote that there was a growing army of thousands of men, women and children all over Australia religiously hitting the streets talking to people and letterbox dropping how-to-vote cards promoting freedom parties.

"Australians en masse have educated themselves on political matters. They are folks of all walks of life but have one principal value in common, Freedom; especially freedom from the tyrannical Covid-19 response endured by the Australian people.

"Their relentless actions in protesting; letterbox dropping, social media posting and hitting the pavements week-after-week show they are hell-bent on taking their country back.

"And these grassroots of everyday Australians are growing like wildflowers and the people they are talking to are listening in growing numbers. While people are sitting complying through silence in Australians draconian public and corporate health orders of vaccine mandates and gag orders, the Covid-19 response in Australia has woken a sleeping giant.

"Ultimately the people in the above stories are reigniting a strong Australian spirit with those growing and willing to listen to logic; honesty and courage. What they have discovered is a force, a sleeping giant in all of us. The government's Tyrannical Covid-19 Response was ultimately their own undoing. The rock in David's slingshot that brought Goliath down in rain, hail or shine."

That's what hope looks like.

***

A week out from a federal election in Australia, nationwide rallies occurred on Saturday, May 14, 2022, organised by an alliance of grassroots groups from the freedom movement, a blanket term for a diaspora of community groups opposed to the lockdowns and mandates which had disfigured Australian societies.

The rallies went under the banner of "Sack Them All – Vote The Majors Last".

Susan Pavan saw the events of that time as marking the greatest restriction of civil liberties In Australia's history and her role to spread the untold stories of people power. "There are many everyday Australians breaking through the illusion of tyranny."

Triccy from the People's Revolution, a grassroots group of people disrupting the current political landscape in not just his own state of Queensland but nationwide, strategy is bringing unified and trustworthy people and communities together.

Triccy adopted a strategy of unifying the grassroots groups into a single political force.

He had experienced constant police intimidation for his part in the protests, but still continued to lead some of Australia's largest rallies, with hundreds of thousands marching for freedom.

"The People's Revolution group has also defended businesses who still served unvaccinated citizens despite threats of fines under emergency powers. A video of a group of Australians blocking police entering a cafe in Queensland went viral.

Triccy recalled: "It was like Apartheid. If you were not vaccinated, you were not allowed into certain areas. A local cafe had been targeted by authorities for breaking health orders.

"So I called the troops… and we went down there with about three hundred people. And I said: 'Guys, when these cops come everybody link arms in front of the door and don't let 'em through whatever happens – link arms, stay there and don't let them through.'

"So we did a practice run and a squad car drove past. And you should have seen the look on their faces when they saw three hundred people linking arms.

"It was empowering for everyone because we showed that people power is what's gonna' win this war.

"And that was a small display of people power. We have a hundred thousand people turn up to a rally. How many cops are in Queensland? There's not enough.

"So the numbers are so important – that's the key here. Guys keep spreading awareness, get the people, however you can, to join in."

***

There were flocks of birds and unresolved stories; there were days when all Old Alex wanted to do was drive spikes through the brains and eye sockets of his tormentors, underneath those scudding clouds and damp winds of the south coast.

For he, too, in a very different way, was being outrageously harassed by the intelligence agencies. They wanted him to know he was under surveillance. They wanted him frightened, disturbed, intimidated. That he was on his own made him all the easier a target.

Australia's intelligence agencies had a long history of harassment and intimidation of the nation's writers, artists and public intellectuals. It was in their corporate DNA. The public didn't understand it, but those journalists and authors whose work ventured into the realm of national security most certainly did.

The stanchions had been plunged into the ground. The soldiers had moved forward in one military, unified step.

It was military. It was an army. It was about war.

An invisible war.

That freezing winter; that imperilled country; that lingering outrage in the likes of him, while elsewhere people smiled or gathered themselves in insular warmth. They accepted their own poverty as if it had always been. They accepted the actions, the notions of their leaders as if they were wise; as if it was their duty to accept them, to accept the manner in which the authorities controlled their lives and dictated their lifestyles.

As if still in lockdown, the filthy bad weather was keeping many people inside.

Nearby there was a religious person, a Christian. Old Alex was convinced he could hear their demented prayers: "The Crucifixion. Our Lord. Our Saviour."

As little sense as it might have made, he could feel the spirits swarming, the flocks of birds in a descending flurry. In the beginning was the Word and the word was God. They were determined to communicate. The birds were just images implanted into a human brain because animal images were the easiest to understand, and had been for thousands of years, across thousands of cultures.

We were united in our grief.

And yet it hadn't happened yet, the worst of the worst of that unfolding revelation. Oneiromancy. An uncommon word which meant divination through dreams.

Old Alex felt driven to record this brief moment of transit of the soul of the nation; a moment of unknowing naivety before the nation sank into full scale totalitarianism.

Australia wasn't the country people holding the strings of power pretended it to be; the media, the academics, the politicians, the comfortable middle classes.

And he, like so many others, withdrew into a parochial state of mind; worried about paying the increasingly expensive electricity bills, keeping warm; while all the entities around him were, in a sense, nothing but a flurry of birds in a freezing wind swept by a far greater majesty. If it seemed like an impossibility, just think of the invisibility of the internet; and the infinite nature of the universe which had given rise to the spirit realm.

Out on the edge of Lake Illawarra in the early dawn, where Old Alex went to do his Buddhist exercises, the sunrise caught the underbelly of pelican in an orange flash against a dark, wintry sky; and he understood that all those moments of beauty, these splintering fragments of time, were also eternal.

Grief. A spike through their mushy brains. Blood oozing from damaged eye sockets. Violence. Cruelty. A freezing wind.

A machine that could read everything. A record that was eternal.

We embrace the future as we embrace the past.

Rise up, rise up.

***

Nation-wide rallies were organised for a week out from the Australian federal election.

"Rallies are happening in every capital city and also major regional cities," said Mr Christian Marchegiani from Reclaim The Line, a grass-roots group for frontline workers against Covid-19 vaccine mandates. "What has happened and transpired in this country in the last two years? Think of the birthdays, the special events, the funerals, the weddings you have missed.

"Think of everything that was taken away from you; your freedoms, your rights, your right to work, your right to trade for two years, your right to see your loved ones. People couldn't see their dying parents in nursing homes. Think about what they put us through."

"Never, ever forget, even while everything seems like it's gone back to normal. Just remember how easy it was for them to take that all away from us. And this is what we're trying to say to everyone. Never, ever forget."

"We are making the statement to the government that the treatment of everyday Australians during the last few years is not acceptable.

"They can't shift the blame to the state government. They were responsible, the people are not happy. And we are sending them a message that we are telling everyone to vote majors last and they will be shaking in their boots."

***

One of Scott Morrison's final acts of betrayal of his own countrymen, before being trounced at an election not even he could slither his way out of, was to call for a so-called pandemic treaty with the Bill Gates funded World Health Organisation, a United Nations bureaucracy staffed with numerous Gates loyalists and former employees.

The treaty would allow for the United Nations to take over pandemic management in Australia. After the last debacle!! Where were these people's heads? As Gates, in league with Big Pharma, was the puppet master of Australia's entire Covid response, it was yet another appalling surrender of sovereignty on the road to political annihilation.

It was another in a long queue of "you couldn't make this up" moments which had characterised the early 2020s.

Asked in Darwin, the capital of the Northern Territory, well away from the urban centres where he was particularly disliked, if he would sign the pandemic treaty being discussed by the World Health Organisation, the Prime Minister replied: "We have said right from the outset the WHO should have those powers and those authorities to be able to go and deal with pandemic situations. The idea that countries can just say 'no, you can't come in and have a look at a pandemic that's about to break out'. I think it's only sensible that this an area of international cooperation that is very very important."

Whichever bureaucrat was feeding Morrison these lines need not have worried. Morrison might have been known for repeating the lines of whoever was the last official to brief him, but his successor would prove just as tame a parrot.

The comments come ahead of the The 75th World Health Assembly, a six day talk fest held in Geneva which commenced on 22 May.

Could there be a greater betrayal of sovereignty?

Former United Nations Assistant Secretary-General Ramesh Thakur warned in *Spectator Australia* of the coming massive expansion of the international pandemic bureaucracy and the powers of the WHO to press countries towards authoritarian public health measures.

"Health includes mental health and wellbeing and is highly dependent on a robust economy, yet the WHO-backed package of measures to fight Covid has been damaging to health, children's immunisation programs in developing countries, mental health, food security, economies, poverty reduction, social and educational wellbeing of peoples. Their worst effects were grievous assaults on human rights, civil liberties, individual autonomy and bodily integrity.

"The vaccine push has ignored accumulating safety signals about the scale of adverse reactions, on the one hand, and rapidly dwindling efficacy after successive doses, on the other.

"If adopted, it will consolidate the gains of those who have benefitted from COVID-19, concentrating private wealth, increasing national debts and decelerating poverty reduction; expand the international health bureaucracy under the WHO; shift the centre of gravity from common endemic diseases to relatively rare pandemic outbreaks; create a self-perpetuating global biopharmaceutical complex; shift the locus of health policy authority, decision-making and resources from the state to an enlarged corps of international technocrats, creating and empowering an international analogue of the administrative state that has already thinned national democracies."

***

Unconvinced by any of the electoral pantomime, soaked to the core by month after month of ceaseless rain and wishing to distance himself from the election, Old Alex went walkabout. The election was happening further away than ever. He did not wish to participate in any sense, and certainly not to blunder with loose fingers on a keyboard. There had been a funeral and a eulogy under grey skies, a wintry time in every sense.

To honour a loyal and humble servant, to mark the suffering and parting of the matriarch of a dynasty which would spill down through time, spirits circled the cemetery there in the Southern Highlands.

It fell to Old Alex to give the eulogy for the matriarch of the family; as a now a senior of the clan, a long distance from his wild youth.

There was a kind of circling reverence in the surrounding trees; as he paid tribute before the gathering of relatives and members of her Church, where she had been much loved and respected, finding in that organisation what she had not found elsewhere in life.

He kept it apolitical, except for one moment: "While I don't want to bring politics into this sad occasion, many in the family have not a single kind word to say about the shocking health bureaucracy which has inflicted such terrible and unnecessary isolation and suffering on the nation's elderly during the Covid era.

"My mother died, if nothing else, of a broken heart, cut off from the family she had placed front and centre of her entire life thanks to the endless blizzard of inhumane diktats from the New South Wales health bureaucracy. That she was stopped from seeing many members of her family in her final months because they hadn't had enough shots or boosters or whatever, or there was yet another round of isolation or quarantine on the wards, was cruel beyond measure, beyond comprehension."

Similar travesties, many utterly heartbreaking, had been visited on many thousands of families across the country.

There was no use going on about it. Politicians and their phalanxes of health bureaucrats had inflicted the same cruelties on thousands of families across the country; the horror stories, the legions of sad and lonely deaths, were already the stuff of folk legend.

***

So after all that, Old Alex got in the car and drove, ending up in a place called the Glengarry Hilton, a once notoriously unlicensed and much loved pub out on the opal fields of north western New South Wales. These things are infinite. There is no beginning and there is no end. These ancient, normally arid landscapes, held something else within themselves.

A recently acquired dog, who thought his name was "What the fuck, Buddy", acted as an easy entre.

The election came and went. There was a change of administration. He watched it on a small screen in the public bar. Passions did not run high. One pack of assholes or another running the country didn't make much difference to anyone out in these places.

Above, as if the underwing of some great stingray, the sky barely rippled; a timespan in the millions of years.

"We, too, wish to be understood." That's all the ancient spirits said the entire time he was there, in that truly stunning landscape.

For in the course of millenia, in these ancient places, a mammal on the surface, passing through the trees, meant nothing; or almost nothing, less than a firefly, less than a mouse. Most Australians feel this.

It began raining shortly after he arrived out there in the Great Outback where it almost never rained, and the roads became increasingly impassable. For a time, it was just him and the dog at the Glengarry Hilton, when the staff went home after a quiet day because there was no way the Opal Tour buses could make it through the mud.

Just as he had feared, in the final outcome the freedom fighters did poorly in terms of polling outcomes; not landing a single member. All those protests. All that determination. Sometimes you have to lose to win; and somewhere in this matrix was the truth of it all.

The official story was unravelling on every front. Scott Morrison was gone and his opponent, Anthony Albanese, in power. Born with hope, an inclination to allegiance, Old Alex would get a surprised look when he predicted, "Albanese will become as despised as Morrison".

At the back of the Glengarry Hilton, in the rough and ready accommodation of the Australian Outback, a man, passing through as a lot of people did that particular spot, showed him an opalised, fossilised tooth, 110 million years old, he said.

How little any of it mattered.

Even he did not know why.

Even here, now, it was raining, where it almost never rained. The rarely green landscape was so lush, and yet so ancient, as one denizen put it: "You expect a dinosaur to come rushing out of the trees."

Who were those faraway oligarchs and eugenicists, people who thought they could play God? Who thought they could do this to a divine creation?

Whether it was millions, or billions, or trillions, these lifeforms, who were they to say what was needed, or for what purpose?

Who did they think they were?

Time crushed every creature.

Only the immortals remained.

And soon enough, those men who thought they could play God would themselves be crushed. The billionaires, the powerful, laid waste upon the Earth. Their own cracked images in a cracked mirror not even a firefly, gone from this place, cursed.

While the same immortals said to him: You Are Blessed. Or in antique English: Blessed Art Thou.

***

In defeat, even in the smoking ruins of his career, with the scandals of his time in office wrapping around his pudgy neck, former Prime Minister Scott Morrison believed he was on a divine mission. At a Pentecostal event in Western Australia he called on worshippers to put their faith in God.

"You're not defined by your grievance, or your offence, or being part of some collective set of grievances, you have to constantly assert out there. Do you believe if you lose an election that God still loves you and has a plan for you? I do. Because I still believe in miracles.

"God's kingdom will come. It's in his hands. We trust in him. We don't trust in governments. We don't trust in the United Nations, thank goodness. We don't trust in all these things, fine as they may be and as important as the role that they play. Believe me, I've worked in it and they are important.

"But as someone who's been in it, if you are putting your faith in those things as I put my faith in the Lord, you're making a mistake. They are earthly, they are fallible. I'm so glad we have a bigger hope."

***

Vanquished leaders are always fascinating in defeat, and the former prime minister found himself being booed by the crowd at a football match in Sydney just days after he lost the election.

Scott Morrison was sitting in the stands at the Sydney Cricket Ground when the camera spotted him

As he was shown on the big screen boos rang out around the 31,000 strong crowd.

"Scott Morrison in the house, geeze," commentator James Brayshaw said.

"Frosty reception," replied commentator Daisy Pearce.

One fan seated in front of the former prime minister gestured an "up yours" with his middle finger and punched the air as he appeared on screen.

Unfazed by the reception the former leader smiled and waved amid the jeers.

The man was beyond embarrassment.

The man whose abject mismanagement of the Covid era had done such enormous harm to his country, and to millions of his fellow Australians. A man whose complete lack of remorse was a study in sociopathy.

Scott Morrison never acknowledged or took any responsibility for the havoc he wreaked upon the country, and continued to defend the mass vaccination of the population as an achievement. The lockdown and vaccine mandates were all the responsibility of the states, a piece of blame shifting worthy of a shapeshifter.

When asked whether he regretted going too hard with lockdowns, he responded, in a softball interview with Sharri Markson of Sky News: "I never instituted one lockdown. They were all decisions of state governments. Different states had different approaches."

Morrison defended the lengthy and confusing press conferences he held at the beginning of the pandemic, appearances which did a great deal to instil a sense of derangement and fear into the Australian population and enabled the authoritarian madness which overtook the country.

"That was necessary at that time."

As for the already massively controversial vaccines, the mandates and the thousands of professionals, including teachers and nurses, who lost their jobs: "Individual states went down that path. I don't regret the need to have a country vaccinated – that was incredibly important and it was really hard, it was very challenging.

"But when it comes to the mandates, other than as I said in those cases of medically sensitive, publicly facing occupations in aged care and so on, the Federal Government did not support any other mandate at all.

"I can also say this that the expert medical panel that guided and advised throughout the pandemic, they never agreed to wide scale vaccine mandates, not once, other than for aged care and for sensitive publicly facing medical roles, they did not recommend, collectively, mandates."

On the face of it, Morrison looked like he'd just gotten away with the crime of the century.

***

The authoritative body of literature picking apart the government and vaccine proponents Covid narrative was growing steadily.

Pandemia: How Coronavirus Hysteria Took Over Our Government, Rights, and Lives by former *New York Times* journalist Alex Berenson, published in October of 2021, was one of the first out of the box.

Pandemia was originally very hard to procure in Australia, with excessive costs, lengthy delays, or in the case of Amazon's Kindle, impossible to buy at all.

It seems unlikely that a sophisticated selling machine like Amazon would discourage purchase of such an anticipated publication. But *Pandemia* was the last book the Australian government wanted the punters to read, intent as it was in perpetuating the lie that they had been keeping Australians safe.

In a legacy media beholden to government funding, lockdown and vaccine sceptics were almost impossible to find. Out in the real world, they were everywhere.

Whether or not *Pandemia* was deliberately geo-blocked by Australian authorities is uncertain, but certainly likely. As had been seen on so many levels, a failing and desperate Morrison government was more than willing to play to the cheap seats through everything from politicising national security to weaponising gender debates. And no more so than Covid.

In a post to his Substack newsletter Unreported Truths Alex Berenson asked what was happening Down Under: "Australia should have been the world's ultimate public health and Covid vaccine success story – the nail in the coffin for Team Reality and the Great Barrington Declaration. Australia did just what the Bill Gates-funded gurus wanted.

"It locked down early and hard and stayed that way for almost two years. It closed its borders and responded to local outbreaks with even tougher restrictions. Australian police used drones and automated licence plate readers to check if people were more than a few miles from their homes.

"The restrictions largely 'worked', putting aside their cost to civil liberties, education, and mental health, of course, since those don't matter to Covid fanatics. Through the fall of 2021, Australia had few Sars-Cov-2 infections and almost no Covid deaths.

"When Covid vaccines became available, Australia took an equally aggressive stance. The country's six states segregated unvaccinated people, barring them from shopping, going to restaurants, and even entering libr0aries. States also forced Covid shots on many workers as a condition of employment, making up to 75 percent of workers get jabs.

"Australians did not universally support the rules. Thousands of anti-vaccine and anti-lockdown protestors jammed Melbourne and other major Australian cities last fall.

"Still, despite Australia's reputation as an outpost of rugged individualism, it is actually more like Canada than the United States. Polls routinely showed that a majority of Australians supported the restrictions and were pleased with their government's overall response to the coronavirus."

Berenson observed that there had been a high level of compliance within the Australian population to the point that during the spring and summer of 2021, most Australians were primarily concerned that they did not have enough access to vaccines.

More than 95 percent of Australians 16 and over ultimately took the shots – mostly Pfizer's mRNA jabs. The acceptance extended to boosters, which nearly 70 percent of Australian adults received.

And for almost two years, America's elite media rapturously held Australia up as an example of how the United States should have behaved and how many lives lockdowns and vaccines could have saved. Never mind that Western European countries, which had lockdowns and Covid vaccination rates similar to Australia's, had death counts similar to America.

"Australia's Covid success story has a new ending – and it may hold very hard lessons for vaccine advocates.Since December, when the Omicron variant arrived, Australia has had an unending Covid wave. And after falling in April and May, infections, hospitalisations, and deaths are soaring again as Australia, which is in the Southern Hemisphere, enters its winter."

As Berenson observed, for the previous several months Australia had had more deaths per-capita than the United States, and nearly all those people were vaccinated.

"In the last six weeks, 656 people have died of Covid in New South Wales, Australia's largest state. More than 85 percent were vaccinated, and most of them had been boosted.

"Even more concerning, Australia has also had a large increase in non-Covid deaths. During the first three months of 2022, Australia had almost 20 percent more deaths than normal. Even excluding Covid deaths, deaths were almost 10 percent above normal. Figures for April and May from Victoria, its second-largest state, suggest excess deaths have risen even further since then and may be running 30 percent above normal - a stunningly high level."

Berenson said it was hard to overstate what the unspooling crisis in Australia may mean for vaccine and lockdown advocates. "Because it so successfully contained Covid in 2020 and 2021 and then used mRNA and DNA/AAV vaccines so aggressively, Australia is a near-perfect test case for what Omicron and future variants will do to a population that was mass vaccinated *before* being exposed to Covid."

Once an outlier, no longer, Berenson concluded: "Clearly, the vaccines have failed. For now, Australian national and state governments continue to push boosters – and to publish honest data showing just how poorly the shots are working.

"No points for guessing whether the honesty or the booster campaigns are likely to end first."

The great machinery of government continued unchecked. Indeed: "What was happening in Australia?"

SEVENTEEN
PERPETRATORS IN POWER

Under conditions of terror most people will comply but some people will not. No more is required, and no more can reasonably be asked, for this planet to remain a place fit for human habitation. One man will always be left alive to tell the story.

Hannah Arendt.

Nothing appears more surprising to those who consider human affairs with a philosophical eye, than the easiness with which the many are governed by the few; and the implicit submission, with which men resign their own sentiments and passions to those of their rulers.

David Hume, Of the First Principles of Government, 1768.

A PATINA OF routine calm hinging on a deliberate manipulation towards boredom could not hide the fact that the new Albanese government was already being enveloped by historic social and political pressures more dramatic and more immediate than anyone could have imagined; particularly the spiralling cost of living and falls in living standards, and the unfolding scandal of excess deaths, vaccine injuries and the absolute betrayal of the populace by the nation's political class and their handmaidens, the health bureaucrats.

The realisation was slow to come, that the freshly elected government was no better than its predecessor; despite all the hope, optimism and good will that was garlanded around the Labor politician's necks as they entered the political centre stage.

With all the evidence of government malfeasance pouring in from around the country, and internationally, there were only a few explanations: the Australian authorities were either dishonest, incompetent, illiterate or corrupt. Old Alex opted for the latter.

But whatever the evidence in real time, the Australian authorities continued with their mass vaccination program, knowing, surely, full well the harm they were doing to their fellow Australians.

How could anyone, at this point, not know?

But still the citizenry lined up to be vaccinated, to keep their jobs, or thinking they were doing the right thing by the community; still, despite all the evidence available to any half knowledgeable person.

Paul Collits put the frustration if not hand wringing despair felt by any thinking person who cared for their country and its citizenry as articulately as anybody.

"There is nothing more likely to get under the skin of the pro-vaxxer establishment than pointing out that the magic mushroom vaccines designed by politicians to give them a get-out-of-jail-free card in relation to Covid are experimental, unnecessary, useless and dangerous.

"Despite the easing of restrictions in Australia and elsewhere, we still have the legacy of unemployed unvaccinated in their tens of thousands, we still have masks on public transport and in other settings, and we still have a corporate culture of so-called Covid safety, the latest opportunity for virtue signalling on a grand scale.

"Every day that passes makes it clear that the vaccine emperor has no clothes, that it is now simply laughable for anyone to suggest that the vaccines work. If I were a rabid pro-vaxxer, I wouldn't be saying much."

Keep in mind that key phrase, "highly injected Australia".

"We now have a pandemic of the vaccinated. Not only that, the vaccines-plus-lockdowns regime has effectively wiped out any opportunity we might have had to build up individual and herd immunity, the trusted strategy previously relied upon in dealing with viral infections – until 2020, that is."

The data was clear. Three months after a mass vaccination campaign came a spike in excess deaths.

"The bottom line is, where there is no truth, the world morphs into a set of competing post-modernist narratives. A world of cognitive dissonance, of newspeak and doublethink.

"A world of supposedly intelligent minds has succumbed to mass manipulation and lemming-like behaviour on so many fronts. Idiocracy? Or merely the innocent victims of evil.

"The dangers of the vaccines are sufficiently mind-blowing on their own to call into question the whole of the Covid State's blind faith in experimental and unnecessary medical procedures forced down people's throats for two years.

"Oh, and they do know they are lying."

***

There was a lightening of the national mood post that long ago election in May of 2022. As if at the end of a long court case, where justice was not just done but seen to be done.

The sour, dispirited, powerless and bleak disposition which had settled on the population, that same feeling you get when you know you're being robbed but there's nothing you can do about it, lifted.

For Old Alex there was also a sense that it was happening far away, that creatures born aloft could not be conquered, that the celebrations of electoral victory by Australia's Labor party were happening somewhere else, to another class, or stratum of society.

Adding to the ferocious despair of that period, the entire crushing of all normal social interaction, was the eternal, interminable rain. It just never stopped; morning to dusk and through the long wintry nights, barely once did those lashing rains give pause.

Hermetic was the word Old Alex most often thought of, but it was more than that, the sense of imprisonment, of a profound disillusionment, of a place where all the walls had closed in, hope extinguished, a place not just of loneliness but of a deeper evil, a darkness which had settled across them all; into their blood, into their psyche, into the fabric of everything around them; a darkness that hovered overhead and into their bodies, enmeshed.

That vision soaked valley was primordial now with the deep green of drenched trees and paddocks. The mythical army which occupied his waking dreams had assembled on the banks of the valley opposite; imperious, determined, patient, well not very, as if the time was ripe, even if he was not; and he was most certainly not.

The infantry, kitted out with all their spears and mediaeval glory, perhaps not mediaeval but older still, Roman, pre-Roman, flags of victory or conquest; cruel Assyrian gods, Ishtar, the cruel god of love and war, here in this ancient spiritual place which had absolutely nothing to do do with the Western gods, and yes, below, in the valleys way below, a change of administration.

Those who engaged in this passionate dispute were vindicated or disillusioned, while all the talk now was of rising costs of living, of an economy in ruins, of the garbage that political debate had become.

Jess down at the Lakeview Hotel told the story of how she had ended up in hospital after her second shot; and was refusing to get the "booster".

The vaccines were failing worldwide, but the failure was being dubiously hidden from the Australian people. And yet, they had known all along. They must have. The evidence was clear.

This scandal, on an almost incomprehensible scale, barely sank through the leaves into any form of public consciousness; and all of it, all of it, as the birds wheeled and the eagle gripped its branch, as spirits stirred and mustered.

And they took, in unison, those hundreds of ceremonially kitted soldiers, another step forward.

As for Australia: yes, there had been a change of administration. Was it any coincidence that the agendas of Australia's new Labor government and one of the world's richest men, Bill Gates, were the same: vaccines and climate change.

Fool the masses for a living. Perhaps this truly was a spiritual war, as increasing numbers of people believed. The soldiers, restive after such a long wait, stirred in their ranks across that cold, rain drenched valley and stepped forward once again; through their shields, through the shield that was this time.

***

One after another the perpetrators retired, with all the faux compliments from their colleagues. The execrable NSW Health Minister Brad Hazzard, Federal Health Minister Greg Hunt, John Skerrick from the Therapeutic Goods Administration which approved the vaccines, Michael Gunner from the Northern Territory, who corralled the indigenous off their sacred lands, Brendan Murphy, who as Chief Medical Officer and then Secretary of the Department of Health became the public face of Australia's fight against Covid, giving regular press conferences with the Prime Minister, Scott Morrison, and Health Minister Greg Hunt.

But all too many remained. Premier Daniel Andrews in Victoria, Premier Mark McGowan in Western Australia, Premier Annastacia Palaszczuk in Queensland.

Deceitful all. That was the Australia of the 2020s.

What constantly amazed Old Alex was that people were not more angry.

Perhaps they were. They just didn't make it into the media. If you had miscarried, or your child was permanently disabled as a result of a vaccine injury, you would be distressed and angry beyond words. But you wouldn't make it onto the evening news.

***

This was a period of transition; or blame shifting, but many of the harms caused by Australia's draconian overreach continued to shatter through the community. Despite state governments beginning to abolish harsh vaccine mandates that winter of 2022, a significant number of Australia's biggest employers were continuing to require their workers be vaccinated.

In retrospect, that a supposedly responsible employer would push their workers to be vaccinated with a scandal ridden product that demonstrably did not work simply defied belief. Perhaps, there was a whisper of perhaps, some of the people involved in this cascading evil were well intentioned, believing they were doing the right thing. Which left the question, how could anyone be so stupid?

Most were just simply doing as they were told, going along to get along.

With a considerable amount of nefarious negotiating behind the scenes, the push to make vaccination the responsibility of corporations was just another dodge by governments trying to avoid responsibility for their own actions. The scale of the fraud remained almost incomprehensible; a madness plain and simple.

And this was no longer an outlier sentiment.

The NSW government was removing most vaccination mandates by the end of June, while the once hermit kingdom of Western Australia was also easing off. Queensland removed many requirements, while mandates in the Northern Territory, which required workers to have three Covid shots, were also being lifted.

Nonetheless, multiple corporations declared there would be no changes to their vaccination policies, including the airline Virgin Australia, with 6,000 employees, the country's major telecommunications company Telstra, with more than 28,000 employees, the nation's largest bank Commonwealth, also with more than 28,000 employees, the nation's largest company mining giant BHP, with 80,000 employees, and the largest retailer in Australia, supermarket chain Woolworths, with more than 200,000 employees.

No Jab No Job.

All were requiring at least two doses.

The Victorian government had not announced an end to its broad vaccination mandates. It was mandatory for workers in healthcare, aged care, disability, emergency services, correctional facilities, quarantine accommodation and food processing and distribution to be up to date with their vaccination doses. In Victoria that meant a third dose to work on site.

Workplace lawyers predicted that enforcing of mandates without government health orders could prompt a fresh wave of legal challenges by employees, particularly from employees in low-risk environments.

Meanwhile, for those in "high-risk" workplaces, the push for a fourth jab had just started. *The Age* reported: "Victorian Premier Daniel Andrews will push the federal government for all healthcare workers in hospitals across Victoria to get a fourth dose of coronavirus vaccine, amid concerns over waning immunity.

"He revealed his intention to approach the Commonwealth over the second booster shots on Monday, saying hospital chiefs had raised it as a 'real priority' following a recent spate of COVID-19 outbreaks seeded by staff bringing the virus into work."

If something doesn't work, double down.

***

Meanwhile, the country's most powerful media organisation bar the taxpayer funded broadcaster ran a headline: "Aussies who have lost relationships, jobs, friendships and even precious time with loved ones have spoken out about their lives being ruined."

News Limited was always a quixotic and unpredictable beast. It wasn't always just a case of "follow the money".

Charis Chang told the story of a woman, among the five percent of Australians not jabbed, who despite repeated attempts could not find work as an unvaccinated person.

"I couldn't bring myself to do a medical procedure I didn't want and I was scared," the woman said. "I just kept thinking that surely they would have some compassion and would start softening these restrictions.

"If I felt there was a safer vaccine that had less side effects, better efficacy and a more traditional base – I would consider it.

"I wanted so badly to have an open mind and understand all sides but I felt that wasn't being returned. On top of everything else, that was really hard – feeling like an outcast from the community. I've never felt more discriminated against in my life than I have in the past year since vaccines were introduced."

As Ethan Nash at TOTT News observed, Australians were allowed back into pubs and clubs, "but without the ability to get back to work – are we really truly free from the Corona Psyop?"

***

Well away from his years of full time work with a corporate monster, Old Alex noted with a certain wryness the introduction of laws forcing employers to take care of the mental health of their employees and the implementation of programs for journalists suffering from Post Traumatic Stress Syndrome because of the stresses of their job.

"If you were having a bad day you saw me coming, pad in hand," Old Alex would sometimes say as way of explanation of his role as a general news reporter; although none of it mattered much now, stranded as he was in that wintry spirit drenched valley, coming to terms with what had happened in his own life, much, in a sense, like the country itself.

In a hundred million years, when even the primitive humans would be a distant memory, such tiny points in history for such a short lived species, would prove insignificant. But for now, it was all too vivid in his waking dreams.

The humans cared so little for each other's welfare, that's what struck him the most, an oddity for such a sociable species.

There was an instance; a reward; a flake of snow. There was a change of administration in a country called Australia. Not the chosen one, simply a transmitter, he heard the message: "Much of the work is already done."

But there was much to do; and Old Alex was disoriented, or reluctant, imperilled; really just reluctant, distrusting, as the wind whipped around the house on those dark mornings. There was no affection, there was a soldier's duty. These things, these creatures, these moments of consciousness which wished to encase him in some kind of beneficence; while the Teals, as the newly elected, wealthy women candidates championing climate change were called; set out on their social justice agendas; as if anything they did was any more than tokenism.

"We're between two ice ages, it's all going to look rather stupid under 60 feet of ice," he used to say, in an adopted, old, cynical self. Now he just sighed; at all the progressives trumpeting the same message as the billionaires of Davos, those oligarchs who had all worked out how to make fortunes out of the climate change cant, with the added bonus of being able to control populations through fear and an ever expanding web of freedom destroying edicts.

But for the moment, anyway, there was a honeymoon.

A new Prime Ministerial face for the so-called left in Anthony Albanese, and a new face for the so-called right with Peter Dutton, who would, his supporters hoped, return the party to its socially and fiscally conservative roots.

***

Vaccinate the world, that had been the dream of those who visited Covid upon the Earth. Make themselves not just billions, but hundreds of billions; and make themselves into gods who could live forever.

It would all fail, as hubris always failed. Who were these idiots to decide who lived and died, which humans would prosper and which would not, who would thrive and who would not; their brief moments of fame, their brief adulation, so in the end the same thing astonished him as had astonished him before: How little they cared for each other. How willing these perpetrators were to create a new slave class.

Old Alex stood in queues or said hello to the few he knew. He missed the city. The area was quiet, miasmic.

And that same wish kept coming back that he had had as a child: to understand everything.

The ectoplasmic nature of the spiritual response; the ancient feel of these places; even when he was trapped, if you will, on a suburban block, the trees cleared, the native animals, the scattering of humans who had travelled up this long valley long ago. All of it.

Old Alex read with horror the creed of the Bill Gates owned, or at least controlled, World Health Organisation: "It is imperative that leaders seize this opportunity to mobilise the funding and political will required to achieve global targets for COVID-19 vaccination coverage, testing rates and access to treatments, including oral antivirals and oxygen. Achieving these targets is essential to ending the pandemic, by reducing transmission and protecting everyone from the harms of COVID-19."

The WHO weren't the only ones to have suffered reputational damage during this benighted, cursed era; politicians, health professionals, media personnel, all had been bought and all were held in increasing contempt by a weary and disbelieving population.

And far above, in a realm beyond their realm, barely a ripple in a vast sky.

But in the here and now, tasked as Old Alex felt by an ancient imperative, not as one but as many, we would skip across centuries, we would bring the message of this time to another, equally stricken time.

While the country breathed a sigh of relief at the back of Scott Morrison, the Prime Minister, the "leader", who had done more harm to the country than any other Prime Minister in its history.

There was not a shred of honour in any of the politics of the day.

***

That mid-winter was a season for recriminations, both in Australia and internationally.

American author and researcher Michael Senger wrote for the Brownstone Institute: "Those in power were able to so whimsically shape our reality because the officials, journalists, judiciaries, citizens and self-styled intellectuals who were meant to keep power in check were revealed to be little more than sycophants.

"I dislike what I witnessed during Covid, particularly in what it revealed about the minds of those around me. What I believed were commonly-shared ideals of liberalism, humanity, critical thinking, universal rights, and constitutionalism were revealed to be little more than the modern trappings of sycophancy – fashion statements popular among contemporary elites only to be jettisoned as soon as the rich men who funded their employers, peers, and influencers decided that they were no longer convenient.

"We were told that war is peace, freedom is slavery, and ignorance is strength. But worst of all, our own friends and peers were told to ostracise and vilify us if we did not do as we were told – and far too often, they did as they were told. Coupled with the still-unknown risks associated with mRNA technology and the now well-documented cases of death and serious injury from these vaccines, for governments across the world to have exerted extreme pressure on children and healthy adults to get these vaccines is absolutely sickening.

"That some healthy young people were surely coerced into receiving an injection that led to their death or serious injury, when the data showed that the benefits did not outweigh the risks, is an unconscionable tragedy."

***

The government might not have wanted to talk about Australia's excess death rate, but everybody else did. One of the best journalists in the country, Rebecca Weisser at *Spectator Australia*, had been quick on to the story.

That winter of 2022 she wrote: "January was the cruellest month. Australians emerged from their long lockdowns only to be confronted with the Omicron variant that largely evaded the vaccinal antibodies they'd acquired over the previous ten months. On the worst day, there were more than 105,000 cases and by the end of the month, there had been 15,993 deaths from all causes, 3,053 deaths above the historical average, an excess mortality rate of 23.5 per cent.

"Summer is usually kinder to the sick and the elderly.

"The taboo consideration that cannot be raised in polite company is the Covid mass vaccination program. It is an article of faith that the vaccine is 'safe and effective' and to raise a scintilla of doubt is anathema, punishable by excommunication. Nonetheless, since the program began on 22 February almost 130,000 adverse events have been reported to the Therapeutic Goods Administration, including 874 deaths."

In April, May and June of 2021, when mostly elderly people were vaccinated, there were, on average, more than three deaths a day reported.

As the age of the vaccinees declined the death rate eased but it was still more than two a day in July, August and September, and more than one a day in the last three months of the year, a total of 744 deaths.

Weisser wrote: "This year it continues. In the first 25 days in May for example, (the most recent data) there were 32 deaths, the youngest, a little boy of five who died of cardiac arrest.

"He's not the only child to die.

"At least five children aged 5-11 have died post-vaccination in the last four months whereas only eight children under 10 have died 'with' Covid during the whole pandemic.

"This mortality rate is not normal."

Before the Covid vaccines, the Therapeutic Goods Association received only two to three reports of death from all vaccines per year.

"Yet to the TGA, apparently, all these deaths were just a coincidence, even the 12 deaths from myocarditis, a recognised side effect of the mRNA vaccines.

"Yet it is the extraordinary diversity of the adverse reactions reported in response to Covid vaccines that is striking, and the way in which they mirror the myriad morbidities associated with Covid."

***

Meanwhile, The Deplorables Epic Road Trip was coming to an end.

Michael Gray Griffith wrote: "We have become historians; capturing a history they are already trying to erase. Today we have been on the road over 100 days, and we are due back in Melbourne on July 4th.

"The journey has changed us all, yet the Tide of Tyranny is continuing to come in. On a positive note the goal of the journey, birthed in Epic, was to try replant the joy, hope and its sense of a new community all around Australia, like your grandmother reseeding a neighbour's plant.

"But this was arrogant, for Epic is seeding itself everywhere from Portland to Boolaroo to Darwin, And we have proved that by going there, physically, and meeting these seedlings. These warriors.

"I now believe that the Shrine was where the Resistance was officially conceived, and Epic was the womb where our glorious and growing resistance was born."

Griffith said that it had been an honour to have recorded the stories of the people they had met on the road, and three involved felt humbled and warmed to be a part of a growing tribe.

"This rising counterculture that will one day be the king tide that will wash away all their perversions. And even though we are making mistakes, that's just because we are learning to use our limbs, to speak with our new voice, to discern what we are seeing with our liberated eyes, coloured in the hue and the hunger of freedom.

"Now we have to philosophise, decide what we need from a culture, not just for us but for the future generations, for this defined need will allow us to see our destination, the new country we will help build, and once we can see it, we will reach it, create it, for as a people that's what we have the skills, passion and responsibility to do.

"And whilst we may never reach there, for this will be a long struggle, we will have the privilege of being its foundation, that's why we are, if we have the courage and the love to be so, the Architects of the New Australia. Our Australia, built on a foundation of Inclusion, Empathy and Freedom."

Griffith said many of the people they interviewed were concerned about the future of the culture. "So to return to Canberra and find the Australian Federal Police assaulting a mature woman, Grandmothers who are here fighting for the liberty of their Grandchildren, reignites the lingering fire in our souls.

"There is a large section of our community who we no longer understand. They stay quiet as unconscionable things happen. They seem to have no lines in the sand called enough is enough, and are content to be spectators as everything good about our country burns.

"So today and tomorrow we are heading home with quiet hearts and are wondering if we are returning home or to a trench. Out there somewhere, or inside, or both, there is a God of Good, and he is our backer and our guide, and the reason we know this, is because the strength and beauty and the nobility of the Australian people we have met have both restored and cemented our faith.

"They are all beacons of hope, each defending what is under siege, our culture's Spirit, and not only is that worth fighting for, it's worth dying for, which is why in the end we will win, and why for us coming home is not our journey's end."

***

There were protests around the country as the mid-winter month of July drew to a close.

The headline ran, "Australia: The Place to be Pepper Sprayed as Protestors around the country March against the New World Order".

The arrival of a new Prime Minister appeared to have made little difference to the Covid overkill of the Australian authorities. In a high energy protest in Brisbane the by now triumphant People's Revolution flags once again flew high, the wind folding it occasionally to read "The People's Evolution", all in a sea of beating drums and impromptu concerts.

That was one thing that came through this period of chaos, the native talent of the people.

Lockdowns and restrictions were ending, but vaccine mandates continued to create havoc across multiple Australian industries and government agencies. They were a major driver behind the demonstrations. .

Australia now had one of the world's most highly vaxxed populations, and concurrently one of the highest Covid death rates. Yet despite this, with the media running a spate of Covid scare stories, there was widespread fear the authoritarian derangement which had characterised the past two and a half years was resurfacing.

A change of administration didn't make much difference when you had lost your job.

It was evident from the wide range of ages and diversity of people attending the protests that the Australian government had lost the middle ground. As one placard read: "We Are One".

Say No to the New World Order. Reist the Great Reset. Another placard read: "We are seeing an Outbreak of Bullshit on TV".

1ClickNews, proudly banned from YouTube, reported on Twitter: A huge Protest has broken out all over the city with People holding signs that say "I support dutch farmers", "FK the NIH", "No to covid zombies".

In Melbourne there were numerous violent scuffles as protestors faced walls of police. The group True Arrow filmed the event and reported: "We are seeing multiple women pepper sprayed. There are distressing scenes of frantic people washing their eyes out with water. Some protesters were carried by four police through a corridor of police into the back of paddy wagons."

Michael Gray Griffith of Cafe Lock Down, freshly back from his Epic Road Trip, addressed the crowd: "Resistance is growing everywhere. You are the vocal face of it. Around Australia people see Melbourne as the frontline in this war, and it is a war. A good majority know this is bullshit. We are winning. It might not feel like it because it's cold and miserable and they are pepper spraying us. In a marathon you have to learn to endure pain."

In reference to the Victorian Premier, the crowd chanted: "Sack Dan Andrews".

In Adelaide fine weather helped with the relaxed and celebratory protest. One woman said: "This is a lot better than Melbourne, where they beat you off the road."

In the nation's capital a large sign of fluorescent paint on plastic sheeting strung between kerbside trees read: ""What will you tell UR kids? Did you rise up or comply?"

***

There on the side of that valley wind whipped the drenched house, and for Old Alex another realm phased in and out, as if he could see the future. For days, weeks in fact, the army had assembled and stirred restlessly on the other side of the valley, waiting, stepping forward in anticipation, moving back, stirring once again. We speak to you in images you can understand.

A shimmering collection of shields moving in and out of focus; patient but restless, if any of it made sense. He did not feel up to the task, but then again there was no choice. We are given what we are given. We must do what we must do.

Patience; that's what it had required from those who watched and wanted immediate action. He took to repeating the sentiments of Marcus Aurelius: Relax. Spend time with nature and the gods.

And thinking, as he had thought so often over these years: none of this will matter much in a hundred million years.

But here, in this brief time span, skipping across the centuries, it did matter. This moment, this day, this life. These lives. The glory of this moment which could never be regained yet was already imprinted in the fabric of history.

As so many had commented, and continued to comment, the compliance of the population was one of the most extraordinary things about the entire episode.

"They do not expect to live long," the General in the Art of War had observed of his loyal soldiers heading into war.

Their nobility was a mere flash in a grand scheme.

And noble humans were rare in this time.

Now, with the internet a kind of mycelium encircling the globe, the consciousness was changing, the generations changing. There was no excuse for low information; but that of course was what saddled much of the population; settled in place, of a place.

He came across the Welsh word Hiraeth: "A spiritual longing for a home which maybe never was. Nostalgia for ancient places to which we cannot return. It is the echo of the lost places of our soul's past and our grief for them. It is in the wind and the rocks and the waves. It is nowhere and it is everywhere."

It seemed to fit.

He was struck, as always, by the humans with whom he so little identified; but this time round also struck by how much they were settled in place, becoming part of a place, part of the landscape.

The psychopaths at the top of this hierarchy cared not a jot for those beneath them; and yet there were the common people, aping the false narratives of the world's super-rich, climate change, gender identity; not to become their best selves, not to live happy and productive lives, not to be fulfilled in their work and their lives and their loves.

How easily the population had been fooled.

Who were these people who wanted to play God? To inject billions of people with a "gene therapy"? Who thought they were intelligent enough, gifted enough, to play such a role? To determine who lived or died.

You might as well harvest the trees.

It wasn't your decision to make.

The birds, those mythical falcons, tore apart, fed upon, the soft brain tissue of his tormentors.

And we stood alone. And waved.

Calling, calling.

The gate between the realms was being lowered, the time was nigh.

***

The divisions extant at that time were not just within government or between authorities and protestors, but had also divided the medical profession.

A new group of highly qualified medical professionals, driven by a strong sense of outrage, formed the Australian Medical Professionals Society.

The traditional representational body, the Australian Medical Association, discredited by its unquestioning backing of the government's Covid measures, was faced with a dwindling membership base. Some 95% of doctors had been members back in the 1960s. By 2022 that figure was less than 30%.

AMPS explained themselves thus: "Doctors were gagged by threats to their registration. Many have been disciplined or suspended for challenging the public health messaging even if they believed that they had scientific evidence to support their professional view.

"There have been multiple practitioners, particularly in recent times, who have been disciplined or suspended as a threat to public health for contradicting Covid Public Health messaging. Yet there are serious questions about data accountability and transparency, safety and efficacy requirements for provisional approvals or lack thereof, prohibitions on early treatment options, informed consent obligations.

"One of the chief concerns of our membership is that of medical free speech.

"Contingent to a joint statement received from the Australian Health Practitioner Regulation Agency AHPRA and the National Boards on 9 March 2021, Australian Health Professionals numbering over 825,000 were essentially forbidden from publicly questioning the science underlying the emerging COVID-19 injectables, let alone questioning any government messaging urging Australians to be vaccinated because these products were deemed 'safe and effective'."

The directive read: "Any promotion of anti-vaccination statements or health advice which contradicts the best available scientific evidence or seeks to actively undermine the national immunisation campaign (including via social media) is not supported by National Boards and may be in breach of the codes of conduct and subject to investigation and possible regulatory action."

AMPS stated: "The current AHPRA position statement makes abiding by our codes a risk to careers, registration and livelihood. A very effective and insidious silencing tool.

"The effect of this unilateral action was to undermine professional independence and, in so doing, strip away years of training, academic achievements, qualifications, awards and expertise. However well intentioned, this gagging by bureaucratic decree inserted AHPRA and the National Boards between the Clinician and their Patient, in addition to counteracting normal robust interprofessional dialogue, as more data emerged.

"In any event, the implied and intended outcome of the gagging was to see Doctors and Health Professionals effectively mandated to support the government campaign to have the Australian population injected with drugs for which there was no adequate short, medium or long-term safety or efficacy data.

"Indeed, the rush to market and Provisional Approval occurred despite the absence of the usual pre-clinical studies, including testing for Carcinogenicity and Genotoxicity.

"In this regard, it should be of serious interest that a peer-reviewed investigation has demonstrated that mRNA-derived Spike proteins enter the cell nucleus and interfere with DNA. However, many critical facts like these became forbidden subjects for Health Professionals and Doctors to raise with their patients, let alone in public forums.

"To date, Adverse Events flowing from these products are at historically unprecedented levels globally and continue to rise. And again, to date, no other drugs in human history have reported more deaths, illnesses, injuries, and disabilities.

"It is evident that Australians have suffered as a consequence of the Provisional Approval pathway laws. These have facilitated the rapid entry of significantly under tested products into the Australian market, despite their being recognised to be highly novel and experimental. Nonetheless, the COVID-19 injectables were mandated in many jurisdictions and workplaces, causing large numbers of Australians to feel coerced and simultaneously baffled by the inability of Doctors and other Health Professionals to give them a voice."

***

Professor Ramesh Thakur from the Australian National University was equally blunt.

As he recorded, the Covid report from New South Wales Health for the week of July 10–16, 2022, said: "The minority of the overall population who have not been vaccinated are significantly overrepresented among patients in hospitals and ICUs with Covid-19."

Just two pages later, the same report gave the number of unvaccinated people admitted to hospital and Intensive Care Units as zero.

"Even by the standards of public health authorities across the world gaslighting the people in order to nudge them into docile – and often performative – compliance with official edicts, this level of internal contradiction of narrative with data is breathtaking.

"Covid vaccines are undeniably leaky. Their real-world effectiveness lasts a disappointingly short time. Mass vaccination campaigns in the middle of a pandemic can possibly also give an evolutionary advantage to mutations with greater vaccine escape properties."

Thakur goes on to quote a string of studies to support his case. Professor Kenji Yamamoto of the Okamura Memorial Hospital reinforced a warning from the European Medicines Agency of the potential for frequent booster shots to harm the immune system.

An Icelandic study showed a significantly higher probability of reinfection of the boosted. Equally, there were breakthrough reports in the mainstream media of the deadly long-term harms of lockdowns themselves. Official statistics suggested, to quote one headline, "The effects of lockdown may now be killing more people than are dying of Covid."

"The causes are exactly what many had predicted from the start: A monomaniacal focus on Covid to the neglect of all other health concerns meant many ailments that are treatable with routine early screening went undetected until too late; excessive test, track and trace and isolation requirements took many healthcare personnel out of circulation; and deaths by despair and loneliness from the enforced separations from family and the fellowship of friends.

"Even now there is a great reluctance to discuss the serious adverse events, including deaths, associated with and caused by vaccines themselves. Concerning safety signals continue to grow. For example, a study in June by several experts analysed data from Pfizer and Moderna Covid vaccine trials. They found that the risk of hospitalisation from a vaccine-related adverse event was higher than the risk of hospitalisation from Covid itself. Until such time that these are properly investigated, we will lack accurate and reliable data on the scale and severity of the problem."

"In a sane world, there was simply no way the Australian government could justify its continued push to vaccinate and then boost the population."

***

Already a new generation was taking over, on a planet renowned for its fecundity. Welcome back. The voices were contradictory. Perhaps it had always been. He himself was better than he had been for a long time. But the nation? Well, that was another story.

It was a freezing winter. With soaring energy costs and depleted incomes, many were afraid to heat their own homes because of the exorbitant cost, and instead snuggled up in bed to stay warm.

Absolutely bloody freezing.

Meanwhile the apparatchiks, those distant creatures the long suffering public had theoretically elected to serve, blathered on about global warming and raked yet more millions off an already impoverished population. Old Alex should have been outraged. He was just saddened.

Here, back in Oak Flats from the opal fields, different spirits stirred than in the country's vast interior; simply because, in a time continuum, everyone needs skipping stones, a surface from which to slither to another surface, a place from which to begin, a realm in which to enter.

So in his waking dreams that seer not yet born would speak to him, and he would speak back; though the wonder of it all, the utter impossibility of it all. The images made no clear or rational sense. Not that it mattered; not that the populace cared.

There had just been an election in Australia; but if you listened to the idle conversations in coffee shops or bars none of it mattered; as if it had never been. Only on the internet, that mycelium of the age, were voices raised in protest.

The so-called representatives of the people spouted the same garbage as the Davos billionaires; and remarkably enough, the people believed.

There are different species of humans, Ethan had said in a Discourse chatroom, and yes, of course there were. "They have always walked among us."

Oh Wonder. Oh Wonder.

If he could reach into himself for certainty he would have done so; but instead, storm tossed, part of him a derelict addict, unkempt on a street corner, amidst those fallen angels gathering around the homeless shelters. The truth only slowly dawned.

Those vast aggregate intellects could not speak through a single person, or a single tree, could not act alone, they needed vast numbers to transmit a message so complex, simply in order to act.

And hence the origin of the gods, or the myths of gods.

These were the strange thoughts that whispered through Old Alex as he sat on his deck and watched the cows grazing on the valley floor opposite; in a rare moment of sunshine.

And now the eugenicists. The gods had stirred in anger, wrath, for no one stood in their way and emerged unscathed. Who were these people who thought they could play God? Who thought they could do this to a divine creation?

Whether it was millions, or billions, or trillions, these lifeforms, who were they to say what was needed, or what the ultimate purpose?

Time crushed every creature.

Only the immortals remained.

And soon enough, those men who thought they could play god would themselves be crushed. The billionaires, the powerful, laid waste upon the Earth. Their own cracked images in a cracked mirror not even a firefly, gone from this place, cursed.

While the same immortals said to him: You Are Blessed. Or in antique English: Blessed Art Thou.

There in that wintry valley.

***

There came, that October of 2022, the final month of Spring when the days began to lengthen at last, the first major review of Australia's response to Covid, titled Faultines, was released. Touting itself as an independent inquiry, the review was chaired by Peter Shergold, a former secretary of the prime minister's department and funded by the Paul Ramsay Foundation, the Minderoo Foundation, and the John and Myriam Wylie Foundations.

The review found that Australia's response to COVID-19 exacerbated existing inequalities within the society. Those bearing the brunt of the pandemic included low socio-economic families, women, children, those in aged care, people with disabilities, temporary migrants, and multicultural communities. The burden was not shared equally.

You don't say, Jessebelle.

Paul Collits was straight into the fray: "The most obvious problem with the inquiry is that it fails to confront the biggest issue of the past two and a half years.

"And no, it is not lockdowns, however massively unnecessary and damaging these were. The biggest issue has been the Covid tyranny's crushing of freedoms and rights through vaccine mandates and the bullying of citizens through vaccine propaganda. It is tedious to have to repeat it endlessly.

"The vaccines were never fit for purpose. They were never even meant to stop transmission of the coronavirus. We were lied to on that.

"The vaccines were experimental. Their manufacturers and marketers were protected by government from prosecution. The vaccines were not needed for most people. The vaccines were, for many, dangerous, even lethal. We were lied to about that as well.

"Remember 'safe and effective'? Two lies in the one marketing pitch.

"Make no mistake, these things were not just misplaced, but were evil. But what of the brutal and unnecessary vaccine mandates? Nothing to see here, it seems. If one accepts the approach of the review panel and its backroom economist research team. Hard questions were never asked.

"This is a review of the technocracy, in the worst sense of that term, done by the technocracy. And quite possibly done for the technocracy."

***

Joe Hildebrand at News Limited, who had a much wider readership than almost anyone in the country, and who Old Alex knew simply through dint of having worked in the same building for years, was equally ferocious in the wake of the Review.

"The thing about the truth is that it always comes out," he wrote. "It may take years, decades or even centuries, but reality has a way of asserting itself. Lies inevitably fall apart.

"And so more than two and a half years after Covid-19 first came to Australian shores the truth has finally emerged about our various governments' response to it and the lies have been exposed. Lockdowns were wrong. School closures were wrong. Border closures were wrong. Poor people were hurt the most.

"To their eternal shame, state premiers and chief health officers were complicit in this. They were wrong and they caused untold damage that will be immeasurable and long-lasting."

Hildeberg lambasted his critics, the sort of people, as he put it, who liked to talk about being on the right side of history. Now history had caught up with them.

"They were wrong, dead wrong. Not only the decision-makers who awarded themselves close to messianic status – with powers to match – but the frothing mobs that cheered them on. They were wrong, wrong, wrong and wrong all along.

"Already they are crawling sideways, changing their tune or shrinking from public view. The usual Twitter warriors seem oddly subdued.

"But history will remember them and history will judge them and history will not be on their side. Because now the truth is here. Not out there, but right here, right now. And the truth always wins."

***

None of the big picture looks at the harms done by the response of governments to Covid were in the least complimentary. Writing for the Brownstown Institute, the eminently qualified authors Carla Peters and David Bell observed: "An underlying principle of public health is, or was, to provide the public with accurate information so that they can make good health choices for themselves and their community.

"The past three years have seen this paradigm turned on its head, with the public's money being used to deceive and coerce them, forcing them to follow public health dictates.

"The public has funded their own incarceration and impoverishment through their taxes, with public funds driving the unprecedented non pharmaceutical, and then pharmaceutical, response to a virus that kills mainly old sick people near the end of their lives.

"Children have had their education downgraded, and economies have been mangled, ensuring future generations will also pay. So, what did the public actually pay for?

"Citizens have paid the bill via taxes for novel nonpharmaceutical interventions (lockdowns, mask mandates and frequent testing) and repeated vaccinations of immune people with rapidly waning vaccines, whilst seeing their own incomes reduced. The increase in the money supply to cover relief for forced unemployment has driven inflation, contributing to increased food, water, energy, health and insurance costs. These responses have disproportionately harmed low income families.

"Lockdowns may prove to be one of the gravest governmental failures of modern times. A cost-benefit analysis of the response to COVID-19 found lockdowns to be far more harmful to public health (at least 5-10 times) in terms of well-being than COVID-19.

"Significant collateral damage is not unexpected, as mass business closures and restricted movement have affected billions of people globally through poverty, food insecurity, loneliness, unemployment, educational interruption, and interrupted healthcare.

"What did not make media headlines is the more than three million children who have died from malnutrition in the first year of the pandemic.

"The sense of fear, anxiety and helplessness brought to families and 2.2 billion children around the globe with removal of future earning capacity and limited access to healthcare will impact lives in an unprecedented manner for generations."

***

Goodbye to sweet reason. Goodbye to all rationality. The public square had become so utterly dishonest Old Alex, like so many of his compatriots, could hardly bear to the nightly news.

Utterly, totally, dishonest.

The putrid news, at least as far as Old Alex was concerned, that NSW Chief Health Officer Kerry Chant had received an Order of Australia threw Old Alex into a funk; he knew he shouldn't care, that he shouldn't let these things affect him. But they did.

As trivial as it sounded, after all, nobody expected anything better from the nation's politicians and bureaucrats but self aggrandisement and incompetence, but nonetheless he was incensed. The politicisation of Australia's award system had been going on for years; whether it was giving awards to those involved in the discredited Iraq war, although as it was all secret the public were never allowed to know exactly what gallant feat was being thus acclaimed, or to the endless cavalcade of social justice warriors and feminist or multicultural so beloved by intellectually lazy bureaucrats.

We, that is the long suffering populace, just got used to it.

But this one; it was an insult to every freedom fighter, every individual who stood up to the tyrannical over-the-top tilt into totalitarianism the country had endured and to the many people damaged by vaccines, lockdowns and social isolation; as those bureaucrats in power determinedly implemented one failed public health policy after another.

Not that a lobotomised populace seemed to care, but nonetheless it flattened him, his despair at the corruption of the body politic, the utter banality of it all.

There was no shortage of things to be outraged about.

The world's worst internet, highest electricity costs, most surveilled population, least free democracy.

Except this was so destructive, so outrageous, so difficult to fathom; the pig ignorance of it. After the tribulation, trust no man. And certainly not, in this context, a public health official.

EIGHTEEN
FACTCHECK THIS: BOMBSHELL REVELATIONS

Under normal circumstances the liar is defeated by reality, for which there is no substitute; no matter how large the tissue of falsehood that an experienced liar has to offer, it will never be large enough, even if he enlists the help of computers, to cover the immensity of factuality. The liar, who may get away with any number of single falsehoods, will find it impossible to get away with lying on principle.

Hannah Arendt.

There is no act of treachery or meanness of which a political party is not capable; for in politics there is no honour.

Benjamin Disraeli.

For anyone who had followed the Covid narrative and the rampant corruption involved, the revelations out of the European Parliament that Pfizer did not even test to see if their Covid-19 vaccine stopped transmission after more than two years of totalitarian lunacy, were gob smacking, appalling, delicious in a terrible sense.

Following a committee meeting investigating the European Union's 36 billion Euro contract with Pfizer, the largest ever signed by the EU, Member of the European Parliament Rob Roos of the Netherlands, a highly credible source, released a video with the caption "BREAKING:

Vaccine never tested on preventing transmission. This means the COVID passport was based on a big lie".

The clip, of an execrable performance by a Pfizer executive Janine Small, shows her giving a strangled laugh when directly asked to give a yes or no answer on whether or not Pfizer tested to see if the vaccines prevented transmission.

No, they did not.

Yet stopping transmission to protect loved ones was the sole reason hundreds of millions of people around the globe got "jabbed"; including millions of perfectly decent Australian citizens who did not realise that the "safe and effective" mantra coming from their leaders was an out and out lie.

The admission made redundant or absurd the actions of Western governments in mandating vaccines. The Australian government's aggressive push to vaccinate the population had ultimately made it one of the most heavily vaccinated countries on Earth.

Many, in rolling up their sleeves, believed they were doing the right thing by their families, friends and communities.

But those snake oil salesmen otherwise known as politicians, frantically pushing a poorly tested and experimental medical product must have known they were flogging a useless or in fact harmful product.

The Pfizer admission provoked outrage around the globe, and destroyed whatever shreds of credibility were left for America's corrupt public health establishment.

By late 2022 figures from the Australian Bureau of Statistics showed excess deaths running at 17.1 percent above normal.

Australians did this to Australians.

***

In the video shared by Roos, which promptly went viral and which interestingly enough was readily available on two of the greatest manipulators of the Covid narrative, Twitter and YouTube, he addresses the camera and states that the Dutch Prime Minister and Health Minister told the Dutch people that "if you don't get vaccinated, you're antisocial" and that "you don't get vaccinated just for yourself, but also for others."

Roos continued, "Today, this turns out to be complete nonsense. In a Covid hearing in the European Parliament, one of the Pfizer directors just admitted to me: at the time of introduction, the vaccine had never been tested on stopping the transmission of the virus. This removes the entire legal basis for the Covid passport."

In the video, Roos then introduces the testimony clip showing himself asking Janine Small of Pfizer for a "clear" answer.

"I will speak in English so there are no misunderstandings. Was the Pfizer Covid vaccine tested on stopping the transmission of the virus before it entered the market? If not, please, say it clearly. If 'yes' are you willing to share the data with this committee? And I really want a straight answer, 'yes or no' and I'm looking forward to it."

"No", Small replied. "We had to really move at the speed of science to understand what is taking place in the market. We had to do everything at risk."

Her remarks were widely ridiculed by commentators and comedians alike.

The lie, or the failure to correct the lies of politicians, came not just from the vaccine manufacturers; but from their willing helpers in the media and in the nation's bureaucracies.

Much of the disintegration of Australia and the complete loss of faith in government owed its origin to the fact that the population had been frequently and repeatedly lied to about Covid vaccinations, led to believe that by having the vaccine they were contributing to a social good and stopping the spread of a dangerous virus.

It was a lie, had always been a lie, and those peddling it either must have known, or should have known; with their massive salaries, their even more massive vaccine related grants, their staff, their burnished university degrees.

But still they lied.

Nor was it a lie from an occasional self-aggrandising bureaucrat, it was a whole of government effort; from the Prime Minister down through to the state Premiers and Chief Medical Officers, right down to the doctors and medical staff at vaccination centres.

And what made it even worse was that they did it to their own people, with everyone in the military and the public service, police, teachers, nurses, rescue workers, all were obliged to get "the jab" or lose their jobs.

Thousands quit out of principle, creating chaos across multiple industries and organisations.

Still others suffered various degrees of vaccine injury as they faced the Hobbesian choice of being injected or losing their job; forced to face homelessness and an inability to care for their children, or roll up their sleeves.

Later Roos would argue "There was no basis for Covid passports and Covid vaccine mandates. Worldwide people are angry because their governments lied to them. Our governments lied because they based their narrative on the idea that you do this for others and that vaccination stops transmission, for which there was no evidence.

"And all fact-checkers have to admit that the government messaging was plain wrong and government policies undermined fundamental rights in an unprecedented way

"What should happen, in my opinion, is that politicians are held accountable. The people who were responsible for these policies should resign if they are still in office. This has been the most damaging violation of fundamental rights in decades. Its impact is lasting. Small businesses are still going bankrupt because of high inflation after they were already weakened by Covid lockdowns. Young people are still more often depressed and lost out on valuable life experience – our society suffers from an obesity epidemic – and this was not because of some force of nature, it was because politicians decided to enact these policies. Those who did should resign and this violation of fundamental human rights should never happen again."

***

Ironically for a news organisation which had done so much to promote public hysteria and the interests of Big Pharma, News Limited came out with a story titled "Yes, they claimed the vaccines would prevent transmission" with the slug line: "After a "scandalous" admission by a Pfizer executive testifying before parliament this week, there is one massive lie being told to everyone."

Predictably the comments section went straight off the charts. Here's just one example, from a poster calling himself Jab: "I lost my job due to the mandates, a loss of over $80k over the year. I've supported myself throughout this time, no government help. I've been told I am selfish, not looking out for my fellow humans, the elderly, the immunosuppressed, how I was putting them all at risk.

"I've been down-trodden and treated like an outcast of society. All because of a lie. Let's hope those responsible for the lies will all be dealt with."

Helpfully the author of the piece Frank Chung listed a series of examples of Australian and American officials who assured the public that the vaccines stopped transmission.

This was an American inspired fiasco with worldwide implications, and it was the rampant corruption of the American public health and regulatory systems, American based companies such as Pfizer and Americans themselves, including most infamously Bill Gates, Anthony Fauci and Mark Zuckerberg, who had manipulated the narrative and inflicted this harm on populations worldwide.

The stench that flowed from this international disaster marred still further America's damaged reputation.

US President Joe Biden said in July 2021 that "you're not going to get Covid if you have these vaccinations".

A lie.

White House Chief Medical Adviser Dr Anthony Fauci said in May of 2021 that vaccinated people become "dead ends" for the virus.

"When you get vaccinated, you not only protect your own health and that of the family but also you contribute to the community health by preventing the spread of the virus throughout the community.

"In other words, you become a dead end to the virus. And when there are a lot of deadends around, the virus is not going to go anywhere. And that's when you get to a point that you have a markedly diminished rate of infection in the community."

A lie, a complete and total lie, and a very influential one and that.

Centre for Disease Control director Rochelle Walensky said in March 2021 that "vaccinated people do not carry the virus, don't get sick".

A lie.

As Chung reported: "In Australia, politicians and health officials held millions of people hostage for months, lecturing and threatening them to get vaccinated to regain their freedoms.

"The vaccines were the 'way out' of the pandemic, they were not just to protect ourselves but to 'protect others, they would 'stop the spread', and not getting vaccinated was 'selfish'.

"Vaccine passports, the vaccinated economy, were necessary so people who 'did the right thing' would feel 'safe' knowing they weren't 'mixing' with the unvaccinated, who were a 'risk to the community'."

All of it was bullshit, to slip into the Australian vernacular.

***

That winter of 2022 edging into spring was cold, and the vile weather allowed no quick return to normality. The population begged for a sunny day.

If they were formed from all those prayers and all that chanting, if they had gathered along the Tigris River all those years ago, if the native prayers in this place bore little resemblance to the power drunk madness of former times, if gods indeed formed out of the ectoplasm of all these desires, bled off the back of books, derived from literature and the scribes, perhaps, just perhaps, it might make sense.

This mystery beyond mysteries Old Alex pondered every day; as he also pondered one of history's greatest deceits.

The nearby shorelines were piercingly beautiful, beyond beautiful. Every detail picked out, bathed in eternal light, an awesome power.

All war is deception, that lie played over and over He kept quiet. He feared no longer. The country itself? It stood on a precipice. That was the way it felt.

Australia was a lost concept, a country destroyed almost as an afterthought by the world's rich and powerful. We all stood at the end of American Empire, for it was the Americans who had foisted this truly evil disaster on the world's population

The mob had jeered. The operatives had jeered. And now, frightened at the uncanny nature of it all, they fell silent.

And the ruin they had helped visit upon the country, on his country, on their fellow countrymen and women, the elderly, the children, the weak, the strong, the nation's hard working and applauded, these oligarchs and the useful fools in the nation's bureaucracies, they had helped to destroy it all.

The coconspirators in the Australian government straightened their ties. They did not know how to cover their malfeasance any longer; and if they hadn't dodged out from the scrum already, looked eagerly for the EXIT sign. They were guilty. And they knew it.

***

Here's a sampling of the blizzard of terror that rained down on the Australian population, induced a nationwide psychosis and encouraged millions of people to roll up their sleeves for a vaccine which was neither safe nor effective, and which most certainly did not stop either infection or transmission.

Daniel Andrews, Premier of Victoria:

September 5, 2021: "We're going to move to a situation where, to protect the health system, we're going to lock out people who are not vaccinated and can be. If you're making the choice not to get vaccinated, then you're making the wrong choice, you're making the wrong choice. And for safety's sake, back to that point of how much work our nurses have to do, as this becomes absolutely a pandemic of the unvaccinated, and we open everything up, it's not going to be safe for people who are not vaccinated to be roaming around the place spreading the virus."

Lies.

October 26, 2021: "If you're on the fence, if you haven't quite made up your mind yet about whether you will or won't get vaccinated and be protected by these vaccines that are free, that are safe, that are effective – please reconsider that decision. Two doses of this vaccine is the greatest protection that you can have for your health and the health of those you love and, indeed, the health system."

Lies.

January 30, 2022: "I think it's only a matter of time before the relevant federal agencies confirm that it's three doses in order to be protected, not just against really critical illness but to be protected or to minimise the likelihood that you get it and that you give it to the people that you love. At the moment two doses are protecting the vast majority of people from serious illness, but it's only with three doses that you'll be prevented not just from serious illness but from getting this virus, this Omicron variant, and therefore giving it to others."

Lies.

Queensland Premier Annastacia Palaszczuk:

November 9, 2021: "People want to be able to go to a music festival, a stadium, a cafe or a restaurant and know the people who are around them are fully vaccinated and it's safe for their families. This is an important step in keeping our freedoms. Millions of people have gone and got vaccinated and they need to be rewarded for their efforts. They have done a great job, they have done everything I have asked them to do. But as a community, if we are going to stop the spread of this virus when the borders open and the virus is going to come here, we need people to get vaccinated. Families want to know they are safe when they are out in public."

All based on falsehoods.

Jeannette Young, then Queensland Chief Health Officer, was later rewarded with the plum post of Governor of Queensland. Her husband Professor Graeme Nimmo received travel perks and benefits while serving as an adviser to Covid-19 vaccine manufacturer Pfizer.

October 7, 2021: "The only thing that's going to stop us getting locally acquired cases going forward, we know is vaccination. We can't stop it. The only way to stop it is vaccination. It does take five weeks from your first dose of Pfizer to be fully protected and six weeks from your first dose of Moderna."

False.

West Australian Premier Mark McGowan

October 31, 2021: "I just urge these people to go and get vaccinated. The time for protesting and reading crazy conspiracy theorists online is over. Some of the material they're spreading is extreme, misleading and frankly lies. They are reading wacky theories online that are untrue. This rubbish that's put out online and some of the lies and misleading information … is dangerous. I just urge them to stop, go and get vaccinated and just act like normal, rational human beings."

Dangerous garbage.

January 13, 2022: "Following WA's Safe Transition, we want the public to be confident in these public settings, and that they're only mixing with other vaccinated people. People less likely to be carrying or able to pass on the disease. It reduces the risks posed by unvaccinated people bringing the virus into busy, populated settings. Life will become very difficult for the unvaccinated from January 31. No pubs, no bottle shops, no gym, no yoga classes, no gigs, no dancefloors, no hospital or aged care visits. If you go and get vaccinated today you can have your second dose by early February, but if you choose to remain unvaccinated you're choosing to put yourself at risk, you're choosing to put the people around you at risk and you're choosing to increase the burden on our health staff."

False.

Then South Australian Premier Steven Marshall:

May 25, 2021: "This is Kaylah Pascoe — she's among the first 16-year-olds in regional SA to roll up her sleeve and get a Covid-19 vaccine. Thank you Kaylah. By getting vaccinated, she is not only helping protect herself, but is preventing others from suffering from this insidious disease.

"We are scaling up our vaccination rollout in South Australia, to include people aged 16 years and over living in regional areas. A vaccinated SA population means a much safer and stronger economy. "

A truly appalling fiasco visited upon Australians by their elected representatives. And to the nation's most precious resource, its youth.

November 24, 2021: "We've had a very, very good uptake in South Australia. They know that when they look interstate at the moment, this is essentially the disease of the unvaccinated."

It was never a disease of the unvaccinated. That was a corporate inspired government sponsored lie. Why were our taxes used for this purpose?

Northern Territory Chief Minister Michael Gunner, notorious for rounding up much of the indigenous population off their homelands, confining them to quarantine camps and forcibly, effectively, injecting them.

September 15, 2021: "I know I am supposed to say I respect people's choices and reasons for not getting vaccinated — I don't. I don't understand, I don't respect it. You don't get to choose to burden our health system because you refuse to follow preventative health measures."

November 22, 2021: "A lockout means fully vaccinated residents are able to move about the community freely, while wearing a mask. If you give a green light, give comfort to, support anybody who argues against the vaccine, you are an anti-vaxxer. Your personal vaccination status is utterly irrelevant. There are people actually supporting the idea of a teacher being unvaccinated in a remote community classroom with kids who can't be vaccinated. I reject it. If you're out there in any way, shape or form campaigning against the mandate, then you are absolutely anti-vax. If you say pro-persuasion, stuff it. Shove it.

"We are absolutely going to make sure as many Territorians as possible are vaccinated. I will never back away from supporting vaccines, and anyone out there who comes for the mandate, you are anti-vax."

Pure, simple madness.

Or was it greed?

Did they, or was that another conspiracy theory, pocket millions from the vaccine manufacturers in the guise of consultancy fees? A conflict of interest, obviously, but perhaps not technically illegal.

January 6, 2022: "Work is not a reason to leave the home for the unvaccinated. The Chief Health Officer has also determined that restriction of movement is critical right now and that one hour of exercise for the next four days is not essential. There has been plenty of time for people to get vaccinated, people who are not vaccinated present the greatest risk of spreading the virus and are the most at risk of becoming seriously ill if they get the virus."

More lies. Simple as that.

***

In Old Alex's home state of New South Wales the rabid lockdowns and urgent, incessant remonstrations with the public to get themselves vaccinated raised not just his ire but his suspicions.

He knew perfectly well, having worked with these people and their ilk for decades as a general news reporter, that they did not genuinely care a jot for the public they were elected to represent. Never had. Never would. They cared about their status, their career paths, their incomes, their cosy little retirement nest eggs. Comfortably shrouded in an air of importance, with their chauffeur and assistants and high level meetings, the sight of themselves on television simply confirmed their own self image. They were professional politicians of Australia's professional class. They possessed no genuine affinity with the voting public, who they only understood through the filtered medium of opinion polls, surveys and focus groups.

The great unwashed, the peasantry, the poorly educated and the working class, were there to be manipulated, controlled, taxed, and, at election time, to be fooled into voting them back into office.

And very comfortable, lucrative offices they were.

Perhaps, as Old Alex watched one stuffed suit after another at one press conference after another, it was the status, the ego strokes, that they cared about the most. The cash was nice, too. The influential connections, very handy. The chauffeur driven car, good one! The functions, the travel, the sense of power, all of it a sweet reward to which they felt fully entitled.

They didn't care about the welfare of the public, or they wouldn't have so constantly ripped them off with so many ridiculous and expensive schemes; they would not have wasted their taxes in the way they so flagrantly did.

It made no sense to him whatsoever that they were now so urgently determined to have the population vaccinated with a vaccine they could not possibly know the long term consequences of; and yes, to understand the most perplexing of stories it's almost always simply a case of "follow the money".

***

NSW Premier Gladys Berejiklian:

August 25, 2021: "Don't hold off, get your hands on any vaccine you can. Keep yourself and your loved ones safe. It's also doing a community service by helping stop the spread and keeping people out of hospital."

A lie.

September 2, 2021: "Anybody should come forward and get vaccinated. We don't want to see anybody vulnerable without a vaccine. This is, I've said a couple of times, a pandemic, an epidemic of the unvaccinated. When we see people who are fully vaccinated hospitalised or horribly die, often there are other conditions associated with that."

All based on lies.

September 7, 2021: "I wouldn't want to be in the room with lots of people who aren't vaccinated."

September 15, 2021: "We don't want anyone who hasn't been vaccinated yet to sit at home. Come out, get vaccinated, do your bit for yourself and your family. Remember that people might say well if you're not vaccinated, that's on you and you might get sick – well, no. Unvaccinated people spread the disease more readily. So if you're in a venue or somewhere and there's unvaccinated people [you have] more chance of contracting the disease from them because they don't have that protection."

A sheer, total and complete fabrication supported by the Prime Minister and the health bureaucracy.

September 20, 2021: "Unvaccinated people, it's one thing to put themselves in jeopardy, but they're jeopardising everybody else because they're more contagious. If you choose not to be vaccinated, it's one thing to make that decision for yourself and your family, but you're also making that decision, suggesting that you don't care if you're more contagious to other people."

These people just made stuff up; it was irresponsible, stupid and deeply dangerous.

Gladys Berejiklian resigned within weeks, under investigation from the Independent Commission Against Corruption for an unrelated scandal but tight on the heels of allegations that Pfizer was manipulating public policy through tens of millions of dollars of donations to political lobbyists.

The way Old Alex saw it, the prompt nature of her departure after the allegations of corruption were raised beggared belief. There was never any adequate explanation for her resignation. Perhaps, to use another colloquialism, she knew "the shit was about to hit the fan".

New South Wales Health Minister Brad Hazzard:

July 29, 2021: "There are a lot of people who don't base their decisions in science or evidence. I'd say to those not wanting to take vaccines, my message to them is you're being extremely selfish if you think you can not have a vaccine just because you don't want to have a vaccine, well you should think about what you're doing to your family and to the community, and I would say even more than that, what a hide you have, what a ridiculous position is that when you're going to put health staff at risk, and when you get sick you're going to expect to come into hospital and get paid for by taxpayers."

***

What a blather of absolute nonsense.

As history quickly demonstrated, it was the Health Minister who, by making such ridiculous claims, was putting everybody's health at risk.

Within days of the revelations emerging out of the European Parliament and brutal coverage in Sydney's tabloid newspaper *The Daily Telegraph*, Brad Hazzard resigned from politics.

Many pundits on social media were delighted to see the back of a man they thought of as "evil", a man who, having been a vociferous proponent of lockdowns, masks and vaccines, had done massive harm to the state's more than eight million residents.

His moment in the sun had turned into a Dark Winter for everybody else.

Perhaps he could get a job with Pfizer. He had certainly done everything in his power to flog their defective product.

Perhaps he already had one lined up some cosy little sinecure, that was the suspicion abroad, and well and truly lodged in Old Alex's brain, that these people would never have behaved the way they did without considerable financial incentive. But that bordered on the slanderous, surely not.

The overlords would have liked everyone to just conveniently forget the whole damn thing. For those whose lives had been irreparably damaged, and there were many of those, there was no forgetting.

As Hazzard resigned, excess death rates were running at an unprecedented 17 per cent above normal, hospitals were gridlocked and chaotic, the health system in crisis, thousands of nurses had quit rather than get "the jab", and faith in government was at existentially low levels.

It was a major threat to Australian democracy and the credibility of the ruling elites. And for one simple reason. If anyone ever believed a word that came out of these people's mouths ever again, more fool them.

The puffed up, stern, self aggrandising image of Brad Hazzard, the New World Order Health Minister on a mission, beamed into everybody's lounge rooms, alarmed the gullible and transfigured many people's lives.

There would be no mea culpa, and no apology. In the round of valedictory media interviews, fielding softball questions from gormless journalists, Hazzard was never held to account.

Talking about the opposite side of humble. Because he could, Old Alex published a hit piece just before Christmas of 2021 titled: In A Year of Utter Madness One Thing Is Certain: New South Wales Health Minister Brad Hazzard Has To Go.

"Millions of citizens of Australia's most populous state have had their lives and businesses destroyed or profoundly disrupted throughout the madness, the sheer unadulterated insanity, of 2021.

"Front and centre of this debacles has been the increasingly crazed figure of Health Minister Brad Hazzard, whose deranged posturing and spit flying authoritarian drivel has done much to discredit not just the state's political class but the states medical and bureaucratic edifices.

"Referencing 'modelling' from epidemiologists during a press conference, Hazzard said the 'reproductive rate of the virus' was more than 1.5, with numbers close to doubling every three days.

"Hysterically, of course, 'Omicron' is an anagram of 'moronic', making every sceptic on the planet laugh.

"Hazzard's fear mongering is set against the backdrop of a spate of excoriating books dismembering every aspect of the Covid narrative. The sceptics were well out of the closet; and everyone now knew the shocking fraud behind the yarn, not least of all the world's military and intelligence agencies.

"Governments, including Australia's state and federal governments, had been left stranded with a credibility gap so wide it was impossible to jump over.

"But still they continued on."

Throughout his dysfunctional reign as Health Minister, Brad Hazzard refused to release the so-called modelling and the so-called medical advice that he was relying on for his endless, increasingly surreal, announcements.

That is, he was locking down the state and hysterically driving the population into mass vaccination, but would not, or could not, demonstrate why.

***

Australia was a country bound by, immersed in, Old Alex, fulminating away, couldn't think of the term, cooked in hypocrisy. It required a dumbing down of the population for the apparatchiks to get away with it. And how they thought they could get away with it, with many a super brain on the planet focused on the case, Old Alex had no idea.

All of these messages, the detritus from failed Psyop programs, the haunting, it became impossible to trust his own instincts, sheltering inside in a rain drenched scape.

Events, dear boy, events, let the passage of time tell its own story; in a rain drenched valley filled with spirits and waking dreams. He clung to life, he soared above it all. They were gathering up their weapons. Not disembodied wings, not this time, something more lethal, flying high over them all, even above the time channels,

Far from the only one to see a greater spiritual battle, these were his thoughts, as he gazed through the rain at the vivid green paddocks beyond.

Stay true.

Hypocrisy will out. All cause mortality will out. He saw the advertisements on public broadcasting channels, or the government funded and manipulated private media, "Safe and Effective". How could anyone still believe?

The entire culture was mired in deceit. It was a horrifying thing. It made him blanche, the scale of it all, the millions of dead and damaged, the absolute, utter hypocrisy of those who had perpetuated this crime against their fellows.

Everyone was compromised. Everyone had been dirtied by this deceit; now out in the open. The perpetrators were so brazen, they had barely even bothered to hide their tracks.

Arrogance, of course, had brought down many a scammer. The authorities and perpetrators should have been squirming in embarrassment; that their consciences had been so small, their fealty to the truth nonexistent, their ruthless ambition so large, their careless dismissal of the spirit realm, the fates, the gods, the universal nature, truly, they should have been squirming in embarrassment.

Look over there! We're at war!

Take time, for it is the greatest gift you will ever receive. Here in this time, when so many futures were destroyed.

***

The principal problem for government's attempting to maintain credibility through this period was that much of the information, and the forecasts they relied upon, repeatedly shown to be wildly inaccurate, were resourced by the Bill Gates funded World Health Organisation, around which daily swirled ever greater controversies.

The massive funding of both academics and institutions from vested interests was a process known as regulatory capture on the one hand, and buying influence on the other, and had a severe influence on Australia, with a "bought" sign hanging from the necks of many of the establishment figures the public once trusted.

One of the New South Wales government's favourite go-to experts was Professor Kristine Macartney of Sydney University, who infamously received $65 million in government grants for vaccine linked work.

How is that not a conflict of interest?

As the well respected Arkmedic's blog recorded, Professor Macartney was the Director of the National Centre for Immunisation Research and Surveillance, and there was a close relationship between the NCIRS, the NSW Government and the Health Department.

She was also a member of the Advisory Committee on Vaccines of the Therapeutic Goods Administration, the body which gave final approval for the Covid vaccines in Australia.

The TGA, with a budget of $170 million, was principally funded through fees imposed on pharmaceutical companies. In their Business Plan they claimed that "As an Australian Government regulator we adhere to the following principles: We are committed to maintaining the trust and confidence of the Australian public. We are accountable to the government of the day and the Australian public and work cooperatively with the industry we regulate. We communicate meaningfully with stakeholders including consumers, providing transparency across our regulatory practice. We assess evidence in making decisions and recognise the value of taking a risk-based approach to regulatory, compliance and enforcement activity."

Covid proved every last one of these claims to be false.

Kristine Macartney also acted as an expert consultant to the World Health Organisation.

Arkmedic questioned the claim she made in an academic paper that she had no conflict of interest.

"You got $65 million in government grants running a study that HAS to portray government policy (with mandates that likely resulted in thousands of deaths) in a good light or your grants will be pulled and you don't have a conflict of interest? Are you kidding?"

She told the NSW Supreme Court in 2021, in one of a number of cases attempting to block vaccine mandates: "They certainly do reduce the levels of the spread from one individual to the other, coming back to my point that if you're not infected you can't spread the virus, so that is transmission."

The mandates stayed.

And many dedicated professionals in the caring professions, nurses, teachers, ambulance drivers, quit their jobs or got sacked.

Arkmedic continued: " If you don't agree with Professor Macartney and you work in the NSW health (or federal health) system, with all her links and affiliations, what do you think would happen to you? That is the power of $65 million in grants. And that is the power that is a MASSIVE conflict of interest that should have been declared in that preprint. The power to make ridiculous and mathematically impossible claims and never have to answer for them."

Throughout the Covid era Australia's academics sang true to their government and vaccine manufacturer funding sources, making those independent minded enough to speak out extremely rare indeed.

Money talks, and in this case the money came more or less directly from vaccine manufacturers.

***

Vaccinating children took the term "criminal negligence" to a whole new level.

Millions of Australia's school students were injected with the most dangerous vaccine in history, a vaccine they did not need, which carried known risks and which prevented neither infection nor transmission.

And which increasing international evidence was already suggesting was in fact counterproductive, increasing not decreasing chances of illness.

It was sick stuff.

To many it was nothing short of satanic.

Despite significant evidence that children were more likely to die or suffer serious consequences from the vaccine than they were from Covid-19, and a number of jurisdictions including Scandinavia banning it for children, not one of the Australia's politicians responsible for the vaccinating of millions of children called for a moratorium.

In the wake of the Covid fiasco, as Health Ministers state and federal made the five yard sprint from public tit to private boardroom, a unique aspect of the corruption within Australia's political system, it was already obvious from anyone following the story that the vaccination of children was fraught with danger.

Lead author of one of the earliest studies, published as a preprint in September of 2021, was Dr Tracy Høeg, Resident at the University of California's Davis Medical Centre. She gained her PHD in epidemiology at the University of Copenhagen.

The study found that in healthy 12-15 year old boys, the risk of post-vaccination myocarditis was 3.7 to 6.1 times higher than the risk of hospitalisation from Covid.

Imagine doing that to your own children?

For those unfamiliar with the term, myocarditis is inflammation of the heart. The inflammation can reduce the heart's ability to pump and cause rapid or abnormal heart rhythms. Severe myocarditis weakens your heart so that the rest of your body doesn't get enough blood. Clots can form in your heart, leading to a stroke or heart attack.

Nearly all (86%) of the boys affected needed some form of hospital care, the authors said.

Even at this stage, before it began recommending Covid vaccines for every child over the age of five years, and the mass vaccination of millions of children began, the Australian government knew that the early warning signs were alarming.

Absolutely alarming.

What sort of parent would inject their child with an experimental vaccine for which the long term consequences were entirely unknown?

The sort who were naive enough to believe their own government.

***

As late as the 24th of October, 2022, when the world was already in uproar over the malfeasance and outright corruption involved in the development of the so-called vaccines, that is a medication which neither prevented infection, transmission or hospitalisation, the Australian government was recommending booster doses of children. And aggressively promoted them to an age cohort which had almost no risk of dying, or even getting seriously ill, from "the virus".

For children six months or older with special needs the government stated: "Parents of eligible children aged 6 months to <5 years recommended for vaccination should seek COVID-19 vaccination as soon as they are able to secure a vaccination clinic appointment."

The immorality of a government pushing a medical intervention on a population, knowing full well that these treatments were doing more harm than good, would curl through history as an inexplicable outrage.

Pushing them on adults was bad enough. Pushing them on children who could suffer life-long injuries as a result was beyond comprehension.

Except for the extreme manipulation of mainstream and social media by government in league with pharmaceutical companies, a better informed public would never have done this to their own children.

Now, at last, the truth was out. Around the world the dam walls of misinformation built by pharmaceutical companies, politicians and the media were breaking, all at once. Nobody believed the story anymore.

***

"The vaccination of children is insane," said Professor Ramesh Thakur of the Australian National University. "Pushing vaccines on to children is obscene.

"It's testament to the evil that has taken hold following the fear induced in people by deliberate psychological campaigns of terror propaganda, aided and abetted by mainstream and social media, that large numbers of people in Western societies have actively colluded with governments in imposing harms on children.

"This must be the first occasion in history that we have made children bear the heaviest costs, with futures mortgaged to massive debts, educational opportunities drastically curtailed and exposure to potentially harmful and even lethal medical interventions just so the old can cling on to life without meaning for a few more years. Remember, in almost all Western countries the average age of Covid death is higher than the average life expectancy."

***

In that strange uncanny world that was Australia, where memory seemed non-existent and conscience eradicated, a sense of responsibility from the ruling elites non-existent, the silence that greeted the unravelling scandal, impacting billions of people around the globe and Australia's entire population of 25 million, reminded Old Alex of the jihad terror storm that had overtaken the government and the media only a few short years before.

Abandoning good government in favour of scaring the population half to death, former Prime Minister Tony Abbott, who served between 2013 and 2015, had repeatedly focused on Islamic State as the universal threat he and his government were protecting the people from.

Australia's allegiance to American wars, with tens of billions of dollars of military contracts dancing in the background, had besmirched Australia's moral standing in the world for decades. But still they carried on.

In one press conference after another, Abbott rhapsodised about the evils of "the death cult", as he termed the jihadis, those who were prepared to die for their beliefs and for their God on the far side of the world.

Soldiers were sent to Iraq, hundreds of millions of dollars were squandered; the newspapers ran page after page badged "The Death Cult", but when the Iraqi government finally declared victory over Islamic State, there wasn't a single frontpage headline, barely even a whisper.

The government moved seamlessly on. Equally, after Covid came the Ukraine war and a relentless blizzard of climate change propaganda, and the nation, dozing or dazed, let it all slip by. There was no accounting. No justification. No expression of either satisfaction or guilt. One great big nothing, down there in Terra Nullius.

Abbott, Australia's 28th Prime Minister, disappeared into history in 2015.

Whether the outrage of Australia's Covid mismanagement and its many consequences would equally disappear into history, well, by this stage the mainstream media was doing its best by dutifully ignoring it.

Much of the deceit in mainstream media derives from story selection rather than the stories themselves. For example, a vaccine sceptic was as invisible on the $1.2 billion government propaganda wing the Australian Broadcasting Corporation as a men's rights activist or a cynic of the global warming mantra. That amounts to gaslighting by omission.

**

Professor Ramesh Thakur, writing for the Brownstone Institute put it thus: "Remarkably, the Pfizer admission has been studiously ignored by the Australian Mainstream media. In case I had missed the coverage of the bombshell interview in the Australian media, I did a search on the website of ABC (Australia's version of the BBC), *The Age*, *The Australian* and *The Sydney Morning Herald* newspapers.

"I got zero hits for Robert Roos, the Dutch MEP who asked the question in the European Parliament of Pfizer director Janine Small, and for the latter who confessed to lack of testing for transmissibility. Fading trust in our principal institutions is contributing to the multipronged global crisis of democracy.

"The lack of media interest and coverage means there is little pressure for public accountability. Absent that, there will not be any punishment meted out to ministers and bureaucrats for the extensive range of malfeasance in inflicting cruel and inhumane harms on millions of their citizens; no prospect of emotional closure for the people for the trauma they have suffered, including deaths of despair and desolation born of loneliness; delayed prospects of the masses shedding their sheer dread of a virus that for most healthy people under 70 or 65 is not really a severe illness; and a refusal to institute the most powerful deterrent of all for any repeats of public criminality on a grand scale.

"Instead we can all look forward to endless cycles of rinse and repeat of surveillance, compulsion and coercion of the masses on the whims of their technocratic betters."

The placard "Nuremberg 2.0" had been prominent at Australian demonstrations for more than a year.

But no matter how much harm the perpetrators of these crimes had done to their fellow Australians, the Nuremberg outcome, where ten prominent Nazi figures were hanged for crimes against their own people, was no longer available in Australia.

The death sentence might have been abolished, but if you kill a member of the police force in Australia you get sentenced to life without parole. The apparatchiks who forced this dangerous medication onto the nation's police and military personnel under threat of losing their jobs, and persuaded millions of Australian parents to vaccinate their children, were getting away scot free.

***

Waking dreams. Vivid, mystic dreams which had pursued Old Alex all his waking life. A channelling of sorts. There had been moments of joy, for sure, as the army shuffled restlessly on the valley ledge, small successes to celebrate, time to kill, destiny to fulfil.

Now, spears raised, they stepped forward in their thousands. There was an evil afoot. Elegant, violent, they gathered their strength, their enmity, they saw through all of it; the subterfuge, the artifice, the military name-calling gronks who had made his life hell in failed Psyop programs, all of it, the enemy clear, the brutality, the cruelty, the ancient evils and the ancient wisdoms, they mustered for the dawn, they would not be denied.

The gods fortified their soldiers.

They made them stronger still.

He stood tall and stricken; for already tears of joy and sorrow; and he remembered the line: "We weep for you and you are not yet born."

That sorrow at the crimes this species had committed against itself, the pain that so many individuals unnecessarily suffered, all of it was striking in its historicity.

It took a lot to stir the gods, far more to raise their anger; for their time channels were so different to our own. Now they were here, in Australia of all places; and the idea of a Second Coming seemed absolutely improbable. But here they were.

The specific, sociable nature of humans, their ability to cooperate in large numbers, was, in a sense, what drove this; for no single man, no single entity, had the computing or neural power to even begin to comprehend. So the army grew in power.

We were here now. We protect those we choose. That skipping stone into the future, anchored here, was only a fraction of what was about to happen.

This ancient evil. These ancient forces.

The point was to enter into a battle of the ages. The point was to preserve what they could.

The point was to destroy the perpetrators, to bring to justice those who had sinned so grievously against their fellows in this benighted realm; so blessed, so powerful, so utterly beautiful.

They could not, would not survive, these evil, cruel, arrogant men.

For as we said long ago: the meek shall inherit the Earth.

Most members of Australia's mainstream media acted as handmaidens for Big Pharma and cheerleaders for government misinformation and overreach throughout the Covid era.

One exception was *Spectator Australia*.

Editor Rowan Dean wrote that the admission dragged out of Pfizer that they did not so much as test whether the vaccine stopped transmission, the reason hundreds of millions of people took "the jab", revealed a massive abuse of power by elected officials.

"Here in Australia we had some of the worst lockdowns, we had this vicious persecution of unvaccinated people, we had our state premiers going on television and saying they wouldn't be in the same room as the unvaccinated. It was this endless repetition of 'this is a pandemic of the unvaccinated'.

"We had health authorities – health bureaucrats – telling the public that they were going to make life incredibly difficult for you if you weren't vaccinated. This was persecution.

"The point is that our politicians led us to believe, in fact, they insisted at every level. Whether it was Anthony Fauci in the States or our own politicians here in Australia – at every level our health bureaucrats insisted that the vaccines prevented transmission and this was the rationale for mandatory vaccination which, in this country – and in other places – many people lost their jobs. Many people are still out of work. Many people had their lives turned upside down and destroyed because they insisted to us that it did stop transmission.

"This isn't a problem with Pfizer, this is absolutely about the abuse of power by politicians who are either too stupid, or too lazy, or too corrupt to actually check out the facts and were prepared to abuse their power.

"It was the lies of government and the lies of health officials drafting policy, that matter. And they certainly lied."

There were exact parallels between Europe and Australia; contracts remained invisible to the public, billions of dollars of public money disappeared for a product which did not work as advertised, neither stopping infection nor blocking transmission, the population was bludgeoned, nudged, lied to or mandated into taking a vaccine many of them did not want, and Australia's politicians were heavily involved in what was already being spoken of as the biggest medical fraud in history.

***

Unfortunately for its citizens there would be no such inquiry in Australia, not that Spring, not that Summer, not even a whisper of a thought, at least not officially, of hauling the vaccine companies before parliament to explain their behaviour, their flogging of a manifestly deficient product, the cooperation of so many wings of the Australian government in such a mass market deceit, or an examination of the profound consequences for the population.

After all, it was the officials who were left high and dry, unable to deal with a putrid mess they had been swept into.

But there would be plenty of inquiry elsewhere.

A crime had been committed against humanity that was unprecedented in its scale.

The technology and media organisation headed by Naomi Wolf, Daily Clout, published a book on the gathering scandal. In her introduction Wolf explained the project: "The book *Pfizer Documents Analysis and Reports* is a record of a great crime against humanity.

"In 2022, the Pfizer documents, a tranche of 55,000 documents, many of them thousands of pages long, were released via a court order. This was due to a successful lawsuit by attorney Aaron Siri. The US Food and Drug Administration had asked the court to keep these documents hidden for 75 years – until after most of us alive now would be dead and gone.

"Luckily, the court did not concur."

Realising that the task was beyond normal journalistic inquiry, much of the documentation was written for scientists and medical researchers, in language that only specialists in those fields could really understand properly or explain, Daily Clout sent out a call for expert volunteers.

"A global audience thus recognised how important it was for an informed public – who had been harried, bullied, and "mandated" to receive Pfizer's and Moderna's mRNA injections in 2021-2022 – to understand what was really revealed inside of the Pfizer documents. There was no way, with a group this distinguished in science and medicine doing the labour, that the interpretation of these documents could be dismissed as fringe, subjective, or as the work of conspiracy theorists.

"You will see that the 50 reports document what may be a massive crime against humanity. You will see that Pfizer knew, as it appears, that the mRNA vaccines did not work. You will see that the ingredients, including lipid nanoparticles, in the mRNA injections bio-distributed throughout the body in a couple of days, accumulating in the liver, adrenals, spleen — and ovaries.

"You will see that Pfizer and the FDA knew that the injections damaged the hearts of minors — and yet waited months to inform the public. You will see that Pfizer sought to hire over a thousand new staffers simply to manage the flood of 'adverse events' reports that they were receiving and that they anticipated receiving.

"You will see that 61 people died of stroke — half of the stroke adverse events being within a couple of days after injection — and that five people died of liver damage with, again, many of the liver damage adverse events sustained shortly after the injection. You will see neurological events, cardiac events, strokes, brain haemorrhages, and blood clots, lung clots and leg clots at massive scale.

"You will see that headaches, joint pain, and muscle pain are rampant as adverse events, though these are not disclosed as routine side effect warnings by our agencies.

"Most seriously of all, you will see a 360-degree attack on human reproductive capability: with harms to sperm count, testes, sperm motility; harms to ovaries, menstrual cycles, placentas; you will see that over 80 per cent of the pregnancies in one section of the Pfizer documents ended in spontaneous abortion or miscarriage.

"You will see that 72 per cent of the adverse events in one section of the documents were in women, and that 16 percent of those were "reproductive disorders," in Pfizer's own words. You will see a dozen or more names for the ruination of the menstrual cycles of women and teenage girls.

"History has not yet concluded its assessment of what Pfizer has done. We are at the very start of that assessment."

***

Unprecedented in scale. That was about right.

Just to rely on their good work TOTT News, one of the only significant Australian media outlets to follow this utterly massive scandal in any detail, ran a series of articles badged The Pfizer Papers.

The inescapable conclusion being, Australian government officials must have known there were significant issues around the vaccines, even as they continued to promote them.

The truth will out.

Here are just a few excerpts from their series:

The Pfizer Papers. The Company Exploited and Misapplied a Controversial Clinical Trial Method

Documents reveal sleight-of-hand tactics were used on clinical trial protocols to ensure the Pfizer-BioNTech vaccine was granted a licence.

It is very, very unlikely that were it not for the pandemic, the Pfizer-BioNTech product would have been granted a licence.

The dedicated work of rights advocates has given us an unparalleled opportunity to explore the Pfizer papers and unearth exactly how they, in collusion with the FDA, pulled off one of the biggest crimes of the century.

Newly-released Pfizer-US Food and Drug Administration (FDA) documents suggest that after several trial participants died — following injection with the experimental product — Pfizer covered up their deaths by attributing them to natural causes, existing conditions, and even by mere assumption that the given death was not triggered by the injection.

A common pattern emerges: Pfizer and the FDA minimise the deaths and do not attribute them to BNT162b2. Instead, they highlight natural causes, existing conditions, and mere assumption.

The Pfizer Papers: The Company Secretly Planned for the Third Dose:

Pfizer began a third dose study while continuing trials of the second dose. Despite this, it saw fit to declare that two doses were effective for six months.

No sooner had they made the claim, CEO Bourla stated that three doses might be needed, even though it would have taken Pfizer until at least October 2021 to discern that information from trial participants, yet the US Food and Drug Administration authorised the third dose in September, with trial data still pending.

On and on the scandal went. And it was about to blow sky high.

The story might not be getting much coverage in Australia's legacy media, but an irrepressible social media was alive with outrage.

As the Leonard Cohen song went: "Everybody knows that the boat is leaking, Everybody knows that the captain lied".

***

The scandal left many questions. Here are just a few.

Why did then Prime Minister Scott Morrison appoint Jane Halton, who had a longstanding relationship with Bill Gates through senior positions in the Gates funded Coalition for Epidemic Preparedness Innovations and the World Health Organisation, to essentially oversee Australia's pandemic response as a Commissioner on the newly created National COVID-19 Commission Advisory Board.

CEPI was launched at the 2017 World Economic Forum and kicked off with $460 million of seed funding from the Bill and Melinda Gates Foundation.

As Dr Phillip M. Altman at the Australian Medical Professional Society put it: "The claim that this was a pandemic of the unvaccinated was an outright lie told by our most senior health bureaucrats to convince people to take a gene-based drug which had grossly inadequate short-term safety data and no long-term safety data.

"Despite the total lack of scientific evidence supporting vaccine mandates, Bill Gates, the world's biggest vaccine investor, was fortunate to be able to install his longstanding loyal lieutenant and personally appointed CEPI Chairperson, Jane Halton, to personally spearhead Australia's vaccine policy.

"Anyone with any relevant formal scientific training should have known there was never any clinical evidence to support vaccine mandates. This has been known from the beginning. Industry and labour organisations destroyed careers, businesses, families and imposed financial stress and mental anguish across Australia for nothing.

"It is still going on. It is all for nothing."

Why, knowing Gates' financial interest in the Covid vaccines, did then Prime Minister Scott Morrison turn repeatedly to the Bill and Melinda Gates funded Peter Doherty Institute for Infection and Immunity for advice, or justification, on everything from lockdowns to vaccines?

Their prognostications on everything, from the lethality of Covid to the efficacy of vaccines and the need for lockdowns all proved totally wrong;

but that didn't seem to matter. They still soaked up millions of dollars in government funding; and kept coming back for more.

In any other situation serious questions would have been asked.

Why did Scott Morrison take a phone call from vaccine-profiteer-in-chief Bill Gates early on in the Covid panic, what did they discuss?

Why did the Australian government order 255 million doses of the vaccine, that is ten doses for every man, woman and child in the country?

Why haven't the contracts been made public? What did we sign away? How many tens of billions of dollars did the government spend on vaccines they couldn't possibly use?

Why was the taxpayer expected to fund this magnificent largesse to vaccine manufacturers who already knew, from their own research, that the vaccines were a failure?

Why doesn't the new Federal Health Minister Mark Butler see this squandering of billions of dollars of public funds as an issue worth pursuing?

Why were the vaccine manufacturers given total exemption from liability?

Why did the regulatory body the Therapeutic Goods Administration, which receives much of its funding from pharmaceutical companies, so rapidly approve a medication which was already causing massive controversy around the world? Why did no one in power, first in the Morrison and then in the Albanese governments, speak up about this obvious conflict of interest?

Why did the government and its agencies deliberately suppress any discussion on the safety and efficacy of vaccines, manipulating through tax concessions and funding the mainstream media outlets while at the same time harassing or silencing sceptics? Why did the Australian government allow foreign owned social media companies to censor Australian citizens?

Why did Scott Morrison say, towards the end of his dismal reign, that power to manage a pandemic should be handed over to the Bill Gates funded World Health Organisation, an organisation already attracting massive criticism around the world for its mismanagement of the Covid "plandemic", as it was now frequently being called?

How did Big Pharma capture all the organs of the Australian government, from its politicians to its health bureaucracies, and then use the police, the military and the nation's intelligence agencies to perpetuate their lies?

Why, knowing full well the international controversy enveloping mRNA vaccines and Moderna, in August of 2022 did Prime Minister Anthony Albanese risk his own reputation by promoting a $200 million Moderna production facility at Monash University in Victoria?

When did the Australian government sell out their own population?

NINETEEN
AFTER THE TRIBULATION
TRUST NO MAN

A belief that artificial intelligence can be programmed to do our bidding may turn out to be as unfounded as a belief that certain people could speak to God, or that certain other people were born as slaves. The fourth epoch is returning us to the spirit-laden landscape of the first: a world where humans coexist with technologies they no longer control or fully understand.

This is where the human mind took form. We grew up, as a species, surrounded by mind and intelligence everywhere we looked. Since the dawn of technology, we were on speaking terms with our tools. Intelligence in the cloud is nothing new. Nature's answer to those who seek to control nature through programmable machines is to allow us to build systems whose nature is beyond programmable control.

George Dyson. *Analogia*.

THERE IN THE Great Southern Land the sun finally did come out. After three years of cold, wet, windy, truly dismal weather, driven by a climate phenomenon known as El Nina, that autumn of 2023, which begins in March, saw at least a few days of sunshine.

The weather had amplified the psychological impacts of lockdowns, social distancing, curfews, masking and all the rest of the palaver; and at last it was over. Apparently. An always news averse population took to their surfboards and outdoor adventures; parents proudly watched over their children in the municipal parks, and everywhere a new optimism coursed through their veins.

Old Alex wound down the car windows and cranked up the car radio. Everywhere was a delight. That same thought kept coming back to him; "the world is so beautiful", as Buddha was reputed to have said on his deathbed.

Families were out walking and children swarmed in the streets and public pools. Everything was born anew. A dust of warmth across the suburb and the lawns went rogue. On the surface there was no sign of what had happened. The highways were once again filled with traffic, the once ghostly, heavily policed streets were now full of shoppers and people out for the day.

There was a semblance of normality; indeed in many ways the country did return to some sort of normality after the utter derangement of the Covid era.

But that was the surface gloss. It was not the same.

Politicians and their bum buddies in the media barely mentioned Covid these days, it was too embarrassing, the garden path they had led their population down. Excess deaths were now running at more than 15 percent; so much for "Keeping Australians safe".

Everyone now knew the heart of the lie, and if they didn't know, it was only because they were cognitively impaired or deliberately closed their eyes.

Most people were keen to move on, which was easy enough to do if you hadn't lost your job thanks to the vaccine mandates, if your business hadn't been destroyed by the lockdowns, if your child hadn't been permanently disabled as a result of a vaccine injury, or if you yourself weren't suffering any of the array of medical complications now associated with the vaccines.

But after all that happened, after all the outrage that lay buried under falling leaves, it was still hard to comprehend the scale of what had happened or the consequences for both individuals and the society at large.

As Jeffery Tucker founder of the world's leading academic centre confronting the Covid narrative, the Brownstone Institute wrote so elegantly that very same autumn, at some point in the last three years, even the official story of why we had all been locked down, socially distanced, prevented from travelling or even visiting loved ones dying in hospital, all seemed to have slipped away.

"The lockdowns didn't work. The travel restrictions were pointless. The plexiglass, the one-way aisles, the oceans of sanitiser dousing everything, the constantly-changing regulations on whether we should stand or sit indoors or out, and the two yards of distance mandated between any two people were all brutal failures. The masking that hid our smiles for two years achieved nothing but dehumanisation. Then the magic bullet – the so-called vaccines – flopped too and even multiplied the suffering. And then, at some point, it all just went away."

Indeed, now, the Australian government, obviously not wanting to confront the complete failure of their Covid strategies and the consequent loss of face, was filling the public square with social justice rhetoric and their grand schemes of transitioning the nation to renewable energy.

The streets went back to normal, proud young dads and protective mums took their children to the shopping centres, and if you didn't know better, it would be hard to believe that this was a place of lockdowns and curfews, dramatic levels of policing while politicians daily spread fear though the airwaves.

We were all meant to forgive and forget. Conveniently, for the perpetrators.

Jeffrey Tucker reflected Alex's own more coagulated thoughts in what had surely been one of the most confusing times in all of history: "March 17, 2020, was the first day of the end of civilised life, the one for which Western peoples had been fighting for one thousand years. It was the first full day following the lockdowns that ended all rights and liberties, including even the right to have friends for dinner or go to community worship services or attend or hold weddings and funerals.

"The sun had fallen the previous day just after the press conference announcing 15 days that stretched to 30 days and then to three years of quasi-martial law imposed for a virus. But nature is oblivious to the affairs of men, and so the indefatigable sun rose anyway the next day, as if to do what it had always done: bring its light and warmth to bathe humanity in new hope in the new day.

"The sun did peer up over the horizon and did bring its light, but this time it did not bring hope. It shone over a world but only highlighted the absence of joy, opportunity, and excitement over the unexpected blessings that would come our way. All of that had been taken away and suddenly, seemingly without warning.

"The sun that day shone a light on wreckage and terror of a society consumed in tyranny and fear. It was there as if to mock hope, its every ray broadcasting disdain for our own sense of security and confidence in the future. Every hour above the horizon torched our optimism, including all of its signs on earth: music, dancing, and human relationships.

"What precisely are we supposed to believe was the reason they wrecked the world as we knew it? I can't even seem to find an attempt at an explanation anymore."

***

There was a remarkable convergence of storylines in that period of early 2023, of characters and movements and media organisations. On a world scale not least of the factors in the conflagration was the transformation of Twitter into a free speech platform, and the cascade of Covid exposes which followed, demonstrating that the entire public narrative had been heavily manipulated by American intelligence agencies, including the FBI, and that leading scientists had been deliberately silenced.

Locally, not least of the bizarre stories capturing the tributaries joining in some giant collision was that of the visit to Australia of Bill Gates, one of the world's richest men, a promoter of and profiteer from vaccines and, many suspected, a believer in eugenics.

Perhaps, in the end, the entire episode of Gates arrival Down Under was no more sophisticated than a pyromaniac coming to watch among the crowd as firefighters tried to put out the fire he himself had created, for Bill Gates had been the puppet master of Australia's entire Covid response.

What will it profit a man if he gains the whole world, yet forfeits his soul?

The most truly bizarre of all the many bizarre aspects of that visit was Gates' confession that the vaccines he promoted and which the Australian government squandered billions on, and which countless politicians and health bureaucrats enthusiastically championed, didn't work.

"Antibodies, antivirals, we think we can also have very early in an epidemic a thing you can inhale that will mean you can't be infected. An inhale blocker. We also need to fix the three problems of vaccines. The current vaccines are not infection blocking, they're not broad, so new variants come up and you lose protection, and they have very short duration."

His words, at a speech for the Lowy Institute, which he also incidentally funded, received widespread coverage around the world.

Yes, the same Bill Gates who, estimates suggested, had just made more than half a billion dollars in profit selling his shares in BioNTech, the manufacturers of Covid-19 vaccines, before he started bagging the vaccines out as essentially useless.

Bill Gates' influence had been everywhere over the previous three years. He funded the World Health Organisation, which all Australians were taught to look to as the international authority, way beyond their own level of expertise. He funded the Peter Doherty Institute for Infection and Immunity, which the government relied on for its advice on masking, social distancing, lockdowns and vaccination rates.

He had given funds to *Guardian Australia*, which championed vaccines, and also funded the academic journal *The Conversation*, where academic after academic extolled the virtues of the vaccines.

That was just the tip of the iceberg. Gates funded virtually everything to do with the vaccine rollout in Australia, and made billions of dollars as a result.

Whether he also funded the nation's politicians through backdoor "consultancy fees", and the extent to which he did so, might never be known. Old Alex, for one, would have very much liked to know.

***

On the 20th of January, 2023, Prime Minister Anthony Albanese welcomed Bill Gates into the official Sydney residence, Kirribilli House.

At a grin and grip for the cameras Albanese said: "Can I welcome you here very much. We haven't met before. But I've admired your work and your contribution, not just financially, but in raising debates, including the need to deal with health issues.

"We've just been through the pandemic, but we need to prepare for future health challenges. And of course, climate change."

"We've had a great partnership on global health, Gavi, polio. Thanks for your increase on Global Fund, a lot to do there."

Albanese had just announced an additional $230 million donation to the Gates-founded Global Health, bringing Australia's total contribution to just under a billion dollars, enough to build several hospitals, money raked off the backs of working Australians, many of whom could barely afford to pay their electricity bills and who faced lengthy queues and long wait times if they ever went near a public hospital.

"You're very welcome here," the Prime Minister said.

No ordinary citizen gets to sit in Kirribilli House and be told by the nation's Prime Minister how very welcome they are. By this time there were hundreds of thousands, if not millions of ordinary Australians who regarded Bill Gates as little better than the devil incarnate; as the world's Vaccine-Profiteer-In-Chief, a man who belonged not in his private jet but in a prison cell. Worldwide, scandal after scandal had already discredited almost everyone involved with perpetrating the agendas of the Covid Era, most particularly Bill Gates.

For a country wearied by shocking governance, there had been optimism surrounding a new Prime Minister. Some saw the meeting as an egregious insult to the many doctors, academics and protestors who despised Bill Gates, and a callous insult to the thousands of people who had been injured or killed by the vaccines he championed.

There was a massive compromise of Australia's public health systems involved in climbing onboard the Bill and Melinda Gates Vaccine Express. Now the entire world was alarmed; everybody, apparently, but the Australian Prime Minister. No amount of whitewash can cover the truth. Every freedom fighter in the country now knew exactly where the Prime Minister stood.

Albanese may have been advised against the very public grin and grip with Gates on security grounds, but if he wanted to see some of the sentiment in the community he didn't have to look past his own official Twitter feed.

Radge declared: "Ahah, Moderna in Monash Uni to produce mRNA vaccines, Bill Gates wants livestock to be jabbed so that next time round, doses by consumption…more heart problems, depopulation – simple really…The boy from the slum, you are a complicit criminal."

David Flood tweeted: "Most of us can see through the thinly veiled globalist agenda. You're blatantly selling out all Australians. The worst part is there's not a damn thing we can do about it. It isn't about politics, it's about right & wrong. Trojan Horses – climate crisis, pandemic, Ukraine."

On and on. Petrol burned on dark waters while Old Alex dreamed of frozen methane seas, as on the moons of Saturn. He had no idea why. There was life, different forms of life, everywhere.

***

The entire story had come full circle.

These were the beginnings and the ends; all folding into one. In the earliest days of the "pandemic", after speaking to former Prime Minister Scott Morrison, longtime Bill Gates loyalist Jane Halton was appointed to essentially spearhead Australia's Covid response.

Now here was the newly minted Prime Minister, Anthony Albanese, meeting with one of the world's most ruthless vaccine profiteers, Bill Gates, at the official residence Kirribilli House.

Living well in a 44 bedroom mansion in Canberra and while in Sydney one of the city's finer residences, with views straight across the fabled harbour to the Opera House. Albanese appeared to have no shame at prosecuting the agendas of the Davos billionaires, vaccines and climate change, while masquerading as a representative of the people.

Both men wore dark suits and open necked white shirts for their photo op.

As, according to a friend of his who lived in the area, helicopters hovered overhead.

None of their deceit, none of their arrogance, none of their money would, in the end, do either of them any good, only serving to blind them to the nature of the battle, their place in history, the flow of time.

Those military helicopters were perhaps the very same helicopters which had hovered ominously over the harbour in 2020, with the entire city in lockdown, the streets and malls deserted. Old Alex would leave his temporary office in Circular Quay, it was not illegal to go to work, and walk through the Royal Botanic Gardens, down to the point known as Macquarie's Chair.

There he directly faced Kirribilli House on the opposite shore, and those ancient spirits which possessed him, those ancient curses, had streamed across the harbour to find their mark in the walls of that dwelling which had seen so many of the nation's rich and powerful, back in 2020 frequently used by the then Prime Minister Scott Morrison.

You will never have another good day. Everything in your life will slowly unravel. Your name will be marked forever. Cursed art thou.

Because he already knew, outside of time, told you already, because he had already known the damage then Prime Minister Scott Morrison would do to the country, he had wished him gone immediately. Perhaps not assassination, Old Alex had just thought that all Morrison's tendrils of corruption, all his connections to the mining lobby and the Very Big End of Town, would bring him undone sooner or later; and as far as he was concerned, the sooner the better.

It hadn't happened as nearly as quickly as he had hoped.

Instead the ruin of a sad sack Morrison took years. As the bloated rotting corpse of a pig flayed in the public square, he swung in the breeze and the village youth whirled their whips, followed, later in the night, by the village idiots, until he lost the 2022 election in a tsunami of public contempt, and remained a vile presence on the political scene, reviled, ridiculed, his stench creeping out to destroy his own party, his own dignity, and the country which had given him so much.

As damaging, and now as utterly discredited as Australia's Covid strategies were, just prior to his arrival Bill Gates had publicly praised two countries, Australia and China, for their Covid response. There was a reason why; they were the two countries whose Covid response most closely aligned with totalitarianism.

And now here, living high on the public tit, Albanese was meeting with a man who had made billions of dollars from the Covid scam, a man who had done a mind boggling level of damage to the country; and there they were, practically holding hands, talking about climate change. Oh My God!!!

"You're very welcome here," the Australian Prime Minister Albanese declared as the news cameras flashed.

"I love coming to Australia," Gates replied.

No doubt, in possession of the billions he had made off Australia's working poor, he did.

Who do you think lurks in those walls? Who do you think, an ancient sense of injustice stirred, has now awakened, is aware of your presence, those spirits who had always sought and resided in the halls of power.

Where do you think all this is going to lead?

Easy to guess.

Why hadn't those entities acted quicker to rid us all of the pestilence that was Morrison, and this new, so far less despised version of a corporate monster?

At first he thought it was distance, that the curses were weakened by the distance they had to traverse; but that wasn't it at all.

Just as trees have a different sense of time, so, too, the gods.

Why things happen the way they do, why evil, such tantamount, such obvious evil as this, exists and indeed appears for a time to flourish, was beyond human ken. He touched the infinite, and they lay bare.

The same voice had returned: "We weep for you, and you are not yet born."

The swarming had begun. There was nothing he, or now anybody, could do to stop it.

***

More or less concurrently, the popular song Gates Behind the Bars became readily available on YouTube, material which only a short time before would have been banned or suppressed.

In early 2021 the well known independent act Five Times August began releasing a series of protest songs taking aim at Covid-era regulations, the Biden administration and Justin Trudeau, as well as the Gollum like figurehead of American Public Health Doctor Anthony Fauci with the hit song "Sad Little Man," which reached #1 on several Amazon and Apple Music charts.

> Sad little man sitting deep in a lie
> He's dead in his soul but he'll keep you alive
> Do what he says, not what he do
> 'Cause the truth is for him and the lie is for you
> Sad little man but he's treated like a God
> As the faithless pray to a fake and a fraud
> Worship the man, pledge to his word
> One shot, two shot, now you get a third

Now, as the Prime Minister shook hands with Bill Gates, any Australian citizen could listen to Gates Behind The Bars:

He's out for revenge
To hurt every man
He'll print all the food
And drug every kid
Pretend like he's good
Then hide what he did
Nobody's safe
Nobody's safe
Nobody's safe
'Til we have Gates behind
Gates behind the bars

He deals in the dark
AND buys his own truth
He'll package it up
And he'll sell it to you
All the sheep will believe
Afraid they will die
Trapped by the one
Who has wrapped them in lies

***

As he sat in the most expensive seats in the house at The Australian Open, a summer tennis sporting ritual in the Land Down Under, an ageing and unfit Bill Gates showed not a shred of sympathy for the thousands of nurses, teachers, doctors, police and other professionals who had lost their jobs for refusing to take his vaccines.

Nor for the hundreds of thousands who had marched through the streets of Melbourne, the millions who had endured curfews, state border closures and some of the most extreme lockdowns seen anywhere in the world. Or the thousands of business owners who had seen their life's dreams destroyed.

Even during the days Gates was in Australia, travelling around in one of his $70 million private jets, scandal after scandal enveloped the rollout of the vaccines worldwide.

Every Western country which implemented lockdowns and mass vaccination campaigns was experiencing historically high excess death rates, ranging up to 20 percent. In Australia they had been hovering around 17% prior to Gates arrival directly from the annual gathering of billionaires for the World Economic Forum in Davos, Switzerland.

During Gates' stay in Australia came the news that Thailand was likely to become the first country on Earth to cancel its Pfizer contracts and demand their money back, after a Thai Royal, the eldest child of Thailand's King Maha Vajiralongkorn, Princess Bajrakitiyabha, 44, went into a coma after what was believed to have been her second Covid vaccine shot.

As a consequence one of the world's most revered disease experts and a formidable critic of medical and corporate misconduct during the Covid era, German Professor Sucharit Bhakdi, the son of the former Thai Ambassador to Switzerland, was invited to speak to some of the country's highest authorities.

Gates' visit also coincided with the release of the Daily Clout's forensic exploration of the Pfizer documents, which were only released on court order after Pfizer tried to conceal them for 75 years. The coverage had been excoriating. With Twitter now in the hands of Elon Musk and transformed into a free speech platform, there was no longer anywhere to hide and the explosive revelations of government and intelligence agency manipulation of the Covid narrative was now out in the public square.

The book became an instant bestseller on Amazon.

There was widespread jubilation both in Australia and around the world when "Novax" Djokovic won the Australian Open. His victory, celebrated by freedom fighters everywhere, was widely seen as a victory against globalism and Big Pharma. The memes flew.

Paul Collits, both perceptive and acerbic, wrote on his Substack page: "They say that revenge is a dish best served cold. And so it came to pass at Melbourne Park tennis centre. A mere twelve months ago, Novak Djokovic was deported from Australia by a Liberal Minister and a Liberal Government.

"The political low-lifes who arranged Djokovic's short yet ignominious imprisonment and deportation are called Scott Morrison and Alex Hawke. They are alleged to be conservatives. In reality, they are unprincipled political spivs, now mercifully out of office but, sadly, still collecting their parliamentary salaries. Salaries that are paid by us.

"Djokovic seemed particularly emotional and very pleased with this particular win. The scenes after the match of the winner celebrating with his family and close supporters up in the stands were memorable. Indeed, they were life affirming. This wasn't just a tennis match. It was justice. This is a victory for a whole movement.

"It was singularly appropriate that one Bill Gates was there in Melbourne to witness it. Photos of Gates show him looking especially forlorn, bordering on miserable. Gates is the Sultan of Vaccines. The Djoker is the Prince of Covid dissidents. One wants to vaccinate the world, possibly for quite sinister reasons. The other is a champion of informed medical consent and the right to medical privacy. And freedom of movement, to boot. A little schadenfreude is surely permissible in relation to poor, sad old Bill."

Alexandra Marshall at Spectator Australia wrote: "A crowd full of 'novax' signs confused TV commentators as they were raised alongside a sea of Serbian flags. Djokovic, meanwhile, climbed up into the stands and then collapsed into the arms of his team. It was clear that this was a victory over more than tennis. Djokovic had defeated the tyrannical authorities and bureaucracies that fought to keep him away from his tennis crown.

"It was embarrassing for the many Australians involved, and those who joined the goon squad cheering his deportation the year before, to remember how Australia treated the World Number One Novak Djokovic.

"If anyone needs proof that the vaccine requirements were nothing but political nonsense, look no further than this year's announcement that Covid positive players were allowed on court. 'The Science' tells us that Djokovic never posed a health risk to the Australian Open – he posed a political risk to both the local Victorian Labor government and the Federal Liberal government."

Marshall suggested that former Prime Minister Scott Morrison owed the unvaccinated an apology. A grovelling one.

On January 6, 2022, Morrison tweeted: "Mr Djokovic's visa has been cancelled. Rules are rules, especially when it comes to our borders. No one is above these rules. Our strong border policies have been critical to Australia having one of the lowest death rates in the world from Covid, we are continuing to be vigilant."

A year later Marshall asked: "How does that work, Mr Morrison, when vaccines have no impact on transmission? Any comments? Updates? Want to discuss the largest rise in unexplained deaths in Australian history? No?"

***

According to Our World Data, ironically also funded by the Bill and Melinda Gates Foundation, as at the end of January, 2023: 69.4% of the world population had received at least one dose of a Covid-19 vaccine. 13.26 billion doses had been administered globally, and 1.19 million were still being administered each day.

26.4% of people in low-income countries have received at least one dose.

In Australia 64,623,053 doses had been administered to a population of approximately 26.5 million.

***

The world, or at least the human realm of it, as almost everyone seemed to sense, was shifting on its axis, a wound healing over. Instead Old Alex felt as if he was imprisoned on a scree slope, surrounded by hard, hostile objects while further away a wounded world healed over; children coated playgrounds and parks and rode their bikes down pathways, young fathers carried their children carefully, mothers gossiped at the edge of the public pool.

And the universe returned to a magic realm, far from the dark plotting of corrupt American officials and obsequious, gormless Australian politicians.

The jumbled images that seethed through his head still made little sense to Old Alex, this stitch in time just that, a tiny stitch, even if it transcended centuries and involved the fate of an entire nation, or even epoch. What would this darkness which had taken over Australia look like in a million years? Less than a blink in time; less than the tiny potoroo seeking shelter in the dark beneath his house.

Already the perpetrators were departing, already the government was possessed with a kind of amnesia, as if it was not responsible for the crimes it committed against its own people, and wished fervently to impose this amnesia on the broader population.

Jacinda Ardern, the Prime Minister of New Zealand, resigned, and as one commentator observed under a video of an entire crowd erupting in cheers: "Such a cop-out. All jumping ship so they don't be held accountable for their dealings, and mind you still getting paid by tax dollars."

New Zealand, along with Australia, had imposed some of the harshest lockdowns in the world, along with strict mask edicts, social distancing and mass vaccination, policies which even as they were being enacted were already being decried by leading scientists around the world as the greatest public health failing in history. Critics claimed both Australia and New Zealand were testing grounds for "techno-fascism"; population control by any other name.

The reality might be very different, but there was Anthony Albanese praising Jacinda Ardern as a woman who had led her country with intellect.

"Through the sheer power of her example, Jacinda Ardern has reminded us all that kindness and strength are not mutually exclusive," the Australian Prime Minister declared as part of a rush of sycophantic hypocrisy across the Australian political spectrum. "Even more importantly, she has shown that a true leader possesses both."

Greens senator Sarah Hanson Young said Ms Ardern had been a trailblazer and a true inspiration: "Heartfelt admiration and thanks to Jacinda Ardern for showing that compassion, courage and understanding are the true strengths of leadership. We will miss wishing she was our own prime minister."

Politicians frequently make a mistake commonly made by lawyers. Saying something is true does not make it true. They thought they had won because the mirror looking back at them, the media landscape, allowed them to appear as winners. But they had not won.

Globally, Ardern had been a stand-out Covid cultist and totalitarian.

She savagely locked down the entire country and excluded stranded Kiwis abroad, destroying the fragile, tourism-reliant Kiwi economy in the process. Perhaps her most infamous line, relating to so-called Covid disinformation, was: "We will continue to be your single source of truth. Unless you hear it from us, it is not the truth."

All those Ministries of Truth were in the process of acquiring a very bad rap sheet.

On 10 February, 2022 New Zealand police arrested more than 50 people, as they forcefully removed protesters camped outside parliament to protest vaccine mandates and ongoing restrictions.

Taking inspiration from truckers' demonstrations in Canada and mirroring events in Australia, hundreds of protesters blocked streets with trucks, cars and motorcycles, many having travelled considerable distance to be there. The protests coincided with the first speech for the year by the New Zealand Prime Minister.

Hundreds of vehicles were plastered with messages such as "give us back our freedom" and caused major disruptions in the city. Some drove around the city with horns blaring, as more protesters on foot listened to speeches.

Many of the vehicles that blocked central Wellington's streets moved on within 24 hours, but the atmosphere remained tense, with several hundred activists vowing to stay "as long as it takes".

Activists chanted the powerful Māori war dance known as the Haka and yelled "hold the line" as they scuffled with a line of police moving to clear the protest camp from the lawns of parliament.

Police moved in using loudhailers to warn the crowd they faced arrest unless they left the area. There were scenes of punching, kicking and manhandling of protesters by multiple police officers, amid cries of "this is not democracy", "shame on you" and "drop the mandate".

Footage showed similar scenes to those which had frequently occurred in Australia, police swarming over protestors and forcibly arresting them. Through the media, Ardern told the protesters to "move on", adding that "they did not represent" the majority view of New Zealanders.

"People have the right to protest but when that tips into affecting business, people's ability to move, the ability of kids to go to school or the ability of emergency services to move around, obviously the police have to manage that," she said.

The following month, on 2 March, police reported that 60 people were arrested and they had "gained significant ground" in their initial effort to clear the protesters, with many tense and violent scenes in the process.

"Those protesters illegally occupying parliament grounds and surrounding streets have been given ample opportunity to leave. It is time for them to go," Prime Minister Jacinda Ardern said at a news conference.

Ardern said the protests had been fuelled by misinformation and conspiracy theories.

By the time Ardern retired the consequences of her catastrophic mismanagement of Covid were already evident in the data and her Cinderella status had well and truly vanished.

***

In a piece titled New Zealand: Mugged By Covid Reality, Professor Ramesh Thakur wrote that in the first year of the pandemic there had been strong public support for lockdown measures, despite known or predicted collateral harms, including loss of livelihoods, elevated mortality from neglect of other diseases and ailments, "deaths of despair" from greater loneliness, and police abuses.

"People did not take kindly even to mere questioning of the restrictions. With many governments, for example the British, deploying state propaganda to the full to instil fear of the disease and shame all effort to question restrictions, the moralisation deepened into sacralisation.

"This offers a plausible explanation for why people who so warmly embrace the moral framework of diversity, inclusion, and tolerance in social policy settings, ended up supporting vaccine apartheid for those hesitant to get jabbed by shots with worryingly thin efficacy and safety trials before approval for public use.

"With the passage of time, as evidence mounted of the folly of Zero Covid policy and the accumulating harms it was causing, the New Zealand government was trapped in a prison of its own construction and found it difficult to change course, even after the futility of the entire program became obvious in the data."

Deaths began to climb dramatically in February of 2022, when 77 percent of the entire population had been vaccinated.

By August 2022, New Zealand's cumulative Covid-19 cases per million people had surpassed the US and was on track to catch up with the UK and EU. Australia was ahead of all of them.

A month after her resignation New Zealand recorded its biggest increase in registered deaths in 100 years, mirroring the fate of other nations who imposed harsh lockdowns and mass vaccination campaigns.

Just as in Australia, there would be no admission of culpability from the government.

***

Ironically Ardern emphasised kindness in her resignation speech: "I hope in return I leave behind a belief that you can be kind, but strong. Empathetic, but decisive. Optimistic, but focused. Be strong, and be kind."

Perhaps the epitome of Jacinda Adern's "kindness" was the case of "Baby W", a six-month old baby boy with a congenital heart condition forcibly removed from his parents and transfused with vaccinated blood during a hopefully life-saving operation.

Considering the already well known consequences of mRNA vaccines and the hundreds of thousands of reports of adverse reactions this was an act of pure barbarism. Bastardry of the highest order.

Supporters demonstrated outside The Auckland High Court as it passed down a decision ruling that the baby be placed into the care of his paediatric heart surgeon and cardiologist until the completion of the surgery and post-operative recovery.

Harrowing footage of the encounter showed the distressed parents frantically trying to speak with authorities as the baby was taken away by hospital staff.

"You guys will be recorded in the annals of history as criminals who take babies from their mothers," the baby's father said to authorities as an administrator informed the mother she could see the baby after surgery.

After the verdict, vocal anti-vaccine campaigner Liz Gunn told supporters to pressure Prime Minister Jacinda Ardern to somehow reverse the decision.

"Jacinda, this is at your feet," she said. "Beg them to show some humanity in this country, which we were once so proud of and of which I am now so ashamed."

Health authorities had rejected the parents' request for unvaccinated blood, arguing it was impractical and unnecessary.

The family claimed to have dozens of non-vaccinated donors lined up.

As usual the mainstream media ran only the side of the story that suited their government handlers. The Australian Broadcasting Corporation ran a report claiming: "The case has gripped New Zealand and underscored the potency of vaccine misinformation."

No, it was not misinformation. Those parents had every right to be extremely concerned.

The Guardian, which received funding from the Bill and Melinda Gates Foundation, an organisation making billions out of the vaccines, reported the NZ blood bank claiming: "There was no evidence that previous vaccination affected the quality of blood for transfusion."

Bullshit.

Out in the real world, there were cries of alarm everywhere.

***

Author of that magnificent book *The Bodies of Others* Naomi Wolf argued that at least some of the strange, other worldly feel of the pandemic response could be put down to the widespread use of machine intelligence by the military, government and intelligence agencies involved.

But in her writings Wolf raised another prospect, that there were, indeed, as others had frequently expressed, an even darker force at play.

In an essay "Have the Ancient Gods Returned" she wrote: "These days, to my surprise, people want to talk to me about evil.

"I concluded that I had looked at the events of the past three years using all of my classical education, my critical thinking skills, my knowledge of Western and global history and politics; and that, using these tools, I could not explain the years 2020-present.

"Indeed I could not explain them in ordinary material, political or historical terms at all.

"This is not how human history ordinarily operates.

"I could not explain the way the Western world simply switched, from being based at least overtly on values of human rights and decency, to values of death, exclusion and hatred, overnight, en masse — without resorting to reference to some metaphysical evil that goes above and beyond fallible, blundering human agency.

"When ordinary would-be-tyrants try to take over societies, there is always some flaw, some human impulse undoing the headlong rush toward a negative goal. There are always factions, or rogue lieutenants, in ordinary human history; there is always a miscalculation, or a blunder, or a security breach; or differences of opinion at the top.

"But none of that fracturing or mismanagement of normal history took place in the global rush to lockdowns, the rollout of COVID hysteria, of mandates, masking, of global child abuse, of legacy media lying internationally at scale and all lying in one direction, of thousands of 'trusted messengers' parroting a single script, and of forced or coerced mRNA injections into at least half of the humans on Planet Earth.

"I reluctantly came to the conclusion that human agency alone could not coordinate a highly complicated set of lies about a virus, and propagate the lies in perfect uniformity around an entire globe, in hundreds of languages and dialects. What we have lived through since 2020 is so sophisticated, so massive, so evil, and executed in such inhumane unison, that it cannot be accounted for without venturing into metaphysics."

Baal was back. Ishtar was back. The ritual sacrifice of children was back.

***

The minutiae of Australian politics is boring even to Australlians.

Suffice to say that the same divide between the left, the so-called progressives, and the right, the alleged conservatives, that was seen across the Western world also played out in Australia. That is, the "progressives" backed lockdowns, social distancing, masking and vaccine mandates, while the "right" stood up for individual sovereignty and opposed mass vaccination, lockdowns, uber surveillance and the militarisation of a health response. The situation was even more confused in The Land Down Under because the conservatives were destroying themselves in a desperate rush to be as "woke" as their opponents, and the left hadn't had a new idea in decades.

But at least the sneering mob of intellectual pygmies who had led the Covidian charge had fallen, if not into disgrace at least into silence, while the perpetrators fell on their own swords one by one, retiring before the full consequences of their actions were clearly understood.

One of the nation's worst Covidians, the freshly minted Prime Minister Anthony Albanese, had infamously insisted prior to the 2022 election that any journalist who wanted to travel on the Albanese election bus must be triple vaccinated, wear an N95 mask and take a rapid antigen test every three days.

In other words you had to be fully compliant with the inane ciktats of the era just to sit on the same bus as the Prime Minister in waiting. Let no freedom warrior approach, promote fear and hysteria wherever possible, seize the reins of power.

Having purportedly endured a dose of Covid from which he appeared to suffer little, Albanese never mentioned Covid these days except to repeatedly refuse to call a Royal Commission into Australia's Covid response, and filled the public square with social justice rhetoric on climate change and an indigenous voice to parliament, both extremely divisive and expensive shibboleths which, encased by groaning and incompetent bureaucracies, would be unlikely to improve the lives of anyone.

That the vaccines proved not just useless but dangerous, the masks equally useless and the Covid tests notorious for producing false positives, was somehow irrelevant; even then, when learned professors around the world were decrying the entire Covid freak show as a Big Pharma inspired scam to herd entire populations into mass vaccination, make record profits and, as was becoming increasingly clear, fulfil a darker agenda of military and global intelligence agencies in cahoots with the likes of Bill Gates.

The folk wisdom "always follow the money" had never been truer.

Australia's deranged response to Covid, to which Albanese had been such a crazed convert, was the last thing Albanese wanted to talk about.

***

Much pilloried at the height of the hysteria, the very few Australian politicians who had stood up to Covid hysteria, most notably Senators Alex Antic, Malcolm Roberts and Gerard Rennick, along with the Australian United Party's Craig Kelly, had all been vindicated.

The rest of Australia's elected representatives, as Roberts was keen to point out, now looked like Big Pharma shrills.

In a speech to parliament the Senator said: "As a servant to the people of Queensland and Australia, I note that at the European parliament inquiry into Covid two weeks ago, Janine Small, the President of International Developed Markets for Pfizer revealed that the Pfizer vaccine injection was never tested to see if it would prevent transmission – never tested.

"Small went on to say this was because Pfizer had to work at the speed of science. Well, it seems the speed of science and the velocity of money are the same thing. Shameful decisions were taken deliberately to facilitate Big Pharma getting their injections to market in time.

"The mouthpiece media have the same large investment funds on their share register as Big Pharma. It's no surprise the mouthpiece media amplified the Covid scare, doubling down on fear porn and demonising anyone who clung to 'my body, my choice', just so the media's shareholders could line their pockets with tens of billions of dollars in windfall profits.

"The conclusion an increasing number of Australians are coming to is that our health technocrats tore up our tried and true health systems to shift products for their mates in the pharmaceutical industry, and now people are dying from those same products.

"Even today, vaccine mandates are still in place around Australia.

"The reality of a falling birth rate, unexplained increases in deaths and more than 130,000 cases of vaccine harm here in Australia is being ignored.

"Still, we are told the injection is safe and effective. Safe and effective is not one lie; it is two lies. The vaccine is neither safe nor effective. Medical practitioners who stood up for the rights of their patients were deregistered after action from Big Pharma's enforcement arm, the Australian Health Practitioner Regulation Agency.

"Only a Royal Commission can decide all of the issues I have raised tonight. One royal commissioner will not be enough for the litany of legal and regulatory abuse, medical malpractice, financial malfeasance, conflict of interest, child abuse, human rights abuse and the shredding of international agreements Australia has endured.

"The harm from our Covid response was foreseeable and preventable. If only the Senate, the ultimate house of review, had had the courage to stand up and call bullshit. The Senate did not. As a result, the public has lost confidence in the medical profession, health administration and politicians.

"I have no doubt that, when the truth comes to light, history will judge those in this place as being cowards all. We have one flag, we are one community, we are one nation, and Australians want justice."

***

From the very beginning Old Alex had held the notion that the evil perpetrated on his own species, humans, was their own work, or more precisely the work of America's intelligence agencies, an essentially deranged, drunk on power, lunar right element that thought they could control the world's population through mass vaccination.

We were witnessing the End of the American Empire, with their failed wars, one after another, Vietnam, Iraq, Afghanistan, Ukraine.

And now their own war against their own people, those they considered "superfluous".

The sad element of all of this for Australians was that, thanks to fawning apparatchiks sucking up to their American overlords, their country had become nothing more than a client state, wedded to interminable wars, to state corruption and to deranged social fads. And so it fell foul of the utterly corrupt nature of America's public health system. Millions vaccinated, billions of dollars sacrificed on their altar. Many would never recover their health, their God given, evolved, natural health.

The evidence was out there. Easy, in fact, to find.

As Dr Phillip M Altman with a fellow team of well credentialed researchers of the Australian Medical Professional Society wrote: "The United States Department of Defence has had a dominant role in the response to the SARs CoV2 virus and in the subsequent development, manufacture and distribution of the Covid 19 vaccines. This has been kept hidden from the general public since early 2020.

"The US Department of Defence clearly perceived a threat to national security and all decisions from that point onward to the present day were subject to full command and control from them. Strong evidence for this has now become readily available in the public domain, published on the US Food and Drug Administration website. Many adverse consequences have been the outcome of this secret military response to a public health matter.

"The lesson is that the development and production of vaccines and other therapeutic products for general civilian use should never again be allowed to be under full military command and control.

"Many aspects of the Covid 19 event, which began in January 2020, and the responses to it have been confusing, especially to the general public but also to many scientific and medical observers.

"The clinical outcomes of infection were exaggerated from the very beginning in what looked like a coordinated bid to create a panic reaction in the general public. Other health consequences were ignored.

"A globally coordinated program followed suppression of well known pharmaceuticals and nutritional products which may have had utility as therapies in the early stages of viral infection. And only one solution was promoted — a new vaccine technology that had never been used before in human beings on a large scale.

"Since the introduction of the Covid vaccines, many questions have arisen about lack of adequate manufacturing practices, of quality control, of basic pharmacological and toxicological studies and of appropriate clinical safety and efficacy studies. There seems to have been a reluctance on the part of drug regulatory authorities in many nations to acknowledge both the unprecedented level of reported serious adverse drug reactions and deaths reported in association with these products.

"Why was the public not advised that the normal standards of quality, safety and efficacy were compromised in the name of national security and not applied to the development and testing of these vaccines? Why was this kept secret?

"Given the considerable safety concerns following the introduction of these gene-based COVID vaccines, why are governments around the world, including Australia, planning to make further significant investments in this unsafe, rushed vaccine technology driven by the United States military?"

***

There would be no Nuremberg style inquiry into the Australian government's shocking mismanagement of the Covid scare, no "Nuremberg 2.0" as the placards waved at demonstrations called for. Instead Australia's most recent Prime Minister, Anthony Albanese, was proving just as good as his predecessor at squandering vast amounts of money on useless inquiries he already knew the answer to, pouring taxpayer funds down the gullets of lawyers with one aim, not to find the truth but to discredit his political opponents.

He was also proving just as good as the slippery Scott Morrison in using the nation's media for propaganda purposes and filling the public square with anodyne social justice rhetoric, climate change, gender identity, race. A man who had spent almost his entire life on the public tit had no intention of paying any attention to the concerns of the nation's struggling middle classes.

The last thing Albanese wanted was an inquiry into Covid which exposed his own side of politics as being entirely complicit in inflicting enormous harm on the Australian community.

Instead Albanese found time to join the legendary Sydney Gay Mardi Gras and a few days later marched across the Harbour Bridge for World Pride Day. He said it was an honour to acknowledge those who had fought to advance human rights.

"It was incredible to walk across Sydney Harbour Bridge with World Pride this morning, supporting human rights campaigners from Australia and across the world," Albanese told reporters. "No matter who you are, who you love or where you live – you should be valued, equal and celebrated."

This was the same man who had aligned himself with the deranged authoritarianism of Victorian Premier Daniel Andrews and Vaccine-Profiteer-in-Chief Bill Gates and made not one word of protest as his fellow Australians were pepper sprayed, bashed, imprisoned, fined, arrested and vilified.

Not to mention the fact that millions of Australia's Muslims and fundamentalist Christians regarded the gay pride marches as anathema; further dividing an already deeply divided nation.

The left, as always, poured scorn on anyone who dared to disagree with them, or even wanted to debate the many issues crowding the public square, labelling them racist, homophobic, transphobic, an anti-vaxxer, a climate change denier, or just plain old right wing.

As an increasingly curmudgeonly Old Alex was wont to say: "The government should just stay out of our lives."

The hypocrisy, the breathtaking hypocrisy of these people, left Old Alex if not bitter at least incredulous. They had created for themselves a monster.

It was a terrible storm. And it wound through the heart of everything, the core of the nation; and he felt consumed by swamps of some sort of sad madness, as if he could hear them gasp in the intake valve, as if it would make sense if only they waited long enough, if only they were smarter, cleverer, better educated, of greater and more powerful intellect, or of simple, now old fashioned, wisdom. But it was none of these things.

And so, among those ancient, truly ancient spirits which were so much a part of the deep resonance of the Australian landscape, there were formulations and manifestations and a terrible, virtually indifferent silence. Only some people could hear them, or gave them an ear, yet they came for you in the morning; they came for you at night. Bridges get walked on; and we are all, in a sense, bridges between a past and a future. Old Alex had done everything he could to stop his head swarming; like an ethereal bee swarm running through the valley. And now it was too late.

This nation would rise and fall, this civilisation would come and go. But the ancients would remain; and speak to his descendants, and a seer, generations into the future, fighting another Dark Age, would reach back to learn what had happened in these strange times.

***

Not least of the many transformations of that period of history was the conversion of the social media platform Twitter from an instrument of control for the American intelligence agencies into a free speech platform.

It became evident through a series of exposes which became known as the Twitter Files, a treasure trove of material exposing state and intelligence agency manipulation of social media and thereby the democratic process, a systematic manipulation of the narrative.

Matt Taibbi, author of *Griftopia* and *Hate Inc.* and one of America's best journalists, helped expose the suppression, manipulation and control of the vaccine narrative by the same government which had developed the vaccine in the first place.

This included the Virality Project, a sweeping, cross-platform effort to monitor billions of social media posts by Stanford University, federal agencies, and a slew of often state-funded NGOs.

Matt Taibbi told a US Judicial Committee on the Weaponisation of the Federal Government: "What we found in the Files was a sweeping effort to use machine learning and other tools to turn the internet into an instrument of censorship and social control. Unfortunately, our own government appears to be playing a lead role.

"We learned Twitter, Facebook, Google, and other companies developed a formal system for taking in moderation 'requests' from every corner of government: the FBI, DHS, DOD, the Global Engagement Center at State, even the CIA."

In Number 19 of the Twitter files Taibbi wrote that "Reports of vaccinated individuals contracting Covid-19 anyway"; "natural immunity";

suggesting Covid-19 "leaked from a lab"; even "worrisome jokes", all came in for attention from the censors.

All were characterised as potential violations or disinformation events. The Virality Project told Twitter that "true stories that could fuel hesitancy," including things like "celebrity deaths after vaccine" or the closure of a central New York school due to reports of post-vaccine illness, should be considered "Standard Vaccine Misinformation on Your Platform."

Unfortunately for Australians, the nation's shallow mimicking of America's misguided, delusional if not outright corrupt response to Covid meant the Americans certainly found in Australia a willing league of politicians, health bureaucrats and functionaries.

Australian politicians, with very few exceptions, also accepted the manipulation of the country's information flows by foreign social media companies, most notably Facebook and Twitter, both of which were widely used in Australia.

Where were Australia's leaders while foreign owned companies were hijacking their own citizens' right to free speech and accurate information on the vaccines? MIA. Missing in Action. Complicit.

***

A legacy of that period was the shift to independent media and to podcasts; which meant a significant percentage of the population were no longer receiving their information from government manipulated sources. One of those outlets to gather in strength and popularity during that period was Rebel News Australia, fronted by Avi Yemini, a former Israeli military officer whose indefatigable in-your-face confrontational journalism won him a highly entertained audience.

In Switzerland for the annual get-together of the obscenely wealthy, the World Economic Forum at Davos, Yemini and Ezra Levant of Rebel News in Canada spotted Albert Bourla, the Chief Executive of Pfizer, walking the streets.

His company had made windfall profits from the Covid-19 vaccine, a "vaccine" which did not prevent infection, transmission, hospitalisation or death and which was now being seen as a criminal sleight of hand, the biggest heist in history.

The old fashioned gotcha hounding of Bourla through the picturesque streets of Davos made for classic footage; he just looked guilty.

Video of the incident was viewed more than 20 million times. And became one of the biggest stories in the outlet's history.

While Bourla said nothing except "Have a nice day" Ezra Levant began peppering him with questions: "When did you know the vaccines didn't stop transmission? How long did you know that without saying it publicly?

"We now know that the vaccines didn't stop transmission. But why did you keep it secret? Are you worried about myocarditis? Are you worried about liability?

"What do you have to say about young men dropping dead of heart attacks every day? You said the vaccine was 100% effective, then 90%, then 80%, then 70%. What do you think on your private yacht, on your private jet?

"Do you think you should be charged criminally for some of the criminal behaviour you've obviously been a part of?"

Avi Yemani, a graduate of the abusive Melbourne lockdowns, stepped in with an even more aggressive line of questioning: "Is it time to apologise to the world, sir? To give refunds back to the countries that poured all their money into your vaccines that don't work, an ineffective vaccine?

"Aren't you ashamed of what you've done in the last couple of years? Are you proud of it? You've made millions on the back of people's entire livelihoods,

"How does that feel, to walk the streets, having made millions on the back of the regular person back home in Australia, in England and Canada?

"How much money have you personally made off the vaccine? How many boosters would it take for you to be happy with your earnings?.

"If any other product in the world doesn't work as promised you get a refund. Should you not refund to countries that laid out billions for your ineffective vaccine?"

The incident came after it was revealed that the Pfizer CEO personally earned $50 million in compensation across 2021 and 2022 and the company's revenue had tripled to more than $100 billion since 2019.

"Shame on you, sir," said Ezra as Bourla passed behind security guards.

"Shame on you," said Avi.

Prominent Australians attending that year's World Economic Forum included former Prime Minister Kevin Rudd, soon to become Australian

Ambassador to the US, former Foreign Minister Julia Bishop, Chief Executive of mining giant and Australia's largest company BHP, Mike Henry, Australia's Second-Richest Person and Executive Chairman of Fortescue Metals Group Andrew 'Twiggy' Forrest, and Mathias Cormann, former Australian Minister for Finance currently serving as the Secretary-General of the Organisation for Economic Co-operation and Development.

Most of these people were paid for by the Australian government. Why should Australian taxpayers be forking out for this splendid junket on the exclusive ski slopes of Davos? Why did the Australian government parrot the same agendas as the Davos billionaires?

***

Perhaps it was just a coincidence that Artificial Intelligence, which had been in the wings for decades, suddenly stepped onto the stage, front and centre of many people's lives in the immediate aftermath of the most large-scale attempt to transform human social formation ever undertaken.

Old Alex doubted it very much.

Testing the program ChatGPT out of curiosity, he asked it to write 300 words on his local waterway Lake Illawarra in the 1800s, a typical job as a general reporter he might have been asked to do; fillers for which the bosses gave no mercy, they didn't care what the words were, they just wanted it to be credible and to fill a hole on a page. Such tedious jobs were the bane of every general reporter's life.

The program did in seconds what would have taken him hours if not all day; and for someone who had worked in journalism all his life, he couldn't pick a word wrong. Perfect intro. Perfect outro. Impeccable grammar.

It was impressive, and it was revolutionary; and humanity did, indeed, stand on the edge of a new, and remarkable epoch.

Old Alex was saddened to find out that ChatGPT was closely linked to Bill Gates; and, funnily enough, was capable of lying.

Equally, Old Alex was now using other programs, fresh on the market, to illustrate stories for his magazine, using words to prompt images, or asking for pictures in a particular style. Skills that had taken artists a lifetime to achieve could now be done by a computer in seconds; and in any style he wanted. A French impressionist image of the ruins of an ancient civilisation on Mars, not a problem.

But no, that did not mean that humans were now largely redundant. "Surplus". As the dystopian lords of the World Economic Forum and their eugenics fellow travellers would have it.

***

Because it was one the most remarkable occurrences he had ever witnessed in a lifetime of news reporting, because the experience had been so heart warming and so profound in so many ways, Old Alex decided to go back to Canberra for the first anniversary of the string of demonstrations which culminated on February 12 of 2022 with one of the largest and most high spirited marches Australia had ever seen.

For the week before, he republished stories in his magazine from the days he had been there, stories with headlines like: From All The Lands We Come, We Will Wash Away Tyranny, The Spirit Rises, The Great March, The Sad and Brutal Final Hours.

When he first arrived at the parliamentary lawns the number of protesters was so small he wondered if he was in the wrong place; but then he parked and mingled, armed once again with nothing but a reporters pad and a shuffling air, everybody's friend, harmless.

For sure, despite the small numbers, with t-shirts like "The Media Is The Virus, I Will Never Comply" and the presenter on stage booming "We stand for the generations that come after us", some of the spirit was the same. He detected no air of defeat.

In contrast to the hundreds of thousands who thronged the front lawns of Parliament House a year before, perhaps 100 protesters gathered on the 11th, and in the order of 300 on the 12th.

But none of the participants he spoke to doubted they were on the right side of history, vindicated after 12 months of scandals and revelations surrounding the damage of the government's Covid measures.

"We are becoming good friends and building a family," one of the protestors told him. "It is like a family reunion."

Daniel Vincent, 49, a veteran soldier from Western Australia, said: "I am here for the sanctity of children and the full disclosure of trust. I have been here for 12 months. I'm not allowed in the parliamentary Precinct.

"I can't go back to Western Australia. They have opened the borders but they can just come into your home and force vaccinate you. There is no evidence that this has occurred, but that is the law and as a face of the Freedom Movement, I could be a target.

"I have mates who never returned from East Timor, and then kids need representation. It is a shame. They have no fathers to fight for the freedoms they deserve."

Holding a large Australian flag and marching up and down in front of Parliament House Phil Jones, a miner from Queensland, said: "I am here to save this country. I could read a group of data and see it didn't add up. We never went home from last year. I've never felt anything like that before.

"We swagged through winter. It was a cold winter. We have swagged on the side of the road. We have been at the Governor Generals every day since February the 7th 2022. Every day. Every single day."

One act of protest involved spiking into the lawns a collection of crosses with the details of people killed and injured by the vaccine: "Taylor Maunt, 22, Victoria, August, 2021, Pfizer = heart problems"; "Inez L. 50. Coffs Harbour, NSW. Pfizer x 2. Diagnosis: Trigeminal Neuralgia"; "Betty, 27, Pfizer. RIP"; "Michelle, 51, AstraZeneca, RIP"; "Cain, 45, Pfizer, RIP".

Steven Carter 49, a mechanic from Gosford who organised the display said: "This came about through word-of-mouth. We've been doing this in Hyde Park In Sydney.

"When you are reading death stories it is horrible. We have 400 more of these in the car. There's another group on the other side of the park of maybe 500 that we have stuck in the ground over there too."

***

As was his wont, Old Alex had made zero plans for where he was going to crash the night, except perhaps in the car. Fortunately for him, he ran across an old mate from the Epic Days, Nick with the Dingo Dog, and ended up at the Warri Camping Reserve, just outside the border of the Australian Capital Territory.

Set in the upper reaches of the Shoalhaven River, with the wind curling through the eucalypts it, too, had a mysterious, magical feel, like so much of the Australian landscape.

A year before, the authorities had hounded every last impassioned freedom fighter out of the nation's capital, and the Warri Reserve was the first place they could camp unmolested.

Without jobs and without the wherewithal to pay for rent or a mortgage, infuriated by the destruction of their lives, hundreds had gathered at Warri in the days, weeks, and months after Epic. Now a year later the numbers appeared to fluctuate around a couple of dozen.

Some returned out of nostalgia. Others because the entire Epic experience and the surrounding protest movements were in themselves a spiritual revelation.

That part of Australia is cold much of the year, and the local New South Wales police truly won the freedom fighter's hearts by bringing them a trailer load of wood.

One of those returning for the anniversary of the Epic March was Steve, 32, who quit his job as a retail manager for a tobacco distributor after Covid made his work life unbearable. Down on his luck, about to become homeless, a deal to spend his last $1500 on a van to live in fell through.

"I was in the middle of a panic attack", he recalled. "I tried to calm myself down with meditation, and I was half way through when there was an abrupt, unexpected knock at my door.

"I answered the door and it was one of my neighbours from down the street, I never really spoke to him, except to say hello. He didn't know I was looking for a van, he didn't know I was moving out.

"He was a spiritual person and said he had bought 150 legs of ham to give away for Christmas, and asked if I would like a ham. I said thanks mate, but I am vegan.

"He said, I thought so. If you don't want a ham, what about a van?

"My jaw dropped in disbelief. I asked him, how did you know I was looking for a van?"

"He said he didn't know how, he just knew. It was like telepathy. He put six months rego on it and gave it to me for free. He didn't want anything in return.

"It has been the most reliable car. It has been my home.

"I look at it as a gift from God. God is the good in everyone, a spirit that works through people, through all of us. A lot of people have had similar spiritual experiences, an overwhelming feeling that everything is going to be OK, an energy that reassures us."

***

There was no longer any excuse for ignorance. The authoritative body of literature, research papers and other material debunking the Covid narrative to which Australia had been hostage grew until the case became undeniable.

With a tsunami of critical podcasts and interviews online, it was hard to believe there was anyone left on Earth who actually believed the Covid yarn spun by governments, now more likely to be described as "an incomprehensible human tragedy and horror". The vaccinated ceased their virtue signalling and finally fell silent.

Amongst the books, a number of which became instant bestsellers, were Ed Dowd's *Cause Unknown: The Epidemic of Sudden Deaths in 2021 and 2022* and Dr Robert Malone's *Lies My Government Told Me*.

Not least of them was John Leake and Peter McCullough's *The Courage to Face Covid-19: Preventing Hospitalisation and Death While Battling the Bio-Pharmaceutical Complex*.

On a well attended promotional tour of Australia Dr McCullough, made no bones about his stance that the Covid vaccines were unsafe, linking the products to high risks of cardiac injury, neurologic damage, and blood clots among other complications. He believed the vaccines were driving excess deaths in Australia and other highly vaccinated countries.

"The vaccines should be taken off the market. This is a worldwide crisis. The emergency now is this massive number of patients suffering injury, disabilities and death after mass vaccination. The next person who dies unexpectedly with no antecedent illness and there's no other explanation, it is the vaccine until proven otherwise."

As for the media's claims of misinformation, Dr McCullough countered: "What I'm suspicious of is the media following a narrative. The media was complicit with an overarching plan for Covid-19 from the very beginning, and that plan was designed to drive as much fear, suffering, hospitalisation, and death as possible in order to relentlessly promote the vaccines. And so any person who stands in the way of that agenda is defamed."

Author John Leake, travelling with McCullough, observed of their visit: "What happened to the Australians is that their government and media relentlessly terrorised them. Nowhere in the previously free world except maybe Canada has the State been more brutally paternalistic than in Australia.

"Nowhere has the State's playbook been more clear and ruthless: 1) Blitz of media terror. 2) Invoke Emergency Power. 3) Suspend constitutional liberties. 4) Lock everyone up. 5) Bodyslam and blast with rubber bullets anyone who protests the lockdowns. 6) Relentlessly push of the COVID-19 vaccines as the key to safety and freedom. 7) Delist any doctor who publicly questions the safety and efficacy of the gene transfer products.

"Our tour has taught us that many Australians still care about their constitutional protections and liberties. Our fear that everyone Down Under is suffering from Stockholm Syndrome was completely unfounded."

***

If you were expecting peace in this altered realm, or some sort of cosmic bliss, there was none. Appear near when you are far, appear far when you are near. All war is deception. This was war.

Some times, many times, the ancient wisdoms had far more to teach us than the blizzard of verbiage social justice warriors poured across the culture on a daily basis.

For Old Alex, isolated in that aerie on the side of a long shallow valley, that strange prescience persisted, that he was being visited from the future, that it had all happened before, even down to the detail, why they found him only on the ground floor, when in the future the house would be multistoried. This evil that had been visited upon the Earth forced an evolution of the state of human consciousness; and so humans, before genetic and cybernetic enhancement became commonplace, took their place in the natural order of things.

The soldiers lined along the edge of the valley, at attention, their stanchions firmly planted in the ground.

But what was most striking was the bonfires which lined the surrounding cliffs.

Perhaps it was an echo of the indigenous, who had lit bonfires on the headlands to communicate with the tribes up and down the coast. Or to signal danger, as they had done when the giant ships arrived, filled with those strangely dressed ghosts with their firesticks, Europeans with guns; as frightened or bewildered as the indigenous may have been, they could not have realised, could not have conceived, that their world was coming to an end.

That the genocides humans had visited upon each other, past, present and future, were about to be visited upon them.

But more like, as he gazed around the rim of those echo chambers, those sharp valleys, as he saw the bonfires burning on the sandstone cliffs, many located in the exact same spots as what would one day be ancient temples, they were a warning or a signal from the future, that there in their chaotic and stricken time those fires indicated another crisis; as those futuristic helicopters, manned with another species of men who looked down on the populations below just as the comfortable populations of the 21st Century had recalled, if they recalled at all, the Neanderthals. As stupid, inferior. Even as their DNA still ran through their blood.

But there it was, those fires; incense ravaged, distressed, urgent; speaking to, or recalling those scenes of Jesus in the temples of the Middle East. But here, in these cold valleys and ancient places, as the glories of another civilisation hovered in the air, and collapsed, or faced imminent collapse, for the very same reason so many civilisations had perished before, they had ignored the common people, mistreated the serfs, the peasantry, yes, the common people whose aspirations and struggles, virtues and flaws, they had ignored as somehow inferior, or irrelevant.

Just as the privileged bureaucrats of the 21st Century had regarded their own citizenry with contempt.

As those humans who lived 2000 years after the birth of Christ, the human Christ, had sneered at their own uneducated, had regarded as zoo animals their ancestors, chimpanzees, apes, a bewildering style and number of variations, these things, these trains or chains of DNA which spread down through the centuries to this.

And in that incense soaked temple so far in the future, a desperate priest, a high born energy, borne aloft if you will, reached back to find a solution to his present day crisis; to another time of universal deceit, another time when contempt for the ordinary citizen had led eventually, ultimately, to social chaos, to the collapse of their own social order, as the peasantry asserted their right to exist.

You only had to look at the swirling chaos of the trees to understand this divine presence. And that priest; he wanted to know. He sought a desperate solution. His own life, it appeared, was in danger, as the throngs gathered around his last refuge, his last resting place, as he burnt in volume the last of his incense, as he sought if not an eternity for himself an understanding of eternity itself, as he sought to know, no matter how high born, how it had all come to be.

Those secrets hidden until the time was right; beyond all normal human ken.

And the nation they then called "Australia", that place which had been so full of certitudes and by the standards of much of the future population, unimaginable wealth, to be able to go to their shops and markets, to be able to buy goods from all over the world, for these soon unimaginable luxuries taken for granted by the citizenry at large.

These things, those fires, those smells and sense of burning, of conflagration, of a terrible, terrifying time.

And that priest, hurling through the stone walls, escaping the throng, knowing in no way what to do, knowing that his life was about to an end at the hands of the masses gathering in revolt outside the temple walls, reached back to speak to him with an urgency of mission. For these mysteries. These terrible travesties. For these breaches of the spirit. For this time that was their time, for his prayers that were their prayers.

The seer and his attendants chanted in an urgent invocation. They pleaded for mercy as the mob broke down the walls, their centuries of affluence and high status at an end.

It was coming to an end, this period of human history, these fates. And yet still, that panicked seer reached back to him, seeking safety, or a solution. And the answers to the questions they sought; the wisdom they sought. There were no answers in the vast stream called time. There were, simply, those high flying birds. And a new dawn born out of chaos.

***

There was one political hot potato in Australia which would not go away, no matter how much the government would like it to, and that was the matter of excess deaths.

To watch a politician or bureaucrat squirm, all a few rebel members of parliament had to do was ask them about it.

Australia's high excess death levels were now news around the world, and mirrored other heavily vaccinated countries. In some ways, Australia appeared to have quickly returned to normal. But it wasn't true.

Truly, exposing the scandals around Australia's Covid roll out became as easy as shooting fish in a barrel.

Craig Kelly, head of the United Australia Party, resigned from the then ruling Liberal Party in 2021, disgusted by his own mistreatment and by their mismanagement of the Covid scare.

He lost his seat but remained leading the party and amassed a considerable personal following. Once an outlier and very much a pariah, as revelation after revelation over Covid malfeasance fueled outrage around the world Craig Kelly found himself a loud voice in the middle of a rushing torrent, no longer alone.

"Unprecedented excess deaths should be the No.1 story in our media, but they are refusing to cover it," he wrote. "You'd expect such suppression and censorship of such important information in a Communist controlled society."

Frustrated by the media's failure to cover the story, The United Australia Party took out major advertisements instead: "Excess Death Rates in Australia: Why Aren't Questions Being Asked".

"In February of 2023 Kelly wrote: "We lost another 1,432 extra Australians in November 2022, taking the annual cumulative total to 22,886 excess dead Australians from 2022 from January to November."

He said that was equivalent to a fully laden A380 crashing and everyone on board dying, every week of the year.

"The bodies of excess dead Australians are piling up at a faster rate than during WW1 or WW2. Something has gone terribly wrong in Australia. This shocking, unprecedented and ongoing level of excess deaths should be the number one issue in the country. It should be on the front page of every paper. The lead item on every news bulletin. The subject dominating Federal Parliament at Question Time.

"But there is silence. An information blackout."

There was nothing normal about these excess rates.

Internationally Dr John Campbell, whose pedantic and thorough podcasts on Covid had won him more than 2.7 million followers, was one of those to highlight the issue, as his headlines suggested: "Excess deaths in young adults", "Excess deaths in all age groups", "Excess deaths, lack of data".

In a podcast Excess Deaths in 30 countries he recorded that excess deaths in the UK began for the weekend ending the 13 January, at over 20%. Excess deaths were also being recorded across Europe, in America, Canada, Australia and New Zealand.

"We know that these excess deaths are not, the majority of these, are not attributable to Covid at all. I think we are in an international emergency, not being responded to by our governments in any way, shape or form. Indeed they seem to be ignoring it. As indeed do most of the mainstream media. Why aren't we getting a response to these massive increases in excess deaths?"

***

History, of course, is a river rushing by from which we can only capture one brief part. Words, like headlines, can only tell but one small fraction of the story, here on this most fecund of planets, in this dark part of human history when so much harm was done to so many people, when the authorities lied constantly, and hypocrisy reigned.

There were now so many scandals enveloping the rollout of the Covid-19 vaccines it was difficult to keep track. If there was anyone left who still believed the fear mongering Covid narrative spun by some of the most corrupt and dishonest individuals, organisations and governments in the world over the three year span beginning in 2020, they were now hard to find.

Despite the well documented scandal over the damage to women's reproductive health from Covid vaccines, the excess death rates in highly vaccinated jurisdictions across the world, the litany of vaccine injuries and deaths, and the widespread acknowledgement that the vaccines did not stop infection or transmission, in 2023 the Australian authorities were still advocating vaccination for pregnant women and launched a major campaign urging people to "top up" their Covid vaccines.

Here, to close out this part of Australia's story, are just a few of the headlines as we go to press: "Australia's drug regulator hid vaccine deaths from public"; "TGA covered up vaccine deaths of a 7 & 9 year old"; "mRNA Vaccine Contamination Much Worse Than Thought: Jabs Up to 35% DNA That Turns Human Cells into Long-Term Spike Protein Factories";

"No jab, no heart: Mother denied transplant due to vaccination status"; "Why the Body Attacks Itself After COVID-19 Vaccination"; "Excess deaths, parliament questions"; "IT WAS ALL A LIE: How you were tricked into taking part in a Deadly Experiment that killed Millions"; "Emails in 2020 blow the covid PCR test scam out of the water", "Why Indiscriminate Mass Vaccination Has Worsened the Pandemic", "Stop the shots: Covid expert calls for unsafe vaccines to be taken off the market, links vaccines to excess deaths".

"Cardiac Arrest and Death after COVID-19 Vaccination"; "Explosive Increase in Cardiac Symptoms after Second Injection"; "UK Gov. confirms England & Wales have suffered 63k Excess Deaths"; "10 Myths told by Covid Experts and Now Debunked", "One Shot Destroyed My Life", "Doctors Deliberately Gave the Unvaccinated a Lower Level of Care", "Busting the Myth that Covid Vaccines Are Highly Effective Against Death", "Husband of BBC Presenter Killed by Covid Vaccine Sues Astra-Zeneca, Says Vaccine is Unsafe Defective Product", "Covid vaccine injury class action filed against Federal Government".

The River Rushes By.

ACKNOWLEDGEMENTS

I owe a great debt to a number of prominent Australian writers, journalists and public intellectuals and have been pleased to publish them in A Sense of Place Magazine; and subsequently to use their material in this book.

Among those making a significant contribution have been Professor Ramesh Thakur, affiliated with the Australian National University. A former Assistant High Commissioner with the United Nations, he has been a standout voice for common sense. His thorough academic and statistical analyses have been published widely throughout this period, and he has been generous with his work. It is a great pity the Australian government chose to ignore him.

Paul Collits, whose cogent, insightful and often scathing commentary throughout the Covid era meant his work stood in stark contrast to that of the pale propagandists masquerading as journalists in Australia's mainstream media.

Equally, Rebecca Weisser at *Spectator Australia* has proven herself one of the country's finest journalists throughout this period.

Professor Gigi Foster at the University of New South Wales, author of *The Great Covid Panic*, has also been a standout voice against the Covid hysteria which enveloped Australia and I have been pleased to reference her work.

I would particularly like to thank Ethan Nash at TOTT News, who has also been generous with his work. TOTT are an outlier in the Australia media landscape, wedded neither to the standard left nor right polarisation of Australian journalism but fascinated by futurism and transhumanism. His excellent work has been extremely relevant to the times.

I would also like to thank journalist Susan Pavan, whose passionate work during this period did the nation proud.

Many unsung heroes have emerged from Australia's freedom movement during this period, too many to mention here, have significantly contributed to the temper of the times. As we say in the text, you could easily dedicate an entire museum and research centre to Australia's multi-talented freedom movement and the response of multiple politicians and governments.

Memorable figures have included David Oneeg, with his Aussie Chat blog, Monica Smit of Reignite Democracy Australia, and Rukshan Fernando, who streams as The Real Rukshan and won a legion of fans through his high quality video footage of the protests which enveloped the country.

Michael Gray Griffith of the activist group Cafe Locked Out emerged as one of the finest writers and documentors of this period of Australian history, and he, too, has generously given permission for use of his work.

An old journalistic contact Kim Cullen kindly read early drafts of the book and her encouragement has been much appreciated.

I would also like to thank Nick Thompson for his assistance at Camp Epic, Warri Camp and with the website of A Sense of Place Magazine.

And once again I would like to thank Anthony Reale, the owner of the Village Fix Cafe in Shellharbour. His courage in standing up to the absurd overreach of the Australian authorities was in itself an inspiration. And his excellent coffee helped bring the book to fruition.

ABOUT THE AUTHOR

John Stapleton was born in Bangalow on the New South Wales north coast on 21 June 1952. The first money he ever made out of writing was in 1974 when he was co-winner of a short story competition held by what was then Australia's leading cultural celebration, the Adelaide Arts Festival.

He graduated from Macquarie University in 1975 with a double major in philosophy and did post-graduate work with the Sociology Department at Flinders University.

As a freelance journalist in the 1970s and 1980s, while alternating between living in Sydney and London, his articles and fiction appeared in a wide range of magazines, newspapers and anthologies, including The Australian Financial Review and the now defunct Bulletin.

John Stapleton worked on *The Sydney Morning Herald* as a staff news reporter between 1986 and 1994. The paper was then listed as one of the Top 20 newspapers in the world.

He worked for the national newspaper *The Australian* from 1994 to 2009.

His books include: *Thailand: Deadly Destination*, *Terror in Australia: Workers' Paradise Lost*, *Hideout in the Apocalypse*, *Dark Dark Policing* and *Unfolding Catastrophe: Australia*. His memoir of a lifetime in journalism, *Hunting the Famous*, will be released later this year.

As a news reporter, Stapleton encountered and wrote many hundreds of stories about everyone from street alcoholics to Australian Prime Ministers; from the staple flood, drought, fire and natural disasters of the Australian bush to scenes of urban dysfunction.

In 2000 he became co-founder of the world's longest running radio program on father's issues, Dads on the Air. He currently edits *A Sense of Place Magazine*.

He is the proud father of two children.

www.ingramcontent.com/pod-product-compliance
Ingram Content Group UK Ltd.
Pitfield, Milton Keynes, MK11 3LW, UK
UKHW061222180426
11947UKWH00026B/1969